SOCIOLOGY FOR A NEW CENTURY

DEVELOPMENT AND SOCIAL CHANGE

A GLOBAL PERSPECTIVE

SECOND EDITION

◆

PHILIP McMICHAEL

PINE FORGE PRESS
Excellence and Innovation for Teaching

For information, address:

 Pine Forge Press
A Sage Publications Company
2455 Teller Road
Thousand Oaks, California 91320
E-mail: sales@pfp.sagepub.com

Sage Publications Ltd.
6 Bonhill Street
London EC2A 4PU
United Kingdom

Sage Publications India Pvt. Ltd.
M-32 Market
Greater Kailash I
New Delhi 110 048 India

Publisher: Stephen Rutter
Assistant to the Publisher: Ann Makarias
Production Editor: Astrid Virding
Editorial Assistant: Nevair Kabakian
Copy Editor: A. J. Sobczak
Typesetter: Lynn Miyata

Printed in the United States of America

00 01 02 03 10 9 8 7 6 5 4 3 2

Library of Congress Cataloging-in-Publication Data

McMichael, Philip.
    Develoment and social change: A global perspective /
by Philip McMichael—2nd ed.
        p.   cm.—(Sociology for a new century)
    Includes bibliographical references and index.
    ISBN 0-7619-8692-8 — ISBN 0-7619-8667-7
    1. Economic develoment projects—History.   2. Economic development—History.   3. Competition, International—History.
I. Title   II. Series.
HC79.E44 M25   2000
306.3'09—dc21   99-050704

For Karen,
with love and gratitude

Contents

ABOUT THE AUTHOR

Philip McMichael grew up in Adelaide, South Australia, and he completed his undergraduate studies at the University of Adelaide. After traveling in India, Pakistan, Afghanistan, and Papua New Guinea, he pursued his doctorate in Sociology at the State University of New York at Binghamton. He has taught at the University of New England (New South Wales), Swarthmore College, and the University of Georgia and is presently Professor and Chair of Rural and Development Sociology at Cornell University. His book *Settlers and the Agrarian Question: Foundations of Capitalism in Colonial Australia* (1984) won the Social Science History Association's Allan Sharlin Memorial Award. He is the editor of *The Global Restructuring of Agro-Food Systems* (1994) and *Food and Agrarian Orders in the World Economy* (1995). He has served as director of Cornell University's International Political Economy Program and as chair of the American Sociological Association's Political Economy of the World-System Section, and he is currently President of the Research Committee on Agriculture and Food for the International Sociological Association. He and his wife, Karen Schachere, have two children, Rachel and Jonathan.

ABOUT THE PUBLISHER

Pine Forge Press is a new educational publisher, dedicated to publishing innovative books and software throughout the social sciences. On this and any other of our publications, we welcome your comments, ideas, and suggestions. Please call or write to:

Pine Forge Press
A Sage Publications Company
31 St. James Ave., Suite 510
Boston, MA 02116
617-753-7512
E-mail: sdr@pfp.sagepub.com

Visit our World Wide Web site, your direct link to a multitude of online resources: www.pineforge.com

Foreword

Sociology for a New Century offers the best of current sociological thinking to today's students. The goal of the series is to prepare students, and—in the long run—the informed public, for a world that has changed dramatically in the last three decades and one that continues to astonish.

This goal reflects important changes that have taken place in sociology. The discipline has become broader in orientation, with an ever growing interest in research that is comparative, historical, or transnational in orientation. Sociologists are less focused on "American" society as the pinnacle of human achievement and more aware of global processes and trends. They also have become less insulated from surrounding social forces. In the 1970s and 1980s, sociologists were so obsessed with constructing a science of society that they saw impenetrability as a sign of success. Today, there is a greater effort to connect sociology to the ongoing concerns and experiences of the informed public.

Each book in this series offers in some way a comparative, historical, transnational, or global perspective to help broaden students' vision. Students need to comprehend the diversity in today's world and to understand the sources of diversity. This knowledge can challenge the limitations of conventional ways of thinking about social life. At the same time, students need to understand that issues that may seem specifically "American" (for example, the women's movement, an aging population bringing a strained social security and health care system, racial conflict, national chauvinism, and so on) are shared by many other countries. Awareness of commonalities undercuts the tendency to view social issues and questions in narrowly American terms and encourages students to seek out the experiences of others for the lessons they offer. Finally, students need to grasp phenomena that transcend national boundaries—trends and processes that are supranational (for example, environmental degradation). Recognition of global processes stimulates student awareness of causal forces that transcend national boundaries, economies, and politics.

The dramatic acceleration of the global economy sets the stage for Philip McMichael's *Development and Social Change: A Global Perspective*, now in its second edition. McMichael explores the complex and evolving interplay between rich and poor countries in the late twentieth century. His starting point is the understanding of international inequality predominant in the 1950s and 1960s. This understanding joined international organizations and Third World governments in a common ideology of state-managed economic and social change. It championed the idea that poor countries, with a little help from rich countries, could become developed countries, in effect pulling themselves up by their own bootstraps. Reality, of course, fell far short of the vision that inspired development thinking, and this view, which McMichael calls the *development project,* gave way to the *globalization project.* Goals of integration with the world economy and openness to its forces supplanted the goal of national development and "catching up with the West." The globalization project, in effect, has provided a convenient rationale for persistent international inequality. McMichael's portrait of global interconnections at century's end spotlights the long reach of international markets and commodity chains and the many, often invisible, connections between producers and consumers worldwide.

Preface to the Second Edition

The subject of development is difficult to teach. Living in relatively affluent surroundings, students understandably situate their society on the
"high end" of a development continuum—at the pinnacle of human economic and technological achievement. They often perceive both the
development continuum and their favorable position on it as "natural"—
a well-deserved reward for embracing the values of modernity. (This is
likely to be the case also for students from the so-called Third World,
although their experiences will be different.) It is difficult to put one's
world in historical perspective from this vantage point. It is harder still to
help students grasp a world perspective that goes beyond framing their
history as a simple series of developmental or evolutionary stages—the
inevitable march of progress.

In my experience, until students go beyond simple evolutionary
views, they have difficulty valuing other cultures that do not potentially
mirror their own. When they do go beyond the evolutionary perspective,
they are better able to evaluate their own culture sociologically and to
think reflexively about social change, development, and international
inequality. This is the challenge.

The narrative that follows presents an overview of social change and
development at the turn of the twenty-first century. It is not organized
around competing theories of social change and development, nor does it
adhere to a single, all-encompassing perspective. Rather, the narrative
retraces the story of development as an increasingly global enterprise. The
tack this book takes is to introduce students to the global roots and dimensions of recent social changes and to the special role filled by the **development project**.* It encourages them to think about development as a transnational project designed to integrate the world, and it helps them to see
how this project is currently undergoing dramatic revision via political
and economic globalization, and by some powerful counter-movements

---

*All boldfaced terms are defined in the Glossary/Index.

within this process. With these understandings in place, they will be better prepared for the many challenges that lie ahead.

Many of the available texts approach development through the lens of theory. Texts are usually organized around competing theories or perspectives (e.g., modernization versus dependency versus world-systems theory, liberal perspectives versus Marxist perspectives, structuralism versus neo-liberalism, and so on). Students find themselves thrown into the task of evaluating abstract perspectives without proper grounding in knowledge of the post–World War II developmentalist era. Presenting competing theoretical perspectives is a fundamental part of teaching social change and development, but students need a basic understanding of the context within which these competing theories arose and then collided.

The post–Cold War world that students live in today is very different from the world that gave rise to development theories. The rapid pace of social change makes the task of understanding this world akin to shooting at a moving target. The established units of sociological analysis (e.g., national societies and citizens, individual rational actors, and so on) are now surrounded by competing organizing principles—sub-national communities and supra-national regions, transnational webs of exchange and transnational communities, ethnic and cultural entities, expressive politics, and so on. It is even questionable whether development theory, as it is now known and debated, will survive the dramatic social changes of the post–Cold War world, as the ground is shifting—even degrading—under the development project.

This book has been designed with these new challenges in mind. My aim is to situate current changes historically, first presenting an overview of the development era (including its theoretical discourses) and then addressing its declining salience as a new global era emerges. Students who are already familiar with such social movements as feminism, grassroots activism, and rain forest protection, will find these issues here in the context of the shifting debates and challenges to the development project.

The text traces the steps in the gradual evolution of the development enterprise into an emerging **globalization project**, outlining the conditions under which the post–World War II managers of states and multilateral agencies institutionalized development as a key organizing principle in the Cold War era. A series of case studies concentrate on the Third World countries' experience of the development project, individualizing this experience and showing how it differed across Third World countries and regions, while at the same time situating those individual experiences in a common process.

The common process of development itself has changed substantially. From the early 1970s, when new global trends begin to override the 1940s Bretton Woods development institutions, a new project of globalization began, gradually supplanting the development project, dramatized by the debt crisis of the 1980s. The text lays out the main features of this trend, including some of the major counter-mobilizations, such as the feminist and the environmental movements. New questions arise in a world that is simultaneously integrating and disintegrating and grappling with environmental problems on a global scale. The scale and style of politics are changing, and new issues of human rights have emerged in a world that is experiencing an increasingly rapid circulation of money, people, goods, electronic impulses, and ideas. All of these issues complicate our once tidy view of development and the problem of international inequality. The goal of this presentation is to offer students an integrated perspective on the forces that have changed how "development" is understood in the last quarter of the twentieth century.

By understanding the construction of the development era, students have a basis from which to begin to make sense of current trends of restructuring. These trends involve new discourses and new institutional developments, with a deep-rooted contention over the shape of the emerging world order.

What Is New in This Second Edition?

This second edition has two tasks: updating and reframing the story of the globalization project.

The world has moved on since 1995, when the first edition was completed, and the author's perspective has shifted since then. The two changes are quite related.

The overwhelming change is that both the global development project and its swelling opposition have grown more urgent. Perhaps the urgency is magnified by the millennium, but it also expresses the fragility of the project of globalization. The late 1990s financial crisis, beginning in Asia and spreading to Eastern Europe and Latin America, was one indicator. The crisis not only destabilized the global financial system and the societies concerned but also destabilized the coherence of vision among the global managers. Another indicator is the movement to protect cultural and bio-diversity against the global development project. A growing opposition to bio-engineered food, for example, has recently captured global attention, giving pause to a confident biotech industry and its vision of a global system of food security, with far-reaching implications for the environment, food safety, and millions of small farmers across the South.

It is this encounter, between the attempt to institute a market culture globally and the alternative visions of cultural diversity and bio-diversity from myriad counter-movements, that defines this revision. I have tried to reframe the projects of development and globalization in such interactional terms to emphasize that cultures (including that of the market) are socially constructed and mutually conditioning. This counters the tendency to see "development" and "globalization" as monolithic forces. It also raises the possibility that, being both interactional and multidimensional, the development and globalization projects are (re)constituted by the very social forces they seek to control. It seems to me that it is important for students to understand that although development may be in crisis, resolution lies in part in recognizing that the market is a political construct and cannot constitute a sustainable culture in itself. There are countless examples of grassroots and transnational movements that start from this proposition, and they are slowly but surely interacting.

This revision weaves new historical and contemporary narrative, as well as a series of new case studies, into the existing text to offer a subtler view of the encounter between the global market and its countermovements. There are new case studies of such counter-movements, presented as effective agents that change the terms of encounter—for example, the protective movement of "informalization" that has obtained a certain legitimacy in the eyes of the Tanzanian state; the perplexing issue of female genital mutilation posing universal human versus specific cultural rights and producing local resolution to women's advantage; and the various labor, farmer, and environmentalist movements to resist and protect against the corrosive force of the global market. The two dozen new case studies enrich the narrative and render the concepts more concrete. They also offer a more interactional and open-ended perspective on social change. Finally, to enhance the overall presentation of the concepts, this second edition includes thirteen new graphics, as visualization is an important part of the learning process.

Organization and Language

In examining the experiences of the development project, I have interwoven global and national issues, which helps both to situate current limits to nationally managed development and to show how even national development strategies had intrinsic global dimensions. For example, Chapter 2's discussion of how Third World industrialization depended substantially on a system of food aid organized by the United States demonstrates how a global food system underwrote national developmentalism, instituting a classic developmentalist rural-urban exchange. Subsequent chapters link national agricultural modernization and rural depopulation in the Third World to global problems of growing political instability and international labor migration.

Finally, a word about language. It has become commonplace to note that the Third World and the Second World have ended as coherent entities, and I have tried to record this change during the narrative by adding the epithet "the former" to each of these terms. Although they certainly violate a heterogeneous reality as omnibus terms, they are useful as shorthand and certainly recognizable to most people. I stick with *First World* for no other reason than convenience. Similarly, in some instances I have used the terms *North* and *South* where these categories have a certain currency as political subdivisions of the contemporary world.

Acknowledgments

I have dedicated this book to my wife, Karen Schachere, for a multiplicity of wonderful reasons over and above her patience.

I also wish to express my thanks to the various people who have helped me along the way. I begin with my publisher and editor-in-chief, Steve Rutter, for his remarkable vision and his enthusiasm and faith in this project, both first time and second time around. Charles Ragin, the series editor, convinced me to present a discussion of development as a narrative of the postwar world, to provide necessary background for post–baby boomers in the first edition. Elizabeth MacDonell performed the unenviable task of copyediting the first draft of the original manuscript—she gave me invaluable advice on presentation of the text. Mary Douglas and Patterson Lamb performed their magic in copyediting the second draft of the manuscript. A. J. Sobczak has copyedited the second edition with great care and foresight. Greg and Anne Draus, typesetters, created the pleasing illustrations and book pages. Rebecca Holland took care of more things behind the scenes in publication than I will ever know in her careful professional way. Similarly, Sherith Pankratz has kept me on task with the second edition and kept me in good humor along the way, as only she can do. She has been ably assisted by Windy Just, Jean Skeels, and Ann Makarias. Astrid Virding and Karen Wiley kept the project humming reliably during the production stage. Jillaine Tyson has improved the text through her creative enhancement of some new graphics I provided. Two reviewers, Charles H. Wood of the University of Texas, Austin, and Valerie Gunter of the University of New Orleans, offered many useful hints on improving the presentation of ideas in this text. Several reviewers helped me think toward the second edition, including:

Kazem Alamdari, California State University, Los Angeles
Jill M. Belsky, University of Montana
Ione Y. DeOllos, Ball State University
David Kyle, University of California, Davis

William Loker, California State University, Chico
William I. Robinson, University of Tennessee

Robert Wood of Rutgers gave additional valuable critical reflections
on the second edition draft. Linda Buttel gave invaluable advice
and generous help on computer programming.

Finally, to my friends and supporters I am extremely grateful for your
encouragement and insight. Fred Buttel pushed me to undertake this task,
and he and Harriet Friedmann both went through the whole first draft
with a fine-tooth comb, helped me bring out the big picture, and rescued
me from inconsistency and omission. Richard Williams offered me
invaluable advice on meanings in the text and how to convey them to students. Michelle Adato steered me toward a richer understanding of social
movements. Dale Tomich insisted that I be as didactic as possible—for
me. Gary Gereffi straightened me out on the global production system.
Dia Mohan provided stimulus to new ways of thinking about a world in
which, arguably, everyone is modern. Raj Patel has pitched many useful
questions about how I think about the world. Amod Lele performed Her-
culean tasks bringing interesting graphics to the second edition. My
undergraduate and graduate students (particularly my Teaching Assis-
tants) at Cornell, and some at other institutions I have visited, have contributed many valuable insights. I may not have succeeded in realizing all
this good advice, but to all of you, my thanks.

A Timeline of Developmentalism and Globalism

WORLD FRAMEWORK	**Developmentalism (1940s-1970s)**
POLITICAL ECONOMY	State-Regulated Markets Keynesian Public Spending
SOCIAL GOALS	Social Entitlement and Welfare Uniform Citizenship
DEVELOPMENT [MODEL]	Industrial Replication National Economic Management [Brazil, Mexico, India]
MOBILIZING TOOL	Nationalism (Post-Colonialism)
MECHANISMS	Import-Substitution Industrialization (ISI) Public Investment (Infrastructure and Energy) Education Land Reform
VARIANTS	First World (Freedom of Enterprise) Second World (Central Planning) Third World (Modernization via Developmental Alliance)

MARKERS

Cold War Begins (1946)	Korean War (1950-1953)	Vietnam War (1964-1973)
Bretton Woods (1944)	Marshall Plan (1946)	Alliance for Progress (1961)
United Nations (1943)	Non-Aligned Movement (1955)	U.N. Conference on Trade Development Group of 77 (1964)

FIRST DEVELOPMENT DECADE   SECOND DEVELOPMENT DECADE

- - - - - - ●———————●—————————●—————————●——————
1940   1950   1960   1970

INSTITUTIONAL DEVELOPMENTS

World Bank/IMF/GATT
(1944)   (1944) (1947)
US$ as   PL-480 Program   Eurodollar/
Reserve Currency   (1954)   Offshore $ Market

COMECON
(1947)

Globalism (1970s-)

Self-Regulating Markets (Monetarism)

Private Initiative via Free Markets
Identity Politics Versus Citizenship

Participation in the World Market
Comparative Advantage
[Chile, South Korea]

Efficiency (Post-Developmentalism)
Debt and Credit-Worthiness

Export-Oriented Industrialization (EOI)
Agro-Exporting
Privatization, Public and Majority-Class Austerity
Entrepreneurialism

National Structural Adjustment (Opening Economies)
Regional Free Trade Agreements
Global Economic and Environmental Management

Oil Crises (1973, 1979)	Cold War Ends (1989)	"New World Order" Begins

Debt Regime
(Supervised State/Economy Restructuring)
(mid-1980s)

New International Economic Order Initiative (1974)	Earth Summit (1992) Chiapas Revolt (1994)	World Trade Organization Millennial Round (1999)

DEBT CRISIS/
THE "LOST DECADE"

1970	1980	1990	2000
Group of Seven (G-7) Forms (1975)	GATT Uruguay Round (1984)	NAFTA (1994) World Trade Organization (1995)	
Offshore Banking	IMF/World Bank Structural Adjustment Loans		

Glasnost/Perestroika

Development and Social Change

Development and the Global Marketplace

What Is the World Coming To?

These days the term *globalization* is on practically everyone's lips. Or so it would seem. One of the distinguishing features of this new century is the powerful apparatus of communication that presents an image of a world unified by global technologies and products and their universal appeal. It is almost as if there is no alternative to this image of globalization. And yet we know that while 75 percent of the world's population has access to daily television reception, only 20 percent of the world's population has access to consumer cash or credit.

We may see television commercials depicting the world's peoples consuming global commodities, but it is not as if everyone actually shares either this reality or this image. We know that the 20 percent of the world's people who do have consumer cash or credit consume 86 percent of all goods and services, while the poorest 20 percent consume just 1.3 percent.[1] The distribution of the world's material wealth is extraordinarily uneven. We also know that although we may be accustomed to a commercial culture, there are other cultures (e.g., Amish, Islamic, peasant, forest-dweller) that are either not commercial or not comfortable with commercial definition. Cultural meaning is not universally defined through the market, so "globalization," as it is currently understood, is not necessarily a universal aspiration.

Why, then, is there so much talk of "globalization"? There is no simple answer, but some explanations follow.

- Although the world's peoples and continents have always been connected through exchanges of goods, literature, ideas, and fantasy, the recent communications revolution makes it possible to connect the world more intensively than ever before.

- Through the communications revolution we gain access to and share knowledge of other cultures, and we evaluate different political cultures and their treatment of subgroups, such as children, women, subsistence dwellers, prisoners, homosexuals, indigenous people, and so forth.

■ In the late twentieth century, "globalization" replaced "development" as a serious discourse and project of political and business elites.

■ The increasingly finite world has become the object of powerful countries and corporations concerned to improve their competitive advantage by "capturing" world resources.

■ The increasingly finite world has made itself known to us through the rising degradation of the environment.

■ Tourism is currently the world's largest industry, especially cultural tourism, in which "otherness" is packaged as a cultural export to earn foreign currency.

■ As the world and its natural and cultural resources are subjected to commercial speculation, media images prompt us to imagine the world's diversity as a source of wealth, simultaneously reducing it to a single, global entity.

As hard as it might be, it is worth trying to imagine what globalization might mean to people who do not consume the material benefits or the images of globalization. There are some who aspire to consume, some who view "globalization" as privileging existing consumers, some who find meaning in their own culture but nevertheless feel somehow diminished by the comparison, and some who simply reject consumerism and affirm their culture. Let me illustrate these types, respectively:

■ Some years ago I attended a village meeting, in New Guinea, at which a well-known "cargo cult" member was instructing his fellow villagers to prepare for a shipment of goods from "the outside." Cargo cults construct millennial fantasies about seen or unseen foreign goods or gifts being bestowed upon non-Western peoples, in the absence of being able to conceive of reorganizing their own culture to actually produce such items. This kind of perception is evident in the New Guinean Pidgin English term for "helicopter"—"mixmaster belongim Jesus"—which suggests that divine providence is somehow connected to the artifacts of industrial civilization.

■ In Judith Hellman's book *Mexican Lives*, a street vendor named Rosario anticipates the impact of globalization (via the North American Free Trade Agreement) on those Mexicans who survive by smuggling goods across the Texan border to sell in Mexico

City: *"You have to understand, thousands of people at the border live from collecting bribes. . . . If free trade comes, they'll find another way to shake us down, or maybe they won't let us cross at all. The NAFTA treaty isn't meant to rescue people like us, it's meant for the rich."*[2]

- Helena Norberg-Hodge's book *Ancient Futures* describes how Ladakhi people, whose economy is not governed by money, perceive Western culture through contact with tourists, armed with cameras and seemingly infinite amounts of money, for which they evidently do not have to work: "In one day a tourist would spend the same amount that a Ladakhi family might in a year. Ladakhis did not realize that money played a completely different role for the foreigners; that back home they needed it to survive; that food, clothing, and shelter all cost money—a lot of money. Compared to these strangers they suddenly felt poor." Here, an invidious comparison with Western culture occurs through quite artificial contact. The author remarks that Ladakhis "cannot so readily see the social or psychological dimensions—the stress, the loneliness, the fear of growing old. Nor can they see environmental decay, inflation, or unemployment. On the other hand, they know their own culture inside out, including all its limitations and imperfections."[3]

- Jose Maria Arguedes, an Andean poet, writes, in "A Call to Certain Academics":[4]

> *They say that we do not know anything*
> *That we are backwardness*
> *That our head needs changing for a better one*
> *They say that some learned men are saying this about us*
> *These academics who reproduce themselves*
> *In our lives*
> *What is there on the banks of these rivers, Doctor?*
> *Take out your binoculars*
> *And your spectacles*
> *Look if you can.*
> *Five hundred flowers*
> *From five hundred different types of potato*
> *Grow on the terraces*
> *Above abysses*
> *That your eyes don't reach*
> *These five hundred flowers*
> *Are my brain*
> *My flesh*

In juxtaposing these images, it is obvious that despite powerful images of a world converging on a common consumer culture, there are alternative currents of meaning and social organization. How the differences will be resolved is, of course, one of the key issues that frames the twenty-first century. Many perspectives and voices express these tensions. Here I offer two such perspectives:

- Renato Ruggiero, the former Director-General of the World Trade Organization, expressed the view of the proponents of economic globalization when he remarked in the late 1990s: "More than ever before, the world's prosperity . . . rests on maintaining an open international economy based on commonly agreed rules. . . . [B]y opening their economies . . . countries accelerate their development." He also stated, "What is at stake as we contemplate the future of the multilateral system is much more than trade and economics. It involves questions of political and economic security. It is about how relations among countries and peoples are to be structured. It determines whether we foster international solidarity or descend into a spiral of global friction and conflict."[5]

- Richard Neville, a consultant to business on alternative futures, remarks in an article titled "The Business of Being Human":

  The point of business is to provide profit. The point of culture is to provide meaning. Can the two be reconciled? Not entirely; and we are doing our best to overlook the fact. This denial fuels our thirst for distraction, glorifies the ugly and endangers the ecosystem. On the other hand, it's kind of fun. Look at the queues outside Planet Hollywood. . . . Each year, the total corporate expenditure on advertising and marketing is more than $US 620 billion, making it the boldest psychological project ever undertaken by the human race. It works out to more than $100 for every person on the planet, most of whom will never have the means to acquire the BMWs, the microwaves, the designer labels."[6]

Taking our cue from these statements, the twenty-first century appears to be shaping up as an elemental conflict between profits and meaning. Although this scenario may be too simplified, it does seem to capture one of the key sources of tension attached to "globalization." In particular, it signals the conflict between the market culture that would unify the world and the popular cultures that differentiate the world as a mosaic of lifestyles. Of course these two cultural types intermingle, but their horizons are "global" and "local," respectively, and the survival of each increasingly depends on limiting the autonomy (or power) of the other. An example of this tension is the controversy regularly generated by animated Disney films that attempt to appeal to consumers' multicultural impulses, but via Westernized cultural images. Critics charge that the characters—whether Aladdin, Pocahontas, or Mulan—reproduce ethnic stereotypes that privilege the commercial success of the global Disney corporation and diminish the dignity and complexity of the historical cultures depicted.

Another, related tension concerns the social and environmental impact of the global market culture. An article in *The Washington Post* addressed to North American coffee drinkers, headlined "Where Were Your Beans Grown," made the observation that coffee farming in Central America is reducing the songbird population. Russell Greenberg, a scientist from the Smithsonian Institute, has documented the decline of bird life in Central America related partly to the boom in coffee drinking. As rain forests disappeared, 150 species of migratory songbirds relocated to the traditional shade trees that protect young coffee plants on the plantations. As coffee drinking intensifies, farmers remove the shade trees and substitute sunlight and chemicals to accelerate bean growth, thereby reducing bird habitats.[7]

This kind of environmental impact is widespread and indicates the conflict between rising market demand for globally produced goods, on one hand, and the sustainability of ecological and social systems at the points of production on the other. The world was shocked in 1998 when tropical hurricanes wrought widespread disaster in Central America, with mudslides destroying thousands of low-income dwellings and the lives of many of their inhabitants. Vulnerability to mudslides was a consequence of over-logging of the rain forests for timber, commercial cropland, and pastures to sustain lucrative exports to the world market. Central America was losing about 180 acres of trees an hour. Global warming was blamed for the torrential rains that fell that year in Central America as well as in China and Bangladesh.[8]

When people read about these disasters and their link to the market culture, inevitably they feel a sense of powerlessness in the face of such huge, transnational dilemmas. As awareness of the connections grows, however, people find ways and means to respond. For example, Russell Greenberg involved himself in the Smithsonian-sanctioned promotion of "shade-grown coffee" beans under a "Café Audubon" brand. He was emulating other consumer-led movements, such as the dolphin-safe tuna campaign and consumer boycotts of soccer balls stitched by children in Pakistan, to use consumer power to arrest social and ecological harm arising from unregulated market practices. In these ways, the tension between profits and meaning finds expression.

The Global Marketplace

Much of what we wear, use, and consume today has global origins. Even when a product has a domestic, "Made In . . ." label, its journey to market probably combines components and labor from production and assembly sites around the world. Sneakers, or parts thereof, might be produced in China or Indonesia, blue jeans assembled in the Philippines, a transistor radio or compact disk player put together in Singapore, and a watch made in Hong Kong. The fast food eaten by North Americans may include chicken diced in Mexico or hamburger beef from cattle raised in Costa Rica. Depending on taste, our coffee is from Southeast Asia, the Americas, or Africa. We may not be global citizens, yet, but we are global consumers.

The global marketplace binds us all. The Japanese eat poultry fattened in Thailand with American corn, using chopsticks made with wood from Indonesian or Chilean forests. Canadians eat strawberries grown in Mexico with fertilizer from the United States. Consumers on both sides of the Atlantic wear clothes assembled in Saipan with Chinese labor, drink orange juice from concentrate made with Brazilian oranges, and decorate their homes with flowers from Colombia. The British and French eat green beans from Kenya, and cocoa from Ghana finds its way into Swiss chocolate. Consumers everywhere are surrounded, and often identified, by world products.

Commodity Chains and Development

The global marketplace is a tapestry of networks of commodity exchanges that bind producers and consumers across the world. In any one network, there is a sequence of production stages, located in a number of countries at sites that provide inputs of labor and materials contributing to the fabrication of a final product. Sociologists call the networks **commodity chains**.* Chains link each input stage, as a local combination of commodities, and together these phases form a finished good sold in the global marketplace. The chain metaphor illuminates the interconnections among producing communities dispersed across the world, and it allows us to understand that when we consume a final product in a commodity chain, we participate in a global process that links us to a variety of places, people, and resources. Although we may experience consumption individually, it is fundamentally social.

---

*All boldfaced terms are defined in the Glossary/Index.

Not everything we consume has such global origins, but the trend toward these worldwide supply networks is powerful. It is transforming the scale of economic development, reaching beyond regional and national boundaries. Some researchers, for example, have noted that the ingredients of a container of yogurt, from the strawberries and milk to the cardboard and ink for the carton, travel more than 6,000 miles to market in Germany, and yet all could be produced within a 50-mile radius.[9] As more and more goods and services are produced on this transnational scale, **development** assumes a different meaning. In the past, we understood development to be a process of economic growth organized nationally, but today, global economic integration is transforming development into a process of *globally organized economic growth.*

As former WTO Director Renato Ruggiero was quoted above as saying, globalization is now perceived as indispensable to development. This is a powerful idea that informs development policies made by national governments and international development agencies, like the World Bank. Most governments across the world are participating in an opening of their economies to global competition, or, in the case of the European Union, synchronizing their macroeconomic policies by adopting a common currency, the euro, in order to streamline the European economy and give it a global competitive edge. This initiative gathered steam when the United States, Canada, and Mexico signed the **North American Free Trade Agreement (NAFTA)** in 1994, providing the United States with a huge open market as a home base. The point is that development and globalization have become synonymous—for business and political elites across the world.

As Rosario the street vendor observed, however, the marriage of development and globalization is spawning quite uneven offspring, as some regions and populations survive and prosper and others decline. On the margins there are new currents of grassroots activity seeking to formulate and implement alternative, locally sustainable forms of development. In many cases these forms of development have different goals: (1) they focus on basic needs rather than the rising material expectations that we associate with the consumer culture, and (2) they view local participation, and therefore cultural meaning, as an indispensable part of the local development process.

These are the two major currents of "development" today, and it is important to understand that they are very much related to each other. For one thing, the global marketplace is quite uneven in its consequences:

- With the collapse of Soviet communism in 1989, Russia joined the global capitalist club only to experience a dramatic compression of living standards for most Russians, as their Gross Domestic Product declined 52 percent through 1995, and this situation has worsened since then.[10]

■ The 1997 United Nations *Human Development Report* noted, for example, that of the 4.4 billion people in developing countries, about 60 percent lack access to safe sewers, 67 percent have no access to clean water, 25 percent have inadequate housing, and 20 percent have no access to modern health services of any kind.

■ The average African household today consumes 20 percent less than it did a quarter of a century ago.

■ The $17 billion spent annually in the United States and Europe on pet food exceeds by $4 billion the estimated annual additional cost of providing basic health and nutrition for everyone in the world![11]

In the context of globalization and rising global inequalities, many marginalized communities are responding by developing their own survival strategies, both material and cultural. As globalization proceeds, local initiatives spring up. Development agencies like the World Bank are noticing this and channeling funds to nongovernmental organizations (NGOs) that are involved in grassroots endeavors, such as micro-credit distribution. Some say that the World Bank is merely trying to stabilize communities that have experienced marginalization from the global marketplace; nevertheless, even here the global developer assumes a local face.

Global Networks

In today's world, the interdependencies among people, communities, and nations are ever present. When we consume, we consume an image (of aesthetic or athletic dimensions, say) as well as materials and labor from many places in the global marketplace. Just as all humans eventually breathe the same air and drink the same water, consumers enjoy the fruits of others' labor.

The *global labor force* is dispersed among the production links of these commodity chains (see Figure 1). In the U.S.-based athletic shoe industry, the initial labor is related to the symbolic side of the shoe design—and marketing. This step remains primarily in the United States. Then there is the labor of producing the synthetic materials; of dyeing, cutting, and

FIGURE 1

A Commodity Chain for Athletic Shoes

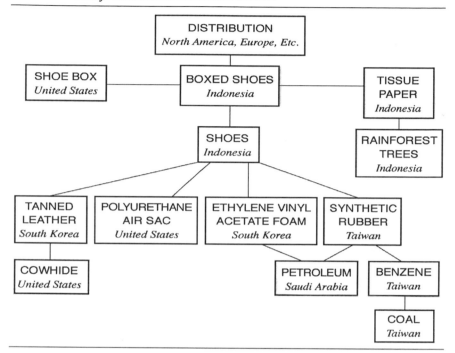

SOURCE: Bill Ryan and Alan Durning, "The Story of a Shoe," *World Watch*, March/April 1998.

stitching; and of assembling, packing, and transporting. These forms of labor are all relatively unskilled and often performed by women, especially South Koreans, Taiwanese, Chinese, Indonesians, and Filipinos. Companies like Nike subcontract with such labor forces through local firms in the regional production sites. South Korea and Taiwan are among the more reliable sites, generally having greater capacity and greater quality control than some other countries, but a shoe that costs Nike $20 on export from South Korea may cost only $15 if made in Indonesia or China. In fact, in 1996, Nike's expensive trainers, worth $150 in the United States and Europe, were assembled by some 120,000 Indonesian contract workers earning less than $3 a day, which, although a starvation wage, met the legal minimum that applies to more than half of Indonesia's 80 million–person labor force. Depending on political and/or economic conditions, a company like Nike will shift a substantial part of its production to these lower-wage sites.[12]

Relocating production is a routine part of any competitive firm's oper-ations today. As fashion and design change, and with them labor costs and management patterns, so may the location of production. Firms reroute the production chains to stay competitive. Any shopper at The Gap, for example, knows that this clothing retailer competes by changing its styles on a six-week cycle. The key to this kind of flexible organization is to use far-flung subcontractors who can be brought on line or let go as the market changes. The people who work for these subcontractors often have little security as one of the small links in this global commodity chain. Of course, job security varies by commodity, firm, and industry, but the insecurity of employment all over the world reflects the uncertain-ties of the global market.

We hear a lot of discussion about whether the relocation of jobs from the United States, Europe, and Japan to the "developing countries" is a short-term or a long-term trend. The topic raises questions.

- First, are "mature" economies shedding their manufacturing jobs and becoming global centers of service industries (e.g., education, retailing, finance, insurance, marketing)?

- Second, do those jobs that shift "south" descend a wage ladder toward the cheapest labor, for example in China?

- Third, are these only temporary competitive strategies by firms to reduce costs, or is the world being restratified into low- and high-wage regions for the foreseeable future?

We examine such questions in the following chapters, because the re-distribution of jobs on a global scale is an indicator of a profound trans-formation underway in the world, a transformation that is redefining the parameters and meaning of development.

Another example from the global marketplace concerns conditions of work, illustrated in the global food industry. More and more fruits and vegetables are being grown under corporate contract by peasants and agricultural laborers around the world. Chile exports grapes, apples, pears, apricots, cherries, peaches, and avocados to the United States dur-ing the winter months. Caribbean nations produce bananas, citrus fruits, and frozen vegetables, and Mexico supplies American supermarkets with tomatoes, broccoli, bell peppers, cucumbers, and cantaloupes. Thailand grows pineapples and asparagus for the Japanese market, and Kenya exports strawberries, mangoes, and chilies to Europe. In short, the global fruit and salad bowl is bottomless. In an era when much of this production is now organized by huge food companies that subcontract with growers and sell in consumer markets across the world, these growers face new conditions of work.

As discussed in Chapter 1, non-Europeans have been producing specialized agricultural products for export for some time, but the scale and profitability of export food production have expanded greatly in recent decades as the number and concentration of world consumers have grown. Firms must remain flexible to compete in the global marketplace. Not only does this need for flexibility bring growers across the world into competition with one another as firms seek to keep costs down, but it also means that the produce itself must meet high standards of quality and consistency. Growers find that their work is defined by the needs of the firm to maintain its market image and a predictable supply of products desirable to consumers across the world. So not only is the job insecure, but its very performance is shaped by global market requirements.

Most contract growing of fruits and vegetables is done by women. Women are considered more reliable as workers than men; they can be trained to monitor plant health and growth and to handle fruit and work efficiently. Employers presume that women are more suited to the seasonal and intermittent employment practices (e.g., harvesting, processing, and packing) necessary to mount a flexible operation.[13] Increasingly, the needs of the global marketplace shape the conditions of work and livelihoods in communities across the world.

Social Dimensions of the Global Marketplace

Globalization is ultimately a local phenomenon. It is difficult to imagine the changing web of social networks across the world that produce our market culture. We do not think about the global dimensions of the product we purchase at a supermarket or store. The market, and its far-reaching effects on our lives, seems almost natural. We disregard these connections at our peril, for several reasons:

- We can no longer understand the changes in our society without situating them globally.

- We are likely to misinterpret social upheavals across the world if we ignore the contributions of global processes to political and economic instability.

- We cannot understand the consequences of disturbances in our complex biosphere without taking account of world-scale social transformations and stress on natural resources.

Along many of the commodity chains that sustain our lifestyle are people who experience globalization in quite different ways. Many are not consumers of commodities: four-fifths of the roughly 5 billion people in the world do not have access to consumer cash or credit.[14] Even so, they are often the producers of what we consume, and their societies are shaped as profoundly by the global marketplace as ours, if not more so. We seldom remember this.

Rain forest destruction, for example, is linked to the expanding global marketplace, although the connections are not always direct. Since the 1970s, Brazilian peasants have been displaced as their land has been taken for high-tech production of soybeans for export to feed Japanese livestock. These people have migrated en masse from the Brazilian southeast to the Amazon region to settle on rain forest land. Their dramatic nonrenewable and devastating burning of the forests captured the world's attention in the 1980s. It forced the industrialized world to see a link between poverty and environmental destruction.

Less obvious, however, is the precipitating connection between rising demand for animal protein in the Northern Hemisphere and rain forest destruction. This connection is obscured by our customary view of development as a *national* process, making it even more difficult for us to view this episode as a global dynamic with particular local effects. The case study of the "hamburger connection" outlines one such instance of world-scale social transformation with distinct local effects.

CASE STUDY

The Hamburger Connection

Between 1960 and 1990 forests disappeared at alarming rates in Central America. During this time, more than 25 percent of the Central American forest was converted to pasture for cattle that were in turn converted into hamburgers. Deforestation was linked, by way of the global marketplace, to an expanding fast-food industry in the United States. About one-tenth of American burgers use imported beef, much of it produced under contract for transnational food companies by Central American meat-packing plants. The Central American beef industry has had powerful institutional support through government loans assisted by the World Bank, the Agency for International Development (AID), and the Inter-American Development Bank

(IADB). The plan was to tie the development of Central American societies to this valuable export earner.

Few people realized that consuming a hamburger might also involve consuming forest resources or that Central America's new beef industry would have vast environmental and social consequences. These consequences include the displacement of peasants from their land and forest-dwellers from their habitat because more than half of Central American land was committed to grazing cattle. As less land was available for farming, the production of peasant staple foods declined. The Costa Rican government had to use beef export earnings to purchase basic grains on the world market to compensate for the declining local food supply and to feed the country's people. The global process of which the hamburger chain is part is thus linked to social and other changes in North and Central America.

Sources: Myers, 1981, p. 7; Place, 1985, pp. 290-295; Rifkin, 1992, pp. 192-193.

A brief examination of the hamburger industry demonstrates how products that may be everyday items of consumption, particularly in the wealthier segments of the global market, may have considerable effects on producers and producing regions where they are made. Not only are producers and consumers linked across space by commodity chains, but these links have profound social implications.

As we begin to examine the social links, we see that they are often tenuous and unsustainable. The more links that are made, the more interdependent become the fortunes of laborers, producers, and consumers across the world. A change in fashion can throw a whole producing community out of work. A footloose firm seeking lower wages can do the same thing. A new food preference in one part of the world will intensify export agriculture somewhere else. Intensification may offer the security of a contract to a grower community for a time, but it may also increase that community's vulnerability to a more competitive producer elsewhere, given the variability of land fertility and wages and the mobility of firms. The intensification of beef exporting not only may displace a peasant community, but also a local culture of mixed economy interwoven with food crops and livestock may give way to specialized pasturing of steers. It also may affect the economic priorities of a nation as well as that nation's (and the world's) resource base.

Dimensions of Social Change in the Global Marketplace

The changing composition and rhythms of the global marketplace connect people and development conditions across the world. Such interconnections have three dimensions:

- First, there is the integration of producers and consumers across space as commodities crisscross political boundaries.

- Second, this spatial integration introduces new dimensions of time as world market rhythms enter into and connect physically separate communities. For instance, a firm that establishes an export site in a community brings new work disciplines required for production of goods for the global market.

- Third, once communities are integrated into the new time and space of the global market, they are increasingly subject to decisions made by powerful market agencies such as governments, firms, and currency or commodity speculators. If oil prices spike, for example, the effect is felt in a variety of ways by a variety of groups in the global economy, from farmers through petrochemical firms to travelers. If there is a run on national currencies, as in the 1997 Asian financial crisis, whole populations can suffer as they have in Indonesia, Thailand, and South Korea.

The market's continual reorganization dramatically affects the livelihoods of people and their life trajectories. Today the global athletic shoe industry, turning footwear into fashion, generates new and evolving employment opportunities in the United States (specialty shoe stores, product design, and marketing) and in East and Southeast Asia (production and assembly). Capturing market shares by designing fashion and finding cheap labor sites is the name of the game, but this game continually reshuffles the employment deck and people's futures. Although money makes this world go around, its accelerated circulation compresses people's lives into a unified social space (the global marketplace) and time (the rhythms and cycles of the global economy).

Consider again the dynamics of the beef chain. Not only does rising hamburger consumption incorporate new grazing regions into the global marketplace, but this new space itself has its own time. In the United States, beef consumption developed and grew throughout the century-long process of settling the American (rural and urban) frontier. The current fast-food demand, however, compresses the modernization process for forest-dwellers and Indian peasants, forcing them to adapt in a single generation, converting their habitats to pasture and displacing many of them to urban fringes. On the broader scale, the burning of forests and grazing of livestock intensify the threat to future generations of global warming. We are seeing the actions of humankind endangering the habitability of the planet. Here the long run, or rather our sense of it, is compromised by the finiteness of biospheric resources: perhaps the most dramatic effect of the compression of space and time.

Development as a Global Process

This introduction illustrates, through the examples of commodity chains and their social and environmental impacts, the global nature of economic activity. It may still be pursued by individual nation-states, but less and less does it resemble the conventional definition of development as *nationally organized economic growth*. In this book, we examine the ways the world has moved from nationally organized growth toward *globally organized economic growth*.

Development and economic growth are active goals, rather than natural processes. We know this from observing still-existing communities of forest-dwellers, who fashion their lives according to natural cycles. With the rise of modern European capitalism, state bureaucrats pursued economic growth to finance their military and administrative needs, but "development" as such was not yet a universal strategy. It became so only in the mid-twentieth century, as newly independent states joined the world community and the rush toward development, with quite varying success.

We are now in an era of rethinking development, given the evident failure of many countries to fulfill the promise of development and the world's growing awareness of environmental limits. In this context, *sustainability* has become a popular issue, forcing a reevaluation of the development enterprise. This book traces the changing fortunes of development efforts, the shortcomings of which have produced two responses. One is to advocate a thoroughly global marketplace to expand trade and spread the wealth. The other is to reevaluate the economic emphasis and to recover a sense of cultural community.

The "development debate" is re-forming around a conflict between privileging the global market and privileging human communities: Do we continue expanding industry and wealth indefinitely, or do we find a way that human communities (however defined) can recover social intimacy, spiritual coherence, healthy environments, and sustainable material practices? Both visions are confronting a changing world, possibly a declining world, of which each is increasingly well aware.

These visions echo the elemental conflict between profits and meaning stemming from the rise of Western rationalism. This draws from an economic model driven by technology and market behavior rather than from existing cultures. The globalization of this model, therefore, is likely to generate cultural tensions, especially where non-Western cultures are affected. The dilemma resides, partly, in the unequal power between Western states and firms and non-Western states, firms, and communities. This inequality is often expressed in the tension between the "haves" and the "have-nots," or between the North (Western Europe, Japan, and North America) and the South (Africa, Latin America, and Asia). It is interesting that inequality and tension are growing within both North and South as globalization intensifies. The major thrust of this book is to make these tensions intelligible by situating them within a global, historical framework.

PART I

The Development Project
(Late 1940s to Early 1970s)

1

Instituting the Development Project

Development is a term we mostly take for granted. But what does it really mean? And to what does it apply? The answer to these questions is surely contextual. From the perspective of the twenty-first century cybernetic age, development is often associated with technological progress. Of course that perspective may not coincide with that of the majority of the world's population, as suggested in the introductory section. Nevertheless, in this view development is understood to be positive because it brings material and psychological improvement as humans learn to manipulate the natural world.

It is, of course, hard to argue with the notion of improving material benefits—but the question, as always, is at what cost? Technological progress does not just come to us; it involves continual (and indeed, accelerating) change in social and environmental arrangements. We tend to evaluate development in terms of outcomes and gains (e.g., incomes, goods and services), but it is also important to evaluate it in terms of what people give up or lose (and why they resist) in experiencing development in these terms. In addition, who gets left out?

Although development certainly is most clearly linked to economic growth, it has other, related, faces. The U.N.'s *Human Development Report* (1990), for instance, stated:

> [T]he basic objective of human development is to enlarge the range of people's choices to make development more democratic and participatory. These choices should include access to income and employment opportunities, education and health, and a clean and safe physical environment. Each individual should also have the opportunity to participate fully in community decisions and to enjoy human, economic and political freedoms.[1]

Our general image of development is of *directional change*. Sociologists characterize such change as occurring in the governing beliefs of societies (from religious to secular rule), in their spatial patterns (from rural to urban living), or in their material means (from animal to machine power).

3

That is, development has come to be identified with a Western lifestyle. Most non-Western cultures have been exposed to this lifestyle, and some of their people (especially their social and political elites) have adopted Western styles of consumption. In addition, many non-Western societies have followed Western patterns in belief, in social patterns, and in material activities. It is almost as if, because of its universal appeal, development is natural.

Lately, however, countertrends have been emerging: some religious fundamentalists challenge westernization; some environmentalists argue that our resource-dependent consumer lifestyle cannot be sustained, that we have in fact depleted our natural environment beyond a point of no return; growing numbers of people across the world inhabit "underground" or informal economies (on the margins of the formal political and economic system); and Western economies face a growing problem of maintaining stable employment. In other words, what might appear natural is not necessarily universally shared or permanent.

How can we untangle this puzzle? The most fruitful way is to think about the *historical* context in which development has evolved. History provides some answers to how development has come to assume a particular meaning—of cumulative change with a specific direction. Further, history allows us to understand how this conception of development has become naturalized as a universal process.

Colonialism

Our appeal to history begins with a powerful simplification. It concerns the social psychology of European colonialism, built largely around stereotypes that have shaped perceptions and conflict for five centuries. (Colonialism is defined and explained in the following insert, and the European colonial empires are depicted in Figure 1.1.) One such perception was the idea among Europeans that non-European native people or colonial subjects were "backward," or trapped in their tradition. The experience of colonial rule encouraged this image, as European and non-European cultures compared one another within a relationship in which Europe had a powerful social-psychological advantage backed up by its military-industrial apparatus. This comparison was interpreted, or misinterpreted, as European cultural superiority. It was easy to take the next step and view the difference as "progress," something the colonizers could impart to their subjects, at will.

FIGURE 1.1

European Colonial Empires at the Turn of the Twentieth Century

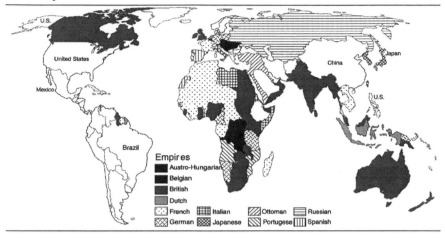

What Is Colonialism?

Colonialism is the subjugation by physical and psychological force of one culture by another—a colonizing power—through military conquest of territory. It predates the era of European expansion (fifteenth to twentieth centuries), extending, for example, to Japanese colonialism in the twentieth century and, more recently, Chinese colonization of Tibet. Colonialism has two forms: colonies of settlement, which often eliminate indigenous people (such as the Spanish destruction of the Aztec and Inca civilizations in the Americas), and colonies of rule, where colonial administrators reorganize existing cultures to facilitate their exploitation (such as the British use of local *zamindars* to rule the Indian subcontinent). The outcomes are, first, the cultural genocide or marginalization of indigenous people; second, the extraction of labor, cultural treasures, and resources to enrich the colonial power, its private interests, and public museums; third, the elaboration of ideologies justifying colonial rule, including notions of racism and modernity; and fourth, various responses by colonial subjects, ranging from death, through submission and internalization of inferiority, to a variety of resistances—from everyday forms through sporadic uprisings to mass political mobilization.

Such a powerful misinterpretation of other cultures appears frequently in historical accounts. It is reflected in assumptions made by settlers in the Americas and Australasia about the indigenous people they encountered. In each case, the Europeans perceived the Indians and aborigines as people who did not work the land they inhabited. In other words, they had no right of "property"—a European concept. Their removal from their ancestral lands is a bloody reminder of the combined military power and moral fervor with which European colonization was pursued. It was buttressed by a process of cultural conquest, whereby Europeans systematically devalued and redefined non-European cultures in terms of European "superiority."

In precolonial Africa, as communities achieved stability within their environment, they developed methods for survival that were related to kinship patterns and supernatural belief systems. These methods were at once conservative and adaptive because, over time, African communities changed their composition, their scale, and their location in a long process of settlement and migration through the lands south of the equator. European colonists in Africa, however, saw these superstitious and traditional cultures as only occupying, rather than improving, the land. This perception ignored the complex social systems adapted first to African ecology and then to European occupation of that ecology.[2] Under these circumstances, the idea of the "white man's burden" emerged, a concept in which the West viewed itself as the bearer of civilization to the darker races. French colonial historian Albert Sarraut claimed in 1923:

> It should not be forgotten that we are centuries ahead of them, long centuries during which—slowly and painfully, through a lengthy effort of research, invention, meditation and intellectual progress aided by the very influence of our temperate climate—a magnificent heritage of science, experience and moral superiority has taken shape, which makes us eminently entitled to protect and lead the races lagging behind us.[3]

The ensuing colonial exchange, however, was captured in the postcolonial African saying: "When the white man came he had the Bible and we had the land. When the white man left we had the Bible and he had the land." Under colonialism, when non-Europeans lost control of their land, their spiritual life was compromised insofar as it was connected to their landscapes. It was difficult to sustain material and cultural integrity under these degrading conditions.

The non-European world thus appeared backward to the colonizers, who assumed that non-Europeans would and should emulate European social organization. *Modernity*, or development, came to be identified as the destiny of humankind. The systematic handicapping of non-Europeans in this apparently natural and fulfilling endeavor remained largely unacknowledged. Being left holding the Bible was an apt metaphor for the condition of non-Europeans who were encouraged to pursue the European way, often without the resources to accomplish this.

Western secular and religious crusades in the forms of administration, education, and missionary efforts accompanied colonial rule to stimulate progress along the European path. The problem was that the ruling Europeans either misunderstood or denied the integrity of non-European cultures. Another problem was that Europeans ignored the paradox of bringing progress to colonized peoples whose sovereignty they denied—a paradox experienced daily by the non-Europeans.

This paradox fuelled the anti-colonial movements that sought to wrest independence from Western occupation. Colonial subjects powerfully appropriated European talk of the "rights of man," employing it as a mirror to their colonial masters and as a mobilizing tool for their independence struggle. But independence for what? In a *post*colonial world, non-European cultures had been either destroyed or irrevocably changed through colonial histories. Newly independent states emerged, and political leaders had to operate in an international framework that was not of their making, but through which they needed political legitimacy. In the first place, their newly independent states were materially disorganized and required economic stimulation. Second, the acceptable model of economic stimulation was the European model of development. Third, the source of stimulation was European economic aid. In short, the framework within which political independence was realized was that of the European conception of development. The adoption of the European model across the formerly colonial world in the post–World War II era was the underpinning of what we shall call the **development project**.

We continually evaluate the terms of the development project throughout this book, because (1) the project has been modified in various ways since the 1950s, as the world has changed, and (2) it is increasingly questioned as some of its expectations have failed to materialize. For the moment, it is important to emphasize that the founding assumptions and practices of the development project represented *historical choices* rather than an inevitable unfolding of human destiny. As we see in this chapter, the development project was an organized strategy to overcome the legacies of colonialism, several of which are discussed below.

FIGURE 1.2

The "Colonial Division of Labor" Between European States and Their Colonial Empires

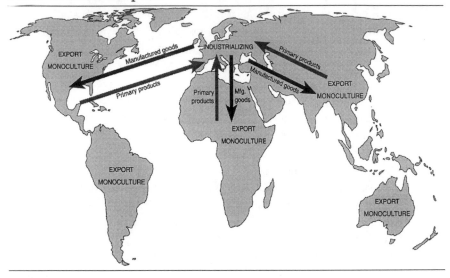

The Colonial Division of Labor

From the sixteenth century, European colonists and traders traveled along African coasts to the New World and across the Indian Ocean and the China seas seeking fur, precious metals, slave labor, spices, tobacco, cacao, potatoes, sugar, and cotton. The European colonial powers—Spain, Portugal, Holland, France, and Britain—and their merchant companies exchanged manufactured goods such as cloth, guns, and implements for these products and for Africans taken into slavery and transported to the Americas. In the process, they reorganized the world.

The basic pattern was to establish in the colonies specialized extraction and production of raw materials and primary products that were unavailable in Europe. In turn, European manufacturing grew on the basis of these products as they became industrial inputs and foodstuffs for its industrial labor force. On a world scale, this specialization between European economies and their colonies came to be termed the **colonial**, or **international, division of labor**, illustrated in Figure 1.2.

The colonial division of labor had two basic effects: it stimulated European industrialization, and it forced non-Europeans into primary commodity production. Such specialization disorganized non-European cultures, undermining local crafts and mixed-farming systems as well as

What Are Some Characteristics of Precolonial Cultures?

All precolonial cultures had their own ways of satisfying their material and spiritual needs. Cultures varied by the differentiation among their members or households according to their particular ecological endowments and social contact with other cultures. The variety ranged from small communities of subsistence producers (living off the land or the forest) to extensive kingdoms or states. Subsistence producers, organized by kin relations, usually subdivided social tasks between men, who hunted and cleared land for cultivation, and women, who cultivated and processed crops, harvested wild fruits and nuts, and performed household tasks. These cultures were highly skilled in resource management and production to satisfy their material needs. They generally did not produce a surplus beyond what was required for their immediate needs, and they organized cooperatively—a practice that often made them vulnerable to intruders because they were not prepared for self-defense. Unlike North American Indians, whose organization provided leadership for resistance, some aboriginal cultures, such as those of Australia and the Amazon, lacked leadership hierarchies and were more easily wiped out by settlers. By contrast, the Mogul empire in seventeenth-century India had a complex hierarchical organization based on local chiefdoms in which the chief presided over the village community and ensured that surpluses (monetary taxes and produce) were delivered to a prosperous central court and "high culture." Village and urban artisans produced a range of metal goods, pottery, and crafts, including sophisticated muslins and silks. Caste distinctions, linked to previous invasions, corresponded to divisions of labor, such as trading, weaving, cultivating, ruling, and performing unskilled labor. Colonizers typically adapted this social and political hierarchy to their own ends.

Sources: Rowley, 1974; Bujra, 1992.

alienating their lands. Not only did non-European cultures surrender their own handicraft industries in this exchange, but they also were often forced to reduce their agriculture to a specialized **export monoculture**, where local farmers became producers of a single crop for export. The disruption caused by this shift is made clear in the preceding insert, which illustrates the interrelation and interdependence of all facets of a precolonial culture.

The destruction of non-European handicraft industries is well known. For example, in the East African kingdom of Buganda, British colonists found a thriving political culture with sophisticated craft production of barkcloth and pottery, neither of which was useful to Europe. Following the creation of the colonial state of Uganda in 1894, these crafts all but disappeared as Bugandan peasants were forced into producing cotton and coffee for export.[4]

Perhaps the best-known subjugation of native crafts occurred through Britain's conquest of India. Until the nineteenth century, Indian muslins and calicos were luxury imports into Europe (as were Chinese silks and satins). By that time, however, the East India Company (which ruled India for the British crown until 1858) undermined this Indian craft and, in its own words, "succeeded in converting India from a manufacturing country into a country exporting raw produce."[5] The company had convinced the British government to use tariffs of 70 to 80 percent against Indian finished goods and to permit virtually free entry of raw cotton into England. In turn, British traders flooded India with cheap cloth manufactured in Manchester. Industrial technology (textile machinery and steam engine) combined with political power to impose the colonial division of labor, as British-built railway systems moved Indian raw cotton to coastal ports for shipment to Liverpool, and returned to the Indian countryside with machine-made products that undermined a time-honored craft.

Social Reorganization Under Colonialism

The colonial division of labor devastated producing communities and their craft- and agriculture-based systems. When the British first came to India, in the mid-eighteenth century, Robert Clive described the textile city of Dacca as "extensive, populous, and rich as the city of London." By 1840, Sir Charles Trevelyan testified before a British parliamentary committee that the population of Dacca "has fallen from 150,000 to 30,000, and the jungle and malaria are fast encroaching upon the town. . . . Dacca, the Manchester of India, has fallen off from a very flourishing town to a very poor and small town."[6]

While native industries declined under colonial systems, local farming cultures lost their best lands to commercial agriculture supplying European consumers and industries. Plantations and other kinds of cash-cropping arrangements sprang up across the colonial world, producing

TABLE 1.1
Selected Colonial Export Crops

Colony	Colonial Power	Export Crop
Australia	Britain	wool
Brazil	Portugal	sugar
Ceylon	Britain	tea
Egypt	Britain	cotton
Ghana	Britain	cocoa
Haiti	France	sugar
India	Britain	cotton, opium
Indochina	France	rubber, rice
Indonesia	Holland	rubber, tobacco
Ivory Coast	France	cocoa
Kenya	Britain	wool
Malaya	Britain	rubber, palm oil
Senegal	France	peanuts
South Africa	Britain	gold, diamonds

specialized tropical exports ranging from bananas to peanuts, depending on local agri-ecologies (see Table 1.1). In India, production of commercial crops such as cotton, jute, tea, peanuts, and sugar cane grew by 85 percent between the 1890s and the 1940s. In contrast, in that same period, local food crop production declined by 7 percent while the population grew by 40 percent, a shift that spread hunger and social unrest.[7]

The colonial division of labor fueled European capitalist civilization (with food and raw materials) at the same time that it disrupted non-European farming cultures. As European industrial society matured, the exploding urban populations demanded ever-increasing imports of sugar, coffee, tea, cocoa, tobacco, and vegetable oils from the colonies, and the expanding factory system demanded ever-increasing inputs of raw materials such as cotton, timber, rubber, and jute. The colonists forced more and more subjects to work in cash cropping, employing a variety of methods such as enslavement, taxation, land grabbing, and recruitment for indentured labor contracts.

As the African slave trade subsided, the Europeans created new schemes of forced, or indentured, labor. Indian and Chinese peasants and handicraftsmen, impoverished by colonial intervention or market competition from cheap textiles, scattered to sugar plantations in the Caribbean, Fiji, Mauritius, and Natal; to rubber plantations in Malaya and Sumatra; and to British East Africa to build the railways that only intensified the two-way extraction of African resources and the introduction of cheap manufactured goods. In the third quarter of the nineteenth century alone, more than one million indentured Indians went overseas. Today, Indians still outnumber native Fijians; they make up 50 percent of the Guyanese population and 40 percent of the residents of Trinidad. In the same period, 90,000 Chinese indentured laborers went to work in the Peruvian guano fields, and 200,000 went to California to work in the fruit industry, in the goldfields, and on the railways.[8]

Colonialism was far-reaching and multidimensional in its effects. We focus here on the colonial division of labor because it isolates a key issue in the development puzzle. Unless we see the mutual dependence created through this division of world labor, it is easy to take our unequal world at face value and view it as a natural continuum, with an advanced European region showing the way for a backward, non-European region. *But if we acknowledge that an uneven world is relational (interdependent) rather than sequential, then the conventional understanding of "development" comes into question.*

The conventional understanding is that development is something that individual societies experience or pursue, one after another. If, however, industrial growth in Europe depended on agricultural monoculture in the non-European world, then development was *more* than a national process. This means that either a developed society needs colonies or development is a global, and unequal, process. Whichever way we look at it, it is questionable to think of development as an isolated national activity. This, however, was the dominant conception in the mid-twentieth century, and our task is to consider why this was so *then,* and why *now,* in a rapidly integrating world, development is increasingly associated with globalization.

Before moving to that task, it is important to summarize the main consequences of colonialism, consistent with the focus on the colonial division of labor:

- Non-European societies were fundamentally transformed through the loss of resources and craft traditions as colonial subjects were forced to labor in mines, fields, and plantations to produce exports. A great deal of colonial labor was channeled away from reproducing local, non-European culture and into sustaining distant European urban and industrial needs. In other words, European development depended on the active disorganization of its colonies, often known as **underdevelopment.**

- New systems of colonial rule secured the reorganization of colonial labor. For example, a landed oligarchy (the *hacendados*) ruled South America before the nineteenth century in the name of the Spanish and Portuguese monarchies. This kind of settler colonialism also spread to North America, Australasia, and Southern Africa, where settlers wrested land from the natives. As the nineteenth century wore on, colonialism grew more bureaucratic and centrally organized. By that century's end, colonial administrations in Asia and Africa were self-financing systems, depending on the loyalty of local princes and chiefs, bribed with titles, land, or tax-farming privileges. In turn, they helped to force colonial subjects into cash cropping to pay the taxes which financed colonial administration.

- The shift of males into cash cropping disrupted formerly complementary **gender roles** of men and women in traditional cultures. Women's traditional land-user rights were often displaced by new systems of private property, which put increasing pressure on food production, normally the responsibility of women. In Kenya, for example, the gender interdependence in the Kikuyu culture was fragmented as peasant land was confiscated and men migrated to work on European farms, reducing women's control over resources and lowering their status, wealth, and authority.[9]

- European societies (especially traders and manufacturers) reaped the benefits of a growing stream of products and profits from the colonial trade, much of which fueled industrialization. This was a single, *global* process, connecting social changes at each pole of the colonial division of labor. At one pole, African slaves toiled in the New World and peasants toiled in Asia and Africa, in mines, on plantations, and in cash cropping for export to Europe. At the other pole, European peasantries disappeared into urban labor forces as commerce grew. They now survived by consuming cheap foods made with colonial products such as sugar, tea, and tropical oils and wearing inexpensive cotton clothing.

- The removal of colonial people from their societies and their dispersion to resolve labor shortages elsewhere in the colonial world has had a lasting global effect—most notably in the African, Indian, and Chinese diasporas. The legacy of colonialism is the cultural mosaic and ethnopolitical tension that has shaped and reshaped regions and states across the world.

Decolonization

As Europeans were attempting to "civilize" their colonies, colonial subjects across the Americas, Asia, and Africa explored the paradox of European colonialism—the European notion of rights and sovereignty juxtaposed against their own subjugation. For instance, in the French sugar colony of Haiti, the late-eighteenth-century "Black Jacobin" revolt powerfully exposed the double standard of European civilization. Turning the rhetoric of the French Revolution successfully against French colonialism, the rebellious slaves of the Haitian sugar plantations became the first to gain their independence, sending tremors throughout the slaveholding lands of the New World.[10]

Resistance to colonialism evolved across the next two centuries, from the early-nineteenth-century independence of the Latin American republics (from Spain and Portugal) to the dismantling of South African apartheid in the early 1990s. Although **decolonization** has continued into the present day, the worldwide decolonization movement peaked as European colonialism collapsed in the mid-twentieth century, when World War II sapped the power of the French, Dutch, British, and Belgian states to withstand anti-colonial struggles.

After millions of colonial subjects were deployed in the Allied war effort for self-determination, the returning colonial soldiers turned this ideal on their colonial masters in their final bid for independence. Veteran Nigerian anti-colonialist and later president Nnamdi Azikiwe characterized African independence struggles by quoting Eleanor Roosevelt: "We are fighting a war today so that individuals all over the world may have freedom. This means an equal chance for every man to have food and shelter and a minimum of such things as spell happiness. Otherwise we fight for nothing of real value."[11] Thus freedom was linked to overcoming the material deprivations of colonialism.

Colonial Liberation

Freedom also involved overcoming the social-psychological scars of colonialism. One profound legacy of colonialism is racism, a legacy that deeply penetrated the psyche of colonist and colonized and remains with us today. In 1957, at the height of African independence struggles, Tunisian philosopher Albert Memmi wrote *The Colonizer and the Colonized*, dedicating the American edition to the (colonized) American Negro. In this work (published in 1967) he claimed:

Racism . . . is the highest expression of the colonial system and one of the most significant features of the colonialist. Not only does it establish a fundamental discrimination between colonizer and colonized, a *sine qua non* of colonial life, but it also lays the foundation for the immutability of this life.[12]

To overcome this apparent immutability, West Indian psychiatrist Frantz Fanon, writing from Algeria, responded in 1963 with *The Wretched of the Earth* (published 1967), a manifesto of liberation. It was a searing indictment of European colonialism and a call to people of the former colonies (the Third World) to transcend the mentality of enslavement and forge a new path for humanity. He wrote:

It is a question of the Third World starting a new history of Man, a history which will have regard to the sometimes prodigious theses which Europe has put forward, but which will also not forget Europe's crimes, of which the most horrible was committed in the heart of man, and consisted of the pathological tearing apart of his functions and the crumbling away of his unity. . . . On the immense scale of humanity, there were racial hatreds, slavery, exploitation and above all the bloodless genocide which consisted in the setting aside of fifteen thousand millions of men. . . . Humanity is waiting for something other from us than such an imitation, which would be almost an obscene caricature.[13]

Decolonization was rooted in a liberatory upsurge, expressed in mass political movements of resistance. Most notably, Indian independence leader Mahatma Gandhi kindled nonviolent forms of resistance that included wearing homespun cloth instead of machine-made goods and forswearing use of the English language. Other forms of resistance included tactics of terror against colonists, national liberation struggles, and widespread colonial labor unrest.

British colonialism faced widespread labor strikes in its West Indian and African colonies in the 1930s, and this pattern continued over the next two decades in Africa as British and French colonial subjects protested conditions in cities, ports, mines, and the railways. In this context, development was understood as a pragmatic effort to improve material conditions in the colonies in order to preserve the colonies—and there was no doubt that colonial subjects understood this and turned the promise of development back on the colonizers, viewing development as an entitlement. As British Colonial Secretary Malcolm MacDonald observed in 1940, "if we are not now going to do something fairly good for the Colonial Empire, and something which helps them to get proper social services, we shall deserve to lose the colonies and it will only be a matter of time before we get what we deserve."[14] In these terms, eloquent appeals to justice in the language of rights and freedom in international forums by the representatives of colonized peoples held a mirror up to the colonial powers, demanding freedom.

National Liberation, Development, and Counter-insurgency

Anti-colonial struggles took different forms across time and space. The struggle for national liberation from Portuguese colonialism in Africa was waged in Guinea (Bissau), Angola, and Mozambique through the 1960s and early 1970s. At this time, 99 percent of the Guinea population was illiterate, infant mortality was at 60 percent, malaria was almost universal, and there was one doctor for every 45,000 Africans. Under these circumstances, anti-colonial struggles were framed in revolutionary terms, linking national liberation to the building of indigenous forms of socialism, with a strong dose of development ideology. Amilcar Cabral, the Secretary-General of the African Party for the Independence of Guinea and the Cape Verde Islands, explained in the Eduardo Mondlane Memorial Lecture Series at Syracuse University in 1970:

> In our opinion, the foundation for national liberation rests in the inalienable right of every people to have their own history, whatever formulations may be adopted at the level of international law. The objective of national liberation, is therefore, to reclaim the right, usurped by imperialist domination, namely: the liberation of the process of development of national productive forces. Therefore, national liberation takes place when, and only when, national productive forces are completely free of all kinds of foreign domination. . . . [Further] if imperialist domination has the vital need to practice cultural oppression, national liberation is necessarily an act of *culture*.

In an earlier interview, Cabral commented on the politics of guerilla warfare:

> We explain to everybody, fighters and villagers alike, that our struggle is being waged not only to drive out the Portuguese but also to build and develop the country; that in order to be free, the people themselves must take charge of the country and that they must be the ones who profit from their labor. . . . After creating a new relationship of forces by virtue of our military action, we have to replace

the colonial infrastructure with our own administrative and economic infrastructure, in order to affirm our presence and take care
of the population's elementary needs.

Of course, the occupying army had a different perspective. A
Portuguese army psychological warfare circular at the time
observed:

> As everyone knows, the guerilla cannot fight against an army like
> ours without the support of the population, which procures money
> and food for him, gives him information about us, and supplies him
> with the shelters and hiding places he needs. . . . What must we
> do? . . . We must control the population; we must force it to leave
> zones where the environment is favorable to guerilla warfare; we
> must get it to settle in regions where we can guarantee protection
> and security.

Interestingly enough, the same kind of guerilla warfare and
counter-insurgency was underway simultaneously in Vietnam,
between the Vietnamese National Liberation Front and the
United States and its allies. Here, the U.S. Army dictum, that a
village had to be destroyed in order to save it, echoed the Portuguese army tactic. The symbolism is hard to ignore—the world
was deeply divided over the Vietnam War, as a confrontation
between foreign high-tech and peasant armies, and the ideologies of free enterprise and socialism. Also, the struggle for hearts
and minds, as it was termed, was arguably a metaphor for the
politics of the development project, which viewed poverty and
indigenous movements as seedbeds of opposition to western
modernization.

*Source: Africa Information Service, 1973, pp. 9, 43; Chaliand, 1969,
pp. 48, 128.*

A new world order was in the making. From 1945 to 1981, 105 new
states joined the United Nations as the colonial empires crumbled, swelling the ranks of the United Nations from 51 to 156. This global transformation, granting political sovereignty to millions of non-Europeans (more
than half of humanity), ushered in the era of development.[15] This era was
marked by a sense of almost boundless idealism, as governments and
people from the First and the Third Worlds joined together in a coordi-

nated effort to stimulate economic growth; bring social improvements through education, public health, family planning, and transport and communication systems to urban and rural populations; and promote political involvement in the new nations. Just as colonized subjects appropriated the democratic discourse of the colonizers in fueling their independence movements, so members of the new nations appropriated the idealism of the development era and sought equality as a domestic and international goal.

Decolonization and Development

The development era was intimately linked to decolonization because political independence was the condition for states pursuing national economic development. We have already noted that the European experience was the obvious model from the perspective of the European colonial subjects, but not all European colonies became independent in the same time period, so development models varied.

Latin America obtained its political independence in the 1820s as the Spanish and Portuguese empires declined. These empires began in the sixteenth century, at least a century before the emergence of other colonial powers, such as Holland, England, and France. Within the international colonial division of labor, Latin American commercial development centered on the prosperity gained through agricultural exports to Europe. Port cities like Rio de Janeiro and Buenos Aires grew as European immigrants came to Latin America to prosper from the commodity boom between 1870 and 1930. Sugar, bananas, and coffee from the tropical regions expanded alongside industrial crops such as cotton, sisal, and rubber, with wheat and livestock products coming from the *pampas* of Argentina and Uruguay. Because of the profitability of export agriculture, Latin American political systems were dominated by powerful land-owning classes in coalitions with wealthy urban traders. In fact, in the pursuit of modern commercial development, Latin American agro-export coalitions complemented European industrial-financier coalitions, in a single global process. Britain dominated the world market during the nineteenth century, generating a development model that was viewed as being "outer-directed."

The commercial development of Latin America distinguishes it from the rest of the colonial world that was under European rule until the mid-twentieth century. Certainly economic and social patterns in Latin America (such as export agriculture and landed oligarchies) reflect the historical legacy of colonialism. The Latin American republics dressed their oligarchic regimes in the French and U.S. revolutionary ideologies of **liberal-nationalism**, which informed nineteenth-century European nation-building with national education systems, national languages and currencies, and modern armies and citizenries.

Elsewhere in the non-European world, these ideologies would also flower with decolonization, but much later. The opportunity of one and one-half centuries of independence, in addition to a substantial settler population that marginalized indigenous cultures, allowed national political and commercial systems to develop, as in the Colombian case study. Indeed, in the early twentieth century, Argentina's gross national product per capita was similar to that of North America. But new Asian and African states formed in a different historical period, following a century of intensive colonialism as European states matured and competed for industrial raw materials and markets in the colonial world. Asian and African decolonization occurred at a time when the United States was at the height of its global power and prosperity, and eager to reconstruct the postwar world to expand markets and the flow of raw materials. Reconstructing a war-torn world was an international project, inspired by a vision of development as a national enterprise to be repeated across the world of newly independent states.

CASE STUDY

Latin American Development: The Colombian Coffee Industry

The Latin American states, with their large European settlements and their early independence, had the opportunity, not available to other colonial regions, of developing a commercial culture around their lucrative export agriculture.

An example was the industrial reorganization of Colombian coffee growing, initiated through a particular combination of public and private enterprise. Coffee was Colombia's premier export crop from the late nineteenth century to the 1970s. It began as an estate crop, organized by large landowners. As international demand for coffee grew, small growers colonized the region of Antioquia in central Colombia. In 1928 a private, quasi-state organization, the National Federation of Coffee Growers of Colombia (FEDECAFE), was founded. The Colombian government ceded control of the country's coffee fund to FEDECAFE in return for its commitment to integrate the small growers into a modern production system based on new technologies such as modern fertilizers, hybrid seeds, and mechanization. Over time, coffee marketing and the provision of credit and banking services were organized through cooperatives and a new bank, Banco Cafetero. The region was integrated through transport systems, rural schools, health centers, and elaborate extension services to growers.

By 1931 the director of FEDECAFE articulated a national development culture, centered on a reorganized coffee industry:

> The coffee industry does not only represent the association of producers . . . rather, today and for many years to come [the industry] can say to the four winds: "I am fiscal equilibrium . . . I am external credit for the nation and the departments, I am the Bank of the Republic . . . I represent and on me depends a healthy monetary system based on the gold standard, exchange rate stability, the possibility of introducing to the country machinery, rails, scientific books, foreign professors, in a word, the civilization of Colombia from a material point of view."

In other words, coffee sustained an elaborate rationalization of Colombian agriculture and prosperity for the estate owners and the urban mercantile elites. As such it was identified as the basis of Colombian modernization.

Source: London, 1993.

The model for this vision was that of the United States. U.S. development was understood to be "inner-directed" as opposed to the "outer-directed" British model. The U.S. model's anti-colonial lineage was compelling: the revolt of the North American colonies against British colonialism in the late eighteenth century, and then the successful Civil War against the last vestige of colonialism in the slave plantation system of the Old South. The former cotton-exporting South was then incorporated into a new *national model* of economic development, built on the mutual integration of agricultural and industrial sectors. The division of labor between industry and agriculture, which had defined the global exchange between colonial powers and their colonies, was now an internal dynamic within the United States. Traders in Chicago, for instance, purchased midwestern farm products for processing, in turn selling machinery and

FIGURE 1.3

Distinguishing Between an International and a National
Division of Labor

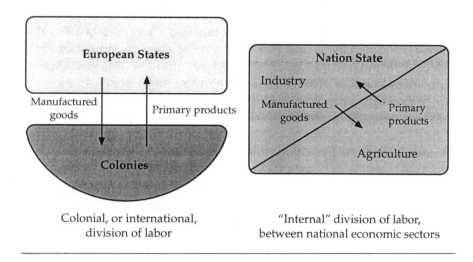

| Colonial, or international, division of labor | "Internal" division of labor, between national economic sectors |

manufactured goods to those farmers. City and countryside prospered
together. The difference between the colonial and the national division
between industry and agriculture is illustrated in Figure 1.3.

Postwar Decolonization and the Rise of the Third World

In the era of decolonization, the world was subdivided into three
geopolitical segments. These subdivisions came about after World War II
(1939-1944) as the Cold War set in and Europe was divided between the
capitalist Western (**First World**) and the communist Soviet (**Second
World**) blocs. The term **Third World** arose in the 1950s and referred to
those countries inhabited by non-Europeans that were poor and for the
most part colonized by Europe (China, for example, was not fully colonized). There were stratifications across and within these subdivisions, as
well as within their national units. The ways we divide the nations of the
world are explained in the following insert.

In the postwar era, the United States was the most powerful state—
economically, militarily, and ideologically. Its superior standard of living
(with a per capita income three times the average for Western Europe), its

How We Divide Up the World's Nations

Division of the nations of the world is quite complex and extensive, and it depends on the purpose of the dividing. The basic division made in the early postwar era was into Three Worlds: the First was essentially the capitalist world (the West plus Japan), the Second was basically the socialist world (the Soviet bloc), and the Third was the rest—mostly former European colonies. The core of the Third World was the group of nonaligned countries that tried to steer an independent path between the First and Second Worlds. These countries included Egypt, India, Indonesia, and Yugoslavia. In the 1980s a Fourth World was named to describe regions that were being marginalized internationally. Then there are the divisions used by the United Nations and other institutions of the development establishment: developed countries, developing countries, and least developed countries. Critics of the development establishment reconceptualized the division as one between the developed and the *under*developed worlds in the late 1960s. In the 1970s the oil-producing countries broke away and formed a producer cartel, becoming the **Organization of Oil-Exporting Countries (OPEC).** At the same time, a group of rapidly industrializing Third World countries became known officially as **newly industrializing countries (NICs)**—they represented a beacon to the rest of the Third World. Alongside this group and overlapping it are the **new agricultural countries (NACs)**, in which industrial agriculture for export had taken hold. Other groupings include the **Group of 7 (G-7)** states (the core of the First World, and de facto global managers) and the **Group of 77 (G-77)** states (the collective membership of the Third World that formed in the mid-1960s).

anti-colonial heritage, and its commitment to liberal domestic and international relations lent it the trappings of an ideal society on the world stage. It was the undisputed leader of the First World, and it came to be the model of a developed society.

Ranged against the United States were the Soviet Union and an assortment of other communist states, primarily those of Eastern Europe. The Second World was considered the alternative to First World capitalism.

The Third World, the remaining half of humanity, was regarded as impoverished in standard economic terms (despite the fact that it had enormous numbers of people who grew their own food). Frantz Fanon added political and cultural dimensions to the notion of impoverishment when he termed these people the "wretched of the earth." Whereas the First World had 65 percent of world income with only 20 percent of the world's population, the Third World accounted for 67 percent of world population but only 18 percent of its income. Many observers believe that much of the gap in living standards between the First and Third Worlds was a result of colonialism.[16]

This comparison of economic conditions between the First and Third Worlds generated the vision of development that would energize political and business elites in each world. Seizing the moment as leader of the First World, President Harry S Truman included in a key speech on January 20, 1949, the following proclamation:

> We must embark on a bold new program for making the benefits of our scientific advances and industrial progress available for the improvement and growth of underdeveloped areas. The old imperialism—exploitation for foreign profit—has no place in our plans. What we envisage is a program of development based on the concepts of democratic fair dealing.[17]

The following year, a Nigerian nationalist echoed these sentiments:

> Self-government will not necessarily lead to a paradise overnight. . . . But it will have ended the rule of one race over another, with all the humiliation and exploitation which that implies. It can also pave the way for the internal social revolution that is required within each country.[18]

Despite the power differential between the United States and the African countries, the shared sentiments affirmed the connection between decolonization and development. For the Americans and their allies, this was the liberal vision projected globally—a vision of universal political opportunity to pursue national economic growth. For the new states, self-government was the opportunity to put their houses in order to this end.

At this point, the discourse of development assumed additional meaning. Until now, development was understood and practiced by the colonizers as a dual mandate: civilization and development. Lord Lugard, a retired British Colonial (Africa) Army General, formulated the dual mandate: to emancipate colonial subjects from their primitive condition and to exploit colonial resources for the benefit of humankind. Later, in the postwar era, development was understood more as a natural process, with universal application, than a colonial initiative. That is, development could be administered by non-Europeans.[19]

President Truman's proclamation confirmed this understanding in suggesting a new paradigm for the postwar era: the division of humanity into the "developed" and the "underdeveloped" regions. This division of the world implied that all societies inhabited a position on a linear path, along which all nations would develop. Mexican intellectual Gustavo Esteva commented:

> Underdevelopment began, then, on January 20, 1949. On that day, two billion people became underdeveloped. In a real sense, from that time on, they ceased being what they were, in all their diversity, and were transmogrified into an inverted mirror of others' reality: . . . a mirror that defines their identity . . . simply in the terms of a homogenizing and narrow minority.[20]

In other words, the proclamation by President Truman divided the world discursively between those who were modern and "developed," and those who were not. *Modern* became the standard against which other societies were judged. This was a new way of looking at the world. It assumed that with the end of colonialism the "underdeveloped" world had only to follow the example of the "modern" world.

This new paradigm produced a strategy for improving the condition of the Third World. It is the premise for what we shall call the **development project**. The difference between the developed world and the underdeveloped world was viewed as a matter of degree that could be set right by the development project. It assumed:

- First, no matter how diverse was the cultural heritage of Third World nations, the Western experience became the universal model for their development.

- Second, conditions in the Third World were but early stages on a universal path to modern society.

The new development paradigm ignored the contribution of the colonies to European development. It tended to deny that the non-European societies had many intrinsic merits. In a postcolonial era, Third World states could not repeat the European experience of developing by exploiting the resources and labor of *other* societies. Development was *modeled* as a national process. As Gilbert Rist observed of post-colonial subjects, "their right to self-determination had been acquired in exchange for the right to self-definition,"[21] suggesting that they chose the fork in the road that proceeded toward a common future for the world, defined by the experience of Western developmentalism. Of course, each culture imparted its own particular style to this common agenda, whether it was African socialism, Latin American bureaucratic-authoritarianism, or Confucianism in East Asia, to name a few.

Ingredients of the Development Project

The linking of human development to national economic growth was a key historical event. This is why the term *development project* is useful. It was a political and intellectual response to the state of the world at the historical moment of decolonization. Under these conditions, development assumed a specific meaning. It imposed an essentially economic understanding on social life. In this way, development could be universalized, unimpeded by specific cultural patterns. Its two universal ingredients were the nation-state and economic change.

The Nation-State

The **nation-state** was to be the framework of the development project. Nation-states were territorially defined political systems based on the government/citizen relationship that emerged in nineteenth-century Europe. Use of this framework was a historical choice based on the West's experience, not on an inevitable unfolding of human destiny. The following insert illustrates the effects of these arbitrarily drawn boundaries, which continue to reverberate in world affairs of the present.

How Was Africa Divided Under Colonialism?

"The colonial powers inflicted profound damage on that continent, driving frontiers straight through the ancestral territories of nations. For example, we drew a line through Somalia, separating off part of the Somali people and placing them within Kenya. We did the same by splitting the great Masai nation between Kenya and Tanzania. Elsewhere, of course, we created the usual artificial states. Nigeria consists of four principal nations: the Hausa, Igbo, Yoruba, and Fulani peoples. It has already suffered a terrible war which killed hundreds of thousands of people and which settled nothing. Sudan, Chad, Djibouti, the Senegal, Mali, Burundi and, of course, Rwanda are among the many other states that are riven by conflict."

Source: Quoted from Goldsmith, 1994, p. 57.

During the 1950s, certain leading African anti-colonialists doubted the appropriateness of the nation-state form to postcolonial Africa. They knew that sophisticated systems of rule had evolved in Africa before colonialism. They preferred an interterritorial, pan-African federalism that would transcend the arbitrary borders drawn across Africa by colonialism. But the pan-African movement did not carry the day. Geopolitical decisions about postcolonial political arrangements were made in London and Paris where colonial powers, looking to sustain spheres of influence, insisted on the nation-state as the only appropriate political outcome of decolonization. Indeed, a British Committee on Colonial Policy advised the Prime Minister in 1957: "[D]uring the period when we can still exercise control in any territory, it is most important to take every step open to us to ensure, as far as we can, that British standards and methods of business and administration permeate the whole life of the territory."[22] Some Africans who stood to gain from decolonization formed an indigenous elite ready to collaborate and assume power in the newly independent states.

Pan-Africanism was short-lived; nevertheless, it did bear witness to an alternative political and territorial logic. As historian Jean Suret-Canale wrote in 1970:

> Like most frontiers in Africa today, those inherited by Guinea from the colonial partition are completely arbitrary. They do not reflect the limits of natural regions, nor the limits of separate ethnic groups. They were shaped in their detail by the chances of conquest or of compromise between colonial powers.[23]

In addition, some of Guinea's rural areas were in fact attached as hinterlands to urban centers in other states, such as Dakar in Senegal and Abidjan in the Ivory Coast. Considerable cross-border smuggling today is continuing testimony to these relationships. The pan-Africanists proposed regional political systems in which colonial states would be subsumed within larger territorial groupings—such as an East African federation of Uganda, Kenya, and Tanganyika. To this end, in 1958 they organized a pan-African Freedom Movement of East and Central Africa, involving independence first, followed by federation.[24]

Fierce civil wars broke out in Nigeria in the 1960s and in Ethiopia in the 1970s, states like Somalia and Rwanda collapsed in the early 1990s, and at the turn of the twenty-first century conflict in the Congo among armies of six different nations threatened a more general repartition of Africa. These eruptions all included ethnic dimensions, rooted in social and regional disparities. In retrospect, they suggest that the pan-African movement had considerable foresight. Furthermore, ideas about the limits to the nation-state organization resonate today in the growing macro-regional groupings around the world. These **macro-regions** involve states and firms that collectively reach beyond national boundaries to organize supranational markets. Examples include the **European Union (EU)**, the **North American Free Trade Agreement (NAFTA)**, and the **Asia-Pacific Economic Conference (APEC)**—regional groupings that are discussed in Chapter 5.

Economic Growth

The second ingredient of the development project was economic growth. Development planning was to focus on economic transformation. The emphasis on economic growth allowed the application of a *universal* standard to national development. The United Nations Charter of 1945 proclaimed "a rising standard of living" as the global objective. In national accounting terms, this "material well-being" indicator is measured in the commercial output of goods and services within a country. It is commonly associated with per capita gross national product (GNP) as a national average. Thus, per capita GNP, increasing annually at the rate of about 6 percent (assuming a lower rate of population growth), became the measure of successful development in the postwar era, in conjunction with increasing industrialization. Social scientist S. C. Dube commented: "Sights were set rather high when developing societies uncritically accepted the development theorists' assumption that life begins at $1,000 per capita and when an economic historian of Rostow's repute suggested that the test of development is one car for four persons in the society."[25]

Per capita income and commodity consumption, of course, were not deemed the sole measures of rising living standards. Other measures included health (e.g., rates of life expectancy and the incidence of doctors), literacy, and so forth. Nevertheless, the overriding criterion was movement up the economic scale toward the "good society," popularized by economist and U.S. presidential adviser Walt Rostow's idea of the advanced stage of "high mass consumption."[26]

In the minds of Western economists, development required a kind of jump start in the Third World. Cultural practices of wealth-sharing within communities—which dissipated individual wealth—were perceived as a *traditional* obstacle to making the transition. The solution was to introduce a market system based on private property and sustained investment. Rostow coined the term **take-off** for this transition. Economist W. Arthur Lewis used the snowball analogy for industrialization: "Once the snowball starts to move downhill, it will move of its own momentum, and will get bigger and bigger as it goes along. . . . You have, as it were, to begin by rolling your snowball up the mountain. Once you get it there, the rest is easy, but you cannot get it there without first making an initial effort."[27] Economic growth required a range of modern practices and institutions designed to sustain the development snowball, such as banking and rational accounting systems, education, private property, stock markets and legal systems, and public infrastructure (transport, power sources).

Limits of Economic Measures

As is now more apparent, however, use of the *economic* yardstick of development is fraught with problems. Average indices such as per capita income obscure inequalities among social groups and classes. Aggregate indices such as rising consumption levels, in and of themselves, are not accurate records of improvement in quality of life. That is, turning on the air conditioner may measure as increased consumption, but it also releases harmful hydrocarbons into the warming atmosphere. Hamburger consumption may improve national growth measures, but public health may suffer and intensive resource consumption—such as of water, grain, and forest land—may compromise the quality of life elsewhere or in the future. Additionally, economic statistics alone cannot evaluate quality-of-life issues such as the desirability of industrialized and large-scale food systems. For example, between 1909 and 1957 the cost of U.S. food consumption, in constant prices, increased by 75 percent. Only 15 percent of this was because of physiological consumption; the remaining 85 percent or so of the statistical increase refers to greater transport and marketing costs.[28] Whether we need or want food produced and delivered under these energy-dependent and industrial conditions does not figure in the statistical representation of economic growth. On reflection, such prescriptions for economic development have key normative assumptions:

1. Living standards can be quantified, or measured, with a monetary index.
2. The common destiny of a society is **monetization**, with the corollary that an ever-expanding world of commodities is desirable.
3. Non-monetary, or non-commodified, social systems of activity (people growing their own food, performing unpaid household

labor, doing community service) are "backward" and are not an appropriate foundation for societal modernization.

4. Development policy should aim at reducing the living standards gap between First and Third Worlds, with the First World (and its consumption patterns) as the standard.

5. Each national society should pursue these goals individually.

These assumptions, which guided the development project, have been seriously questioned by some Third World intellectuals. Environmental constraints and cultural revival have played their part in stimulating the following kind of critique by Vandana Shiva:

> The paradox and crisis of development arises from the mistaken identification of the culturally perceived poverty of earth-centred economies with the real material deprivation that occurs in market-centred economies, and the mistaken identification of the growth of commodity production with providing better human sustenance for all.[29]

We return to this critique in Chapter 7.

CASE STUDY

Internalization of the Development Project, or Internal Colonialism?

Ancient Futures: Learning from Ladakh, by Helena Norberg-Hodge, is an apt description of how a traditional society (Buddhist in this representation) is transformed by the introduction of money. This was a society in which human relations were ordered by the rhythms of nature high on the unforgiving steppes of the Himalayas. Work, performed collectively, was simultaneously culture, as Ladakhis built their annual and daily cultural rituals around the harvest cycle and viewed personal fulfillment as possible only through community life and reverence for the natural universe. Learning, or what we call education, was integral to cultural rituals and the work of manipulating a harsh environment. Extended kin relations and social cooperation encompassed the lives of individuals, and, according to Norberg-Hodge produced a sense of joy in the satisfaction of essential needs through the community.

The nature of human relations changed dramatically when the Indian state built a road into this remote territory in the 1980s. Initially for military purposes, the new infrastructure conveyed the market culture to Ladakh. Ladakhis were now confronted with powerful agents of change, in the form of tourism, education, and commercial pressures via media images and the association of fulfillment through the accumulation of money. Tourists appeared to have endless amounts of money, without having to work for it. This they spent on cultural artifacts, which once defined Ladakhi social life. Young people drifted off the farms into Leh, the capital city, where they embraced the culture of consumerism with its images of machismo for men and submission for women. The new education system schooled Ladakhi children in Western rationality, implicitly denigrating local culture and teaching them skills inappropriate for returning to that culture, and often unrealizable in the emerging, but unstable, urban job market. Material items that were once simply exchanged for each other via community patterns of reciprocity now commanded a price in the new marketplace. Food prices, for example, were now governed by invisible international market forces. The accumulation of money by individuals became the new rationality, discounting the traditional culture of barter and sharing of skills and wealth. New social divisions emerged: urban/rural, Buddhist/Muslim, men/women, young/old, worker/professional, and so forth.

The moral of the story is that modernization fundamentally altered the rationality of Ladakhi behavior: from collectivist to individualist, where sharp divisions among people appeared and a series of invidious distinctions emerged, starting with the self-denigration of Ladakhis when confronted with Western imagery. This is a parable of "internal colonialism," where the consolidation of the Indian state replicates the intrusion of European culture into non-European societies. In other words, colonialism may have had an irreversible impact on the world, but its dynamic is by no means extinguished. The reach of the state, and the market, continue unabated in the post-colonial era.

Source: Norberg-Hodge, 1992.

The Development Project Framed

Perhaps the most compelling aspect of the development project was a powerful perception by planners, governmental elites, and citizens alike that development was destiny. Both Cold War blocs understood development in these terms, even if their respective paths of development were different. Each bloc took its cue from key nineteenth-century thinkers. The Western variant identified **free enterprise capitalism** as the high point of individual and societal development. This view was based in Jeremy Bentham's utilitarian philosophy of common good arising out of the pursuit of individual self-interest. The Communist variant, on the other hand, identified the abolition of private property and **central planning** as the goal of social development. The source for this was Karl Marx's collectivist dictum: "from each according to his ability, and to each according to his needs."

It is noteworthy that although the two political blocs subscribed to opposing representations of human destiny, they shared the same modernist paradigm. *National industrialization* would be the vehicle of development in each.

National Industrialization: Ideal and Reality

National industrialization had two key elements. First, it assumed that development involved the displacement of agrarian civilization by an urban-industrial society. For national development policy, this meant a deliberate shrinking of the size and share of the agricultural sector, as the manufacturing and service sectors grew. It also meant the *transfer of resources* such as food, raw materials, and redundant labor from the agrarian sector as agricultural productivity grew. Industrial growth would ideally feed back and technify agriculture. These two national economic sectors would therefore condition each other's development, as in the post–Civil War U.S. case discussed earlier in this chapter and illustrated in Figure 1.3.

Second, the idea of national industrialization assumed a *linear direction* for development. The goal of backward societies, therefore, was to play catch-up with the West. The Soviet Union's premier, Joseph Stalin, articulated this doctrine in the 1930s, proclaiming, "We are fifty or a hundred years behind the advanced countries. We must make good this distance in ten years. Either we do it or they crush us."[30] Stalin's resolve came from the pressures of military (and therefore economic) survival in a hostile, Cold War world. The Soviet Union industrialized in one generation, "squeezing" the peasantry to finance urban-industrial development with cheap food.

The industrial priority dominated the development vision. Across the Cold War divide, industrialization was the symbol of success in each social system, and beyond the ideological rivalry each bloc shared the goals of the development project. Indeed, industrial development was pursued in each bloc for reasons of political legitimacy; the reasoning was that as living standards grew and people consumed more goods and services, they would subscribe to the prevailing philosophy behind the delivery of the goods and support their governments.

Cross-National Industrial Integration

Leaders of both the United States and the Soviet Union promoted opposing geopolitical spheres of capitalist and socialist development, respectively. Their political leadership strengthened as allied states adopted their preferred industrial growth model. Adoption usually depended on obtaining access to U.S. or Soviet economic resources (aid, trade, and finance). In this way, patterns of economic and political interdependence emerged within each bloc among the member nations. Very little exchange took place between the blocs until the 1970s.

In the Second World, the Soviet system of self-reliant industrialization and collectivized agriculture was extended to East Central Europe. The goal was to reduce Eastern Europe's traditional agricultural exports to Western Europe and to encourage industrial self-reliance. In 1947, the **Council for Mutual Economic Assistance (COMECON)** was established. It coordinated trade among the members of the East European bloc, exchanging primary goods for manufactured goods, and it also planned infrastructural energy projects for the bloc at large.[31]

In the First World, much of the postwar economic boom depended on *cross-national economic integration.* Integration came primarily through U.S. export credits (where reconstruction loans were tied to imports of U.S. technology) and foreign direct investment. The U.S. encouraged "freedom of enterprise" to spur postwar economic recovery and growth as (multinational) firms outgrew national borders, investing in overseas production and managing international trade among countries in the First and Third Worlds.

Such economic integration under the banner of freedom of enterprise actually began to internationalize domestic economies as foreign owner-

FIGURE 1.4

Intra-Industry Specialization via International Integration

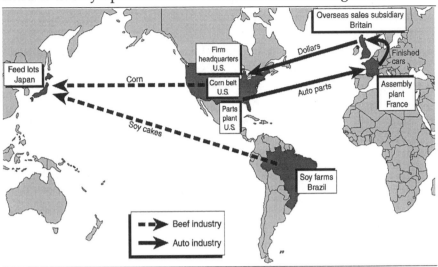

ship of economic sectors grew. Industries came to specialize in producing a part of a product, their output providing the input for the next plant downstream in the production line, which might cross national borders (as a commodity chain). For example, French automobile plants assembled imported U.S. parts and sold the finished cars in England. In the Japanese beef industry, cattle were fed with imported soycakes from specialized soybean producers in Brazil and with corn products from specialized corn farmers in the United States.

In other words, on a foundation of national economic growth, a new global economy was emerging, based on cross-national *intra-industry specialization* (see Figure 1.4). As the development project matured, this new global specialization extended to the Third World, alongside continued Third World specialization in exporting primary products to the First World.

The competitive—and legitimizing—dynamic of industrialization framed the development project across the Cold War divide and propelled member states in the same general direction. Third World states climbed on the bandwagon. The ultimate goal was to achieve Western levels of affluence. If some states chose to mix and match elements from either side of the Cold War divide, well and good. The game was still the same—catch-up. Ghanaian President Kwame Nkrumah claimed: "We in Ghana will do in ten years what it took others one hundred years to do."[32]

Economic Nationalism

Decolonization encouraged a universal nationalist upsurge across the Third World. Such nationalism assumed different forms in different countries, depending on the configuration of social forces (peasant/landowner/professional/trading/manufacturing/labor classes) in each national political system. Nevertheless, the power of the development ideal was universal. It contributed to the establishment of relatively strong **development states** in most Third World countries, advocating variants of economic nationalism. Of course, the ideal was never absolutely realized, as many postcolonial administrations used the development ideal as a means to accumulate wealth and influence in the state—whether through selling rights to public resources to cronies or capturing foreign aid distribution channels. In his study of the postcolonial Indian state, Sugata Bose remarked: "Instead of the state being used as an instrument of development, development became an instrument of the state's legitimacy."[33]

CASE STUDY

The Indian Version of Development

Although there was a universal paradigm of development, every nation had its own version of development, corresponding to cultural and natural resource endowments and the political balance of social forces in each country, and national development paths changed over time. India was rather exceptional in that it embraced elements of First World and Second World development strategies. India defined its development path through Five Year Plans to pursue specific goals. The First Five Year Plan (1950-1955) implemented a series of public infrastructural projects proposed during the closing years of British colonialism. The Second Plan focused on central planning, using a greatly enhanced national savings rate to stimulate industrial capitalist growth. The Third Plan shifted this strategy to the agricultural sector, using income subsidies to consumers to generate demand for foodstuffs and so develop a rural-urban exchange.

This evolving program, however, excluded the rural and urban poor. Accordingly, electoral politics at the turn of the 1970s included broad populist themes, embraced by the successful candidate, Indira Gandhi, as well as by oppositional social movements appropriating the populist promises of developmentalist ideology. Indeed, the Bharatiya Kisan Union (led by rich farmers) critiqued the existing development model and its urban bias:

> The question remains why the condition of the peasant remains what it is despite thirty-eight years of planning in which the progress of agriculture and the development of villages has been so much the focus of discussion . . . the concern for agriculture has been a sham whereas the truth is that from every viewpoint the farmer has been discriminated against and agriculture has been deliberately kept backward compared to industry and other sectors. . . . The price of grain was deliberately kept low right from the beginning so that the urban population and industrial workers could be protected from the burden of expensive food.

While the Fifth (1974) and Sixth Five Year Plans addressed the issue of popular entitlements through a focus on nationally organized food and fuel stocks, a broad redistribution of wealth never took place. This unequal outcome stemmed from three political features of India that shaped its development path: a powerful industrial oligopoly with close ties to the Indian state through the dominant Congress Party, the political and economic power of a class of wealthy farmers enriched by adoption of the yield-enhancing technologies of the green revolution, and a centralized state bureaucracy inherited from the British Raj that used economic development to enhance its power rather than to reduce social inequalities.

In 1991, bowing to globalization pressures, India adopted liberal economic policies, exacerbating social inequalities. While middle-class consumption has expanded, domestic food prices have risen 63 percent, and consumption of cereals and lentils (the staple diet of the poor) has declined—associated with a 70 percent increase in agro-exports (including rice, wheat, and other cereals) and reductions in subsidized food.

Sources: Byres, 1981; Bose, 1997, pp. 52-57; Mittal, 1998, p. 157; Gupta, 1997, pp. 332-333.

The development state characterized the **late starter** on the development path. Planning and public investment were necessary in the strategy of catching up. Three intersecting forces stood behind the ideal of the development state:

1. Development economists encouraged *state planning* to overcome market inefficiencies in Third World countries (e.g., national transport and banking systems).
2. Postcolonial governments inherited a *centralized administration* from colonial patterns of rule.
3. Foreign aid management nourished *bureaucratic growth*, giving planning elites considerable leverage over their society in dispersing largesse. In fact, eligibility for foreign aid often depended on countries having a Western-style state with a bureaucracy composed of ministries, career civil servants, and the like.

Just as *political* nationalism sought to regain sovereignty for Third World populations, so *economic* nationalism sought to reverse the effects of the colonial division of labor. Third World governments were interested in correcting what they perceived as underdevelopment in their economic systems, encouraging and protecting local efforts to industrialize with tariffs and public subsidies and reducing dependence on primary exports (increasingly viewed as "resource bondage").

Import-Substitution Industrialization

Economic nationalism in the Third World arose first among the Latin American states. It was associated with Raúl Prebisch, an adviser in the 1930s to the Argentine military government and then founding director of the Argentine Central Bank. During the world depression of the 1930s, trade links weakened around the world. In Latin America, landed interests lost political power as shrinking primary export markets depleted their revenues. Prebisch seized the opportunity to implement import substitution. Import controls reduced expensive imports of manufactured goods from the West and shifted resources into domestic manufacturing.[34]

In 1951, Prebisch was elected executive secretary of the United Nations **Economic Commission for Latin America (ECLA).** ECLA was central to the early formulation of a Third World posture on reform of the post–World War II global economy. ECLA argued that the impact of the United States on international trade differed from Britain's "outer-directed" impact in the nineteenth century—when countries grew by trading with Britain. U.S. economic growth was, by contrast, much more "inner-directed." Arguing that the United States had less propensity to import primary products, ECLA advocated an "inner-directed" development strategy.

The policy of **import-substitution industrialization (ISI)** became the new economic orthodoxy in the postwar era.[35] But ECLA's view of import-substitution industrialization was in tension with the development project because it transformed the ideal of national economic growth into a potent form of economic nationalism. Economic nationalism potentially threatened the freedom of enterprise (private foreign investment) prescribed in the development project, even though in fact ISI encouraged direct investment by foreign firms.

Foreign Investment and the Paradox of Protectionism

When states erected tariffs in mid-century, multinational corporations hopped over and invested in local, as well as natural resource, industries. For Brazil, in 1956 foreign (chiefly U.S.) capital controlled 50 percent of the iron and rolled-metal industry, 50 percent of the meat industry, 56 percent of the textile industry, 72 percent of electric power production, 80 percent of cigarette manufacture, 80 percent of pharmaceutical production, 98 percent of the automobile industry, and 100 percent of oil and gasoline distribution. In Peru, a subsidiary of Standard Oil of New Jersey owned the oil that represented 80 percent of national production, and Bell Telephone controlled telephone services. In Venezuela, Standard Oil produced 50 percent of the oil, Shell another 25 percent, and Gulf one-seventh. In what Peter Evans has called the "triple alliance," states such as Brazil actively brokered relationships between foreign and local firms in an attempt to spur industrial development. In contrast, several decades later, in a different world, Evans's model of development became that of South Korea, where the state used its financial controls and business ties to nurture strategic domestic investments.

Sources: de Castro, 1969, pp. 241-242; Evans, 1979, 1995.

Promoters of ISI observed that primary goods exporters were paying more every year for imported manufactured goods. Manufacturing technology and unionized industrial labor were evidently more expensive over time, as productivity and wages grew. In fact, apart from the World War II boom, from 1870 to 1947 the **terms of trade** (purchasing power of primary exports in terms of manufactured imports) had declined steadily.[36] The prescription for reversing the discriminatory effects of the colonial division of labor was ISI, subsidized by export revenues.

Import-substitution industrialization largely framed initial economic development strategies in the Third World. Governments pursued ISI policies through exchange rate manipulation, import tariffs, and subsidization of "infant industries." The idea was to establish a cumulative process of domestic industrialization. For example, a domestic auto industry would generate parts manufacturing, road building, service stations, and so on, in addition to industries such as steel, rubber, aluminum, cement, and paint. In this way, a local industrial base would emerge.

Development Alliance

To secure an expanding industrial base, Third World governments constructed political coalitions of different social groups to support rapid industrialization. That is, while development was understood as an economic outcome, it had definite political dimensions. In Latin America, for example, this coalition-building formed a **development alliance**.[37] Its social constituency included commercial farmers, public employees, urban industrialists, merchants, and workers dependent on industrialization. Manufacturers' associations, labor unions, and neighborhood organizations signed on. Policymakers used price subsidies and public services such as health and education programs, cheap transport, and food subsidies to complement the earnings of urban dwellers and attract them to the cause of national industrialization.

The *development alliance* was a centralized and urban political initiative because governments could more easily organize social benefits for urban than for rural dwellers. Providing these social services was a way of keeping the social peace through ensuring affordable food and legitimizing the plan. The development alliance was also a vehicle of political patronage, whereby governments could manipulate electoral support. Mexico's Institutional Revolutionary Party (PRI), which controlled the state for much of the twentieth century, created corporatist institutions like the Confederation of Popular Organizations, the Confederation of Mexican Workers, and the National Confederation of Peasants to channel patronage "downward" in order to massage loyalty "upward."

Employing these kinds of political patronage networks, development states aimed at shifting Third World economic resources away from spe-

What Does a Development State Do?

The development state takes charge of organizing economic growth by mobilizing money and people. On the money end, it uses individual and corporate taxes, along with other government revenues such as export taxes and sales taxes, to finance public building of transport systems and to finance state enterprises such as steel works and energy exploration. States also mobilize money by borrowing in private capital markets, competing with private borrowers. Where state enterprises (financed with public monies, but run on market criteria—such as the U.S. Postal Service) predominate, we have what is called *state capitalism*. Where they complement private enterprise, we simply have a form of state entrepreneurialism. On the people front, typically in postcolonial states, governments mobilized political coalitions of citizens from different social groupings—workers, capitalists, professionals, and small businesspeople. Political loyalty was obtained by the guarantee of certain kinds of social resources to these various groups: public services, price subsidies, easy credit terms to small businesses, tax exemption for capitalists, wage increases for workers, and so on. The development state used these coalitions to support its program of industrialization.

cialization in primary product exports. They redistributed private investment from export sectors to domestic production, and some states used mechanisms like a development alliance to redistribute wealth at the same time. Brazil is often cited as a model of the former strategy, where the state fostered private investment without much redistribution of wealth. Brazil established a development bank to make loans to investors and state corporations in such central industries as petroleum and electric power generation.

Brazilian import substitution catered largely to the demand of relatively affluent urban consumers as well as the growing, but less affluent, industrial workforce. As local manufacturing of consumer products grew, Brazil had to import manufacturing technologies. When the domestic market was sufficiently large, multinational corporations invested directly in the Brazilian economy—as they did elsewhere in Latin America during this period. Latin America characteristically had relatively urbanized populations with expanding consumer markets.[38]

By contrast, the South Korean state centralized control of national development and the distribution of industrial finance. South Korea relied less on foreign investment than Brazil and more on export markets for the country's growing range of manufactured goods. Comprehensive land reforms equalized wealth among the rural population, and South Korean development depended on strategic investment decisions by the state that produced a development pattern in which wealth was more evenly distributed among urban classes and between urban and rural constituencies.

Whatever the form, the power of the development ideal was universal. Political elites embraced the development project, mobilizing their national populations around an expectation of rising living standards. In turn, political elites expected economic growth to give them legitimacy in the eyes of their emerging citizenry.

In accounting for and evaluating the development project, this book gives greatest attention to the Western bloc. There are several reasons for this focus:

- Western affluence was the universal standard.

- Western development patterns generated the concept of "modernity" and theories of "modernization" that became fashionable in the 1950s.

- Much of the Third World was fully exposed to the Western development project, and today this extends to the countries of the now-defunct Second World.

- Western development is viewed in the post–Cold War era as the only game in town that is eligible for multilateral financial assistance.

Summary

The development project stemmed from a specific historical context in which the West offered a model for the future of economic growth. The development ideal was forged during the colonial era, even though colonialism contradicted the ideal. Our brief examination showed that colonialism had a profoundly disorganizing impact on non-European societies through the reorganization of their labor systems around specialized export production. It also had a disorganizing social-psychological effect on these societies. But part of this impact included exposure of non-European intellectuals, workers, and soldiers to the European liberal discourse on rights. Under these conditions, anti-colonial movements emerged, espousing political independence as a liberating act.

The political independence of the colonial world gave birth to the development project. Colonialism was increasingly condemned as individual countries sought their own place in the sun. Finding that place meant also accepting the terms of the development project. Those terms included acceptance of the discursive and institutional relationships that defined the world as an economic hierarchy. Third World states may have become individually independent, but they also came to be defined collectively as "underdeveloped."

Newly independent nations responded by playing the catch-up game—on an individual basis but, as the next chapter shows, within an international framework. The pursuit of rising living standards inevitably promoted westernization in political, economic, and cultural terms, as the non-European world emulated the European enterprise. The influential terms of the development project undercut Frantz Fanon's call for a non-European way, qualifying the sovereignty and diversity that often animated the movements for decolonization. It also rejected the pan-African insight into alternative political organization. Both of these ideas have reemerged recently, and they have a growing audience.

Third World elites, once in power, had little choice but to industrialize. This was the measure of independence from the colonial division of labor. It was also the measure of their success as political elites. The mirrored image of the West was materializing, both in the direction of Third World development and in the collaboration emerging between First and Third World people comprising an international development community.

The development project has come under increasing scrutiny in the 1990s, losing considerable credibility among members of Third World (now Southern) states. It has had quite mixed success, and there is a growing reaction to its homogenizing thrust. Ethnic or cultural identity movements have begun to reassert their political claims in some parts of the world. There is also a growing movement to develop alternative livelihood strategies beyond formal economic relations—to explore new ways of community living or simply to recover older ways of life that preceded the specializing thrust of modern commercial systems. These movements express a loss of faith in the ideals of the development project.

The remainder of this book explores how these ideals have worked out in practice, how they have been reformulated, and how a new project has emerged out of these changes. The next chapter examines the development project in action.

2

The Development Project
in Global Context

Having defined the development project as a postcolonial historical initiative, crystallizing as a national ideal, we now focus on its international dimensions. The development project, spanning a little more than a quarter of a century, was an attempt to universalize the model of European modernization, to create a world in this image. Because the model was an ideal version of development it was unlikely to succeed. That is, Third World needs for external resources were met, not through the ability to colonize other regions of the world as the Europeans had done, but through dependence on First World financial and technological resources. Whether this dependence was a new form of colonialism is an oft-repeated question raised in Third World circles, and it draws attention to the real, global relationships embedded in the development project.

When countries became independent nation-states, they joined the development project. This entailed economic and social changes on both the national and global scales. How could a national strategy be simultaneously global?

- For one thing, the *colonial division of labor* left a legacy of "resource bondage" embedded in the social structure of many Third World countries. Here, powerful social classes (landowners and merchants) favored the primary export specialization deriving from colonial times. Of course, the First World still needed imports of industrial raw materials and agricultural goods, in addition to markets for their industrial products (including technology).

- From another angle, as newly independent states embarked on industrialization programs, they inevitably purchased First World technology, for which they paid with loans or foreign exchange earned from continuing traditional, colonial-style primary goods exporting.

■ Further, nation-states formed within an international framework, which included the economic assistance of the United Nations and the **Bretton Woods** institutions, notably the World Bank, which made project loans for development infrastructure or agro-exporting.

National economic growth depended, then, on the stimulus of these new international economic arrangements. The United Nations (U.N.) declared the 1960s and 1970s "Development Decades" both to mobilize international cooperation in various development initiatives designed to strengthen development at the national level and to mitigate the effects of the international division of labor. In this chapter, we examine the construction of the Bretton Woods system and how its multilateral arrangements framed national development strategies. We then look closely at the ways the development project affected and reshaped the international division of labor, especially in reorganizing agriculture across the world.

The International Framework
of the Development Project

The pursuit of national economic growth by countries across the globe required international supports. These supports were an essential part of the development project. Foreign aid, technology transfer, stable currency exchange, robust international trade—all were deemed necessary to sustain national development policies.

The first order of business was to revive and stabilize the world economy. International trade had fallen by 65 percent during the Depression of the 1930s as countries withdrew from trade. This withdrawal continued during a devastating second world war (1939-1945). Under these circumstances, the United States spearheaded two initiatives to reconstruct the world economy: the **Marshall Plan** and the Bretton Woods program. The former was a **bilateral** initiative because it involved agreements between two states; the latter was **multilateral** because it involved collective agreements by a series of member states. The development project emerged within the bilateral Marshall Plan and became formalized under the multilateral Bretton Woods program. It did not become a full-fledged operation until the 1950s, as newly independent states formed. To understand the origins of the development project, we shall briefly examine the Marshall Plan.

U.S. Bilateralism: The Marshall Plan

In the post–World War II years, the United States was overwhelmingly concerned with the reconstruction of Europe as the key to stabilizing the Western world. European grain harvests in 1946 were expected to reach only 60 percent of prewar levels. Scarcity of labor skills and certain goods depleted transport and communication networks, and countless refugees posed enormous problems. There was also a growing popular desire for social reform.[1] On returning from Europe in 1947, U.S. Assistant Secretary of State for Economic Affairs Will Clayton stated in a memorandum:

> Communist movements are threatening established governments in every part of the globe. These movements, directed by Moscow, feed on economic and political weakness. . . . The United States is faced with a world-wide challenge to human freedom. The only way to meet this challenge is by a vast new programme of assistance given directly by the United States itself.[2]

In these political circumstances, the United States hoped to use financial aid to stabilize discontented populations and rekindle economic growth in strategic parts of the world. The other side of this strategy was to head off, and contain, communism—primarily in Europe, where the Soviet Union had laid claim to territories east of Berlin, but also in the Far East, where communism had gained ground first in China and then in North Korea. The United States sought to gain nations' allegiance to the Western free enterprise system by promoting their economic growth through financial assistance. In 1950, Secretary of State Dean Acheson stressed the urgency of concentrating such assistance in Western Europe, to counter the consolidation of Eastern Europe under Soviet rule: "We cannot scatter our shots equally all over the world. We just haven't got enough shots to do that. . . . If anything happens in Western Europe the whole business goes to pieces."[3]

Meanwhile, since its founding in 1943, the United Nations had organized a collective, multilateral program of international relief. U.S. bilateral initiatives—becoming increasingly importance in the Cold War—complemented and sometimes conflicted with these multilateral initiatives. U.S. bilateral policy overrode the proposals of two multilateral agencies established in 1943: the **Food and Agricultural Organization (FAO)** and the United Nations Relief and Rehabilitation Administration (UNRRA). When these agencies proposed a World Food Board in 1946 to organize reserves and regulate international trade in food, President Harry S Truman's administration declined support. It chose instead to pursue bilateral programs in which the U.S. government retained control of assistance. In the Far East, U.S. food aid replaced UNRRA aid in an effort to bolster Chiang Kai-shek's anticommunist forces in China, and in Europe, the Marshall Plan replaced UNRRA aid.[4]

The Marshall Plan was a vast, bilateral transfer of billions of dollars to European states and Japan, serving U.S. geopolitical goals in the Cold War. The Plan restored trade, price stability, and rising production levels there. It aimed at securing private enterprise in these regions to undercut socialist movements and labor militancy. Dollar exports, allowing recipients to purchase American goods, closely integrated these countries' economies with that of the United States, solidifying their political loyalty to the Free World—the Western bloc of the Cold War world.

U.S. bilateral strategy aimed to consolidate this Western bloc under American leadership. The U.S. State Department considered the economic integration gained through dollar exports a way to stem the Western European trend toward economic self-reliance. The Europeans desired social peace and full employment, to be achieved through closely regulated national economies, but the United States government wanted an open world economy. The Marshall Plan solved this dilemma, using bilateral aid to facilitate international trade and investment arrangements in European national economies.

Because Europe ran a serious trade deficit with the United States (which imported little from Europe), an ingenious *triangular trade system* was set in place to enable Europe to finance imports of American technology and consumer goods. In this arrangement, the United States obtained economic access to formerly protected European colonial territories. Raw materials exported from these territories to the United States produced dollar deposits in European colonial accounts in London banks. From these accounts, Western European states could finance their imports from the United States. In turn, U.S. investments in the colonial and postcolonial territories stimulated demand for European manufactured goods. And so the triangle was complete (see Figure 2.1).[5]

By 1953, the Marshall Plan had transferred $41.3 billion to the First World economies and had sent $3 billion in bilateral aid to the Third World. Post–World War II global economic reconstruction meant containment of communism first, spearheaded by the United States. Military and economic aid complemented each other. With containment in place, fur-

FIGURE 2.1

The Postwar Triangular Trade System Enabled Europe to Purchase American Technology and Goods

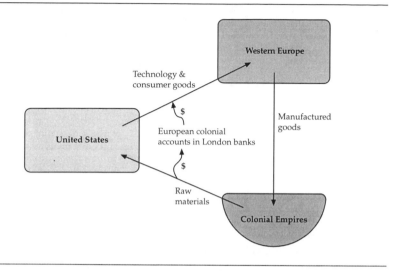

ther reconstruction would be accomplished by a complex multilateral arrangement whereby infusions of American dollars would stimulate the world economy.

Multilateralism: The Bretton Woods System

The idea for an international bank was part of the plan to reconstruct the world economy in the 1940s. Trade was to be restored by advancing credit to revitalize regions devastated by war or colonialism. Through a global banking operation, funds would be redistributed to these regions to stimulate new production. The famous July 1944 conference of forty-four financial ministers at Bretton Woods, New Hampshire, provided the opportunity to create such an international banking system. Here, the United States Treasury steered the conference toward chartering the foundation of the "twin sisters": the **World Bank** and the **International Monetary Fund (IMF)**.

Each institution was based on member subscriptions. The World Bank would match these subscriptions by borrowing money in international capital markets to raise money for development. The IMF was to disburse credit where needed to stabilize national currency exchanges. Once the ministers approved formation of these Bretton Woods institutions, the conference president, Henry Morgenthau, foresaw the

> creation of a dynamic world economy in which the peoples of every nation will be able to realize their potentialities in peace . . . and enjoy, increasingly, the fruits of material progress on an earth infinitely blessed with natural riches. This is the indispensable cornerstone of freedom and security. All else must be built upon this. For freedom of opportunity is the foundation for all other freedoms.[6]

These were the key sentiments of the development project: multinational universalism, viewing natural bounty as unlimited, and a liberal belief in freedom of opportunity as the basis of political development. Human satisfaction was linked to rising living standards. Indeed, on delivering the "Resolution of Thanks" at the conference, the Brazilian delegate, Souza Costa, proclaimed that the Bretton Woods institutions were "inspired by a single ideal—that happiness be distributed throughout the face of the earth."[7]

The functions of the Bretton Woods agencies were

- To stabilize national finances and revitalize international trade (IMF)

- To underwrite national economic growth by funding Third World imports of First World infrastructural technologies

- To expand Third World primary exports to earn foreign currency for purchasing First World exports (for example, industrial technology and consumer goods).

In effect, then, the Bretton Woods system managed an international exchange between the First and Third Worlds that resembled the colonial division of labor, at a more intensive remove. This was not surprising, as this international division of labor was already structured into the very social and economic organization of states across this divide and shaped the way in which they participated in international trade.

The World Bank's mandate was to make large-scale loans to states for national infrastructural projects such as dams, highways, and power plants. These projects undergirded national economic integration and growth, complementing smaller-scale private and public investments. In the first twenty years of the Bank's operation, two-thirds of its loans purchased inputs to build new transportation and electric power systems. Indeed, the World Bank's *Eleventh Annual Report* stated: "Most of the Bank's loans are for basic utilities . . . which are an essential condition for the growth of private enterprise." At the same time, the Bank invested in large-scale cash crop agriculture, such as cacao, rubber, and livestock, deepening the effects of the international division of labor.[8]

The Bretton Woods institutions lubricated the world economy by moving funds to regions that needed purchasing power. Expanded trade stimulated economic growth across the First World/Third World divide. At the same time, these agencies disseminated the development project, tempting Third World states to adopt the industrial and capital-intensive technologies of the West. Whereas Europe had taken several centuries to industrialize, Third World governments expected to industrialize rapidly with multilateral loans and so reduce their specialization in primary goods exporting. Industrialization often substituted capital-intensive for labor-intensive production technologies; the difference between these is explained in the following insert.

Capital-Intensive vs. Labor-Intensive Production

The difference between capital- and labor-intensive activities has to do with the ratio of labor to capital, or tools. The latter lighten labor's load. Ancient pyramid building was a labor-intensive activity—the proportion of slaves to tools was high. Modern dam building tends to be capital intensive because it uses explosives and earth-moving machinery rather than armies of diggers, although large amounts of labor may be used for certain parts of the project—such as erecting scaffolding. In general, as production processes are mechanized, they become capital intensive; that is, they substitute capital for labor.

The Bretton Woods system was unveiled as a universal and multi-lateral attempt to promote rising living standards on a global scale. Of the forty-four nations in attendance at Bretton Woods, twenty-seven were from the Third World. Nevertheless, the system had a predictable First World bias. First, control of the Bank was dominated by the five biggest (First World) shareholders—beginning with the United States, whose representatives appointed their own executive directors to the Board. The remaining seven directors represented the thirty-seven other member states. This asymmetry still exists; in the mid-1990s, the ten richest industrial states controlled 52 percent of the votes, and forty-five African countries controlled just 4 percent of the votes. Second, the president of the

World Bank is customarily an American, just as the managing director of the IMF is customarily a European. Third, the Bank finances only foreign exchange costs of approved projects, encouraging import dependence (in capital-intensive technologies) in development priorities. Finally, the IMF adopted a "conditionality" requirement, requiring applicants to have economic policies that met certain criteria in order for them to obtain loans. International banks and other lenders inevitably adopted IMF conditionality as their own criterion for loans to Third World countries. In this way, Third World development priorities were tailored toward outside—that is, First World—evaluation.[9] Thus, national strategies had global dimensions.

World Bank lending, however effective in its own terms, reflected these First World priorities. The Bank emphasized what were considered to be productive investments, such as energy and export agriculture, rather than social investments, such as education, health services, water and sanitation facilities, and housing. In addition, as a global operation, the Bank found it more convenient to invest in large-scale, capital-intensive projects that might, for example, have common technological inputs and similar appraisal mechanisms.[10] In this way, early Bank lending priorities established large-scale technologies as the basis for borrower country participation in the development project. Not only has the Bank heavily sponsored Western **technological transfer**; it has also established an *institutional presence* in Third World countries.[11] When the Bank finances infrastructural projects, these are often administered through agencies with semi-autonomous financial and political power within host countries, as the case study shows.

CASE STUDY

Banking on the Development Project

The World Bank has always been the premier development institution. In providing loans and expertise, it has exerted considerable influence over domestic development policy. For example, in the late 1950s, as a condition for further power loans the Bank insisted that the Thai government establish the Electrical Generating Authority of Thailand (EGAT). EGAT then supervised a series of loans for large-scale dams, from 1964 (the Bhumibol hydroelectricity project) through the 1970s and 1980s. Thousands of Thai peasants were displaced and resettled under the terms of the dam project, often on poorer lands than those they gave up and at considerable cost to their livelihood. Given EGAT's semi-autonomous status, however, the agency was immune to demands by these displaced peasants for compensation. Such semi-autonomous agencies (**parastatals**) often override domestic political process in the name of technical efficiency.

In Malaysia, a similar parastatal agency called the Federal Land Development Authority (FELDA) was created by the Bank to administer three loans between 1968 and 1973. The purpose of the loans was to finance the clearing of sections of tropical rain forest and the resettling of 9,600 families who would grow oil palms and rubber trees. By 1982, by the Bank's own account, FELDA had developed 1.3 million acres (6.5 percent of Malaysian forest cover in the 1970s) and resettled 72,600 families. In Colombia, between 1949 and 1972, more than 70 percent of Bank loans supported such autonomous development agencies. In spite of the likelihood that World Bank projects would short-circuit the political process, Third World elites embraced them in the interest of development. India's first prime minister, Jawaharlal Nehru, referred to the Rihand dam project as one of "the temples of modern India," especially in generating power for the Singrauli region, India's "Switzerland." The Bank was a leading donor in this project, funding the National Thermal Power Corporation (NTPC) as an alternative to India's infamously inefficient public bureaucracy.

Source: Rich, 1994, p. 75.

In examining how the development project issued from the Bretton Woods institutions, we have focused on the World Bank as the key multilateral agency responsible for underwriting Third World development. In addition to its influence through the parastatals, the Bank framed development priorities through its on-site project agencies and its encouragement of large-scale power generation and transport projects. Such projects stimulated industrialization on a Western scale, often paid for through private investments, increasingly made by foreign corporations and complemented by Bank funds. The Bank also channeled loans into intensive agriculture, requiring fossil fuel, energy-dependent technical inputs such as fertilizers, pesticides, and hybrid seeds. In addition, the Bank catalyzed the central ideas of the development project. For example, in 1956 it created the Economic Development Institute, which trained Third World officials (soon to be prime ministers or ministers of planning or finance in their own countries) in the theory and practice of development as understood in the First World.[12] Finally, Bank lending became a model for other multilateral banks and aid agencies (such as the Food and Agricultural Organization) as they determined priorities for assistance.

In short, multilateralism was more an ideal than a reality in the Bretton Woods system; in reality, Bank policy set the parameters of development. Third World elites by and large embraced these parameters. Arguably, they were hardly in a position to present an alternative blueprint. When individual governments did experiment with socialist alternatives, loan funds rapidly dried up. Multilateral funding was committed to extending the realm of free enterprise.

Interstate Politics in the Postwar World Order

As the realm of free enterprise expanded, the political dynamics of the Cold War deepened. These dynamics had two aspects: the competition between the U.S.-led (First World) bloc and the Soviet (Second World) bloc for spheres of influence, and attempts by the Third World to avoid becoming pawns in this geopolitical game. While the United States and the Soviet Union were busy dividing the world, the countries of the Third World came together to assert their own presence in the international system. We explore the interplay of all these forces in the next sections.

Foreign aid. When we examine the patterns of Western foreign aid in the postwar era, we see that the patterns of development assistance contradicted the universalism of the development project. All states could not be equal; some were more significant players than others in the maintenance of order in the world market system. Western aid concentrated on undercutting competition from states or political movements that espoused rival (that is, socialist) ideologies of development. Its priority was to use funds and trade deals to stabilize geopolitical regions through regionally powerful states like South Korea, Israel, Turkey, and Iran. These states functioned as military outposts in securing the perimeters of the so-called free world and in preventing a "domino effect" of defections to the Soviet bloc.

Cold War rivalry governed a significant part of the political geography of the development project. In the 1950s, the Soviet Union appeared to be gaining on, if not outstripping, the United States in military and space technology. When the Soviet satellite *Sputnik* was first to fly into outer space in 1957, followed by manned Soviet space flights, Second World industrial rivalry gained credibility in both the First and Third Worlds. At the same time, the Soviet Union was expanding economic and political relations with Third World states, especially newly independent states in Asia and Africa. The inherent political rivalry was dramatized in 1956, when the Soviet Union financed and built the Aswan Dam in Egypt. This Soviet initiative followed U.S. pressure on the World Bank not to fund the project, in opposition to the "Arab socialism" of Egypt's new leader, Gamal Abdel Nasser.

By 1964, the Soviet Union had extended export credits to about thirty such states, even though most aid was concentrated among eight countries. Under the Soviet aid system, loans could be repaid in local currencies or in the form of traditional exports, a program that benefited states short of foreign currency. Not only was the Soviet Union offering highly visible aid projects to key states like Indonesia and India, but in its aid policies it was clearly favoring states that were pursuing policies of central planning and public ownership in their development strategies.[13]

For the United States and its First World allies, then, the development project was more than a transmission belt for Western technology and economic institutions to the Third World. So long as the Third World, a vital source of strategic raw materials and minerals, was under threat from an alternative political-economic vision such as socialism, the survival of the First World was at stake. In 1956, this view was articulated clearly by Walt Rostow, an influential development economist:

> The location, natural resources, and populations of the underdeveloped areas are such that, should they become effectively attached to the Communist bloc, the United States would become the second power in the world. . . . Indirectly, the evolution of the underdeveloped areas is likely to determine the fate of Western Europe and Japan, and therefore, the effectiveness of those industrialized regions in the free world alliance we are committed to lead. . . . In short, our military security and our way of life as well as the fate of Western Europe and Japan are at stake in the evolution of the underdeveloped areas.[14]

The United States' foreign aid patterns between 1945 and 1967 confirm this view of the world. Yugoslavia, for instance, received considerable aid as the regional counterweight to the Soviet Union on the western perimeter of Eastern Europe. Elsewhere, aid to geopolitically strategic states (including Iran, Turkey, Israel, India, Pakistan, South Vietnam, Taiwan, South Korea, the Philippines, Thailand, and Laos) matched the total aid disbursement to all other Third World countries.[15]

The Non-Aligned Movement. Parallel with this Cold War world order was an emerging Third World perspective, which advocated a more independent vision. As decolonization proceeded, the composition of the United Nations shifted toward a majority of non-European member states. In 1955, the growing weight of the Third World in international politics produced the first conference of "nonaligned" Asian and African states at Bandung, Indonesia, forming the **Non-Aligned Movement (NAM)**. The NAM used its collective voice in international forums to forge a philosophy of noninterference in international relations. At a subsequent meeting of the NAM, President Nyerere of Tanzania articulated this position in terms of economic self-reliance:

> By non-alignment we are saying to the Big Powers that we also belong to this planet. We are asserting the right of small, or militarily weaker, nations to determine their own policies in their own interests, and to have an influence on world affairs. . . . At every point . . . we find our real freedom to make economic, social and political choices is being jeopardised by our need for economic development.[16]

The subtext of this statement, and indeed of the final Bandung communiqué, was the legitimacy of the economic model of development embedded in the multilateral institutional order. The first bone of contention was the paucity of multilateral loans. By 1959, the World Bank had lent more to the First World ($1.6 billion) than to the Third World ($1.3 billion). Also, loan terms were tough. Third World members of the United Nations pressed for expanded loans, with concessions built in, and proposed that a U.N. facility perform these multilateral development functions. Third World members expected to exert some control over a Special United Nations Fund for Economic Development (SUNFED). The First World's response was to channel this demand away from the United Nations and toward the World Bank. Here a new subsidiary, the **International Development Association (IDA)**, was established to make loans at highly discounted rates (called "soft loans") to low-income countries. Between 1961 and 1971, the IDA lent $3.4 billion, representing about one-quarter of total Bank lending. In addition, several regional banks modeled on the World Bank were established—including the Inter-American Development Bank (IDB) in 1959, the African Development Bank (AfDB) in 1964, and the Asian Development Bank (ADB) in 1966.[17]

The Group of 77. The next contentious issue was the organization of international trade. The **General Agreement on Tariffs and Trade (GATT)**, founded in 1947, enabled states to negotiate reciprocal trade concessions. Because the GATT assumed a level playing field, speakers for the Third World regarded it as discriminatory: many Third World states were economically unable to make such reciprocal concessions.[18] In fact, during the 1950s the Third World's share of world trade fell from one-third to about one-fifth, with declining rates of export growth associated with declining terms of trade.[19] Pressure from the Third World, led by the Latin Americans, resulted in the convening of the **United Nations Conference on Trade and Development (UNCTAD)** in 1964.

UNCTAD was the first international forum at which Third World countries, formed into a caucus group called the **Group of 77 (G-77)**, collectively demanded economic reform in the world economy. They declared that reform should include stabilizing and improving primary commodity prices, opening First World markets for Third World manufactures, and expanding financial flows from the First World to the Third World. Once UNCTAD was institutionalized, it served as a vehicle for Third World views. These were by no means limited to the Third World, however; development lobbies in European countries, left parties and intellectuals, religious and aid organizations, and others in the First World formed a loose alliance during this era dedicated to broadening and realizing the goals of development.

Although UNCTAD had limited effect on world economic relations, its membership of scholars and planners from the Third World infused international agencies with a Third World perspective. Perhaps its most concrete influence was on the World Bank under the presidency of Robert McNamara (1968-1981), who reconceived the Bank's role to link economic growth with the redistribution of wealth. "Growth with equity" was the new catch-cry, and for a while planners embraced the idea of investing in "basic needs." Infrastructural lending continued, but new Bank funds were directed into poverty alleviation projects, with rural development and agricultural expenditure rising from 18.5 percent of Bank lending in 1968 to 33.1 percent in 1981.[20]

As we shall see in Chapter 4, the solidarity of the G-77 lasted to the mid-1970s. At this point the organization of the world economy changed drastically, unraveling the tidy subdivision of the international system into its Three Worlds. This was the beginning of the end of *Third World* as a credible term for a region of the world sharing common historical conditions. It was also a time when the isolation between First World and Second Worlds began breaking down. But until then, the development project framed national economic growth in the Third World through a close relationship between international institutions and national policies. We now take leave of the institutional side of the development project and examine its impact on the international division of labor.

Remaking the International Division of Labor

If the development project was an initiative to promote industrialization in the Third World, then it certainly had success. The result, however, was quite uneven, and in some respects industrialization was quite incomplete. Nevertheless, by 1980 the international division of labor had been remade, if not reversed. The Third World's exports included more manufactured goods than raw materials, and the First World was exporting 36 percent more primary commodities than the Third World.[21] In the remainder of this chapter we examine the shift in the international division of labor and its impact on the *world food system.*

If we look at world manufacturing, the European First World lost its core position as industrial production dispersed across the world. Japan and a middle-income group of Third World states improved their share of world manufacturing output, from 19 percent to 37 percent.[22] In the next chapter we examine the implications of this rising group of middle-income Third World states. Here we focus on the redivision of the world's labor.

From the perspective of agriculture, the Third World's share of world agricultural exports fell from 53 percent in 1950 to 31 percent in 1980, while the American "breadbasket" consolidated its role as the pivot of world agricultural trade.[23] By the 1980s, the United States produced 17 percent of the world's wheat, 63 percent of its corn, and 63 percent of its soybeans; the U.S. share of world exports was 36 percent in wheat, 70 percent in corn, and 59 percent in soybeans.[24] On the other side of the globe, between 1961 and 1975, Third World agricultural self-sufficiency declined everywhere except in centrally planned Asian countries (China, North Korea, and Vietnam). In all regions except Latin America, self-sufficiency dropped below 100 percent. Africa's self-sufficiency, for instance, declined from 98 percent in 1961 to 79 percent in 1978.[25]

Two questions arise: First, why did commercial agriculture concentrate in the First World, while manufacturing dispersed to the Third World? Second, is there a relation between these trends? The answer lies in the political structures of the development project. For one thing, Third World import-substitution industrialization (ISI) protected "infant" industries, swelling the *technological rents* First World firms earned on sales of machinery, equipment, and licenses to Third World industrial enterprises.[26] In addition, First World agriculture was protected by farm subsidies, which were sanctioned by the General Agreement on Tariffs and Trade (GATT).

These policies complemented one another, substantially reshaping the international division of labor. In considering the impact of these intersecting policies on the remaking of the international division of labor, we focus on the shaping of the world food order. This is illustrated in the case study of the South Korean "miracle."

CASE STUDY

South Korea in the Changing International Division of Labor

South Korea is arguably the most successful of the middle-income Newly Industrializing Countries (NICs). In the space of one generation, South Korea transformed its economy. In 1953, agriculture accounted for 47 percent of its gross national product (GNP), whereas manufacturing accounted for less than 9 percent. By 1981, these proportions had switched to 16 percent and 30 percent of GNP, respectively. At the same time, the contribution of heavy and chemical industries to total industrial output matured from 23 percent in 1953-1955 to 42 percent in 1974-1976. How did this happen?

South Korea was heavily dependent on injections of American dollars following the Korean War in the early 1950s, a period during which it pursued the ISI strategy. Initially, imports of cement, metals, chemicals, and fertilizers were banned to promote local production of these products. As the manufacturing base developed, this protection was extended to machinery and transport equipment. The Korean government's 1973 Heavy Industry and Chemicals Plan encouraged industrial maturity in shipbuilding, steel, machinery, and petrochemicals.

To keep industrial growth going, the South Korean government complemented ISI with an **export-oriented industrialization (EOI)** strategy, beginning with labor-intensive consumer goods such as textiles and garments. In the early 1960s, manufactured goods accounted for 17 percent of exports. This figure rose to 91 percent by the early 1980s as increasingly sophisticated electronics goods were added to the basket of exports. Thus,

South Korean manufacturers, nurtured on ISI, gained access to foreign markets (especially the massive U.S. market) for their products.

South Korea exemplifies a development state whose industrial success depended on a rare flexibility in policy combined with the unusually repressive political system of military ruler Park Chung Hee (1961-1979). Koreans worked extremely long hours only to find their savings taxed away to support government investment policies. Industrial labor had no rights. Confucianism was a social cement; as an ethic promoting consensus and the authority of education and the bureaucratic elite, it provided a powerful mobilizing cultural myth. Being situated on the front line of the Cold War helped, as the United States opened its markets for Korean exports.

Wholesale changes were also apparent in the agricultural sector. Before 1960, virtually no Western-style bread was consumed in this relatively small country on the perimeter of the non-communist world. The Korean culture cherishes rice, and at that time the country was self-sufficient in food. By 1975, however, South Korea was achieving only 60 percent of such self-sufficiency, and by 1978 it belonged to what the U.S. Department of Agriculture calls "the billion dollar club." That is, South Korea was now purchasing $2.5 billion worth of farm commodities from the United States, much of which was wheat. In addition, the South Korean government was providing free lunch bread to schoolchildren, and thousands of Korean housewives were attending sandwich-making classes, financed by U.S. funds.

Considering South Korea's history, this was indeed a dramatic transformation, not only in the country's diet and economic organization but also in its world economic relations, as South Korea began to import food and export manufactured goods. After the 1945 partition of North and South Korea, the North had the heavy industry, and the South retained only a light industrial base. The South, however, included 70 percent of the Korean rice bowl, which was forced to supply 40 percent of its rice harvest to Japan during the war.

The South Korean farming population diminished by one-half as industrial expansion attracted rural migrants to the cities. This shift, however, was not because rice farming modernized. Recall that economic development is supposed to transfer labor from a modernizing agricultural sector to a maturing industrial sector.

South Korean rice farming remained extremely small scale, retaining an average farm size of 1 hectare (2.471 acres) during this time. In other words, while South Korean industry modernized dramatically, South Korean agriculture did not.

How did industry manage to modernize without the reciprocal modernization of the farm sector predicted in economic development theory? The answer is twofold. First, the South Korean government was unusually interventionist in economic planning, especially for agriculture, where it closely husbanded a small-scale farming system with farm credit and price supports. Second, this particular national economic strategy depended on the support of the international food order or regime, constructed by the United States in the postwar era.

Sources: Harris, 1987, pp. 31-36; Wessel, 1983, pp. 172-173.

The Food Regime and the Changing Division of World Labor

An international regime is simply a set of rules governing trade among nations. An **international food regime**, it follows, describes the world food order. A food regime connects producers and consumers across the world within a stable trading arrangement.[27]

In the postwar era, the United States set up a *food aid program* that channeled food surpluses to Third World countries. Agricultural subsidies intensified productivity on U.S. farms, generating surpluses for export, which subsidized Third World industrialization with cheap food. It was a massive transfer of agricultural resources to the growing urban-industrial sectors of the Third World. This food regime put into practice the rural-urban prescriptions of the development economists (see Chapter 1), but with a difference: it operated on a global, rather than a national, scale.

The food regime originated in the industrial agriculture established on the North American plains in the late nineteenth century. At that time, along with Canada, Australia, New Zealand, and Argentina, the United States exported grains and meat to Europe to feed its burgeoning industrial labor force. The settler regions were industrial Europe's breadbasket (just as its colonies were suppliers of tropical products), but settler farmers also fed domestic industrial labor forces in a dynamic linking national agricultural and industrial sectors. This, of course, was the "inner-directed" development that informed the development project. As we shall see, this model was difficult to replicate when much of the Third World depended on tropical exports.

Although the "inner-directed" model grew out of the size and wealth of the U.S. national economy, it was also well protected by import controls (institutionalized in the GATT, under pressure from the U.S. government). Tariffs protected producers who specialized in one or two commodities only (such as corn, rice, sugar, and dairy products), and subsidies encouraged overproduction by setting prices for farm goods above their price on the world market.

The Public Law 480 Program

Protected behind import controls and price subsidies, American farmers produced more than they could sell domestically. To dispose of these surpluses, the U.S. government instituted the **Public Law 480 (PL-480) Program** in 1954. It had three components: commercial sales on concessionary terms, such as discounted prices in local currency (Title I); famine relief (Title II); and food bartered for strategic raw materials (Title III). The stated goal of PL-480 was "to increase the consumption of U.S. agricultural commodities in foreign countries, to improve the foreign relations of the U.S. and for other purposes." By 1956, almost half of U.S. economic aid was in the form of food aid. In 1967, the U.S. Department of Agriculture reported: "One of the major objectives and an important measure of the success of foreign policy goals is the transition of countries from food aid to commercial trade."[28]

Title I sales under the U.S. PL-480 program anchored the food regime, accounting for 70 percent of world food aid (mostly wheat) between 1954 and 1977. By the mid-1960s, this food aid accounted for one-quarter of world wheat exports, a quantity sufficient to stabilize the prices of traded food goods. The management of these food surpluses stabilized food prices, and this in turn stabilized two key parts of the development project: the American economy and its breadbasket, and Third World government industrial plans. Through market expansion, each came to depend on the other. The 1966 annual report on PL-480 to the U.S. Congress noted its positive impact on the U.S. balance of payments: "This increase in commercial sales is attributable in significant part to increased familiarity with our products through the concessional sales and donations programs.... [T]he economic development built into food aid programs measurably improves U.S. export sales opportunities."[29]

At this point, in 1966, 80 percent of U.S. wheat exports were in the form of food aid. During the 1960s, the U.S. share of world food aid was more than 90 percent, although this fell to 59 percent by 1973.[30] By then aid had become increasingly *multilateral*, building on a supplementary system of food aid to needy countries that was established in the 1960s at the initiative of the United States. It was funded with financial pledges from the **Organization for Economic Cooperation and Development (OECD)** and administered by the United Nations Food and Agricultural Organization (FAO).[31]

Food Importing

Under the aid program, wheat imports supplied burgeoning Third World urban populations. At the same time, Third World governments intervened in the pricing and marketing of food, establishing distribution programs to pass on the international subsidies to urban consumers (recall the discussion in Chapter 1 of the "development alliance," composed of manufacturers, labor unions, urban professionals, and middle classes). Cheap food thus supported consumer purchasing power and subsidized the cost of labor, in both cases improving the Third World market environment for industrial investments.

Returning to the South Korean case, wheat imports in that country quadrupled between 1966 and 1977,[32] while rice consumption began a gradual but steady decline. Cheap imported food allowed the government to maintain low grain prices to hold down industrial wages. Low wages subsidized the industrial export strategy, beginning with labor-intensive manufacturing of clothing items. Meanwhile, from 1957 to 1982 more than 12 million people migrated from the rural sector to work in industrial cities such as Seoul and Pusan.[33] Thus, rapid industrialization in South Korea, fueled by labor transfers from the countryside, depended on a cheap food policy underwritten by food aid.[34] In this way, the food regime sponsored economic development in one of the "showcase" countries of the Cold War.

The impact of food aid varied elsewhere in the world, depending on the resources of particular countries and their development policies. The Korean case was a success story largely because the government centralized management of its rice culture, its industrial development (balancing establishment of an industrial base with export manufacturing), and the supply of labor to the industrial centers.

By contrast, urbanization in Colombia stemmed from the collapse of significant parts of the country's agriculture under the impact of food aid, followed by commercial sales of wheat. Unlike the government of South Korea, the Colombian government did not protect its farmers. Stimulated by the food aid program, imports of wheat grew tenfold between the early 1950s and 1971. Cheap food imports cut by half the prices obtained by Colombian farmers. They reduced their wheat production by about two-thirds, and other food crops, such as potatoes and barley, virtually disappeared. The displaced peasants entered the casual labor force, contributing to the characteristic urban underemployment and low-wage economy of Third World countries.[35]

Between 1954 and 1974, the major recipients of U.S. food aid were strategic, but not necessarily needy, states: India, South Korea, Brazil, Morocco, Yugoslavia, South Vietnam, Egypt, Tunisia, Israel, Pakistan, Indonesia, Taiwan, and the Philippines (see Figure 2.2). In most cases, it was cheaper and easier for these governments to import wheat and wheat flour to feed their growing urban populations than to bankroll long-term improvements in the production, transportation, and distribution of local foods.[36] Food aid allowed governments to purchase food without depleting their scarce foreign currency.

Shipments of food were paid for in counterpart funds, that is, local currency placed in U.S. accounts in local banks by the recipient government. These funds could be spent only by U.S. agencies within the recipient country. They financed a range of development activities such as infrastructural projects, supplies for military bases, loans to U.S. companies (especially local agribusiness operations), locally produced goods and services, and trade fairs.

Counterpart funds were also used to promote *new diets* among Third World consumers in the form of school lunch programs and the promotion of bread substitutes. As U.S. Senator George McGovern predicted in 1964:

> The great food markets of the future are the very areas where vast numbers of people are learning through Food for Peace to eat American produce. The people we assist today will become our customers tomorrow. . . . An enormous market for American produce of all kinds will come into being if India can achieve even half the productivity of Canada.[37]

In this way, as the food aid program wound down in the early 1970s, commercial sales of American farm commodities often continued, not only because Third World consumers had become dependent on such foods but also because they were mostly newly urbanized consumers. In the case of South Korea, rice consumption per capita continues its annual

FIGURE 2.2

Food Shortage Regions and Food Aid Recipients

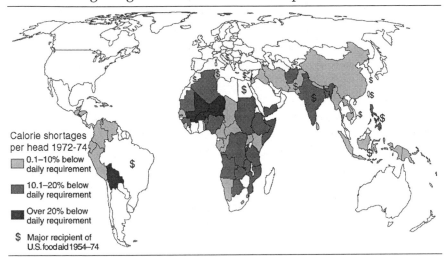

Calorie shortages
per head 1972-74

■ 0.1–10% below
daily requirement

■ 10.1–20% below
daily requirement

■ Over 20% below
daily requirement

$ Major recipient of
U.S. food aid 1954–74

SOURCE: Kidron, Michael, and Ronald Segal, *The State of the World Atlas*. London: Pan, 1981.

decline as Koreans continue to shift to flour-based products and animal protein. In Colombia, where commercial sales were prominent earlier and production of local staples collapsed, imported wheat became the substitute staple food. As we shall see below, when governments can no longer afford such food dependency and when food supplies dwindle, their urban populations will tend to riot.

Food Dependency

Across the Third World in general (with the exception of Argentina), wheat importing rose from a base of practically zero in the mid-1950s to almost half of world food imports in 1971. By 1978, the Third World was receiving more than three-quarters of American wheat exports.[38] At the same time, Third World per capita consumption of wheat rose by almost two-thirds, with no change in First World wheat consumption patterns. Third World per capita consumption of all cereals except wheat increased 20 percent while per capita consumption of traditional root crops declined by more than 20 percent.[39] In Asian and Latin American urban diets, wheat progressively replaced rice and corn. Wheat (and rice) imports displaced maize in Central America and parts of the Middle East, and millet and sorghum in West Africa. Subsidized grain imports also undercut the prices of traditional starches (potatoes, cassava, yams, and taro). Thus, traditional "peasant foods" were replaced by the new "wage foods" of grains and processed foods consumed by urban workers.[40]

The rising consumption of imported wheat in Third World countries was linked to two far-reaching changes in the Third World in this period: (1) the increasingly tenuous condition of peasant agriculture, as subsidized wage foods outcompeted peasant foods because of government-organized urban food markets; and (2) the expansion of an industrial labor force, as small producers (outside the agro-export sector) left the land and sought low-wage jobs in the rapidly growing cities.

In the conventional economic development model, these social trends occur within a national framework. In reality, under the conditions of the development project, they assumed global dimensions as First World farmers supplied food to Third World industrial labor.

Green Power

By the 1970s, Third World reliance on imports for modernized diets was considerable. PL-480 contracts offered incentives to governments receiving food aid to eventually expand their commercial imports of food. The food aid program subsided in the early 1970s in part because Third World commercial imports were swelling. In fact, Third World cereal imports more than tripled during the 1970s. By 1980 the structure of the grain trade had significantly altered, with the Soviet bloc joining the Third World (including China) as the major importing regions and the European Community becoming a major grain exporter, rivaling the American breadbasket.[41] This phase in the international food trade (1973 to the present) has involved cutthroat competition for Third World markets among the grain exporting countries. Commercial exports of food replaced the concessional exports of the postwar food regime.

The centerpiece of this new commercial phase was the U.S. government strategy of **green power**, a strategy of aggressive agro-exporting to consolidate America's role as "breadbasket of the world."[42] The strategy was recommended to President Nixon in 1971 as a means to resolve America's growing balance of payments difficulties at a time when Western Europe and Japan were beginning to erode America's industrial edge in world markets. The Williams Commission recommended that the United States should specialize in high-technology manufactured goods (machinery, computers, armaments) and agriculture. The government removed constraints on the use of American farmland and encouraged export agriculture under the slogan of planting "hedgerow to hedgerow." The green power strategy envisioned a reorganized world agriculture, based in a simple global division of agricultural labor: the United States would expand sales of cheap grain to the Third World, which would pay with exports of labor-intensive crops such as fruit, vegetables, and sugar.[43]

The green power strategy doubled the U.S. share of world trade in grains (peaking at 60 percent) through the 1970s. Between 1975 and 1989, the United States and the European Community used ever-increasing export subsidies to try to corner world grain markets, reducing world agricultural prices by 39 percent.[44] Such food dumping intensified Third World food dependency and destabilized international trade. It is not surprising that the GATT Uruguay Round, which began in 1984, focused on the attempt to establish new rules for agricultural commodity trade—in essence, a potential new food regime. To put this in perspective, we need first to examine how green power affected farming in the Third World.

Remaking Third World Agricultures

Given the emphasis in the development project on industrialization, food aid turned out to be quite fortuitous; by keeping food prices low, it subsidized Third World industrial strategies. Cheap food fed urban populations, leaving urban consumers more income to spend on products of the new industries springing up behind state protection. As we have seen, the intent of the U.S. PL-480 program was also to create future markets for commercial sales of U.S. grains as Third World consumers shifted to wheat-based diets.

Consumption of final products, however, was only part of the strategy. The other thrust of the food aid program was to expand consumption of other agricultural goods, such as feed grains and agricultural technology. Export of these products followed a logic similar to that of the food aid program: finding outlets for surplus products. Behind this stood the massive state-sponsored expansion in American agricultural productivity, which more than doubled that of manufacturing during the period of the postwar food regime (1950s-1970s). The management of agricultural overproduction made disposal of surpluses a matter of government policy.

The Global Livestock Complex

Surplus grain was sufficiently cheap and plentiful to encourage its use to feed livestock rather than people. In this section, we consider how expanding supplies of feed grains stimulated the growth of commodity chains linking specialized feed producers with specialized livestock operations elsewhere in the world. We have already seen how Third World consumers shifted to a wheat-based diet. Here we take that dietary change one step further, as some consumers shifted up the food chain to animal protein (beef, poultry, and pork). It is generally the case that the shift from starch through grain to fresh vegetables and animal protein signifies dietary affluence or modernization. But what historical forces bring this about? If we examine the dynamics of the food regime we can see that such dietary modernization is as much the result of policy as it is the consequence of rising incomes.

Elaborate U.S. grain-processing industries grew in the 1950s as cattle moved from open range feeding to grain feeding, with 75 percent fed on grain by the early 1970s. The grain companies that had formerly sold and processed wheat diversified into the mass production of processed feeds (corn, barley, soybeans, alfalfa, oats, and sorghum) for cattle and hog feedlots as well as poultry motels. Consumption of animal protein became identified with "the American way of life," as meat came to account for one-quarter of the American food bill by 1965.[45]

Poultry consumption more than tripled between the 1930s and 1970, and beef consumption roughly doubled between the turn of the century and 1976.[46] Under the auspices of Marshall Plan export credits for U.S. agribusiness products, this agri-food model spread to Europe and Japan. The European *Common Agricultural Policy (CAP)* allowed free entry to feedstuff imports (cereal substitutes), and the Japanese livestock industry became almost completely dependent on feed-grain imports.

Under the food aid program, exports of feed grains also flourished as animal protein consumption took hold among urban middle classes in the Third World. The U.S. Feed Grains Council routinely channeled counterpart funds into the development of local livestock and poultry industries. Loans were made to more than 400 agribusiness firms to establish subsidiary operations in thirty-one countries as well as to finance trade fairs and educational programs introducing livestock feeds and feeding techniques. By 1966, feed grains were the biggest single earner of export dollars for food companies.[47]

In 1969, four South Korean firms entered joint ventures with U.S. agribusiness companies (including Ralston-Purina and Cargill) to acquire technical and marketing expertise. According to the PL-480 annual report of 1970, these enterprises would use counterpart funds "to finance construction and operation of modern livestock feed mixing and livestock and poultry production and processing facilities. As these facilities become fully operational, they will substantially expand the market for feedgrain and other feed ingredients." In 1972, the annual report concluded that

> these firms were instrumental in accelerating the introduction of US technology and were a major factor in the rapid expansion of . . . the increase in Korea's imports of US corn, soybean meal, breeding stock and other supplies and equipment. For example, annual Korean corn imports increased from about 3,000 tons prior to the conclusion of the first PL 480 private trade agreement in 1967 to over 450,000 tons in fiscal 1972.[48]

CASE STUDY

How Food Commodity Complexes Reveal Social Structuring

The growing feed-grains trade traces changing social diets and, therefore, the transformation of social structures. Animal protein consumption reflects rising affluence in the Third World—the people of these countries embraced First World diets beyond those staple (grain, primarily wheat) diets promoted directly through food aid. German statistician Ernst Engel formulated a law correlating the dietary move from starch, to grain, to animal protein and fresh vegetables with rising incomes. Instead of reflecting individual choice and mobility, the difference in diets has to do with who holds the power to produce certain foods and how patterns of consumption are distributed among social classes.

An example of such intervention in shaping the food chain comes from Costa Rica, a Central American state with a history of government and multilateral support of beef production. Between 1963 and 1973, in Guanacaste province, cattle herds increased by 65 percent while peasant bean production fell 41 percent. Declining food security for the poorer segments of Costa Rica forced its government to use foreign exchange earnings from exported beef to purchase basic grains on the world market to feed its citizens. On the global level, Engel's Law may be in effect, as different classes of people dine on different parts of the food chain, but it is a *managed* effect. As wealthy (often foreign) consumers dine "up" on animal protein, local peasants, displaced by cattle pastures, face an increasingly tenuous low end of the food chain, typically depending on low-protein starchy diets.

Source: Place, 1985, pp. 293-295.

With livestock production expanding throughout the Third World, specialized feed grain supply zones (primarily of maize and soybeans) concentrated in the First World and in "middle-income" countries like Brazil and Argentina. Between the late 1940s and 1988, world production of soybeans increased sixfold. At the same time, maize production was revolutionized as a specialized, capital-intensive agro-industry. In the late 1980s, the value of the maize trade was six times that of the world wheat trade.[49] In other words, livestocking came to be linked, through the grain companies, with crop farming elsewhere in the world. Thus specialized agricultures were linked by chains of commodities organized in global complexes—a pattern common to both agriculture and manufacturing. Indeed, the livestock complex was as central to postwar development and consumption patterns as the automobile complex.

The Green Revolution

The other major contribution to the remaking of Third World agriculture was the **green revolution**. This was a "package" of plant-breeding agricultural technologies originally developed under the auspices of the Rockefeller Foundation (in Mexico in the 1940s) and then in a combined venture with the Ford Foundation (in the Philippines in the 1960s). Scientists focused on producing high-yielding varieties (HYVs) of seeds that allowed intensified cropping patterns. The new hybrid seeds were heavily dependent on disease- and pest-resisting chemical protections in the form of fungicides and pesticides. Intensive irrigation and fertilization were required to optimize yields, a practice that promoted weeds, which then had to be killed with herbicides. In other words, the HYVs came with a considerable package of chemical and infrastructural inputs, encouraging a modern, specialized form of commercial farming. The differences between traditional and modern farming are explained in the following insert.

What a Farm Looks Like Under Traditional and Modern Agriculture

The major difference between traditional and modern agriculture is specialization. Traditional farming is mixed farming that complements crops with livestock that is used as a source of animal power, dung fuel, post-harvest stubble grazing, and various items of subsistence, such as milk, hides, and tallow. Family or village labor is usually the norm. In contrast, modern farms specialize in one or two particular crops or livestock activities. This practice was very pronounced in colonies, where sugar plantations or coffee farms would replace traditional agriculture. With specialization and increasing scale comes capital intensity, as producers add mechanical, biotechnical, and chemical inputs. Agriculture becomes industrialized and may depend on hired labor to complement farm machinery.

In an important trend, a growing number of farmers around the world are redefining modern agriculture along organic and diverse lines (still using some modern technology) because it is a more sustainable form of farming. A resurgence of traditional agricultural practices, such as crop rotation and South American raised bed agriculture, has also enhanced sustainability.

The expansion of green revolution agriculture in the Third World embodied the two sides of the development project: the national and the international. From a *national* perspective, governments sought to improve agricultural productivity and the delivery of maize, wheat, and rice to urban centers. In context of the international food regime, this was an *import-substitution* strategy. The green revolution produced dramatic yields, but they have been highly concentrated in a few ecologically advantaged regions of the Third World. Asia and, to a much lesser degree, Latin America have captured the benefits from the new grain varieties, while Africa has charted few gains. Maize, emphasized early, was not a very successful green revolution crop. The major wheat-producing countries in the Third World—India, Argentina, Pakistan, Turkey, Mexico, and

Brazil—planted the bulk of their wheat acreage in the new hybrid varieties, accounting for 86 percent of the total green revolution wheat area by the 1980s. Meanwhile, six Asian countries—India, Indonesia, the Philippines, Bangladesh, Burma, and Vietnam—were cultivating more than 87 percent of the rice acreage attributed to the green revolution by the 1980s. Because little commercial wheat or rice is grown in much of Africa, the green revolution largely bypassed that continent. Stagnant food production in many African countries stimulated soaring imports of wheat destined largely for the growing urban classes.[50]

Meanwhile, from an *international* perspective, the food aid program helped to spread green revolution technology. A reformulation of PL-480, in 1966, included provisions for "self-help" measures in the contract for food aid. Although varying by recipient, these provisions always included "creating a favorable environment for private enterprise and investment, . . . development of the agricultural chemical, farm machinery and equipment, transportation and other necessary industries, . . . [and use of] available technical know-how." Counterpart funds routinely promoted agribusiness and green revolution technologies, complemented with loans from institutions such as the **United States Agency for International Development (USAID)** and the World Bank.[51] These agencies aimed to weave First World agricultural technologies into Third World commercial farming.

At the same time that it increased crop yields, the green revolution increased *rural income inequalities*. In parts of Latin America, such as Mexico, Argentina, Brazil, and Venezuela, as well as in irrigated regions of India, this high-input agriculture nurtured a process of economic differentiation among, and often within, farming households. Within households, women typically have less commercial opportunity. The green revolution package of hybrid seeds and supporting inputs had to be purchased; to buy them, participants needed a regular supply of money or credit. Women, particularly poor women, usually found themselves "out of the loop"—not only because of the relative difficulty of obtaining financing but also because of institutional barriers in agricultural extension traditions of transferring technology to male heads of households. In Muslim cultures where the tradition of *purdah* keeps women confined, "male agents do not have easy access to the women farmers, and female agents are . . . difficult to recruit."[52]

Among farming households, the wealthier ones were more able to afford the package—and the risk—of introducing the new seed varieties. They also prospered from higher grain yields, often with easier access to government services than their poorer neighbors who lacked the political and economic resources to take full advantage of these technologies. The rising incomes and higher yields of the wealthier households gave them a competitive advantage over their poorer neighbors. Rising land values often hurt tenant farmers by inflating their rent payments. Some poor households were forced to rent their land to their richer neighbors, or lost it through foreclosure to creditors. Finally, the mechanical and chemical technologies associated with the green revolution either reduced farmhand employment opportunities for poor or landless peasants (where jobs were mechanized) or degraded working conditions where farmhands were exposed to toxic chemicals, such as herbicides.[53]

To the extent that we can generalize, the spread of agribusiness typically exacerbates social inequalities in Third World countries. These inequalities take a number of forms. At the village level, gender and household differentiation have occurred, deepening inequities that began with the privatization of formerly communal lands under colonialism. Private property distribution often favors males at the expense of women, whereas commercial agriculture exposes peasants to competitive and unpredictable market forces, often to the disadvantage of poorer, and therefore more vulnerable, households. At the regional level, yield disparities increase between irrigated and nonirrigated districts. Such disparities and the emphasis on marketing of wage foods for urban consumers discriminate against the production of rain-fed grains, beans, and root crops.[54] At the national level, governments have often centralized their power over rural areas through their role in administering aid and development programs such as the green revolution. Indeed, when the Indian government tried to assume control of the Punjabi "breadbasket" in order to stabilize the national food system in the 1980s, a separatist movement generated violent clashes between the central government and the Punjab, an essentially Sikh state.[55]

Anti-Rural Biases of the Development Project

Within the framework of the development project, Third World governments wanted to feed growing urban populations cheaply, both to maintain their political support and to keep wages down. Indeed, the term **urban bias** has been coined to refer to the systematic privileging of urban interests, from health and education services through employment schemes to the delivery of food aid.[56] This bias was central to the construction of development political coalitions in the postwar era. Such coalitions were firmly based in the cities of the Third World.

Attention to the urban areas, however, did not go unnoticed in the countryside, which was neither silent nor passive. Growing rural poverty, rural dissatisfaction with urban bias, and persistent peasant activism over the question of land distribution put **land reform** on the political agenda in Asia and Latin America. When the Cuban Revolution redistributed land to poor and landless peasants in 1959, land reforms swept Latin America. Between 1960 and 1964, Brazil, Chile, Costa Rica, the Dominican Republic, Ecuador, Guatemala, Nicaragua, Panama, Peru, and Venezuela all enacted land reforms. The **Alliance for Progress** (1961)—a program of nationally planned agrarian reform coordinated across Latin America— provided an opportunity for the United States to support land reforms as part of a strategy to undercut radical insurgents and stabilize rural populations. Land reforms attempted to reproduce the American family farm model, first introduced in the late 1940s in East Asia (Japan, South Korea, and Taiwan), which was at that time under occupation by U.S. military forces. These land reforms were a model in two senses: first, as interventions to quell peasant militancy, and second, as a method of reducing tenancy and promoting owner-occupancy on a smallholding basis.[57]

CASE STUDY

The Green Revolution and the Development Mentality

One of the underexplored dimensions of development is the change in the way people think and act in the world. Most studies, including this one, foreground the social-structural changes, leaving changes in systems of thought and cultural identity in the background. This is perhaps because of the ingrained rationalism of the categories through which we conceptualize the world, categories such as "market," "class," "peasant," and "urban" that sociologize individuals and their relationships. In a study of the adoption of green revolution technology in the Colombian coffee industry, Christopher London has examined the process by which coffee growers rethink their cultural identity in the process of technification of coffee production. London's archetype grower, Santiago Mejía, reproduces in his production practices and in his self-understanding the essential ingredients of the conception of development advocated by The National Federation of Coffee Growers of Colombia (FEDECAFE). In an interview, Mejía expresses the shift in his beliefs, devaluing farming with the traditional coffee variety,

pajarito, now that he has adopted the scientific practices of
FEDECAFE-style technification:

> Before . . . [we planted] *pajarito* because there wasn't any other more
> productive variety, so indisputably it had to be the one we used.
> What else could a coffee grower sow? . . . One cultivated *pajarito* in a
> rustic manner, rudimentary, with whatever resources one happened
> to have because he didn't have anyone who could say "we have a
> much better system," or that "it's already been tested and proved"
> like the extension agents do. . . . So, for that reason we and our
> grandfathers had to do it that way because it was the first thing that
> appeared. But as all things evolve so one has to be in agreement
> with development.

London observes that, in embracing the new agricultural technology, the grower is also embracing, to a greater or lesser extent,
the modern mentality, where "his own past . . . is seen as being
primitive and better for having been left behind. One has to be in
agreement with development." The point, of course, is that while
there are powerful institutions like the state, development agencies, the market, and private property that shape conditions and
possibilities for populations (including understandings of development), the variety of ways in which people respond to development as a belief system is a key to understanding its
relative currency, its legitimacy, and/or its enabling role for
disadvantaged groups who appropriate its promises, across
the social world.

Source: London, 1997.

The land reform movement, however, focused on redistributing only
the land that had not already been absorbed into the agribusiness complex. In effect, the reforms exempted farmland undergoing modernization and dealt with what was left, including frontier lands. Indeed,
alongside the strengthening of the agribusiness sector, considerable "re-
peasantization" occurred during this period. In Latin America, two-thirds
of the additional food production between 1950 and 1980 came from frontier colonization, and the number of small farmers with an average of two
hectares of land grew by 92 percent. Arable land overall increased by as
much as 109 percent in Latin America and 30 percent in Asia, but possibly

declined in Africa.[58] Resettlement schemes on frontiers, including forests, were typically financed by the World Bank, especially in Indonesia, Brazil, Malaysia, and India. These strategies sometimes simply relocated rural poverty and resembled "a war against the earth's rapidly dwindling tropical forests." In Brazil, for example, between 1960 and 1980, roughly 28 million small farmers were displaced from the land by the government's sponsorship of agro-industrialization to enhance foreign exchange earnings from agricultural exports, notably soy products. The displaced farmers spilled into the Amazon region, burning the forest to clear new, and often infertile, land.[59]

Persistent rural poverty through the 1960s highlighted the urban bias of the development project's industrial priorities. At this point the World Bank, under President McNamara, devised a new poverty alleviation program. It was a multilateral scheme to channel credit to smallholding peasants and purportedly to stabilize rural populations where previous agrarian reforms had failed or been insufficient. The Bank itself acknowledged that almost half of its eighty-two agricultural projects between 1975 and 1982 were unsuccessful in alleviating poverty. Instead, the outcomes included displacement of hundreds of millions of peasants throughout the Third World, leakage of credit funds to more powerful rural operators, and the incorporation of surviving peasant smallholders, via credit, into commercial cropping at the expense of basic food farming.[60]

The lesson we may draw from this episode of reform is that neither the resettlement of peasants nor their integration into monetary relations is always a sustainable substitute for allowing peasant cultures to adapt to their surrounding environment themselves. The dominant assumptions of the development project heavily discriminated against the survival of peasant culture, as materially impoverished as it may have seemed.

Through a combination of state neglect and competition in national and world markets, the long-term decline of Third World peasant agriculture, begun in the colonial era, has accelerated. Land reforms and land resettlement programs (mainly in Latin America and Asia) notwithstanding, these interventions typically have done little to halt the deterioration of the peasant economy.[61] The commercialization of agriculture undermines the viability of household food production as a livelihood strategy for peasant populations and a subsistence base for the rural poor. The environmental stress associated with population growth and land concentration steadily downgrades survival possibilities for the rural poor as common lands and forest timbers for fuel disappear. The result is a growing stream of peasants migrating to overcrowded metropolitan centers of Latin America, Asia, and Africa.

Summary

Like the example of the Russian doll, the development project was a multilayered enterprise; its components are delineated in the following insert. National strategies of economic growth, extending all the way down to farming technology, depended on international assistance in a variety of forms, from foreign aid through vocational education and rural extension agents to subsidized machinery and agricultural inputs. The Bretton Woods institutions complemented bilateral aid programs in providing the financial conditions for Third World countries to pursue a universal goal of "catch-up." Third World governments embraced national industrial growth as the key to raising living standards. Third Worldism came to mean correcting the distortions, or imbalances, of the colonial division of labor. The key was industrialization. In this way, the Third World as a whole was incorporated into a singular project, despite national and regional variations in available resources, starting point, and cultural and ideological orientation.

Aid programs bound Third World development to the overall enterprise of global reconstruction. Military and economic aid programs

---

What Are the Ingredients of the Development Project?

The development project was an organized strategy for pursuing nationally managed economic growth. As colonialism collapsed, newly independent states embraced development as a legitimating and revenue-generating enterprise. The Western experience of economic growth provided the model, and an international institutional complex provided financial and technical assistance for national development across the world. Some ingredients, then, were (1) an organizing concept to provide universal meaning (e.g., development as emulating Western living standards, rationality, and scientific progress), (2) a national framework for economic growth, (3) an international framework of aid (military and economic) binding the developing world to the developed world, (4) a growth strategy favoring industrialization, (5) an agrarian reform strategy encouraging agro-industrialization, and (6) central state initiatives to stimulate and manage investment and mobilize multiclass political coalitions into a development alliance supporting industrial growth.

shaped the geopolitical contours of the "free world" by integrating countries into the Western orbit. They also shaped patterns of development through technological transfer and subsidies to industrialization programs. We have reviewed here the significance of food aid in securing geopolitical alliances as well as in reshaping the international division of labor. As development economists had predicted, Third World industrialization depended on the transfer of rural resources, but this transfer was not confined to national arenas. Indeed, exports of First World food and agricultural technology revealed a *global* rural-urban exchange.

This global dimension is as critical to our understanding of the development processes during the postwar era as is the variety of national forms. We cannot detail such variety here, and that is not the point of this story. Rather, we are interested in understanding how the development project incorporated national policies within an international institutional and ideological framework. The international framework was theoretically in the service of national economic growth policies, but when we look closer, we find that the reverse also was true. Social changes within Third World countries had their own local face; nevertheless, the local face of development was at one and the same time a local and globally organized process, linking changes in the First World with changes in the Third World. One could say that all change under these circumstances was conditioned by global relationships, especially geopolitics and international transfers of economic resources.

In this chapter, we have examined one such example of these international transfers, and we have seen how they condition the rise of new social structures. Transfers included basic grains directly supplying working-class consumers, as well as feed grains indirectly supplying more affluent consumers through the livestock complex. In this way, First World agricultural expansion conditioned the rise of new social classes in the Third World. At the same time, the export of green revolution technology to Third World regions stimulated social differentiation among men and women, as well as among rural producers, laborers, and capitalist farmers. Those peasants who were unable to survive the combined competition of cheap foods (priced to subsidize urban consumers) and high-tech farming in the countryside commonly migrated to the cities, further depressing wages. Not surprisingly, this scenario stimulated a massive relocation of industrial tasks to the Third World, reshaping the international division of labor. This is the subject of Chapter 3.

PART II

The Development
Project Unravels

3

The Global Economy Reborn

The development project was driven by the idea of parallel national programs of industrial development. Each nation would raise its standard of living by producing a series of "national products" with as coherent an industrial structure and cohesive an industry-agriculture partnership as possible. "Catch-up" meant raising living standards and emulating the U.S. model of balanced or "inner-directed" growth. Public resources and planning were considered legitimate partners of private enterprise, with programs of multilateral and bilateral assistance.

From an international standpoint, the development project reconstructed the world economy along particular lines. U.S. President Franklin D. Roosevelt evoked an image of "one worldism." Global unity would be expressed politically in the United Nations and organized economically through the Bretton Woods institutions. However, as the Cold War intensified in the late 1940s, "one worldism" yielded to "free worldism" under President Truman. With the focus now on *containment* of Soviet and Chinese power, the world economy and the development project came to rest on the twin foundations of *freedom of enterprise* and the U.S. dollar as the international currency. In this arrangement, bilateral disbursements of dollars wove together the principal national economies of the West and Japan. As the source of these dollars, the U.S. Federal Reserve System led those countries' central banks in regulating an international monetary system.[1]

Under these conditions, the former colonies pursued the universal project of development. Of course, countries differed in their resource endowments and the character of their political regimes—ranging from military dictatorship through one-party states to parliamentary rule. Nonetheless, the image was of a *convergent* world of independent states at different points along a single path of modernization. Divergent forces, however, soon emerged. These included a growing, rather than diminishing, gap between First and Third World living standards and a substantial differentiation among states within the Third World as the newly industrializing countries shot ahead of the rest. In this chapter we consider the link between differentiation within the Third World and the growing First World/Third World gap. These two indicators signaled a dramatic reorganization of the international economy as an emerging global production system spun a giant web across the world. This chapter details this emerging process, but it is important to remember that the web continues to be spun and respun today.

Divergent Developments

Between 1950 and 1980, the rate of economic growth in the Third World exceeded that of the First World. It also exceeded the rate of growth of European countries during their early, comparable phases of development. When we consider population growth rates and per capita income, however, the game of "catch-up" appears to have been only that: a game.

In the postwar era, the per capita income of the Third World, as a proportion of that of the First World, remained steady—about 7 percent to 8 percent—but the difference in GNP per capita between First and Third Worlds widened from $2,191 in 1950 to $4,839 in 1975 (in constant 1974 dollars).[2] In the mid-1970s, the official multilateral definition of the absolute poverty line was an annual income of $50. At the time, about 650 million people were estimated to be living in absolute poverty around the world, with another 300 million living in relative poverty—with annual incomes between $50 and $75. By 1980, the numbers of the world's absolute poor had increased to 1 billion, according to calculations for the Brandt Report, *Common Crisis: North, South & Cooperation for World Recovery*.

These estimates may overstate poverty because in subsistence regions of the Third World, per capita income calculations fail to include alternative survival possibilities. In so doing, they misrepresent local culture. Nevertheless, they express the unequal global distribution of income as purchasing power, and, because purchasing power commands resources, such global inequality is cumulative.[3] This situation was demonstrated in the example in Chapter 2 of the greater market power of animal protein consumers, a circumstance in which the demand for higher-value meat and thus indirectly for feed crops outcompetes food crops, thereby depleting local food security. This disparity is amplified on a world market scale.

Thus, the evidence in the late 1960s to early 1970s suggested that most Third World countries were running hard only to fall increasingly behind.

The wealth gap between First and Third Worlds was evidently enlarging despite the promise of the development project. Moreover, the figures cited earlier do not reveal the growing inequalities of income and access to resources *within* these countries.

Industrial growth fueled by international assistance often brought economic development that relied on imported capital-intensive techniques and neglect of food production. The typical social consequence of these patterns was that growing numbers of rural and urban poor were deprived of the benefits of economic growth. The severity of this pattern often depended on the character of the particular country's political regime.

The so-called Brazilian economic miracle followed the pattern described above, with the economy expanding at an annual rate of around 10 percent during the decade of military rule after 1964.[4] But there was also a *net loss* of industrial jobs, a rising share of the total income gained by the top 10 percent of the population, and a growing number of people living at or below the poverty line, variously estimated at 50 percent to 80 percent of the population.[5] It was Brazil's enormous population and resource endowments that fueled the miracle.

By contrast, South Korea, with a much smaller population (it had only one-third as many people as Brazil), followed a different course. The South Korean regime enlarged the domestic market and consumer purchasing power by controlling the differentiation of income between rich and poor, which was roughly one-quarter of the distributional spread of income in Brazil.[6] Although the South Korean regime was authoritarian, its pattern of industrialization depended on implementing a comprehensive land reform program, setting a floor on rural incomes, and enjoying preferential access to the U.S. market for manufactured exports.

Differentiation among Third World countries increased, too, as a select few played the catch-up game more successfully than others and sprinted ahead. The average growth rate for the Third World in the 1960s was 4.6 percent, with per capita growth rates of 1 percent or less; six Third World newly industrializing countries (NICs),[7] however, grew at rates of 7 percent to 10 percent, with per capita growth rates of 3 percent to 7.5 percent.[8] These six countries were Hong Kong, Singapore, Taiwan, South Korea, Brazil, and Mexico.

The rise of the NICs revealed two sides of the development project. On one hand, NICs appeared to fulfill the expectation of upward mobility in the international system. The central tenet of the development project was that living standards in each country would be raised by industrialization. The NICs evidently succeeded in this task, lending legitimacy to the project. They belonged to a group of other middle-income Third World countries whose annual manufacturing growth rates, 7.6 percent in the 1960s and 6.8 percent in the 1970s, exceeded those of their low-income Third World associates (6.6 percent and 4.2 percent, respectively) as well as those of the First World (6.2 percent and 3.3 percent, respectively).[9] The other middle-income countries—for example, Malaysia, Thailand, Indonesia, Argentina, and Chile—were expected to follow the same path.

On the other hand, the rise of the newly industrializing countries also demonstrated the *selectivity* of the forces released by the development project. In the first place, the NICs cornered the bulk of private foreign investment.[10] Much of this was concentrated in developing export production facilities in textiles and electronics in South Korea, Taiwan, Mexico, and Brazil. In 1969, for instance, most of the foreign investment in electronic assembly centered in the Asian NICs—Hong Kong, South Korea, Taiwan, and Singapore.[11] Between 1967 and 1978, the share of foreign direct investment in tax havens (offshore banks) and NICs increased from 50.6 percent to 70 percent, and the share of manufactured exports from the NICs that were controlled by transnational corporations already ranged in the early 1970s from 20 percent in Taiwan through 43 percent in Brazil to 90 percent in Singapore.[12]

In addition, the distribution of industrial growth in the Third World was highly concentrated. Between 1966 and 1975, more than 50 percent of the increase in value of Third World manufacturing occurred in only four countries, and about two-thirds of the increase was accounted for by only eight countries: Brazil, Mexico, Argentina, South Korea, India, Turkey, Iran, and Indonesia.[13]

On the global scale, there was considerable differentiation among Third World countries and regions in levels of industrialization (the measure of development). The manufacturing portion of GDP in 1975 was 5 percent in Africa, 16 percent in Asia, and 25 percent in Latin America and the Caribbean.[14] By 1972, the Organization for Economic Cooperation and Development (OECD) reported: "It has become more and more clear that measures designed to help developing countries as a group have not been effective for [the] least-developed countries. They face difficulties of a special kind and intensity; they need help specifically designed to deal with their problems."[15] The notion of a universal blueprint clearly was fading.

Acknowledging the limits of standardized remedies in the development project was one thing. It was quite another to recognize that the NICs were not simply an arbitrary grouping of middle-income states; there were, in fact, strong geopolitical forces contributing to their industrial success. All states may have been equal in the Bretton Woods system, but some states were more equal than others when it came to their global position.

Hong Kong and Singapore are peculiar because of their historic role as entrepôts (port cities) in South China and the Malaccan Straits, respectively. They have shared in the East Asian expansion of the last quarter of the twentieth century, serving as vital centers of marketing, financial, and producer services. In addition, they are coordinating centers of the ethnic Chinese entrepreneurial networks in the region.

Within the context of the Cold War, the other four states—Taiwan, South Korea, Mexico, and Brazil—held strategic geopolitical positions in the international order, namely as consequential states in their regions. Their higher rates of economic growth draw attention to the dimension of the development project that included the transfer of enormous amounts of direct and indirect economic assistance from the Western powers. Military aid and preferential access to the U.S. market helped sustain authoritarian regimes that stabilized economic growth conditions for a time through such measures as investment coordination and the political control of labor, whether through repressive forms in East Asia or corporatist forms in Latin America. During the period of maximum growth, Taiwan, South Korea, Mexico, Singapore, and Brazil were distinguished by one-party or military rule. South Korea and Taiwan garrisoned U.S. troops, given their proximity to North Korea and China, respectively.

The Newly Industrializing Country (NIC) Phase in Context

The rise of the newly industrializing countries is part of a new historical phase of industrialization. The first historical phase of industrialization matured in Britain, which manufactured textiles and processed food, then exported these products. The second phase of industrialization matured in Britain's rivals in the late nineteenth century—Germany, France, the United States, and Japan—as they built an industrial base around the production of steel, chemicals, and machinery. The NICs combined both phases.

Early Third World industrialization has been termed *primary import-substitution industrialization (ISI).*[16] In ISI, a country shifts from importing manufactured goods to the local manufacturing of basic consumer goods such as textiles, clothing, and footwear, and may engage in food processing. Secondary ISI enlarges local industrial capacity for consumer durables such as automobiles, intermediate goods such as petrochemicals and steel, and capital goods such as heavy machinery. Whereas the Latin American NICs (Mexico and Brazil) began primary ISI in the 1930s and graduated to the secondary phase in the 1950s, the Asian NICs (Taiwan and South Korea) began primary ISI in the 1950s and did not move to the next stage until the 1970s.

The Asian NICs financed their import-substitution industrialization (ISI) via primary export-oriented industrialization (EOI), based on the export of labor-intensive products. They graduated to secondary EOI (exporting higher-value-added products) once their industrial base had matured. That is, the Asian NICs, lacking the resource base of the Latin American ones, had to shift to exporting manufactured goods earlier than did their Latin American counterparts, with their more diversified array of exports (from minerals to foodstuffs).

With the exception of Hong Kong, most of the newly industrializing countries had strong states that guided considerable public investment into infrastructure development and industrial ventures with private enterprise. The South Korean state, in particular, virtually dictated the investment patterns in that nation. Success in ISI depended on the size of a country's domestic market as well as a ready supply of foreign exchange that would allow the country to purchase from the First World the capital equipment technologies necessary to sustain the new industrialization.

Export-Oriented Industrialization (EOI) Displaces
Import-Substitution Industrialization (ISI)

The ISI strategy emerged in the 1930s when international trade collapsed and independent Latin American states had the opportunity to build industrial capacity in the absence of foreign imports. Tariffs sustained this process in the postwar era, encouraging considerable foreign investment (chiefly by U.S. corporations) in domestic manufacturing, even while international trade expanded once again. But there were limits to this intensive mode of industrialization, not the least of which was the saturation of consumer markets. Remittance of corporate profits, in addition to the cost of purchasing or renting First World technologies, led to a mounting foreign exchange bill. Under these constraints, Latin states moved into an export mode, a strategy of broadening markets and earning foreign exchange. The newly industrializing countries of East Asia were already selling in the United States, to which they had special access because of their geopolitical significance.[17] For them, export orientation accompanied import substitution.

Widespread EOI signaled a significant change in strategies of industrialization. The NICs broadened from supplying domestic markets to supplying foreign markets, using transnational corporate (TNC) investment and marketing networks. Industrial exporting had begun in the large states that had relatively mature industrial bases (Argentina, Brazil, Mexico, and India), starting with traditional labor-intensive manufactures—textiles and footwear, for example—and processing of local primary goods such as foodstuffs, tobacco, leather, and wood.[18] But EOI was also a process of relocation of First World manufacturing, of consumer goods followed by machinery and computers, to the Third World. It all depends on how you look at it. Furthermore, the relocation was often of partial, rather than integrated, manufacturing processes to specific sites, as discussed below.

The export-oriented industrialization strategy, in a world economy buoyed by rising First World consumer incomes, nurtured the phenomenon of the newly industrializing countries. In the 1950s, Hong Kong, an exceptional case, was already exporting manufactures, beginning with textiles and garments. From 1960 to 1978, as manufacturing grew in middle-income countries by about 7 percent annually, in the NICs the rate of growth was often twice that. Third World manufacturing exports outpaced the growth in total world trade in manufactures during this period, increasing the Third World share of world trade from 6 percent in 1960 to more than 10 percent in 1979. The bulk of this export growth was attributable to the newly industrializing countries, and its composition broadened from textiles, toys, footwear, and clothing in the 1960s to more sophisticated and competitive exports of electronics, steel, electrical goods, machinery, and transport equipment by the 1970s.[19]

The destination of these products diverged, however, with light manufactured exports (such as clothing, toys, and electronic items) going mostly to the First World (north) and heavy manufactured exports (such as steel and machinery) going to the Third World (south). There was also a significant subdivision among the Third World industrial exporters. The faster growth in manufactured exports occurred (from the late 1960s) in the East Asian states, which specialized in modern industrial products such as clothing, engineering goods, and light manufactures. The difference between these countries and the Latin American states is that the East Asian nations lack a natural resource base and have comparatively small domestic markets. Their success in export manufacturing was achieved by rooting their industrial base in the world economy. Thus,

Mexico, Brazil, Argentina, and India . . . accounted for over 55% of all Third World industrial production but only about 25% of all Third World manufactured exports (narrowly defined). Hong Kong, Malaysia, Singapore and South Korea . . . were responsible for less than 10% of Third World production but 35% of all Third World manufactured exports (narrowly defined).[20]

The newly industrializing countries of Asia were quite exceptional in their export orientation for two primary reasons, both geopolitical. The first is that the East Asian perimeter of the Pacific Ocean was a strategic zone in the U.S. Cold War security system. Military alliances with these states were matched with U.S. openness to exports from this region, often of goods assembled for U.S. corporations. The second is that Japan's historic trade and investment links with this region have deepened as Japan has based its economic power in regional investments in low-wage assembly production. In each case, the Asian NICs have reaped the benefits of access to the insatiable markets of the United States and Japan. Global and regional context has been as influential in their growth as domestic policy measures and economic cultures.

The World Factory

The expanding belt of export industries in the Third World, led by the newly industrializing countries, provides a clue to a broader transformation occurring within the world economy at large. There was a new "fast track" in manufacturing exports that was superseding the traditional track of exporting processed resources. This new export arrangement resembled a **world factory**. It involved production for world, rather than domestic, markets, through chains of production sites differentiated by their function in a global production system.[21]

The phenomenal growth of export manufacturing using labor-intensive methods in the East Asian region, as well as in regions such as Mexico's border-industrial zone, signaled the rise of a global production system and a world labor force. In Asia, the stimulus derived from the regionalization of the Japanese industrial model of hierarchical subcontracting arrangements. The Mexican Border Industrialization Program (BIP) paralleled this reorganization of industrial production. In 1965, the Mexican government implemented the BIP to allow entirely foreign-owned corporations to establish labor-intensive assembly plants (known as *maquiladoras*) within a twelve-mile strip south of the border. Concessions to firms, which employed Mexican labor at a fraction of the U.S. wage and paid minimal taxes and import duties to the Mexican government, were part of a competitive world factory strategy. As reported in *The Wall Street Journal* on May 25, 1967, the Mexican minister of commerce stated: "Our idea is to offer an alternative to Hong Kong, Japan and Puerto Rico for free enterprise."[22]

U.S. firms establishing assembly plants in the BIP concentrated on garments, electronics, and toys. By the early 1970s, 70 percent of the operations were in electronics, following a global trend of U.S. firms relocating electronic assembly operations to Southern Europe, South Korea, Taiwan, and Mexico, seeking low-cost labor in response to Japanese penetration of the transistor radio and television market. The 168 electronics plants established by 1973 on the Mexican border belonged to firms such as General Electric, Fairchild, Litton Industries, Texas Instruments, Zenith, RCA, Motorola, Bendix, and National Semiconductor. There were also 108 garment shops, sewing swimsuits, shirts, golf bags, and undergarments; some subsidiaries of large companies like Levi Strauss; and other small sweatshops (unregulated workplaces) subcontracted by the large retailers.[23]

CASE STUDY

The World Factory in China

China has become a prime location for low-wage production in the global economy. The communist government anticipated this development by establishing "special economic zones" in coastal regions in the 1980s to attract foreign investment. By the mid-1990s, when the East Asian NICs had emerged as "middle-income countries" with relatively high-skilled labor forces, China became the preferred site for foreign investors—especially Korean and Taiwanese investors, who were experiencing rising labor costs at home. In 1995, the ratio of factory wages in China to South Korea/Taiwan to Japan was approximately 1:30:80. In her investigations of the shoe factories (producing Reebok and Nike products, among others) in Dongguan City, sociologist Anita Chan observes that vast concrete industrial estates have mushroomed on former rice paddies. Local farmers now live off the rents from the factories, while tens of thousands of migrants from China's poorer hinterland swell the low-wage workforce. Twelve-hour shifts (with enforced overtime) and seven-day work weeks are common, with Korean or Taiwanese managers using militaristic methods to break in and control the migrant labor force (in addition to requiring a deposit of two to four weeks' wages and confiscation of migrant ID cards). As the cash economy has expanded in China, a huge migrant labor force has gravitated toward coastal industrial regions, attracting foreign investment. Between 1985 and 1996, the portion of Chinese exports from foreign-owned plants grew from 1 to 40 percent. China now produces about half of the world's shoes and a proliferating array of electronic items, toys, and garments for the global economy.

Sources: Chan, 1996; p. 20; Faison, 1997a, p. D4.

The global proliferation of low-wage assembly marked the strategic use of export platforms chiefly in the Third World by competing **transnational corporations (TNCs)** from the United States, Europe, and Japan, and, later, from some Third World countries. As these companies seek to reduce their production costs to enhance their global competitiveness, so export platforms have spread. Thus the NICs' strategy of export-oriented industrialization sparked the generalization of the world factory phenomenon across the globe: from the sweatshops of Los Angeles to the subcontractors in Bangladesh, Ireland, Morocco, and the Caribbean.

The Era of Information Technologies

The world factory system is nourished by the technologies of the "information age." Especially important in the latest of these revolutions is the semiconductor industry. Semiconductors, in particular the integrated computer chip, are the key to the new information technologies that undergird the accelerating globalization of economic relations. Advances in telecommunication technologies enable firms, headquartered in New York, Tokyo, or Singapore, to coordinate production tasks distributed across sites in several countries. These technologies allow rapid circulation of production design blueprints among subsidiaries, instructing them in retooling their production. If a transnational corporation wants to redesign its product to accommodate changing fashion, for example, it can instantaneously reorganize production methods in its offshore plants, using the new information-processing and telecommunication technologies.

Telecommunication technologies allow firms to organize globally, moving components and software among offshore sites and selling end products in world markets. Thus we find "global assembly lines" stretching from California's Silicon Valley or Scotland's Silicon Glen to assembly sites in Taiwan, Singapore, Malaysia, or Sri Lanka.[24] These global assembly lines are extremely fluid commodity chains, as production organization among the links of the chains is centrally coordinated. That is, the pattern and content of these chains is continuously regulated at the headquarters of transnational companies according to market conditions.

If we consider the spread of electronics assembly in the Third World from a national accounting perspective, it is just another indicator of export manufacturing expansion. If instead we look at it from the perspective of the transnational firm, the microelectronics industry integrates global production systems, rendering individual national production sites increasingly substitutable. How has this come about? First, electronics was itself a leading industry in establishing the world factory, given the low-skill character of much electronic assembly and its global dispersion to export platforms across the world. Second, information technology is rooted in microelectronics and underlies the global coordination of production and circulation in other industries, from banking to textiles to automobiles. In this way, the third phase of industrialization (information technology) reformulates and globalizes industrial production.

The Global Production System

The consolidation of the world factory system spun a giant web of exchanges across the world, but the web lacks the symmetry of the spider's creation. Economic globalization is neither uniform nor stable. Global production systems consist of multilayered divisions of labor among plants sited in global or regional networks. Relations across and among these plants are vertically and/or horizontally ordered, depending on the relative hierarchies of skill involved in producing the commodity.

The combination of vertical and horizontal relationships is perhaps best captured in Robert Reich's portrayal of a U.S. corporation that coordinates multinational inputs in an integrated transnational process. He views the corporation as "no longer even American. It is, increasingly, a façade, behind which teems an array of decentralized groups continuously subcontracting with similarly diffuse working groups all over the world." Reich uses the example of a $10,000 Pontiac:

*How Do Transnational Corporations Organize
Their Global Production Systems?*

Transnational corporate organization employs vertical and/or horizontal arrangements among specialized units. Ankie Hoogvelt claims this "loosely confederated network structure" allows firms to survive in and negotiate an environment where markets and technologies are in constant flux. Firms combine global coordination with regional marketing strategies (including purchasing local firms to establish a regional foothold). Informational technologies facilitate this but are both expensive and rapidly obsolescent, necessitating access to financial resources, multiplant production, and extensive marketing networks.

The vertical arrangement derives from the American (Fordist) model of transnational corporate organization. This uses production hierarchies, which centralize and locate information and control of technology in the parent country while transferring standard process technologies to host sites to reduce labor costs and produce standardized components. Thus the industrial assembly-line system is reproduced on a world scale, linking differentiated production sites in a hierarchically ordered global commodity chain.

Alternatively, there is the horizontal arrangement pioneered by the Japanese (Toyotist) model of transnational corporate organization. Here technology is more decentralized, and, arguably, there is opportunity for local development. The emphasis is on flexibility. Management and workers, as well as the parent firm and suppliers, collaborate in continually adjusting to changing (world/regional) market demand. Lean inventories ("just-in-time" production), product design, and responsiveness to fashion are as important as cost reduction. These qualities substitute for the Fordist emphasis on efficiency at all cost. Toyotism encourages horizontal intra-firm as well as inter-firm networks, which are interactive webs exchanging technological and market knowledge. Information and telecommunication technologies facilitate networked organization, by which spatially dispersed production can be coordinated electronically.

Sources: Fujita & Hill, 1995; Castells, 1996; Hoogvelt, 1997, p. 127.

FIGURE 3.1

Global Sourcing: A $10,000 "American Pontiac"—Where the Money Goes

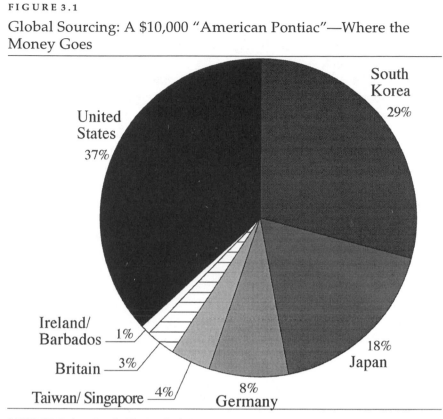

SOURCE: Robert Reich, *The Work of Nations: Preparing Ourselves for 21st Century Capitalism* (Vintage Press, 1992), p. 11.

Of which about $3000 goes to South Korea for routine labor and assembly operations, $1,750 to Japan for advanced components (engines, transaxles and electronics), $750 to West Germany for styling and design engineering, $400 to Taiwan, Singapore, and Japan for small components, $250 to Britain for advertising and marketing services, and about $50 to Ireland and Barbados for data processing. The rest, less than $4000 goes to strategists in Detroit, lawyers and bankers in New York, lobbyists in Washington, insurance and health care workers all over the country, and General Motors shareholders—most of whom live in the United States, but an increasing number of whom are foreign nationals.[25]

With the opportunity for global coordination (and mobility) embedded in informational technologies, TNCs subdivide production sequences according to technological or labor skill levels, and they shift labor-intensive activities to offshore export platforms or processing zones. Thus General Motors drastically cut costs in 1999 by subcontracting with South Korean and Japanese tool makers mired in the depressed conditions of the Asian financial crisis. Parent firms tend to monopolize high technologies, with component processes (assembling, etching, and testing computer chips), component goods (pharmaceutical stock, engines, auto parts), and consumer goods (cameras, electronic games, TVs, and videotape recorders) moved offshore for production in cheaper sites, export processing zones, or sweatshop districts (which mushroom across the world). Transnational corporations often organize production hierarchies and alliances based on joint ventures with firms in other countries. Joint ventures may be used to gain access to technology, markets, or finance—for example, Hyundai improved its computer memory chip production capacity through a joint venture with Texas Instruments in the 1980s, and, in 1999, Renault teamed up with Nissan to exchange its finance for Nissan technology, in the process forming the world's fourth largest auto firm after General Motors, Ford, and Toyota.[26]

The global production system depends on a *technical division of labor* among specialized processes located in different world sites. Here, instead of countries specializing in an export industry (manufacturing or agriculture), world production sites specialize as part of a production chain linking several countries. This *transnational* specialization spread across the First World in the 1960s as firms integrated the production of inputs for a final product. The change was essentially from producing a national product to producing a world product.[27] The following case study of the world car illustrates this change.

CASE STUDY

The World Car: From Ford and Mitsubishi

In the postwar era, the Ford Motor Company invested directly in a United Kingdom affiliate that produced the British Ford Cortina for local consumers; it had a British design and was assembled locally with British parts and components. At that time, no matter where the capital came from, supply linkages and marketing services were generated locally in import-substitution industrialization. In fact, governments pursuing import-substitution policies encouraged foreign investment in the domestic product.

This pattern has since changed. The Ford Cortina has now become the Ford Escort, the "world car" version of the original British "national car." Assembled in multiple national sites (including Britain), the Escort is geared to production for the world market. It uses parts and components from fourteen other countries, including Germany, Switzerland, Spain, the United States, and Japan. Given the larger production run of a world car, Ford claimed a saving of 25 percent over the earlier method of building new cars separately for the North American and European markets.

Similarly, the Mitsubishi Motor Corporation, which is headquartered in Japan, has subsidiaries producing components in South Korea, Indonesia, Thailand, Malaysia, the Philippines, Australia, and even the United States (as joint ventures with the Chrysler Corporation and the Ford Motor Company). Mitsubishi cars, assembled in Thailand or Japan, are sold in the United States, Canada, the United Kingdom, New Zealand, and Papua New Guinea as Dodge or Plymouth Colts.

Sources: Jenkins, 1992, pp. 23-25; Stevenson, 1993, p. D1; Borthwick, 1992, p. 511; Sivanandan, 1989, p. 2.

Dispersal of specialized production tasks across national borders accounts for the growing scale and reach of transnational corporations. The rise of the newly industrializing countries signaled, in part, the extension of global sourcing to some Third World sites. In the 1970s, 50 percent of all manufactured exports from U.S.-based TNCs were from Brazil, Mexico, Singapore, and Hong Kong.[28] For a decade from the end of the 1960s, there was a marked relocation of *industrial* investment from the First World to the Third World. Such industrial "decentralization" was the combined result of declining profitability on investments in the First World and Third World state entrepreneurship to attract foreign investment into local industrialization programs, some of which involved sponsorship of industrial (and agricultural) export zones.

The Export Processing Zone

Export processing zones (EPZs) are specialized industrial export estates with minimal customs controls; they are usually exempt from labor regulations and domestic taxes. EPZs serve firms seeking lower wages and Third World governments seeking capital investment and foreign currency to be earned from exports. The first EPZ appeared at Shannon, Ireland, in 1958; India established the first Third World EPZ in 1965, and as early as the mid-1980s roughly 1.8 million workers were employed in a total of 173 EPZs around the world. By the late 1990s, more than 200 EPZs employed about 4 million workers.[29]

The dynamics of EPZs are not synonymous with the development project, since they favor export market considerations over the development of domestic markets (local production and consumption). Export processing zones typically serve as enclaves—in social as well as economic terms. Often physically separate from the rest of the country, EPZs are built to receive imported raw materials or components and to export the output directly by sea or air. Workers are either bused in and out daily or inhabit the EPZ under a short-term labor contract. Inside the EPZ, whatever civil rights and working conditions that hold in the society at large are usually denied the workforce. It is a workforce assembled under conditions analogous to those of early European industrial history to enhance the profitability of modern, global corporations.

Much of the world's EPZ labor force is composed of women, who usually are treated worse than men.[30] In Mexico, roughly 85 percent of the workforce of the *maquiladoras* is young women, supposedly more docile, agile, and reliable than men in routine assembly work—and certainly cheaper. When Motorola shifted its electronics plant 200 miles south from Phoenix to Nogales in the 1970s, its annual wage per worker for assembly work fell from $5,350 to $1,060. The following description of a worker at an electronics *maquiladora* near Tijuana captures the conditions of this kind of labor:

> Her job was to wind copper wire onto a spindle by hand. It was very small and there couldn't be any overlap, so she would get these terrible headaches. After a year some of the companies gave a bonus, but most of the girls didn't last that long, and those that did had to get glasses to help their failing eyes. It's so bad that there is constant turnover."[31]

Meanwhile, the transnational corporations that employ workers in export processing zones obtain other concessions, such as free trade for imports and exports, infrastructural support, tax exemption, and locational convenience for reexport. For example, for *maquila* investment in Sonora, one of the poorest border states, the Mexican government's most favorable offer was 100 percent tax exemption for the first ten years, and 50 percent for the next ten.[32] In short, the EPZ is an island in its own

FIGURE 3.2

Locations of Export Processing Zones

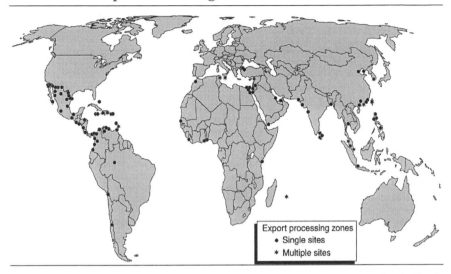

Export processing zones
• Single sites
* Multiple sites

SOURCE: From *Global Shift: Transforming the World Economy*, Dicken, © 1998 by Guilford Press.

society, separated from domestic laws and contributing little to domestic economic growth, other than some foreign currency earned on exports. It belongs instead to an archipelago of production sites dotted across the world (but concentrating in Latin America, the Caribbean and Asia), serving world markets.

The Corporate Dimension of World Markets

Export markets concentrate in the First World, where markets are a great deal denser than Third World markets. For example, the average proportion of the population owning a TV, car, or telephone is 0.1 percent in Asia (excluding Japan), 1 percent in Africa, and 6 percent in Latin America, but 60 percent in North America, 50 percent in Japan, 33 percent in Western Europe and Oceania, and 10 percent in the former Soviet Union.[33] Export, or world, markets are typically organized by transnational corporations (TNCs).

Recent U.N. data reveal that TNCs account for two-thirds of world trade. TNCs control most of the world's financial transactions, (bio)technologies and industrial capacity—including oil and its refining, oil, coal, gas, hydroelectric and nuclear power plants, mineral extraction and processing, home electronics, chemicals, medicines, wood harvesting and processing, and more. The top five TNCs in each major market (such as jet aircraft, automobiles, microprocessors, and grains) typically account for between 40 and 70 percent of all world sales.[34] Further, about 50 percent of world trade takes place inside the TNCs, as components move within corporate networks including subsidiaries of allied firms and parent corporations in the construction of a final product. In the 1970s, the growth rate in the global trade of components came to match that of the global trade in final products.[35] In 1991, for the first time, according to estimates from the U.N. Conference on Trade and Development, sales internal to transnationals exceeded their overall trade in final products, including services. From 1970 to 1998, the number of TNCs rose from 7,000 to 60,000, with more than 500,000 foreign affiliates accounting for roughly 25 percent of global output.[36]

The combined sales of the largest 350 TNCs in the world total almost one-third of the combined GNPs of all industrialized countries and exceed the individual GNPs of all Third World countries. The majority of these firms are headquartered in the centers of the world economy: France, Germany, Japan, the United Kingdom, and the United States account for 70 percent of all transnational investment and about 50 percent of all the companies themselves. The scale of the TNCs is enormous. For example, Pepsico, one of the largest beverage firms in the world, operates more than 500 plants with 335,000 workers in more than 100 countries.[37]

The growing weight of transnational corporations in international trade has increased the pressure on other firms to go global. Firms do this either to reduce their labor costs or to expand sales by gaining access to broader markets. The revolution in communications and the development of transport and financial services has allowed firms to tap into the global labor force.

Manufacturing and the Global Labor Force

The formation of the global labor force had its roots in the development project. It began with urban bias, which disadvantaged rural communities and actively expelled producers from the land. From 1950 to 1997, the world's rural population decreased by some 25 percent, and today 45 percent of the world's population dwells in cities. This worldwide dynamic was the fundamental source of the global labor force. Historian Eric Hobsbawm observed: "Between 1950 and 1975 . . . in Europe, in the Americas, and in the western Islamic world—in fact everywhere except Continental South and East Asia and sub-Saharan Africa—peasants now form a minority of the population. And this process occurred with dramatic speed."[38]

For European societies, the process of depeasantization was spread over several centuries. Even then the pressure on the cities was relieved as people emigrated to settler colonies in North America and Australasia. For Third World societies, this process has been compressed into a few generations, a little longer for Latin America. Rural migrants in many places have overwhelmed the cities and continue to do so.

Dispossessed people entering the manufacturing workforce reduced global labor costs. Once First World firms developed technologies of mass production, they began relocating manufacturing to employ cheaper Third World labor. Mass production developed around large, routinized production runs that could be broken down and subdivided into specialized tasks. The assembly line that emerged in the automobile and meat-packing industries was archetypal. Each worker on the line did a simplified task that contributed to an overall production process. The simplification of specialized tasks is known as the deskilling of work.

Today, tasks deskilled through specialization—such as cutting and stitching in the garment or footwear industry, or assembly in the electrical, automobile, or computer chip industry—are often relocated to cheap labor regions. At the same time, the technologies to coordinate those tasks generate needs for new skilled labor, such as managerial, scientific, engineering, and technical labor.[39] This bifurcation of the labor force means that skilled labor tends to concentrate in the First World, and unskilled labor is often consigned to the Third World. The coordination of both types of labor is the province of TNC enterprise, as detailed in the following description from the 1970s, when this kind of bifurcation first became prominent:

> Intel Corporation is located in the heart of California's "Silicon Valley." . . .
> When Intel's engineers develop a design for a new electronic circuit or process, technicians in the Santa Clara Valley, California, plant will build, test, and redesign the product. When all is ready for production of the new item, however, it doesn't go to a California factory. Instead, it is air freighted to Intel's plant in Penang, Malaysia. There, Intel's Malaysian workers, almost all young women, assemble the components in a tedious process involving hand soldering of fiber-thin wire leads. Once assembled, the components are flown back to California, this time for final testing and/or integration into a larger end product. And, finally, they're off to market, either in the United States, Europe, or back across the Pacific to Japan.[40]

In the 1970s, the relocation of deskilled tasks to lower-wage regions of the world was so prevalent that the concept of a **new international division of labor (NIDL)** was coined to describe this development. Briefly, NIDL referred to an apparent decentralization of industrial production from the First to the Third World. The conditions for this movement were defined as endless supplies of cheap Third World labor, the new technical possibility of relocating the unskilled portions of manufacturing processes to the Third World, and the development of transport, communications, and organizational technology, reducing the significance of distance in the coordination of activities by global firms.[41]

Skilled labor inputs concentrated in the North, except where enterprising states such as the newly industrializing countries of East Asia (South Korea, Taiwan, Singapore, and Hong Kong) used public investment to upgrade workforce skills. The upgrading was necessary because their wage levels were rising in relation to other countries that were embracing export production, such as Malaysia, Indonesia, and the Philippines. In 1975, if the hourly wage for electronics work in the United States was measured at 100, the relative value for equivalent work was 12 in Hong Kong and Singapore, 9 in Malaysia, 7 in Taiwan and South Korea, 6 in the Philippines, and 5 in Indonesia and Thailand.[42] This wage differentiation made the East Asian NICs' labor-intensive production less competitive, forcing them to upgrade their portion of the global labor force.

These Asian countries improved their competitiveness by specializing in more sophisticated types of export manufacturing for First World markets, using cheap skilled labor rather than cheap semiskilled and unskilled labor. After upgrading their labor force, the NICs attracted skilled labor inputs to their countries as a regional growth strategy. As the skilled work came, these states became headquarters, or cores, of new regional divisions of labor patterned on the production hierarchy between Japan and its East and Southeast Asian neighbors.

An East Asian division of labor in the semiconductor industry for U.S. firms formed by 1985 through the upgrading of this production hierarchy. Final testing of semiconductors (capital-intensive labor involving computers with lasers) and circuit design centers were located in Hong Kong, Singapore, and Taiwan; wafer fabrication in Malaysia; and assembly in Malaysia, Thailand, the Philippines, and Indonesia. Whereas in the 1970s semiconductors were assembled in Southeast Asia and then flown back to the United States for testing and distribution, by the 1980s Hong Kong imported semiconductors from South Korea and Malaysia to test them for reexport to the First World as well as for input in Hong Kong's fabled watch-assembly industry.[43]

Patterns of global and regional sourcing have recently mushroomed across the world, particularly under the stimulus of the electronics revolution. Firms establish either subsidiaries in other countries or extensive subcontracting arrangements—such as in labor-intensive consumer goods industries like garments, footwear, toys, household goods, and consumer electronics. For example, the Nike Corporation produces most of its athletic shoes through subcontracting arrangements in South Korea, China, Indonesia, and Thailand; product design and sales promotion are reserved for its U.S. headquarters, where the firm "promotes the symbolic nature of the shoe and appropriates the greater share of the value resulting from its sales."[44] U.S. retailers of every size also routinely use global subcontracting arrangements in the Asia-Pacific and the Caribbean regions to organize their supplies and reduce their costs, as illustrated in the following case study on Saipan.

CASE STUDY

Global Subcontracting in Saipan

One of the production sites used over the past two decades as a supplier in global subcontracting is the tiny island of Saipan, in the Philippine Sea of the western Pacific. The commonwealth of Saipan has been a territory of the United States since the end of World War II, and the islanders are American citizens. In the early 1980s, new federal rules for the garment industry allowed duty free (and virtually quota free) imports from Saipan into the United States as well as liberal foreign investment conditions. Companies involved in garment production on Saipan include Arrow, The Gap, Montgomery Ward, Geoffrey Beene, Liz Claiborne, Eddie Bauer, and Levi Strauss. For certain of these companies, Saipan has strategic importance. Even though its exports make up only about 1 percent of all clothing imports into the United States, they account for roughly 20 percent of sales for some large American companies.

Saipan has a major advantage as a production site: although the "Made in USA" label can legitimately be put on any item produced there, the island was exempted from the federal minimum wage in 1976. The commonwealth government has maintained a minimum wage of $2.15 an hour since 1984 (compared with the federal minimum of $4.25 on Guam, another U.S. territory 120 miles to the south).

Saipan shipped about $279 million worth of wholesale garments to the United States in 1992, and, despite the label, more than half the labor force contributing to these exports is foreign—predominantly Chinese recruits. The clothing factories resemble sweatshops in their working conditions; they have recently attracted the attention of American labor unions and investigators from the U.S. Department of Labor and the Occupational Safety and Health Administration. These inspectors found Chinese workers whose passports had been confiscated and who were working eighty-four-hour weeks at subminimum wages. One of the companies involved, Levi Strauss, responded by establishing new subcontract guidelines requiring improved conditions, which were also to be implemented in other sites in Myanmar and China. Monitoring of conditions continues.

Sources: Shenon, 1993, p. 10; Udesky, 1994; The Economist, *June 3, 1995, p. 58.*

The Saipan case study illustrates the dark side of subcontracting—a pattern of abuse commonly experienced by unprotected labor throughout the world. About 46 million children work for American firms in nineteen different countries, with half this child labor in India alone. Many of these children work fourteen-hour days in crowded and unsafe workplaces.[45] Regardless of whether transnational corporations offer better conditions than local firms, the rise of global subcontracting permits little opportunity for regulation of employment conditions. The global labor force exists on such a broad scale across cultures, out of sight of regulators, that global working situations increasingly resemble the harsh conditions of early European industrial work before labor protections appeared. Some of today's global labor force has been generated by the expansion of agribusiness on a world scale, to which we now turn.

Global Agribusiness

Just as the manufacturing transnational corporations use global sourcing strategies, so do agribusiness firms. The food trade is one of the fastest-growing industries in the world today, especially in processed foods like meat and flour products, and in fresh and processed fruits and vegetables. Food companies stretch across the world, organizing producers on plantations and farms to deliver products for sale in the higher-value markets. As we have seen, the livestock complex was one of the first segments of the food industry to internationalize. It is the basis of the following case study on the making of the "world steer."

CASE STUDY

Agribusiness Brings You the World Steer

The "world steer" resembles the "world car." It is produced in a variety of locations with global inputs (standardized genetic lines and growth patterns) for global sale (standardized packaging). Like the world car, the world steer is the logical extension of the mass production system that emerged in the development era. The beef industry is subdivided into two branches: intensive lot-feeding for high-value specialty cuts and extensive cattle grazing for low-value, lean meat supplying fast-food outlets.

From the 1960s there was an explosion of cattle ranching in Central America (Costa Rica, Nicaragua, Honduras, Guatemala, and El Salvador) as the North American fast-food industry took off. Brahman bulls (or their semen) imported from Florida and Texas were crossed with native criollo and fed on imported African and South American pasture to produce a more pest-resistant, more heat-resistant, and beefier breed of steer. From conception to slaughter, the production of the steer is geared entirely to the demands of a global market. Animal health and the fattening process depend on medicines, antibiotics, chemical fertilizers, and herbicides supplied from around the world by transnational firms. In addition to these global inputs in the production of the world steer, there are the "local" conditions of beef production.

Postwar development strategies favored agro-exporting for foreign exchange to purchase industrial technologies. Central American states complemented their traditional exports (coffee and bananas) with beef when import restrictions on beef exports to the United States were eased by the Alliance for Progress (a hemispheric security project of economic reform sponsored by the United States). Governments obtained loans from the World Bank, the Agency for International Development (AID), and the Inter-American Development Bank (IADB) to fund the expansion of pasture and transport facilities. Beef exporting from the region rose eightfold in twenty years, resulting from a 250 percent expansion of Central America's cattle herds. By 1978, Central American herds totaled 10 million head of cattle, supplying 250 million pounds of beef annually and accounting for 15 percent of U.S. beef imports. Among the foreign investors in this industry were large transnational companies such as International Foods, United Brands, Agrodiná mica Holding Company, and R. J. Reynolds.

World steer production has redistributed cattle holdings and open-range woodland from peasants to the ranchers supplying the export packers. More than half the rural population of Central America (35 million) is now landless or unable to survive as a peasantry. World steer production not only reinforces inequality in the producing regions but also threatens craftwork and food security.

Domesticated animals traditionally have provided food, fuel, fertilizer, transport, and clothing, in addition to grazing on and consuming crop stubble. In many ways, livestock have been the centerpiece of rural community survival over the centuries. Peasants have always used mixed farming as a sustainable form of social economy, hunting on common lands to supplement their local diets with additional protein. Elimination of woodlands reduces hunting possibilities, shrinks wood supplies for fuel, and destroys watershed ecologies. Also, development policies favoring other cattle breeds over the traditional criollo undermine traditional cattle raising and hence peasant self-provisioning. Peasants forfeit their original meat and milk supplies and lose access to side products such as tallow for cooking oil and leather for clothing and footwear. In short, the spread of the world steer industry supplies distant mass consumer markets at the same time that it undermines local agro-ecologies. The world economy does not get something for nothing.

Sources: Sanderson, 1986a; Friedmann & McMichael, 1989; Williams, 1986, pp. 93-95; Rifkin, 1992, pp. 192-193.

Global sourcing also sustains the intensive form of livestock raising that requires feedlots. Three agribusiness firms headquartered in the United States operate meat-packing operations across the world, growing cattle, pigs, and poultry on feedstuffs supplied by their own grain marketing subsidiaries elsewhere in the world. Cargill, headquartered in Minnesota, is the largest grain trader in the world, operating in seventy countries with more than 800 offices or plants and more than 70,000 employees. It has established a joint venture with Nippon Meat Packers of Japan, called Sun Valley Thailand, from which it exports U.S. corn-fed poultry products to the Japanese market. ConAgra, headquartered in Nebraska, owns fifty-six companies and operates in twenty-six countries with 58,000 employees. It processes feed and animal protein products in the United States, Canada, Australia, Europe, the Far East, and Latin America. Tyson Foods, headquartered in Arkansas, runs a joint venture with the Japanese agribusiness firm C. Itoh, which produces poultry in Mexico for both local consumption and export to Japan. Tyson also cuts up chickens in the United States, using the breast meat for the fast-food industry and shipping leg quarters to Mexico for further processing (at one-tenth the cost of preparing them in this country) for the Japanese market.[46]

The New Agricultural Countries (NACs)

Despite the far-flung activities of these food companies, agribusiness investments have generally concentrated in select Third World countries such as Brazil, Mexico, Argentina, Chile, Hungary, and Thailand. Harriet Friedmann has called these countries the **new agricultural countries (NACs)**.[47] They are analogous to the newly industrializing countries insofar as their governments promote agro-industrialization for urban and export markets. These agro-exports have been called *nontraditional exports* because they either replace or supplement the traditional tropical exports of the colonial era. Nontraditional exports are high-value foods such as animal protein products and fruits and vegetables. To carry the analogy further, the term the *new international division of labor* has been extended to these agro-exports because they supersede the exports associated with the colonial division of labor.[48] An example is Thailand, as illustrated in the following case study.

CASE STUDY

Thailand Becomes a New Agricultural Country (NAC)

Thailand's traditional exports of rice, sugar, pineapples, and rubber are complemented with an expanding array of nontraditional primary exports: cassava (feed grain), canned tuna, shrimp, poultry, processed meats, and fresh and processed fruits and vegetables. Former exports, corn and sorghum, are now mostly consumed domestically in the intensive livestock sector. Raw agricultural exports, which accounted for 80 percent of Thailand's exports in 1980, now represent 30 percent; processed food makes up 30 percent of manufactured exports. In other words, Thailand has become a New Agricultural Country.

Seen as Asia's supermarket, Thailand has rapidly expanded its food processing industry on a foundation of rural smallholders under contract to food processing firms. Food companies from Japan, Taiwan, the United States, and Europe use Thailand as a base for regional and global export-oriented production. Since the 1970s, Japanese firms have invested in Thai agriculture to expand feed (soybeans and corn) and aquaculture supply zones for Japanese markets. Typically, Japanese food companies enter into joint ventures with Thai agribusinesses, providing high-technology production facilities and market access abroad.

Thai poultry production is organized around small growers who contract with large, vertically integrated firms. The Thai government established the Fourth Sector Co-operation Plan to Develop Agriculture and Agro-Industry in the mid-1980s, linking agribusiness firms, farmers, and financial institutions with state ministries to promote export contracts. In this way, the government provided support with tax and other concessions to agribusinesses and, through the Bangkok Bank's Agricultural Credit Development, underwrote the distribution of land to landless farmers for contract growing and livestock farming. Thailand's mature feed industry, coupled with low-cost labor, makes its poultry producers very competitive with their counterparts in the United States, especially in the Japanese market. By 1987, this market was supplied equally by U.S. and Thai poultry exports, but since then China has emerged as Japan's major supplier. Shrimp is now Thailand's most valuable agro-export, and Thailand is the world's largest producer of farmed shrimp. Thailand's agro-exports are linked to the rich and growing markets in the Pacific Rim (especially those of Japan, South Korea, and Taiwan), accounting for more than 60 percent of Thailand's foreign exchange reserves in the 1990s.

Sources: Philip McMichael, 1993a; Watts, 1994, pp. 52-53; Goss, Burch, & Rickson, in press.

The Second Green Revolution

As we saw in Chapter 2, the green revolution encouraged agribusiness in the production of wage foods for urban consumers in the Third World. Since then, agribusiness has spread from basic grains to other grains such as feedstuffs, to horticultural crops such as fresh fruits and vegetables. More recently, agribusiness has created feed-grain substitutes such as cassava, corn gluten feed, and citrus pellets, and biotechnology is creating plant-derived "feedstocks" for the chemical industry. This kind of agriculture depends on hybrid seeds, chemical fertilizers, pesticides, animal antibiotics and growth-inducing chemicals, specialty feeds, genetically modified plants, and so forth. In other words, it is a specialized, high-input agriculture servicing high-value markets, as well as food processors and agro-chemical firms. It extends green revolution technology from basic to luxury foods and agro-industrial inputs, and it has been termed the second green revolution.[49]

The second green revolution is a reliable indicator that high-income, consuming classes are increasing in the Third World, adopting the affluent diets associated with the First World. It involves, most notably, substituting feed crops for food crops, a move that further exacerbates social inequalities (in access to land and basic foods). In Mexico, for example, U.S. agribusiness firms promoted use of hybrid sorghum seeds among Mexican farmers in the late 1950s. Then, in 1965, the Mexican government established a support price favoring sorghum over wheat and maize (products of the green revolution). As sorghum production doubled (supplying 74 percent of Mexican feedstuffs), wheat, maize, and even bean production began a long decline. Meanwhile, between 1972 and 1979, meat consumption rose among wealthier Mexicans, with increases of 65 percent in pork, 35 percent in poultry, and 32 percent in beef. At the same time, no kind of meat was available for about one-third of the population.[50]

The second green revolution also underlies the globalization of markets for high-value foods such as off-season fresh fruits and vegetables. This market is one of the most profitable for agribusinesses; high-value foods have become the locus of their growth. For example, as global markets have deepened and transport technologies have grown alongside distribution systems, we now have "cool chains" that maintain chilled temperatures for moving fresh fruit and vegetables grown by Third World farmers to supermarket outlets across the world. U.S. firms such as Dole, Chiquita, and Del Monte have moved beyond their traditional commodities such as bananas and pineapples into other fresh fruits and vegetables, joined by British firms Albert Fisher and Polly Peck. By coordinating producers scattered across different climatic zones, these firms are able to reduce the seasonality of fresh fruits and vegetables and thus create a global supermarket. Year-round produce availability is complemented with exotic fruits like breadfruit, cherimoya (custard apple), carambola (star fruit), feijoa (pineapple guava), lychee, kiwi, and passion fruit; vegetables such as bok choy, cassava, fava beans, and plantain; and salad greens like arugula, chicory, and baby vegetables.[51]

In this new division of world agricultural labor, transnational corporations typically subcontract with Third World peasant/farmers to produce specialty horticultural crops and off-season fruits and vegetables. They also process foods (such as fruit juices, canned fruits, frozen vegetables, boxed beef, and chicken pieces), often in export processing zones, for expanding consumer markets located primarily in Europe, North America, and Pacific-Asia.

Global Sourcing and Regionalism

Global sourcing is a strategy used by transnational corporations and host governments alike to improve their world market position and secure predictable supplies of inputs. But it is not where our understanding of global dynamics stops. Indeed, during the 1980s, there was a marked decline in the rate of TNC investment in the Third World,[52] which had become destabilized by debt stress (see Chapter 4). The decline of foreign investment coincided with a corporate restructuring trend in the First World. This decade of restructuring marked a new direction in firm marketing strategies: market segmentation.

The new direction represents a shift from standardized mass production to flexible production, using smaller and less specialized labor forces (as explained in the earlier insert on TNC organization of their global production systems). Whether flexible production is actually replacing mass production is a matter of considerable debate. In fact flexible, or "lean," production is reorganizing mass production to address the rapid segmentation, or differentiation, of consumer markets. Marketing now drives production, and a system of "mass customization" has developed to allow firms to mass produce essentially similar products with multiple variations to suit individual needs—the sneaker industry, with its endless variations in style, is a clear case in point.

The size of market segments depends on social class incomes. We have seen a considerable stratification of consumption over the past decade—in the broad quality range of cars and clothing items, and, as suggested above, in the segmentation of the beef market into high-value beefsteak and low-value hamburger. With a global market, firms are increasingly under pressure to respond to changing consumer preference as the life span of commodities declines (with rapidly changing fashion and/or technologies). Shifting consumer tastes require greater flexibility in firms' production runs, use of inputs, use of inventory, and selling strategies.

In the 1980s, the Toyota Company introduced the just-in-time (JIT) system of "destandardized or flexible mass production."[53] With JIT, simultaneous engineering replaces the sequencing of mass production— the "just-in-case" system in which materials are produced on inflexible assembly lines to supply standardized consumer markets. By contrast, simultaneous engineering allows quicker changes in design and production, so firms can respond to volatile consumer markets. The Gap, for example, changes its inventory and "look" every six weeks. As the company's Far East vice president for offshore sourcing remarked, "The best retailers will be the ones who respond the quickest, the best . . . where the time between cash register and factory shipment is shorter."[54]

The JIT system lends itself to the promotion of global and regional corporate strategies. In the clothing industry, for instance, commodity chains for shoes and garments can be dispersed globally and centrally coordinated by the parent firm. In the garments trade, a global fashion designer typically purchases a Paris-designed shirt for US$3 to $4 in Bangladesh, Vietnam, or Thailand and sells the shirt in the European market at five to ten times that price. In the shoe trade, for instance, Vietnamese workers make about US$400 a year stitching sneakers, while corporate celebrities are paid US$10 to $20 million a year to "sell" these products. Changing fashions favors flexible subcontracting arrangements in the "field," where labor costs are so low. In more capital-intensive sectors, where automated technologies are less transferable, firms tend to invest in regional sites so they can respond quickly to local/regional market signals as fashions change.[55]

Recent concentration of investment flows in the First World regions of the world market reflects this corporate strategy. These are the regions with the largest markets, where an integrated production complex based on the JIT principle has the greatest chance to succeed. In other words, even if the commodity life cycle has quickened, demanding greater production flexibility, mass consumption of such commodities still occurs, so firms will locate near the big markets.

Regional Strategy of a Southern Transnational Corporation

We tend to think of TNCs as Northern in origin. The Charoen Pokphand (CP) Group was formed in Bangkok in 1921 by two Chinese brothers to trade in farm inputs, including seeds. In the 1960s, CP expanded into animal feed production, from which it began to vertically integrate poultry production, providing inputs (chicks, feed, medicines, credit, extension services) to farmers and, in turn, processing and marketing poultry domestically and then regionally in East Asia. In the 1980s, CP entered retailing, acquiring a Kentucky Fried Chicken (KFC) franchise for Thailand, and now controls about one-quarter of the Thai fast-food market, as an outlet for its poultry, including 715 7-Eleven convenience stores. By the mid-1990s, CP was Thailand's largest TNC and Asia's largest agro-industrial conglomerate, with 100,000 employees in twenty countries. It was an early investor in China, establishing a feed mill in Shenzhen in 1979, in a joint venture with Continental Grain. In 1995, CP was operating seventy-five feedmills in twenty-six of China's thirty provinces; controlled the KFC franchise rights for China, operating in thirteen cities; and with its poultry operations accounted for 10 percent of China's broilers, producing 235 million day-old chicks per annum.

By now, CP has investments in fertilizers, pesticides and agro-chemicals, vehicles, tractors, supermarkets, baby foods, livestock operations in poultry and swine, milk processing, crop farming and processing, seed production, aquaculture, and jute-backed carpets, as well as in telecommunications, real estate, retailing, cement, and petrochemicals. CP produces poultry in Turkey, Vietnam, Cambodia, Malaysia, Indonesia, and the United States, as well as animal feed in Indonesia, India, and Vietnam. Through a public joint venture, CP is involved in China's fourth and sixth largest motorcycle manufacturing operations and in the development of an industrial park and satellite town in Shanghai. CP's current initiative is in shrimp farming; it controls 65 percent of the Thai market and is the world's largest producer of farmed shrimp. CP has used joint ventures to expand shrimp farming to Indonesia, Vietnam, China, and India, which are likely to replace Thailand as the regional source of shrimp because they are cheaper sites for an industry that is beset by ecological stress. In these ways, CP exemplifies the global/regional strategy of flexible sourcing, maintaining offices in Singapore, Hong Kong, Malaysia, Korea, Taiwan, Japan, Belgium, Germany, Vietnam, and the United States.

Source: Goss et al., in press.

The shift to flexible production encourages economic regionalism. Regionalism means that strategic countries act as nodes in the trade and investment circuits stemming mainly from the key First World states. Thus, countries like Mexico and Malaysia become important investment sites precisely because of the new regional complexes of the North American Free Trade Agreement (NAFTA) and the Asia-Pacific Economic Conference (APEC).

In fact, the new industrial corridor in Mexico (from Mexico City north to Monterey) demonstrates this effect. U.S. and Japanese auto companies are currently expanding their operations there, with the North American market in mind. Car and light truck production in Mexico was projected to triple between 1989 and 2000. The city of Saltillo, which used to manufacture appliances and sinks, is building one of North America's larger auto-making complexes, including two General Motors plants, a new Chrysler assembly plant, a Chrysler engine plant, and several parts facilities. Meanwhile, in Southeast Asia, General Motors opened twenty-three factories in the Southeast Asian region in the mid-1990s—fifteen in China, four in South Korea, three in Malaysia, and one in Indonesia; Ford expects to match this by capturing 10 percent of the Asian market by the end of the first decade of the twenty-first century; and Toyota and Honda continue their interest in this regional market.[56]

In the context of NAFTA, U.S., Japanese, and European firms are rushing to invest in food processing operations in Mexico, consolidating its status as a new agricultural company supplying the North American market—similar to Thailand's new regional supermarket role. Firms such as Coca-Cola, Pepsico, General Foods, Kraft, Kellogg's, Campbell's, Bird's Eye, Green Giant, Tyson Foods, C. Itoh, Nestlé, and Unilever are investing in fruits and vegetables, meat, dairy products, and wheat milling to supply regional markets.[57] In fact, U.S. corporate investment in Mexican food processing, after declining 17 percent annually through the 1980s, rebounded by 81 percent in 1989, coinciding with Mexico's preparations to join NAFTA and with changes in the country's investment regulations allowing 100 percent foreign ownership of companies.[58]

New strategies of regional investment partly explain the repatterning of investment flows in the 1990s. As that decade began, foreign direct investment (FDI) in the Third World increased as global FDI declined.[59] By 1992, public and private funds flowing into the Third World had surged 30 percent, exceeding aid to developing nations for the first time since 1983. Just as in the 1970s, when the newly industrializing countries were the locus of world economic expansion, the majority of foreign investment is going to regionally significant states like China, Mexico, Indonesia, and South Korea. These states are significant because they have large and growing domestic markets and/or they are located near other large, affluent markets in East Asia and North America.

Different firms have different production strategies, whether regional or global, depending on the need for proximity (e.g., automated technologies or fresh vegetables) or on sourcing from cheap labor zones (e.g., low-skill labor processing). In the service industry, regional strategies may be necessary to cultural preferences. McDonald's, for instance, may sell Big Macs and Happy Meals in Vienna, Indonesia, and South Korea, but in Vienna it caters to local tastes in blended coffee by selling "McCafes," in Jakarta rice supplements french fries on the menu, and in Seoul McDonald's sells roast pork with soy sauce on a bun. However, the low-to-mid-value retailer Wal-Mart has broad, standardized consumer segments in mind. A spokesman remarked: "With trade barriers coming down, the world is going to be one great big marketplace, and he who gets there first does the best."[60] Thus McDonald's, the firm with the global brand, deploys flexible menus to retain local market share, while Wal-Mart sees the consumer world as its oyster.

The world economy has tendencies toward both global and regional integration. Regional integration may anticipate world integration—especially as it promotes trade and investment flows among neighboring countries. But it also may reflect a defensive strategy by firms and states, who distrust the intentions of other firm/state clusters. At present, the world economy is subdivided into three macro-regions, centered on the United States, Japan, and Germany/Western Europe—each with hinterlands in Central and Latin America, Southeast Asia, and Eastern Europe/North Africa, respectively. Within those macro-regions, there are smaller free trade agreements in operation, often based on greater economic affinity among the members in terms of their GNPs and wage levels. How the near future will unfold—with global or regional integration as the dominant tendency—is not yet clear.

Summary

This chapter has examined the phenomenon of the newly industrializing countries from a global perspective, situating this series of national events in the rise of a global production system. In other words, the emergence of the NICs did not simply represent a possibility of upward mobility for individual states in the world economic hierarchy; it also altered the definition of "development." Until the 1970s, development was understood as primarily a national process of economic and social transformation, but by then two trends were becoming clear. First, the First World was not waiting for the Third World to catch up. Indeed, the gap between these two world regions was expanding. Second, a strategy emerging among some Third World states was to attempt to reduce that gap by aggressive exporting of manufactured goods.

In the 1970s, "development" was redefined by the World Bank as successful "participation in the world market." The prescription was that Third World countries should now follow the example of the newly industrializing countries, pursuing a strategy of export-oriented industrialization. Specialization in the world economy, rather than specialization of economic activities within a national framework, was emerging as the criterion of "development."

Export expansion in the Third World can now be understood from two angles. On one hand, it was part of a governmental strategy of export growth in both manufacturing and agricultural products. The successful governments have managed to convert liberalized policies regarding foreign investment into a recipe for what some term *upward mobility*. Indeed, the exponents of this strategy, the East and Southeast Asian NICs (South Korea, Taiwan, Singapore, and now possibly Malaysia), have displayed an unusual capacity for a flexible form of state capitalism, accompanied by considerable political authoritarianism, including labor repression. They were able to attract foreign capital with promises of stable political conditions and to anticipate industrial directions in the world economy. This ability permitted them to develop human and public capital and upgrade their export composition, in each case securing the benefits of riding the world economic curve. The result was a growing differentiation among Third World countries on the economic development index.

On the other hand, export expansion was part of a global strategy used by transnational corporations to "source" their far-flung activities. Certainly some middle-income Third World states converted domestic production into export production on their own as domestic markets became saturated; however, the transnational corporations were building a truly global economic system—in manufacturing, agriculture, and services. Global sourcing merged with the export-oriented strategy, especially as a result of the debt regime, as we see in Chapter 4. In effect, a new global economy was emerging, but it was no longer composed of national economies. Now it was embedded in those parts of Third World societies that produced or consumed commodities that were marketed on a global scale. The global economy is largely organized around the web of transnational activity, a web that is in constant flux because of competition. For any one state, the corporate-based global economic system is unstable and difficult to regulate. States attempt to address some of the labor and infrastructural needs of the global corporate economy—and their own foreign exchange needs—by organizing zones of export production.

As states absorb global economic activity into their internal organization, they subordinate their future to the global economy. Development has begun to shed its national identity and to change into a global enterprise in which individual states must participate—but tenuously.

4

International Finance and the Rise of Global Managerialism

The separation of the newly industrializing countries (NICs) from the rest of the Third World forced a reevaluation of the development project blueprint. The Third World was, of course, always quite heterogeneous— culturally, politically, and geopolitically as well as in its variety of resources and ecological endowments. The development project, however, had viewed the non-European world as homogeneous, classifying it as "undeveloped" and offering one model for its development. This universal assumption began to unravel in the 1970s as a group of Third World states, defined by their rate of export-oriented industrialization, broke out of the pack. They were not merely pacesetters for the rest to follow; their example served to recast the terms of the entire development enterprise. "Development," which had been defined as nationally managed economic growth, was redefined in the World Bank's *World Development Report 1980* as participation in the world market.[1]

The redefinition prepared the way for superseding the nationally oriented development project. If development was no longer simply national economic growth but world market participation by producers and states, the world economy was emerging as the unit of development. States and even colonies had always participated in the world market. What was so different or significant, then, about the world economy from the 1970s on? We examine this question in this chapter as we look at the institutional changes in the world economy.

The rise of a global banking system, matched by international financial liberalization, laid the foundations for what is now termed "globalization." Money became increasingly stateless and easy to get. In the 1970s, Third World states borrowed from global banks as if there were no tomorrow. In the 1980s, this mountain of debt crumbled as interest rates were hiked to relieve an oversubscribed dollar. The resulting debt crisis drastically reframed the development agenda, through the institution of global

FIGURE 4.1

Representation of Offshore Banking

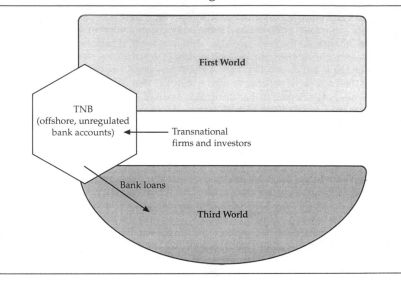

debt management. The debt managers compelled states to look outward, rather than inward, for their development stimulus. The questions we explore in this chapter are (1) from where did the debt managers come and (2) whether and to what extent global economic management overrides national development possibilities.

Financial Globalization

Transnational or global banks (TNBs) formed in the 1970s. They were helped by the burgeoning *offshore capital market* that evaded the regulatory power of states. The TNBs were banks with deposits that were beyond the jurisdiction or control of any government or deposits that were in a country that offered a haven from regulation, such as Switzerland, the Bahamas, or the Cayman Islands. TNBs used these deposits to make massive loans to Third World governments throughout the 1970s (as shown in Figure 4.1). International bank lending, at $2 billion in 1972, peaked in 1981 at $90 billion, then fell to $50 billion in 1985 as a debt crisis followed the orgy of overextended, or undersecured, loans.[2] To learn why this financial globalization occurred, we need to look at the duality of the Bretton Woods system, in which national economic growth depended on the international circulation of American dollars.

The Bretton Woods arrangement maintained stable exchanges of currency between trading countries. To accomplish this stability, the American dollar was used as the international reserve currency, with the multilateral financial institutions (the World Bank and the IMF) and the U.S. Federal Reserve Bank making disbursements in dollars. At the same time, fixed currency exchanges stabilized countries' domestic interest rates, which in turn stabilized their economies. Governments could therefore implement macroeconomic policy "without interference from the ebb and flow of international capital movements or flights of hot money," said J. M. Keynes, the architect of the postwar world economic order.[3] Within this stable monetary framework, Third World countries were able to pursue development programs with some predictability.

The Offshore Money Market

Foreign aid and investment, in the form of American dollars, underwrote national economic growth during the 1950s and 1960s. It also bred a growing offshore dollar market (accessed also by the Soviet Union). This was the so-called Eurocurrency market, initially centered in London's financial district. By depositing their earnings in this foreign currency market, transnational corporations evaded the central bank controls associated with the fixed exchanges of the Bretton Woods system. The Bretton Woods controls limited the movement of capital across national borders, constraining the global activity of the transnational companies.

Eurodollar deposits ballooned with the expansion of U.S. military and economic spending abroad during the Vietnam War. Between 1960 and 1970, they grew from $3 billion to $75 billion, and by 1984 they had risen to more than $1 trillion. As overseas dollar holdings grew, dwarfing U.S. gold reserves, they became a liability to the U.S. government if cashed in for gold. With mounting pressure on the dollar, President Richard Nixon burst the balloon by declaring the dollar nonconvertible in 1971. This was the end of the gold-dollar standard by which all currencies were *fixed* to a gold value through the American dollar. From now on, currencies would *float* in relative value, with the ubiquitous American dollar as the dominant (reserve) currency. That is, national currencies continued to be linked to a dollar standard, but this was more volatile than the gold standard had been because it fluctuated with changes in U.S. domestic and foreign policy. The termination of the Bretton Woods system of fixed currency exchanges was the beginning of the end of the development project.

Just as the development project was politically managed, expressing the superior power of the United States and its development model, so the development project's demise was politically managed. In the early 1970s, contrary to the wishes of Western Europe and Japan, the United States pursued a unilateral initiative to institute a liberal financial regime in the world economy. Given the global reach of the American dollar, removal of exchange controls was designed to protect the autonomy of U.S. policy by separating it from financial claims in the offshore markets. U.S. officials correctly perceived that floating exchange rates would allow the U.S. to shift the adjustment burden associated with its large current-account deficit on to other states, via their own speculative purchases of the dollar or revaluation of their own currencies. Of course, this policy of financial openness was backed up by the relative size of the U.S. economy, the dollar's prominence, and the attractiveness of U.S. financial markets. The U.S. government fully expected that its deficits would be financed by foreign public and private investors buying dollars and American assets. This was made explicit when it reversed a proposal for petro-dollars to be recycled through the IMF, to allow the U.S. Treasury unrivaled access to OPEC funds.

This profound policy shift, from a regulated to a deregulated international financial system, expressed a change in the balance of forces both internationally and domestically within the United States. Internationally, U.S. power was waning with the emergence of rival economies, the bloodletting of the Vietnam War, and mounting financial deficits associated with the war and multinational corporate investments. Domestically, conservative political forces, including an increasingly coherent and orthodox neo-liberal camp in favor of economic liberalism, and multinational corporate interests favored financial liberalization. The latter was viewed as a mechanism to assert American power in the world market as the U.S. lost institutional power vested in the Bretton Woods system.[4]

The shift from fixed to floating currency exchanges ushered in an era of uncontrolled—and heightened—capital mobility as speculators anticipated variation in values by buying and selling different currencies. Financial markets, rather than trade, began to determine currency values, and speculation on floating currencies destabilized national finances. The new way of establishing monetary values has been a continuing problem in the absence of new monetary rules, especially with the magnitude of the international currency transactions. By the early 1990s, world financial markets traded roughly $1 trillion in various currencies daily, all beyond the control of national governments.[5] Thus the mid-1990s saw massive speculation in the Mexican peso, when investors expected NAFTA to strengthen the Mexican economy. When it didn't, traders tried to sell their peso holdings, a move that severely destabilized the Mexican economy and sent shudders through world financial markets, given Mexico's connection with the United States through NAFTA. The peso hemorrhage was so threatening to world financial markets that the United States stepped in to support the Mexican currency with billions of dollars of new loans. The bailout deal required Mexican oil revenues to be deposited in the U.S. Federal Reserve System; if Mexico defaulted, the United States would have access to those funds.

The dramatic loss of currency control by governments threatens nations' economic and political sovereignty. National planners cannot adequately regulate the value of their national currency because currency traders and financiers can influence policy just by moving funds around the world in search of financial profit. Global circulation of huge amounts of money causes national currencies to fluctuate in value. In 1992, *The New York Times* published an op-ed article in which the former chairman of Citicorp described the currency traders, facing 200,000 trading room monitors across the world, as conducting "a kind of global plebiscite on the monetary and fiscal policies of the governments issuing currency." He found this system to be "far more draconian than any previous arrangement, such as the gold standard or the Bretton Woods system, because there is no way for a nation to opt out."[6]

As we return to events of the 1970s, the next shock to the international financial system was the quadrupling of oil prices in 1973, as the thirteen members of the **Organization of Petroleum Exporting Countries (OPEC)** formed a sellers' cartel and agreed on a common price for oil. Fueled by the dollars earned on rising oil prices in the mid-1970s, the offshore capital market grew from $315 billion in 1973 to $2,055 billion in 1982. The seven largest U.S. banks saw their overseas profits climb from 22 percent to 60 percent of their total profits in the same time period.[7] By the end of the 1970s, trade in foreign exchange was more than eleven times the value of world commodity trade. This was a remarkable development! Because the circulation of money around the world continually altered profitability conditions by changing currency values, transnational corporations reduced their risk by diversifying their operations across the globe.[8]

Through its effect on the transnational companies, the financial revolution accelerated the formation of a global production system. It also redistributed economic growth in the world economy. Oil-price inflation led to higher energy prices, which were passed on in higher prices for food and manufactures. This increase produced a severe downturn in the First World, and global economic growth fell by 50 percent in the mid-1970s. Meanwhile, the rise in oil prices greatly expanded the offshore money market, as OPEC states deposited their oil revenues (petro-dollars) in the offshore banks. As the pools of offshore money mush-roomed, so did the power of the global banks. With the First World in recession, the banks turned to Third World governments, eager to borrow and considered unlikely to default. By encouraging massive borrowing, the banks brokered the 1970s expansion in the middle-income Third World countries, which functioned now as the engine of growth of the world economy.

Banking on Development

The move by the banks into the Third World marked a *second* departure from the original institutional structure of the development project, as commercial bank lending effectively displaced official loans from bilat-eral and multilateral sources. With First World economic growth rates slowing and petro-dollars flooding world financial markets, bankers looked to the Third World as a new source of income and began aggres-sively pursuing any and all takers. In the early 1970s, bank loans accounted for only 13 percent of Third World debt, while multilateral loans made up more than 33 percent and export credits accounted for 25 percent.[9] By the end of the decade, the composition of these figures had reversed, with banks holding about 60 percent of the debt. The various shifts from the original development model are summarized in the box on the next page.

The presence of willing private lenders was a golden opportunity for Third World states to exercise some autonomy from the official financial community. Until now, they had been beholden to powerful First World states for foreign aid and to multilateral agencies for funding of their development programs. The Latin American states especially had ab-sorbed considerable foreign investment in their programs of import-substitution industrialization. Now, the money they borrowed from the global banks came not only with no strings attached but also with easy repayment terms because there was so much money to lend. Of the twenty-one Latin American nations, eighteen were ruled in the 1970s by military regimes committed to investing in huge infrastructural projects, particularly in the energy sector. The composition of Latin American bor-rowing shifted dramatically: official/public loans fell from 40 percent in 1966-1970 to 12 percent in 1976-1978, and private foreign direct invest-ment fell from 34 percent in the late 1960s to 16 percent in the late 1970s; concurrently, foreign bank and bond financing rose from 7 percent in the early 1960s to 65 percent of all foreign financing in the late 1970s.[10]

Departures from the Development Model in the 1970s

The 1970s were the decade of transition away from the terms of the development project. One indication was that fixed currency exchanges ended when the dollar was removed from gold parity in 1971. Currencies now floated in value relative to each other rather than being linked to a single standard. The currency instability was fueled through speculation, the instability undercutting possibilities for stable national macroeconomic planning. Another indicator was the displacement of official, multilateral lending to Third World states by unregulated private bank lending. Because it was unregulated, the debt-financing system of the 1970s was unsound; too much money was lent on the assumption that countries could not go bankrupt. In a sense they did, however, and that is what the debt crisis was all about. Yet another indicator was the growing priority of producing manufactures and agricultural products for the world rather than the domestic market. During the 1970s, the G-77 countries attempted to reform the international economy, faced with the collapse of the Bretton Woods system. They tried unsuccessfully to revive ideas for public global economic management that had been introduced in the 1940s and rejected. Also, critics in the development establishment began to reformulate ideas of development, with greater emphasis on poverty alleviation.

With dramatic advances in telecommunications, global banking was a new option for national and, indeed, subnational banks, just as it was for firms competing for a share of an increasingly globalized marketplace. Regional banks from America's declining industrial heartland in Michigan, Ohio, and Pennsylvania, for example, established international portfolios as a surge in lending rose through the decade. The regional BancOhio, for one, expanded foreign lending from zero in 1979 to more than $1 billion in 1983.[11]

With the collapse of the Bretton Woods monetary regime, financial regulation was practically nonexistent. Governments were even borrowing to finance short-term correction of their balance of payments following the oil shock. In this environment, commercial bank loans financed all manner of projects: meeting short-term liquidity needs, underwriting showcase modernization projects that legitimized governments by bankrolling corrupt leaders and their cronies, and supporting legitimate industrial development. By 1984, all nine of the largest U.S. banks had extended more than 100 percent of their shareholders' equity in loans to Mexico, Brazil, Argentina, and Venezuela, while Lloyds of London had lent a staggering 165 percent of its capital to these countries.[12]

The big borrowers—Brazil, Mexico, and Argentina—channeled funds into enlarging their industrial plant and energy production. Mexico claimed to have almost tripled its industrial facilities since 1970, and

> Brazil transformed itself from a country earning 70 percent of its export revenue from one commodity, coffee, into a major producer and exporter of a multiplicity of industrial goods including steel, pulp, aluminum, petrochemicals, cement, glass, armaments and aircraft, and of processed foodstuffs like orange juice and soybean meal. Rio de Janeiro and São Paulo have new subway systems, railroads have been built to take ore from huge mines deep in the interior to new ports on the coast, and major cities are linked by a modern telecommunications network.[13]

Much of this expansion was organized by public or *state-owned enterprises* (like a national postal service), and much of it was designed to generate export earnings. Between 1970 and 1982, the average share of gross domestic investment in the public sector of twelve Latin American countries rose from 32 percent to 50 percent. State managers borrowed heavily to finance the expansion of public enterprise. Often this was done to establish a counterweight to the foreign investor presence in these economies, which accounted for about 50 percent of the Brazilian and 28 percent of the Mexican manufacturing sectors in 1970.[14] It was also done to improve the political standing, and private incomes, of state managers and military elites.

During the 1970s, public foreign debt grew twice as fast as private foreign debt in Latin America. In Mexico, state enterprises expanded from 39 in 1970 to 677 in 1982 under the rule of the Institutional Revolutionary Party (PRI). By 1978, foreign loans financed 43 percent of the Mexican government's budget deficit and 87 percent of state-owned companies. All across Latin America, public largesse supplemented and complemented foreign and local private investment and subsidized basic goods and services for the largely urban poor. Regarding the Argentine military's holding company, Fabricaciones Militares, an Argentine banker claimed: "No one really knows what businesses they are in. Steel, chemicals, mining, munitions, even a whore house, everything."[15]

As public foreign debt grew in the Third World, governments reached beyond the terms of the development project. Those terms centered on the management of private enterprise to build an industrial economy. In the

1970s, states borrowed heavily to make up lost ground. A great deal of the private enterprise involved unmanaged lending to governments by unmanageable global banks. Because it was so uncontrolled, this excessive debt financing inflated the foundations of the development state by severely stretching its commitment to debt repayment.

For a time, public borrowing legitimized the idea of state capitalism, in actively complementing private investment. Third World development states appeared to be successfully in the driver's seat. There were of course variations, from the South Korean state's centralization of financial control over private investment patterns; through the Brazilian model of **corporatism**, in which nine of the ten largest firms were state enterprises and the state monitored financial investment; to the Mexican model of state entrepreneurship, which complemented private investment with productive public investment. The type of state capitalism practiced in Mexico was the more common kind, also practiced by Turkey, Peru, Venezuela, Indonesia, Tunisia, India, and Algeria. During the 1970s, state enterprises across the Third World enlarged their share of GDP by almost 50 percent. Needless to say, there was a high correlation between borrowing and public sector expansion.

State managers, driven by the promise of political glory and the financial spoils associated with economic growth, thus mortgaged the national patrimony. Borrowing in the Euromarkets was an effective counterweight to transnational corporation investment, even when it enabled states to insist on joint ventures with the transnationals.[16] But it also deepened the vulnerability of the development state to the banks and the global debt managers, who began appearing on the scene in the 1980s. Before we address the debt crisis, however, we must consider global political maneuvers in the 1970s, as they presaged the global politics of the 1980s.

The New International Economic Order (NIEO) Initiative and the Politics of Development

The surge of borrowing privately matched what the G-77 Third World states publicly demanded in their proposal, made to the U.N. General Assembly in 1974,[17] for a **New International Economic Order (NIEO)**. This proposal demanded reform of the world economic system to improve their position in international trade and their access to technological and financial resources. The NIEO included the following program:

- Opening Northern markets to Southern industrial exports
- Improving the terms of trade for tropical agricultural and mining products
- Providing better access to international financing
- Facilitating more technology transfers.[18]

The NIEO initiative derived its legitimacy from the historical record. That is, the development project was patchy at best, with some middle-income countries like Brazil and Mexico recording strong growth rates, and a failure at worst. Despite exceeding the growth target of 5 percent per annum (in aggregate) set by the United Nations for the second development decade of the 1960s, economic and social indices suggested that most Third World countries were not achieving the rising living standards promised by the development project. The World Bank reported in 1974:

> It is now clear that more than a decade of rapid growth in underdeveloped countries has been of little or no benefit to perhaps a third of their population. Paradoxically, while growth policies have succeeded beyond the expectations of the first development decade, the very idea of aggregate growth as a social objective has increasingly been called into question.[19]

In the first place, the First World was not providing financial assistance for price stabilization measures for Third World primary exports such as tin, cocoa, and sugar. In addition, the *general system of preferences* (GSP) was quite skewed. GSPs were established under pressure from the U.N. Conference on Trade and Development (UNCTAD) to reduce tariffs on Third World exports of manufactured goods under the GATT agreements. The goods selected by the First World for reduced protection turned out to be those originating in industries controlled by transnational corporations, while those that were excluded tended to originate in domestic industries.[20] This finding lends weight to the observation in Chapter 3 that a global economy was forming alongside and across the set of national economies.

Further, the multilateral and bilateral programs established through the development project had been quite selective. Aid funds were unequally distributed across the world, with the smallest amounts reaching the neediest cases. In the light of stagnating living standards, the international aid community changed its development strategy. This strategy, known as the **basic needs approach**, derived from writings by development scholars such as Dudley Seers. In 1969, Seers had redefined "development" as realizing the potential of human personality. In this formulation, "economic growth is for a poor country a necessary condition of reducing poverty. But it is not a sufficient condition."[21] Development was redefined here as targeting basic human needs rather than simply raising income levels.

This micro-level approach to development appeared in a World Bank report entitled *Redistribution with Growth* (1974), coinciding with Bank President McNamara's concern for improving bank access to the poorer segments of the Third World. It focused on alleviating rural poverty by promoting agrarian reforms in land tenure, credit opportunities for poor peasants, improved water delivery systems, agricultural extension services, and increased access to health and education. As a result, Bank lending shifted its focus toward rural development and agriculture, increasing its annual loan commitments to these areas from 18.5 percent to 31 percent between 1968 and 1981.[22]

The World Bank's "Assistance to the Rural Poor" scheme has been termed an intensification of "global central planning" insofar as it repeated the top-down technical relationship with rural communities.[23] While professing to assist 700 million smallholders (not the landless) with credit, the scheme's net effect tended to integrate subsistence farmers into the agricultures associated with the second green revolution. Furthermore, data from the Organization for Economic Cooperation and Development (OECD) demonstrate that the basic needs emphasis did not produce a fundamental redirection of aid flows in the 1970s, despite the International Development Association's greater attention to sub-Saharan Africa and increased bilateral aid to the poorest Third World countries.[24]

The Third World argued that focusing on inequalities within the Third World as the source of poverty neglected global inequalities. Of course, both sets of relationships were responsible and mutually conditioning, but the interpretive stakes were high. As Honari Boumedienne, the Algerian president, told the U.N. General Assembly in 1974:

> Inasmuch as [the old order] is maintained and consolidated and therefore thrives by virtue of a process which continually impoverishes the poor and enriches the rich, this economic order constitutes the major obstacle standing in the way of any hope of development and progress for all the countries of the Third World.[25]

The Group of 77 nations within UNCTAD duly prepared the statement regarding the New International Economic Order (NIEO). This was a charter of economic rights and duties of states, designed to codify reform of the global system along Keynesian lines (public initiatives). The

NIEO charter demanded reform of international trade, the international monetary system (to liberalize development financing, debt relief, and increased financial aid), and technological assistance. In addition, it proclaimed the economic sovereignty of states and the right to collective self-reliance among Third World states.[26] Although the NIEO also embraced the Second World, the Soviet Union declined involvement on the grounds that the colonial legacy was a Western issue.

The NIEO initiative was perceived as "the revolt of the Third World." It was indeed the culmination of collectivist politics growing out of the Non-Aligned Movement, but it was arguably a movement for reform at best, and, at worst, a confirmation of dependency insofar as the proposal depended on Northern concessions which would in turn increase external revenues available to Third World elites. Interestingly enough, its prime movers were the presidents of Algeria, Iran, Mexico, and Venezuela—all oil-producing nations distinguished by their very recently acquired huge oil rents, as opposed to the impoverished "Least Developed Countries" (LDCs) and the NICs.[27]

Coinciding with the G-77's proposal for global reform was a new development in the core of the First World. This was the formation of what would become the **Group of Seven (G-7)** states. The finance ministers of the original four members (the United States, the United Kingdom, France, and West Germany) met in the White House Library in April 1973. By 1975 Japan, Italy, and Canada were included in the G-7, which had annual secret meetings in which the first five finance ministers shaped economic policy for the seven states (which in turn set the Northern agenda). Also, in 1974, central bankers of the G-10 (G-7 plus Sweden, the Netherlands, and Belgium) responded to a financial crisis stemming from the deregulation of international finance, agreeing to use the Bank for International Settlements (BIS) to organize a "lender of last resort" function in the event of future crises.[28]

Although the G-7 went public in 1986, it played a key role earlier, behind the scenes, in *crisis management*. Its origins coincided with a profound shift in the organization of the world economy—with the demise of the Bretton Woods regime, the excess liquidity during the mid-1970s when the First World stagnated and the world was awash in stateless money and petro-dollars, and an increasingly unruly Third World. Not only did the NIEO and the OPEC episode present the possibility of a *united South*, controlling strategic commodities like oil, but also between 1974 and 1980 national liberation forces came to power in fourteen different Third World states, perhaps inspired by the outcome of the Vietnam War. Under these circumstances, the G-7 provided First World backbone, which included ensuring that the NIEO and its symbolic politics would not amount to much.

The First World's official response was to affirm cooperation and to assist the Third World cause—where it strengthened the world economic order, that is. There were several parts to this response, including the World Bank's basic needs strategy. Among the provisions of the strategy were stabilization of rural populations and extension of commercial cropping, stabilization of the conditions of private foreign investment by improved coordination of economic policy across the North/South divide, and a U.S. strategy of buying time by trying to institutionalize the dialogue within forums such as the French-initiated Conference on International Economic Cooperation (1975-1977), which met several times but reached no agreement.[29]

The First World response combined moral themes with governance, but the master theme was really time: as it passed, so did the energy of the NIEO initiative. In the short term, the unity of the Third World fragmented as the prospering OPEC states and the newly industrializing countries (NICs) assumed a greater interest in *upward mobility* in the international order. In the long term, the redistributive goals of the NIEO would be overridden by the new doctrine of **monetarism** that ushered in the 1980s debt crisis through drastic restrictions in credit and, therefore, social spending by governments. An official of the U.S. National Security Council referred quite deliberately to the expectation that the differentiation among Third World states would promote a form of *embourgeoisement* as prospering states sought to distance themselves from their poorer neighbors.[30]

The moral of this story is that Third World elites attempted to assert political unity in the world at just the time when economic disunity was spreading, as middle-income states and poorer states diverged. The ease of debt financing by way of the offshore capital markets was a key to promoting individual mobility and fracturing collective solutions among the Third World states. The First World's representatives had an interest in fostering the private solution, as expansion of the global production system was necessary to First World economic health. The idea of encouraging a country's participation in the world market as the new development strategy was already strongly rooted. In short, the First World managed to sidetrack the Third World's collective political initiative and assert the market solution to its developmental problems.

In the meantime, the goal of the NIEO in redistributing wealth from First to Third Worlds in some ways actually came to pass. Although much of the wealth was oil money, recycled through bank lending to the Third

World, it nevertheless met the demands of Third World elites for development financing (in addition to financing rising costs of imported fuel as well as rising military expenditures, which contributed to about one-fifth of Third World borrowing). Much of this money was concentrated in the middle-income states and considerably undercut Third World political unity. The marked differentiation in growth patterns of countries intensified in the ensuing debt crisis of the 1980s, which crystallized global power relations.

The Debt Regime

The 1980s debt crisis consolidated two distinct trends that had been emerging in the 1970s: (1) the undoing of the Third World as a collective entity, as economic growth rates diverged among states; and (2) global managerialism, in which the world economy was managed through coordinated, rule-based procedures—the **debt regime**. The breakup of the Third World enabled global elites in the Bretton Woods institutions and the First World to argue that the international economic order was not responsible for the crisis centered in Latin American and African states. They claimed that the experience of the newly industrializing countries proved this. In other words, debt stress and economic deterioration in the poorer zones of the world, they said, stemmed from a failure to copy the NICs' strategy of export diversification in the world market. As we know, however, the NICs, though held up as examples of market virtue, were in fact state-managed economies, suggesting that this diagnosis justified emerging global power relations.

The export-led strategy informed the 1989 World Bank report *Sub-Saharan Africa From Crisis to Sustainable Growth*—regardless of whether the world market could absorb such a proliferation of exports:

> Declining export volumes, rather than declining export prices, account for Africa's poor export revenues. . . . If Africa's economies are to grow, they must earn foreign exchange to pay for essential imports. Thus it is vital that they increase their share of world markets. The prospects for most primary commodities are poor, so higher export earnings must come from increased output, diversification into new commodities and an aggressive export drive into the rapidly growing Asian markets.[31]

Debt was of course not new to these regions of the world. Between 1955 and 1970, several countries (including Argentina, Brazil, Chile, Ghana, Indonesia, Peru, and Turkey) had the terms of their debt rescheduled—

sometimes several times—to ease the conditions of payment, and debt servicing (paying off the interest) was consuming more than two-thirds of new lending in Latin America and Africa by the mid-1960s. The difference now was the combination in the 1970s of oil shocks and unsecured lending by the banks, which intensified debt. During the 1970s, an average of three countries a year rescheduled their debts, and after 1974 debt-servicing capacity declined.[32]

The real debt crisis began in 1980, when the U.S. Federal Reserve Board moved to stem the fall in the value of the dollar resulting from its overcirculation in the 1970s lending binge. The United States adopted a monetarist policy of reducing the money supply. This in turn restricted credit and raised interest rates as banks competed for dwindling funds. Lending to Third World countries slowed, and shorter terms were issued—hastening the day of reckoning on considerably higher-cost loans. Some borrowing continued, nevertheless, partly because oil prices had risen sharply again in 1979. Higher oil prices actually accounted for more than 25 percent of the total debt of the Third World. Previous debt had to be paid off, too, especially the greater debt assumed by over-confident oil-producing states like Nigeria, Venezuela, and Mexico.[33]

Third World debt totaled $1 trillion by 1986. Even though this amount was only half the U.S. national debt in that year, it was a significant problem because countries were devoting new loans entirely to servicing previous loans.[34] Unlike the United States, which was cushioned by the dollar standard (the de facto international reserve currency that countries and traders preferred), Third World countries were not in a position to continue this debt servicing. There are several reasons for this dilemma. For one thing, real interest rates had grown by a factor of fourteen between 1974-1978 and 1981-1982, meaning that the dollar reserves countries used for repayment had lost value against other currencies. In addition, the credit crunch in the early 1980s produced a recession in the First World, which therefore could not keep consuming Third World products at the same rate. Third World export revenues took a dive. On top of this, primary export commodity prices fell 17 percent (relative to prices of First World industrial exports) during this period. The Third World lost about $28 billion in export revenues.[35] Finally, the Third World's share of world trade fell from 28 to 19 percent between 1980 and 1986.[36]

The World Bank estimated the combined average annual negative effect of these "external" shocks in 1981-1982 to be 19.1 percent of GDP in Kenya, 14.3 percent in Tanzania, 18.9 percent in the Ivory Coast, 8.3 percent in Brazil, 29 percent in Jamaica, and more than 10 percent in the Philippines.[37] The result was that many Third World countries were suddenly mired in a *debt trap*: debt was choking their economies. To repay the interest (at least), they would have to drastically curtail imports and drastically raise exports.

Reducing imports of technology would jeopardize economic growth. Expanding exports was also problematic, as commodity prices were at their lowest since World War II and would only slide further as world markets were flooded with more commodities. Some of these commodities were also losing markets to substitutes developed in the First World. Since the mid-1970s sugar price boom, the soft-drink industry, for example, had steadily replaced sugar with fructose corn syrup, a biotechnological substitute. (Sugar is no longer listed as an ingredient in soft drinks.) Other substitutes include glass fiber for copper in the new fiber-optic telecommunications technology, soy oils for tropical oils, and synthetic alternatives to rubber, jute, cotton, timber, coffee, and cocoa.[38] The market was not going to solve these problems alone.

Debt Management

The chosen course of action was debt management. The Bretton Woods institutions once again were in the driver's seat, even though around 60 percent of Third World debt was with private banks. The International Monetary Fund (IMF) took charge because it had originally been given the task of evaluating a country's financial condition for borrowing (even though this function had broken down in the 1970s). The IMF now had a supervisory status that individual banks did not have in the financial system at large.

Debt management took several forms, beginning with stabilization measures. Stabilization focused on financial management—such as cutting imports to resolve a country's imbalance of payments. **Structural adjustment** measures take a more comprehensive approach by restructuring production priorities and government programs in a debtor country—basically reorganizing the economy. In combination with the World Bank and its **structural adjustment loans (SALs)**, the IMF put restructuring conditions on borrowers to allow them to reschedule their loans and pay off their debt. By the mid-1980s, loan conditions demanded a *restructuring of economic policy*, the idea being that debtors should follow multilateral prescriptions for political and economic reforms to ensure economic growth and regular debt service.

Under this regime, the responsibility for irredeemable debt fell on the borrowers, not the lenders—unlike U.S. bankruptcy law. Debt was defined as a liquidity problem (shortage of foreign currency) rather than a systemic problem.[39] With this perspective, the *debt managers* placed the blame on the policies of the debtor countries rather than on the organization of the global financial system. This view was possible for two reasons. First, the International Monetary Fund was in a position to insist that debt rescheduling (including further official loans) was possible only if individual states submitted to IMF evaluation and stabilization measures, which included World Bank structural adjustment loans. Second, despite attempts at debt strikes (by Peru, among others), debtors collectively were in a weak bargaining position, especially because of the great differentiation among Third World countries in growth rates and size of debt. In addition, an individual solution for debt rescheduling was often preferred by indebted governments to the uncertainty of a collective debtors' strike.

In 1982, Mexico and Brazil became the first countries to reschedule their debt in this new way, signaling the start of the debt regime—when global management swung into gear. This new management drew on the example of the 1973 coup in Chile, where a military junta instituted the first experiments in monetarist policies by slashing social expenditures. The Mexican bailout institutionalized debt rescheduling, with new terms of repayment. Mexico was the first real "ticking bomb" in the global financial structure. By 1982, it was $80 billion in debt; more than three-quarters of this amount was owed to private banks, with U.S. banks having almost half their capital in Mexican loans.

Debt management was, and remains, highly political (as the case study in Chapter 6 on the IMF food riots shows). In Mexico, political forces were divided between a "bankers' alliance" and the "Cárdenas alliance," representing a nationalist coalition rooted in the labor and peasant classes. The outgoing president, José López Portillo, allied with the latter group, linked the huge capital flight from his country ($30 billion between 1978 and 1982) to the international financial order and recommended controls on "a group of Mexicans . . . led and advised and supported by the private banks who have taken more money out of the country than the empires that exploited us since the beginning of time." Portillo opposed debt management proposals by nationalizing the Mexican banking system and installing exchange controls to prevent capital flight. He shocked the international financial community when he declared in his outgoing speech:

> The financing plague is wreaking greater and greater havoc throughout the world. As in Medieval times, it is scourging country after country. It is transmitted by rats and its consequences are unemployment and poverty, industrial bankruptcy and speculative enrichment. The remedy of the witch

doctors is to deprive the patient of food and subject him to compulsory rest. Those who protest must be purged, and those who survive bear witness to their virtue before the doctors of obsolete and prepotent dogma and of blind hegemonical egoism.[40]

Portillo's conservative successor, Miguel De La Madrid, guaranteed a reversal, forcing Portillo to back down and concede to an IMF accord, initiated by the U.S. government and the BIS. To effect the bailout, the IMF put up $1.3 billion, foreign governments $2 billion, and the banks $5 billion in "involuntary loans."[41] A global managerial group, including the banks, the multilateral financial community, and the First World governments, put together the bailout package.

The Mexican bailout became a model for other bailout programs, primarily because the Mexican government effectively implemented the stabilization measures the IMF demanded in return for debt rescheduling. Also, Mexico, under President De La Madrid, proved to be one of the states that undermined the possibility of a collective debtor strike. It was in fact rewarded for its refusal to participate in a regional effort to form a debtors' club in 1986. Mexico also engaged in **debt swapping**, whereby foreign investors purchased its debt at a discount in world financial markets in return for ownership of Mexican equity.[42]

Reversing the Development Project

As countries adopted the rules of the debt managers and restructured their economies, they reversed the path of the development project. These rules had two key effects. First, they institutionalized the new definition of development as participation in the world market. In particular, the debt managers pushed for export intensification as the first order of business—as we saw in the World Bank's 1989 report on sub-Saharan Africa mentioned above. Second, the rescheduling conditions brought dramatic adjustments in economic and social priorities within indebted countries. These adjustments overrode the original development goal of managed *national* economic growth with managed *global* economic growth. In effect, these actions stabilized indebted economies so they could at least service their debt—that is, repay the interest due the banks and the Bretton Woods financial institutions. Rescheduling bought time for debt repayment, but it also came at a heavy cost.

Adjustment measures included drastic reduction of public spending (especially on social programs, including food subsidies), currency devaluation (to inflate prices of imports and reduce export prices and thereby improve the balance of trade in the indebted country's favor), privatization of state enterprises, and reduction of wages to attract foreign investors and reduce export prices. Most of these measures fell hardest on the poorest and least powerful social classes—those dependent on wages and subsidies. While many businesses prospered, poverty rates climbed. Governments saw their development alliances crumble as they could no longer afford to subsidize urban social constituencies. The erosion of living standards across the former Third World is illustrated in the following case study of Mexico.

CASE STUDY

The Social Costs of Mexican Debt Rescheduling

According to the National Nutrition Institute, about 40 percent of the Mexican population is malnourished—their diets have little rice, eggs, fruit, vegetables, milk, and meat. As part of the IMF loan rescheduling conditions in 1986, food subsidies for basic foods such as tortillas, bread, beans, and rehydrated milk were eliminated. Malnourishment grew. Minimum wages fell 50 percent between 1983 and 1989, and purchasing power fell to two-thirds of the 1970 level. The number of Mexicans in poverty rose from 32.1 to 41.3 million, matching the absolute increase in population size during 1981 to 1987. By 1990, the basic needs of 41 million Mexicans were unsatisfied, and 17 million lived in extreme poverty.

Meanwhile, manufacturing growth rates plummeted, from 1.9 percent in 1980-1982 to 0.1 percent in 1985-1988, leading to a considerable decline in formal employment opportunities. Coupled with drastic cuts in social services, the reduction in manufacturing led to further deterioration of living standards. By 1987, 10 million people could not gain access to the health system, a situation that contributed to the "epidemiological polarization" among social classes and regions—such as the difference between the infant mortality rates of northern and southern Mexico, and between those of rural and urban areas and lower and upper classes.

Agriculture was also restructured. Mexico had assumed the role of a new agricultural country with extensive state-sponsored agro-industrialization. By 1986, Mexico was exporting to the United States more than $2 billion worth of fresh fruits, vegetables, and beef, but also importing from that country $1.5 billion in farm products, largely basic grains and oil seeds. IMF strictures made dependency on staple foods more expensive and reduced the government's role in subsidizing food staples. The loan conditions also deepened Mexico's agro-food exporting role by expanding the use of land for export agriculture and setting the stage for the early 1990s agrarian reform that has eroded the *ejido* system (small-farmer rural collectives).

Sources: George, 1988, pp. 139, 143; Barkin, 1990, pp. 101, 103; de la Rocha, 1994, pp. 270-271.

In Africa, the severity of the debt burden meant that Tanzania, the Sudan, and Zambia were using more than 100 percent of their export earnings to service debt in 1983. In Zambia, the ratio of outstanding debt to GNP increased from 16 percent to 56 percent in 1985. African economies were particularly vulnerable to the significant fall in commodity prices during the 1980s: copper accounted for 83 percent of Zambia's export earnings and 43 percent of Zaire's, coffee for 89 percent of Burundi's export earnings and 64 percent of Ethiopia's, cotton for 45 percent of Sudan's and 54 percent of Chad's export earnings, and cocoa for 63 percent of Ghana's total exports. As primary commodity prices fell while the cost of imported technology and manufactured goods rose, the terms of trade moved against Africa. During the 1980s, an African coffee exporter had to produce 30 percent more coffee to pay for one imported tractor, and then produce even more coffee to pay for the oil to run it.

IMF/World Bank adjustment policies in Africa reduced food subsidies and public services, leading to urban demonstrations and riots in Tanzania, Ghana, Zambia, Morocco, Egypt, Tunisia, and Sudan. In Zambia, for example, the price of cornmeal—a staple—rose 120 percent in 1985 following such an adjustment policy. School enrollments declined at the same time, as skilled Africans migrated in droves. Between 1980 and 1986, average per capita income declined by 10 percent, and unemployment almost tripled.[43] In effect, all the development indicators, including infant mortality, took a downturn under the impact of adjustment policies. The greater impact on the poor, compared with higher-income groups, is borne out in an internal report of the International Monetary Fund on cost increases as a result of adjustment in Kenya. Relatively speaking, the poor shouldered an extra burden as the price of basic goods and services increased, from 10 percent for food to 95 percent for clothing and shoes.[44]

Oxfam reported in 1993 that World Bank adjustment programs in sub-Saharan Africa were largely responsible for reductions in public health spending and a 10 percent decline in primary school enrollment. In the late 1980s, UNICEF and the U.N. Commission for Africa reported that adjustment programs were largely the cause of reduced health, nutritional, and educational levels for tens of millions of children in Asia, Latin America, and Africa.[45]

Much has been written about the "lost decade" of the 1980s for the poorer regions of the world economy, meaning that the debt crisis set them back considerably. If we combine per capita GDP figures with changes in terms of trade and debt rescheduling, average per capita income is estimated to have fallen 15 percent in Latin America and 30 percent in Africa during the 1980s. In South and East Asian countries, by contrast, per capita income rose. These Pacific Asian states were more in step with the global economy. Along with the South Asian states, they benefited from the oil boom in the Middle East, the most rapidly growing market at this time. The Pacific Asian states exported labor to the Middle Eastern countries, from which they received monetary remittances. One particular reason the Pacific Asian states were relatively immune to the "lost decade" was that the ratio of their debt service to exports was half that of the Latin American countries during the 1970s.[46] Besides their geopolitical advantage, they were less vulnerable to the contraction of credit in the new monetarist world economic order.

The debt crisis certainly exacerbated the demise of the Third World. It continued to lose collective political ground as governments yielded sovereignty to the debt managers, and it fractured into several zones, including what some refer to as the emerging "Fourth World"—particularly impoverished regions, especially countries in sub-Saharan Africa. At the same time, the debt crisis enhanced the power of global management, to which we now turn.

Global Managerialism

Global managerialism is the reformulation of economic policy making according to global, rather than national, considerations. Under debt regime conditions, the multilateral institutions compelled states to adopt policies privileging global, over national, economic relationships. But it is important not to view "global" versus "national" in zero-sum terms. Each conditions the other. Put simply, national institutions embrace global goals. This is not clearly understood because national governments appear to continue to make policy. Where policy enhances the liberalization of flows of money and goods, governments are adopting policies favored by the **global managers**—officials of the multilateral institutions (IMF, World Bank) and executives of transnational corporations and global bankers. In that sense, national policy embodies a global logic.

The conditions laid down during the debt regime initiated this form of surrogate global management. Indebted states agreed to implement certain policy changes and restructuring of economic priorities in order to reestablish creditworthiness in the eyes of the global financial community. When a state gives priority to export production over production of domestic goods to repay debt, for example, it appears to be putting the national financial house in order. This policy may affect the flow of money, but it also attaches the economic fortunes of that country to the global economy. Global managerialism does not necessarily come from the outside; it can be expressed in the very policies and procedures of states as they attempt to reposition their producers in the global economy.

Global managerialism embraces the whole world, not just the formerly colonial countries. Indeed, IMF debt-rescheduling measures were common in the First and Second Worlds, beginning with Britain in the 1970s. Poland's massive debt and subsequent austerity programs had much to do with destabilizing the perimeter of the Second World, leading to the collapse of the Soviet bloc in the late 1980s. Further, from 1978 to 1992, more than seventy countries of the former Third World undertook 566 stabilization and structural adjustment programs imposed by the IMF and the World Bank to control their debt.[47] All this restructuring did not necessarily resolve the debt crisis. In fact, the debtor countries collectively entered the 1990s with 61 percent more debt than they had held in 1982.[48]

Privileging the Banks

As a consequence of growing debt, many countries found themselves under greater scrutiny by global managers. This circumstance put them in a position where they were surrendering greater amounts of their income to global agencies. In 1984, the direction of capital flows reversed—that is, the inflow of loan and investment capital into the former Third World was replaced by an *outflow* in the form of debt repayment (see Figure 4.2). The (net) extraction of financial resources from this poorer world zone during the 1980s exceeded $400 billion.[49] Massive bank debt had become public debt, the repayment of which now fell on the shoulders of the governments themselves.

FIGURE 4.2

Net Transfers of Long-Term Loans to Third World States, 1980-1990

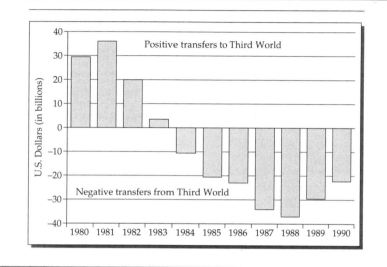

SOURCE: United Nations Development Programme, *Human Development Report 1997* (p. 64). New York: Oxford University Press.

The balance of power under this system of global management has been quite unequal. Indebtedness was considered as an individual state's problem even though the banks wrote off some debt. The banks were protected from complete debt loss by the First World governments, whose central bankers had agreed in 1974 (with the Bank of International Settlements) to stand behind the commercial bank loans, as lenders of last resort.[50] In fact, the banks not only recovered some of their outstanding loans, but the recovery was managed for them by the global managers. As in the case of Mexico, a condominium of First World governments, Bretton Woods institutions, and global banks came together to determine debt rescheduling procedures on a case-by-case basis. The conditions were laid down by the IMF, in consultation with the World Bank. These conditions forced a reshuffling of national priorities. Althought this procedure was universal, it had drastic effects in the poorer regions of the world economy.

An example of the universal impact of debt management policies concerns unemployment. The collapse of economies in the poorer zones drastically reduced the growth rate of exports from richer to poorer countries.

Up to 3 million person-years of employment were lost in North America in the 1980s as a result of declining exports, and Great Britain lost exports equivalent to 49 percent in real terms in the early 1980s, thereby contracting jobs in its export sector. The debt crisis was handled primarily as a banking crisis, leaving national economies to respond however they could.[51]

Challenging the Development State

Privileging the banks in the debt crisis meant that global financial health overrode other considerations, including the viability of government management of national economies. Keynesian (state interventionist) policies had steadily eroded through the 1970s in the First World as the ideology of economic liberalism spread its message of giving the market a free rein. Public expenditure fell; so did wage levels as organized labor lost ground because firms were moving offshore and/or cheaper imports from the newly industrializing countries were flooding domestic markets.

Under the new monetarist doctrine in the 1980s, this trend was extended south. The debt regime directly challenged the development state. Debt managers demanded a *shrinking* of states of the former Third World, both through reduction in social spending and through the **privatization** of state enterprises. To reschedule their debt, governments sold off the public companies that had ballooned in the 1970s. As a result, the average number of privatizations in this region of the world expanded tenfold across the decade. From 1986 to 1992, the proportion of World Bank SALs demanding targeted privatization rose from 13 to 59 percent, and by 1992 more than eighty countries had privatized almost 7,000 public enterprises—mostly public services like water, electricity, or telephones.[52]

Although there is no doubt that development state elites had pursued excessive public financing, privatization accomplished two radical changes: (1) it reduced public capacity in developmental planning and implementation, thereby privileging private initiative; and (2) it extended the reach of foreign ownership of assets in the former Third World— precisely the condition that governments had tried to overcome in the 1970s. Between 1980 and 1992, the stock of international bank lending rose from 4 percent to 44 percent of the GDP of the countries of Organization for Economic Cooperation and Development.[53] Rather than losing the money they had loaned in such excessive amounts, banks earned vast profits on the order of 40 percent per annum on Third World investments alone.[54] At the end of the decade, foreign investment in the Third World countered a global declining trend between 1989 and 1992, increasing from $29 to $40 billion (especially in Mexico, China, Malaysia, Argentina, and Thailand).[55] The restructured zones of the global economy were apparently now quite profitable for private investment: wages were low, governments were not competing in the private capital markets, and an export boom in manufactured goods and processed foods was under way.

Through a case-by-case adjustment, the debt regime transformed the discourse of development in two distinct ways. First, the conditions imposed on debtors for renewal of credit enabled the debt managers to reframe the national project. There was no longer a question of pursuing the goals of the original development project; rather, wholesale restructuring (to compete in the global economy) was necessary to guarantee repayment of debt. Second, austerity measures, privatization, and export expansion renewed the global economy rather than individual national economies. Austerity measures lowered wages to encourage foreign investment, privatization revived the principle of the global freedom of enterprise, and export expansion sustained the flow of products to the wealthier zones of the global economy. Martin Khor, Director of the Third World Network, Malaysia, views structural adjustment as "a mechanism to shift the burden of economic mismanagement and financial mismanagement from the North to the South, and from the Southern elites to the Southern communities and people. Structural adjustment is also a policy to continue colonial trade and economic patterns developed during the colonial period, but which the Northern powers want to continue in the post-colonial period."[56]

Each measure either undermined the coherence or commercialized the sovereignty of national economies. Lowered wages reduced local purchasing power. Wage earners had to tighten their belts; as a result, the market for goods produced locally contracted. Privatization of public enterprises reduced the capacity of states. They were no longer in a position to enter into joint ventures with private firms and lay plans for production priorities; instead, private firms undertook formerly public functions (those that were profitable). Reduction in public expenditure generally reduced states' capacity to coordinate national economic and social programs. Finally, export expansion often displaced local production systems—as we saw, for example, in the case study about the "world steer" in Chapter 3. The following case study of the Dominican Republic offers a parallel but different example of the challenge to state developmentalism under the conditions of the debt regime.

Turning the Dominican Republic Inside Out

Historically, the Dominican Republic was a plantation economy established under Spanish colonialism. Ever since the country achieved independence in the nineteenth century, sugar exporting has been its overwhelming economic activity; other exports are coffee, cocoa, and tobacco. National economic development has depended centrally on the health of these exports. In the 1980s, the contribution of these primary commodity exports to the total export earnings fell from 58 percent to 33 percent. The Dominican government responded to this shortfall, under pressure from the International Monetary Fund, with an export-substitution strategy to generate new sources of export revenues to service its substantial foreign debt. This strategy was encouraged by the 1980s U.S. Caribbean Basin Initiative (CBI) to promote foreign investment in agro-export sectors. Nontraditional exports included tropical root crops such as yams and taro; vegetables and horticultural crops such as peppers, tomatoes, green beans, and eggplants; and tropical fruits such as melons, pineapples, and avocados. Beef products were the most significant agro-industrial export.

The adoption of this broad agricultural restructuring involved policy reversals that removed government supports for basic food production; these fell substantially, with the result that more than 50 percent of the Dominican household food basket was now imported. In addition, social programs that redistributed some wealth were undermined in the rush to subsidize firms in the nontraditional agricultural sector.

As in most countries, domestic food production in the Dominican Republic depended on state support, restriction of imports, subsidized credit and technical assistance for small producers, and regulation of local markets and stabilized prices for the more vulnerable classes in Dominican society. Via structural adjustment, the national agricultural bank was reorganized, reducing available credit for these social programs. Rice, produced under heavy state assistance with guaranteed prices, was "liberalized" in 1988, leading to the demise of the national rice crop and greater reliance on rice imports.

Meanwhile, the state leased the previous sugar plantation lands to transnational corporations such as Chiquita and Dole for the production of pineapples. These transnationals, with plantations elsewhere—in Hawaii, Thailand, the Philippines, Guatemala, and Honduras—are able to negotiate favorable conditions from host governments. Laura Raynolds observes that "most of the roughly 2,000 workers in the new pineapple plantations are casual day laborers who are unprotected by national labor legislation. These workers, many of whom are women, have no job security and are paid less than even the subminimum wage. Labor unions have either been crushed outright or co-opted by the combined forces of the state and the transnational corporations." Regarding the concessions made by the government to the TNCs to attract them to the Dominican Republic, she adds that "these concessions increase the likelihood that production will relocate if the state does not maintain a satisfactory level of subsidization. . . . [T]he Dominican state has forfeited direct control over critical national land resources and rural labor forces."

In short, the makeover of the Dominican state's national economic priorities combined multilateral and state initiatives. The outcome has been a considerable weakening of the state's capacity to pursue a viable and stable national economic plan in the interests of the majority of its citizenry, who depend on the government to redistribute economic opportunity and regulate domestic markets. If states undertake economic reforms to expand agro-industrial production to benefit their wealthier citizens, and expand exports to attract foreign investors, are they not pursuing short-term profits at the expense of long-term national stability?

Sources: Raynolds, 1994, pp. 218, 231-232; Raynolds, Myhre, McMichael, Carro-Figueroa, & Buttel, 1993, p. 1111.

As economic activity became embedded more deeply in global enterprise, the reach of the global economy strengthened at the expense of national economies. This situation was not unique to the 1980s, but the mechanisms of the debt regime institutionalized the power and authority of global management within states' very organization and procedures. This was the turning point in the story of development.

Restructuring States and Societies

Internalizing the authority of global management involves two significant and related changes in the structure of power. First, debt rescheduling conditions actively reorganize states and societies. Second, the reorganization has a profoundly unrepresentative character to it, as bureaucrats in the global agencies exert influence on how states should conduct their economic affairs. Reform policies are routinely imposed by the global agencies with little or no scrutiny by the citizens of the state undergoing restructuring. Chapter 2 reported that the World Bank established local agencies to administer its projects as a matter of course. Under the debt regime, this practice blossomed under the pretext of shaking markets loose from government regulation. Giving the market free rein is arguably a euphemism for allowing such bureaucrats, global banks, and global firms a stronger hand in determining what should be produced, where, and for whom.

The power of global management is typically institutionalized through the administration of adjustment programs. Throughout the Bretton Woods era, the International Monetary Fund exerted considerable influence on the fiscal management of states by applying conditions to the loans it made to adjust the short-term balance of payments.[57] This influence involved merely financial stabilization measures. Structural adjustment loans, by contrast, restructure economic initiatives in debtor countries and redistribute power within the state. The most widespread restructuring redistributes power from program-oriented ministries (social services, agriculture, education) to the central bank and to trade and finance ministries.[58] The importance of this shift is the loss of resources to state agencies that support and regulate economic and social sectors affecting the majority of the citizenry, especially the poorer classes. These resources are shifted to the agencies more directly connected to global enterprise, where economic criteria replace the social criteria that define the national project. Perhaps the most dramatic example of state restructuring in recent years is illustrated in the following case study of Mexico.

CASE STUDY

Restructuring the Mexican State/Society

In preparation for the implementation of the North American Free Trade Agreement (NAFTA) in the 1990s, Mexico undertook a major restructuring plan. For two decades, the Mexican state had been guiding agro-industrialization and regulating the basic grains sector. Centralized control over the production and sale of grain encouraged corruption and political patronage, especially through one-party rule under the legendary Institutional Revolutionary Party (PRI). Although modernization priorities favored the development of irrigated commercial agriculture in the context of the two green revolutions, President Echeverría's 1971 revision of the agrarian reform code, under pressure from *campesinos* (peasants and farm workers), renewed financial and institutional support for the *ejido* sector—community-controlled landholdings deriving from the Mexican Revolution of 1910. Basic grain prices were subsidized, and various forms of agricultural credit assisted the small farm sector. In other words, the state managed both an extensive rural social system, based on *campesino* agriculture that supplied foods to domestic markets, and a profitable commercial agribusiness sector. But the government supported the *campesino* sector with multilateral loans rather than a national progressive tax. When Mexico's oil prices fell in 1981, the debt financing of the basic grains sector could no longer continue. Nor could the national food security system, a grain production and distribution scheme that had begun the previous year under the López Portillo government. These essential national institutions therefore were scrapped.

Between 1980 and 1991, Mexico negotiated thirteen adjustment loans with the World Bank and six agreements with the IMF. The World Bank proposed an agricultural structural adjustment loan in 1986 requiring the elimination of imported food subsidies, the privatization of rural parastatal agencies, the liberalization of trade and domestic food prices, "sound" public investment, and cutbacks in the size of the agricultural ministry. Rural social services were subordinated to economic criteria that focused on agro-industrial priorities. This was a marked turnaround from the days of the Bank's basic needs strategy in the 1970s, which had supported a program of integrated rural development in Mexico. Equity concerns were giving way to the rush to open national economies in the interest of stabilizing the global financial system.

In 1991, a follow-up sectoral adjustment loan for Mexican agriculture further liberalized food importing, privatized state-owned monopolies, and eliminated price guarantees on corn—a drastic step. The social repercussions were sufficiently severe that the Bank subsequently supported the government's Pronasol and Procampo programs, which offered financial assistance to poor rural producers.

Overall, however, the country went through a decade of liberal reforms, mandated by the global managers and pursued by the Mexican government to maintain its creditworthiness—made essential by the prospect of joining NAFTA. The state abandoned its substantial role as manager and regulator of the enormous agricultural sector. It shifted financial support from *campesinos* to agro-export production.

With this drastic shrinking of state involvement in the rural sector, the percentage of *campesinos* with access to official credit fell from 50 percent to less than 20 percent at the end of the 1980s. To fill the void left by the state, *campesino* organizations have mobilized to create new and locally controlled credit systems. Their dilemma is that now they must negotiate credit with the National Banking Commission (CNB), which adheres to the new principles of global competitiveness; these are quite different from the principles on which *campesino* communities run.

In sum, when states restructure, they may improve their financial standing and their export sectors, but the majority of citizens and poorer classes find their protections stripped away in the country's rush to participate in the world market.

Sources: Salinger & Dethier, 1989; McMichael & Myhre, 1991; Myhre, 1994; Barry, 1995, pp. 36, 43-44, 144.

In another part of the world, structural adjustment policies pursued by the multilateral agencies in Africa reveal a telling rethinking of the state's role in development. Initially, as presented in the World Bank's 1981 (Berg) report, the goal of "shrinking" the state was justified as a way to improve efficiency and reduce urban bias.[59] **Structural adjustment programs (SAPs)** directly challenged the political coalitions and goals of the national development state. At the same time, SAPs strengthened finance ministries in the policy-making process.[60] In other words, within the African countries, power moved from the development coalitions (urban planning, agriculture, education) to the financial group, which was most concerned with a country's ability to obtain international credit. The report revealed a shift in Bank lending practices from providing assistance for development concerns to tying aid to "comprehensive policy reform."[61]

The World Bank's premise for the shift was that the postcolonial development states were overbureaucratic and inefficient, on one hand, and unresponsive to their citizenry on the other. In the World Bank's major report of 1989 on sub-Saharan Africa, "shrinking" the state was now reinterpreted as a political reorganization of state administration to encourage populist initiatives. Of course, some of these observations are credible; there are many examples of authoritarian government, corruption, and "hollow" development financing—such as Zaire President Mobutu's lavish global-set lifestyle and Ivory Coast President Félix Houphouët-Boigny's construction in his home village of a larger-than-the-original replica of St. Peter's basilica in the Vatican. Nevertheless, the solutions proposed, and imposed, by the Bank substitute growing external control of these countries in the name of financial orthodoxy.[62]

In its 1989 report entitled, significantly, *Sub-Saharan Africa From Crisis to Sustainable Growth: A Long Term Perspective Study*, the Bank advanced the idea of "political conditionality." It proposed "policy dialogue" with recipient states leading to "consensus forming." This is a sophisticated way of constructing political coalitions within the recipient state that embrace economic reforms proposed by the multilateral agencies.[63] One observer noted: "It has become an explicit target of the institutions, and the World Bank in particular, to shift the balance of power within governments towards those who expect to gain from the policy reforms encouraged by the institutions and/or those who are in any case more sympathetic towards such changes."[64]

This strategy is actually a way of remaking states, through "institution building." It continues the practice discussed in Chapter 2, whereby the administration of Bank projects gives greatest weight to the input of technical experts in national planning. The new phase of Bank involvement deepens by organizing coalitions in the state that are committed to the redefinition of the government's economic priorities. The state sheds its accountability to its citizens, who lose input into their own government. One response is to withdraw into a parallel economy and society, as illustrated in the Tanzanian case study.

CASE STUDY

Tanzanian Society Absorbs Structural Adjustment

Although structural adjustment involves standard prescriptions, its implementation varies from country to country, depending on government capacity and the level of social and political resistance from the citizenry. Resistance takes both formal and informal paths. Political democratization may be one outcome of urban grassroots resistance to a government's betrayal of the development alliance's social pact in implementing austerity measures. Another outcome may involve retreating to the "informal economy" as a survival strategy. This has been the case in Tanzania, a country founded in President Julius Nyrere's vision of a benevolent state anchored in rural villages practicing an African socialism of shared property, collective labor, and a social ethic derived from the traditional African family.

Aili Mari Tripp shows that Tanzania experienced deepening economic crisis at the turn of the 1980s, so that the state, with an already weakened capacity to extract resources, initiated a policy of economic liberalization prior to an agreement with the IMF in 1986, which deepened economic distress. While public sector managers and the mass party organizations opposed structural adjustment, urban dwellers in general were surprisingly quiescent. Between 1974 and 1988, with real wages falling by 83 percent, Tanzanians intensified their income-generating activities "off the books," which involved crop sales on parallel markets in the agricultural sector; sideline incomes for wage workers such as baking, carpentry, or tailoring; absenteeism of schoolchildren; supplementary tutorials by schoolteachers; moonlighting by physicians; and so forth. As Tripp remarks, austerity "was somewhat softened by the fact that more than 90 percent of household income was coming from informal businesses, primarily operated by women, children and the elderly. By providing alternatives to the state's diminishing resource base, these strategies diverted demands that otherwise might have overwhelmed the state. . . . In the end, little was demanded of a state that had placed itself at the center of the nation's development agenda and had established itself as the guarantor of society's welfare."

Sources: Rist, 1997, pp. 130-132; Tripp, 1997, pp. 3-6, 13.

Jonathan Cahn, using information from confidential Bank documents, told of the conditions imposed on an unnamed debtor country. The Bank provided $9 million to an interministerial commission to manage the structural adjustment process, with a "technical committee" established to perform the commission's work.[65] In the Bank's words, this new administrative unit was "designed to assist . . . the Government in implementing its structural adjustment program successfully."[66]

One clear implication of this practice is an expanding trusteeship role for the multilateral agencies. This procedure not only compromises national sovereignty but also subordinates national policy to the demands of the global economy. It illustrates the growth of global regulatory mechanisms that may override national policy making. Under these conditions, the World Bank, now the principal multilateral agency involved in global development financing, has played a definite governing role. It "dictate[s] legal and institutional change through its lending process," and, since its 1989 report, it now asserts that evaluating governance in debtor countries is within its jurisdiction.[67]

Despite the new emphasis on human rights and democratization as conditions for reform and financial assistance, the World Bank remains unaccountable to the citizenry in developing countries. When the IMF and the Bank stabilize and make long-term loans to a debtor, they assume "a governance role that may best be likened to that of a trustee in bankruptcy," except that trustees are accountable to the bankruptcy court. The IMF and the Bank remain accountable to no one other than their powerful underwriters.[68] Further, after a loan is approved, U.S. corporations and citizens are given access to economic—and political—intelligence reports prepared by the Bank. The political asymmetry is obvious, lending support to the idea that global rule without law is being institutionalized.[69]

In sum, the debt regime reformulated the terms of economic management, shifting power from former Third World states to global agencies. Countries surrendered economic sovereignty as First World governments and financiers, both private and public, concentrated managerial control of the global economy in their own hands. World Bank and IMF programs of adjustment were substituted for a true multilateral management of the debt crisis. These conditions imposed standard rather than locally tailored remedies on indebted states. Governments and business elites in the former Third World countries certainly collaborated in this enterprise, often for the same reasons they had promoted development financing in previous decades. They are usually well placed to benefit most from infusions of foreign capital, some of which is used for patronage. Meanwhile, the debt burden is borne disproportionately by the poor. The social and political consequences of restructuring are examined in Chapter 5.

Summary

The divergence of growth patterns in the former Third World intensified through the 1980s. According to the World Bank, the East Asian share of Third World real incomes rose from 22 percent to 33 percent while all other regions had lower shares, especially Latin America and sub-Saharan Africa, where income share fell by 6 and 5 percentage points, respectively.[70]

Two trends were emerging. One was the further polarization of wealth and growth rates within the Third World. The rising tide was lifting some regions and swamping others. The countries of the Third World, which had stood together as the Group of 77, were no longer able to identify and pursue common interests because some were experiencing a level of prosperity so much greater than that of others. The defeat of the New International Economic Order initiative was a turning point. The other trend was the consolidation of the organizational features of the global economy, with the lending institutions assuming a powerful trusteeship role in the debtor nations.

The new global financial organization matched the global production system emerging through Third World export strategies. Offshore money markets redistributed private capital to states as loans, and transnational corporations invested capital in production for global markets. These two trends combined in a frenzy of development projects as Third World states sought to equal the success of the newly industrializing countries. Public investments complemented and underwrote private enterprise. When credit dried up in the 1980s, debt repayment schemes reversed both aid-for-development programs and investment by the transnationals. Debt rescheduling was conditioned on the privatization of state agencies and projects, and the rescheduling process concentrated financial power in the hands of the multilateral agencies. Development states were turned inside out. Global managerialism emerged institutionally as the multilateral agencies initiated the restructuring of policy priorities and administrations in these states, and it gathered ideological force in the growing faith in the authority of the market. In short, the debt crisis was a rehearsal for the globalization project, which we shall discuss in Chapter 5.

PART III

The Globalization Project
(1980s–)

5

Instituting the Globalization Project

The globalization project succeeds the development project. Like the development project, the globalization project is a political-economic construct, framed by a dominant idea. Whereas development was a public undertaking in the development project, it is viewed as a private undertaking in the globalization project. The dominant idea is that of market rule on a global scale. In other words, the development project did not complete its task, which is now redefined as giving the market free reign.

Global economic integration played a substantial role in the development project. Right from the start, the postwar world order rested on two pillars. One was the nation-state, the arena in which development was to be pursued. The other was an international institutional complex, formed to support national development programs with financial aid, currency stability, and technological and professional assistance. International institutions included the Bretton Woods agencies and various public and private agencies of the development establishment, including the U.N. agencies, the British Overseas Development Institute, multilateral regional development banks (such as the Inter-American Development Bank), the international agricultural institutions (the International Wheat and Maize Improvement Center [whose acronym in Spanish is **CIMMYT**] and the **International Rice Research Institute [IRRI]**), and the Ford and Rockefeller Foundations. These institutions, however distinct in function, shared common assumptions regarding development.

The development project had offered a *universal* blueprint for all nations. Technologies and infrastructural programs were universal hardware. Modernization was a universal ideal. The nation-state was to be the vehicle of these shared goals in the postwar era (see Chapter 1). It was the logical political unit in which to mobilize populations around the ideal of modernization—not only because national independence and material advancement were high on the agenda but also because states themselves were power centers that were able to coordinate such mobilization. Membership in a system of states, formally respecting sovereignty, oriented states toward multilateral and bilateral programs of assistance. In this way, national and international development initiatives were inter-twined.

Now we begin our evaluation of the global era. It did not begin on any particular date, but it signifies a new stage of thinking about develop-ment, as represented in the timeline at the beginning of this book. The debt crisis shifted the terms of development from a national to a global concern. States still pursue development goals, but these goals have more to do with global positioning than with management of the national "household." Certainly some specific assistance projects are cast in terms of national development (often at the sub-national level), but even here "development" is associated with the ability to compete in the global mar-ket. In short, development has shed its national characteristics and is now undergoing reformulation as a global project.

The rise of global managerialism was examined in Chapter 4. Its roots go back to the Bretton Woods and Cold War institutions, which coordi-nated a framework for managing national economies, but the global man-agers emerging privately in the 1970s (the G-7) and publicly on the scene in the 1980s made explicit claims about managing a global economy. These managers included the development establishment in the Bretton Woods institutions as well as governments reformed by monetarism and debt rescheduling. They also included transnational corporate and politi-cal elites across the world—arguably a global ruling class, whose shared interest in an expanding global economy was embedded in the multilat-eral and restructured national institutions. A consensus, with a good deal of financial coercion, formed around the redefinition of development to mean *participation in the world market.* The task of this chapter is to explore the elements of this consensus and how they contribute to the new global-ization project. As we shall see, the globalization project is not the only game in town, nor is it particularly stable as a project. There is a prolif-eration of alternatives to globalization on one hand, and there is consid-erable tension among the global elites, in part because of the counter-movements, regarding the speed, means, and direction of globalization. In this chapter we focus on the project itself.

Beyond National Development

The development project dovetailed with nation-building in the postcolonial world. It had a definite political arena: the national territory. This initiative is now disintegrating. We see this in, for example, the disillusionment with conventional development initiatives (expressed in counter-movements from **fair-trade coalitions**, through **eco-feminism**, to **informalization** of economic activity), the current fragmentation of some nation-states into ethnoregional segments (e.g., Yugoslavia, Somalia), and the universal erosion of public supports for populations, especially the underprivileged sectors. The Islamic rejection of westernism is one such counter-movement, illustrated in the case study below.

CASE STUDY

The Islamic Counter-movement

In the early 1970s, with oil prices rising sharply, the Shah of Iran boasted that Iran would catch the West. His country, he predicted, would be the world's fifth greatest military power by 1980, would equal West Germany's per capita income by 1986, and would eradicate class divisions on the way. Iranian oil revenues financed more than $10 billion worth of military hardware purchased from the United States, identifying Iran (with Israel) as the guardian of the Middle Eastern status quo. Meanwhile, the Shah plunged Iran into a modernization program designed to reduce its dependence on oil. Land reforms were ineffectual because their recipients had no technological assistance, and agricultural modernization relied on capital-intensive agribusiness investments from abroad. Between 10 percent and 20 percent of oil revenues financed food imports. The focus on militarization choked industrial growth. In the end, conspicuous consumption by the beneficiaries of rising oil revenues intensified inequality and cultural divisions. Mohammed Reza Shah Pahlavi's westernizing regime was ultimately overthrown in 1979 by a conservative Islamic-led counterrevolution.

The limits of the development project in this case were not set simply by a reliance on oil-financed militarization. Its uneven social impact empowered a growing opposition to modernity and its symbols. Leadership of the opposition was claimed by the Ayatollah Khomeini and the urban network of fundamentalist *mullahs*, Islamic leaders who sought power through a reassertion of Islamic rule. The revolution was multiclass in its composition, including students, intellectuals, middle-class professionals, the traders of the bazaar, and workers, particularly those in the oil fields. A good part of the social base of the counterrevolution

was the mass of displaced peasants driven into the cities at the
rate of 8 percent a year in the 1970s.

Fundamentalist opposition to westernization was a powerful
symbolic movement that served the interests of the Islamic establishment in Iran. The fundamentalists attacked various secular
interests in Iran, including nontraditional women, leftist organizations, and liberal or centrist political groups—in fact, anyone
who espoused democratic-secular rather than Islamic rule.
In Nigeria, in the same year the Shah of Iran was deposed, a
Muslim president used his army to suppress a radical Muslim
fundamentalist movement (lacking a social base) against Western
consumerism and elite corruption generated by new oil wealth.

The content and appeal of fundamentalism depend largely
on its context. Indeed, Islam is known for having two faces.
It has been used conservatively (in Iran, Turkey, Pakistan, and
Indonesia) to secure the status quo and radically (in Algeria,
South Yemen, and Libya, and within the Palestine Liberation
Organization) to promote egalitarianism. Either way, Islam presents a cultural challenge to Western developmentalism, fueled
by the inability of governments to cope with the stresses of
hyperurbanization, evident in Istanbul and Cairo today. Historically, Western and Islamic civilizations have conditioned
each other—the axis of political interaction is now the global
market, tempered by world soccer competition.

Sources: Stavrianos, 1981, pp. 657-660; Araghi, 1989; Watts, 1992;
Cowell, 1994, p. A14; Ibrahim, 1994, pp. A1, 10.

Some of these changes express, in quite varied ways, the emergence of
a new globalization project. That is, these changes are either direct effects
of this project or responses to it. In either case, the globalization project
itself needs to be understood through these counter-movements as much
as through its own discursive and institutional initiatives, which are the
subject of this section of the book. Unlike the development project, the
globalization project no longer simply addresses the postcolonial world.
It is universal, and it concerns the attempt to promote and manage global
markets in order to sustain the Western lifestyle (which also means incorporating, eliminating, or containing alternatives). All states are involved,
even those of the Second World, now that the Soviet bloc has unraveled

and China, Vietnam, North Korea, and Cuba are entering the world market.

In this era of globalization, states are exploring new ways of governing. On one hand, there is a decentralization of central state authority (for example, many governments are divesting themselves of certain social budgetary responsibilities, shifting these down to sub-national entities such as municipalities), allowing space for nongovernmental organizations (NGOs) to coordinate local developments. On the other hand, there is a supra-national centralization of power (such as the formation of macro-regional groupings in which member states agree to certain common economic rules about trade and investment). Everywhere, states are renegotiating their reach, often along bureaucratic lines beyond the control of their citizenry. Some of this has to do with global integrating trends. As sociologist Anthony Giddens has observed: "In circumstances of accelerating globalization, the nation-state has become 'too small for the big problems of life, and too big for the small problems of life.' "[1] Upon this uncertain foundation, the globalization project arises.

In 1980, the World Bank proclaimed the model postdevelopmentalist strategy for development to be *successful participation in the world economy*. The newly industrializing countries were held up as exemplars of the new strategy of export-led growth. During the 1980s, the definition of development was extended to include a policy of broad *liberalization*—in particular, privatization of public functions and the application of market principles to the administration of wages, prices, and trade. President Reagan reiterated this theme in his 1985 State of the Union address: "America's economic success . . . can be repeated a hundred times in a hundred nations. Many countries in East Asia and the Pacific have few resources other than the enterprise of their own people. But through free markets they've soared ahead of centralized economies."[2] These principles guided the structural adjustment measures imposed on debtor nations by the debt managers in the 1980s.

As we know, the successful newly industrializing countries (NICs) of East and Southeast Asia did not actually follow these principles. South Korea was notorious for its "centrally managed capitalism," and the pretenders to NIC status—Malaysia, Thailand, and Indonesia—combined successful export-led growth with strong import-protectionism. Their strategy depended on growing Japanese offshore investment in the 1980s (compared with the dearth of foreign investment in Latin America).[3] In East and Southeast Asia, then, a managed "flying geese" pattern of regional expansion, with Japan in the lead, scored enormous success without adhering to the free market ideal.

Two trends resulted from these developments. First, like the idealized Western model that inspired the development project, the NIC model has also been idealized. Neither model corresponded to historical reality; each merely represented an ideal version of that reality. That is, they served to legitimate a specific configuration of world power. In fact, the free market ideal has been turned *against* the protectionism of the Asian NICs as well as Japan, principally by U.S. bilateral trade pressures on these states since the mid-1980s to open up to foreign trade and investment. Second, the United States has led a parallel attempt to institutionalize this free market consensus globally. Thus, the long, drawn-out negotiations of the GATT Uruguay Round (1984-1994) led to the formation of a World Trade Organization (WTO) designed to anchor a new "free trade regime" on a global scale. These trends are central to the emerging globalization project.

The Globalization Project

Although the globalization project replaces the development project, "development" has not so much lost its currency as changed its meaning. Its frame of reference has shifted, both "upward" and "downward." Development has shifted downward largely at the initiative of proliferating **nongovernmental organizations (NGOs)** that fill the vacuum as states withdraw, or lose, their capacity to assist sub-national groups and causes. Thousands of community and regional development projects continue at the local level, attempting to improve local conditions or stabilize communities affected one way or another by the restructuring of their states. In the other direction, development has been reframed as globally managed growth, with information technologies, and possibly biotechnologies, as the leading sectors.

This bifurcated reformulation of development is telling. It suggests two items to which we shall pay attention:

- First, there are two opposing conceptions of development, distinguished by scale and agency. The community-oriented conception proposes participatory models of **sustainable development**, while the globally oriented conception continues to work through state organizations, but with the goal of privileging corporate actors in the global market. There are, to be sure, points of potential convergence (e.g., the World Bank employs the discourse of sustainable development), but there remains a fundamental difference between popular-democratic versus corporate visions of social organization here.

■ Second, the bifurcation of fields of action expresses the crisis of development as a social model in itself. Localists question the fixation on industrialization and political and corporate centralism, at the expense of the environment and participatory politics. Globalists see a world economy and enlist multilateral institutions and states in an attempt to stabilize currencies and liberalize national economies to reposition economic activity in the global market.

These new frames of reference thus express the demise of the development project's singular framework and provide the ingredients of an intensifying debate over the future organization of the world. Here we examine the elements of the project of globalization.

The Strategy of Liberalization

The globalization project emerges in the *wake* of the development project. Its centerpiece is the belief in market liberalization that took hold under the debt regime. Debtor governments that reduced their size and role were rewarded by the debt managers with credit released in tranches (staggered portions) to ensure their continuing compliance with loan conditions. Thus, national economies were opened up to global forces; they were increasingly globalized, or turned inside out. National governments, in varying degrees, have embraced global rather than national criteria of economic growth. As suggested in the following case study of Chile, such pressure to gain international financial solvency has its costs and consequences—polarizing wealth, compromising the security of domestic populations, and threatening the sustainability of local resources.

CASE STUDY

Chile—The Model of Economic Liberalization

Chile is perhaps the model case of economic liberalization. Although not regarded as a newly industrializing country, Chile has significance that lies in its political history. A military coup in 1973 that eliminated the democratically elected socialist president Salvador Allende was followed by detention, torture, and execution of thousands of Chileans as part of an eight-year period of debilitating authoritarian rule. General Augusto Pinochet pursued a radical free market reform, otherwise known as "shock treatment," masterminded by economists trained at the University of Chicago, a center of neoclassical economics. Over the next two decades, 600 of the country's state enterprises were sold; foreign investment expanded into strategic sectors like steel, telecommunications, and airlines; trade protection dwindled; and the dependence of the Chilean GDP on trade grew from 35 percent in 1970 to 57.4 percent in 1990. In other words, Chile was structurally adjusted before structural adjustment became fashionable. Sergio Bitar, Allende's minister of mining, remarked that privatization was "the greatest diversion of public funds that has occurred in our history, without the consultation of public opinion or accountability to a congress."

The Chilean experiment was hailed as a miracle. U.S. President Bush declared in Chile in 1990: "You deserve your reputation as an economic model for other countries in the region and in the world. Your commitment to market-based solutions inspires the hemisphere." Between 1977 and 1981, private consumption, especially of consumer durables, increased by about 10 percent a year, with some "trickle-down" of consumption from middle to skilled working classes. Real wages went up by roughly a third for the employed, and improvement was made in other social indicators, such as infant mortality rates. Poverty rates remained high, however, at around 35 percent; unemployment rates among the poorer, unskilled segments of the population were at least 15 percent; and social amenities were maldistributed across classes and across the urban-rural divide.

Chile was always known as the most democratic of Latin American nations prior to the assault on its parliamentary and civil institutions by the Pinochet military junta and its economic reforms. In the 1980s, however, when Chile restructured its debt, social polarization increased. The share of national income of the richest 10 percent of the people rose from about 35 percent to 46.8 percent, while that of the poorest half of the population declined from 20.4 percent to 16.8 percent. Chilean social spending continued to fall, wages were frozen, and the peso was seriously devalued. Under these conditions, domestic production faltered as deindustrialization set in, unemployment levels rose to 20-30 percent, and real wages suffered a 20 percent reduction.

At the end of the decade, about 40 percent, or 5.2 million, of the 13 million Chilean people were defined as poor in a country once identified by its substantial middle class. In sum, the pursuit of "efficiency in the global marketplace" had weakened the domestic fabric of social security and local production. In consequence, a sustained grassroots movement, centered in the *poblaciones* (slums) and active from the mid-1970s, succeeded, through painstaking organization and bloody uprisings in the 1980s, in regaining elections in October 1988, when Pinochet was defeated. But Chilean political parties have since become centrist and disconnected from the grassroots movement.

In conjunction with military rule, socioeconomic polarization compromised democratic renewal. This is evident in the recent privatization of Chile's health and social security system (closely observed in northern countries). As a result of privatization, the working poor disproportionately subsidize the health needs of the two million poorest Chileans, and pension coverage of citizens has declined (in part because of workforce informalization). Cathy Schneider observed: "The transformation of the economic and political system has had a profound impact on the world view of the typical Chilean. . . . It has transformed Chile, both culturally and politically, from a country of active participatory grassroots communities, to a land of disconnected, apolitical individuals."

Sources: Bello, Cunningham, & Rau, 1994, pp. 42, 44-45, 59; George, 1988, pp. 131-132; Schneider, quoted in Chomsky, 1994, p. 184; Schneider, 1995, pp. 3, 194, 201; Collins & Lear 1996, pp. 157, 162.

Another dimension of liberalization concerns the commercial exploitation of national resources to service international debt. This exploitation is universal; for example, in Canada, which is home to 10 percent of the world's forests, about 1 million hectares of woodland disappear annually to logging. In the province of British Columbia, the Mitsubishi Corporation has the largest chopstick factory in the world, converting aspen stands into chopsticks at the rate of 7 to 8 million pairs a day.[4] Under the debt regime, natural resources were routinely mined beyond sustainable proportions. The close correlation between debt and high rates of deforestation worldwide is well known.[5]

In Chile, timber exports doubled in the 1980s, reaching beyond industrial plantations to the logging of natural forests. Illegal cutting spread among Chile's poor rural population, about half of whom (700,000) live on native forest land; this is a survival strategy in the context of Japan's insatiable demand for wood chips and depletes Chile's old-growth rain forest.[6] In addition, toxic runoff from unregulated mining and from pesticides used on fruits grown for export has combined with overfishing to jeopardize the annual sardine catch. Chile's export boom in the 1980s overexploited the country's natural resources beyond their ability to regenerate[7] (see Figure 5.1).

Ghana, the World Bank's model of structural adjustment, had a 3.8 percent growth rate in the 1980s, stimulated by extensive aid. Exports of mining, fishing, and timber products accelerated to close the widening gap between cocoa exports and severely declining world prices of cocoa. From 1983 to 1988, timber exports increased from $16 million to $99 million, reducing Ghana's tropical forest to 25 percent of its original size.[8] Development GAP, an NGO, reported that deforestation

> threatens household and national food security now and in the future. Seventy-five per cent of Ghanaians depend on wild game to supplement their diet. Stripping the forest has led to sharp increases in malnutrition and disease. For women, the food, fuel, and medicines that they harvest from the forest provide critical resources, especially in the face of decreased food production, lower wages, and other economic shocks that threaten food security.[9]

Widespread exporting to service debt involves two dynamics: (1) selling domestic resources to firms supplying global markets and delivering the revenues to multilateral lenders as debt repayment, and (2) eroding the country's natural resources (the "commons") that provide subsistence security to the poor. In the long run, removing domestic protections to meet short-run payment schedules threatens social and environmental sustainability.

Expanding exports to earn foreign currency with which to service debt appears to be a logical strategy for individual debtor nations to pursue, but when all debtor nations try to export their way out of debt, the fallacy of the structural adjustment blueprint becomes clear. When seventy countries submitted to the liberalization programs of the multilateral agencies, the resulting glut of exports produced the lowest commodity prices seen on the world market since the 1930s. For example, in West Africa, between 1986 and 1989, cocoa producers expanded their exports by 25 percent only to suffer a 33 percent price fall on the world market. Oxfam, an NGO, named this syndrome the "export-led collapse."[10]

FIGURE 5.1

Debt and Deforestation

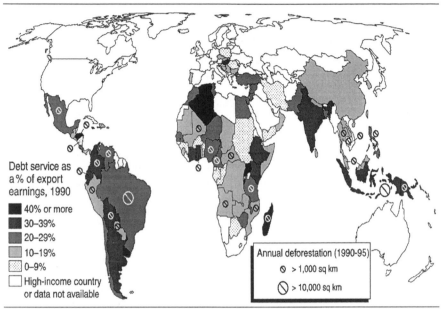

SOURCES: Thomas et al., 1994; World Bank, 1999.

Biotechnical substitution compounds the problem of export reliance. Many prepared foods and drinks now substitute high-fructose corn syrup for sugar. Before 1985, sugar was the common sweetener; since that time, all U.S. soft drinks have been sweetened with sugar substitutes, and U.S. sugar imports have fallen by half. As a result, producers in Brazil, India, the Philippines, Thailand, and several poor African and Caribbean countries lost markets just at the time when their debt servicing demanded increased exports.[11]

It appears, then, that the push to liberalize national economies severely compromises the capacities of governments to deliver on the promise of the development project. The flow of credit to debt-stressed nations depends on the renunciation of national development criteria, but the example of the export-led collapse reveals the risks associated with greater participation in an unequal world market. The terms of participation are not necessarily favorable. Thus, in place of national priorities, global priorities such as debt service, expanded trade, and renewal of foreign investment opportunities gain the upper hand. The next case study illustrates these effects in Eastern Europe.

CASE STUDY

Restructuring in Eastern Europe

The restructuring programs of the International Monetary Fund and the World Bank extended to more than half the former Second World. By 1986, Hungary, Romania, the former Yugoslavia, Poland, Vietnam, and China were subject to IMF supervision of their economies. Many of these states had started borrowing from Western financial institutions during the 1970s, often to pay for basic consumer items demanded by their increasingly restive civilian populations. In 1986, Mikhail Gorbachev was formulating plans for *perestroika* (restructuring) in exchange for membership in the Bretton Woods institutions.

Earlier, in 1982, the IMF had tendered an austerity plan in Hungary on condition that centrally planned production be replaced by "market-responsive" and "financially disciplined" enterprises, along with reductions in subsidies of food, transportation, heating fuel, and housing. These subsidies were the foundation of the well-established basic *economic* rights of the socialist systems. During the 1980s, most commodity prices were shifted to a supply/demand basis, small-scale state enterprises were privatized, and assembly line workers found that instead of a steady wage they were now earning piece rates determined not by the work performed (as with the union contract common in the United States) but by the profit rate of the enterprise. Social equality was being redefined as the equality of private opportunity that characterizes Western market ideology. Of course, former public officials had the lock on private opportunity, not only in Hungary but throughout the former Second World. They enriched themselves and their relatives at the moment of transition from state to private ownership of property. When Eastern European economies were opened to the world market through massive IMF loans of foreign currency, domestic prices moved up to world price levels while wages held constant. As Joyce Kolko remarks: "During the 1980s there was growing resentment in the general population at the rising prices, falling living standards, and the new rich."

Deregulations throughout these once centrally regulated social systems had consequences quite similar to those in the former Third World. By the early 1990s, Eastern European per capita income levels resembled those of the former Third World.

The per capita incomes of Poland and Mexico were about the same, as were those of Hungary and Brazil. Because Eastern European populations have higher levels of education and stable population growth rates, they differ from former Third World societies, but the collapse of their formerly comprehensive system of state subsidies and social consumption put their populations, in a short span of time, at the mercy of the market. This is the reason some observers say Eastern Europe has experienced "Third Worldization."

In Vladivostock and other cities of far-eastern Russia, South Korean companies outsource garment production to beat the quotas on apparel imports into the United States under the Multi-Fiber Arrangements. Only 440 miles from Seoul, where average hourly labor costs in apparel production were $2.69 in 1998, Vladivostock labor costs just 56 cents an hour—and some of that labor is Chinese! Because Chinese workers are used to twelve-hour days and two days off a month, Korean employers use Chinese labor to pressure desperate Russian seamstresses and cutters into accepting sweatshop working conditions. This is one of the replacement sites for Caribbean and Latin American factories established by Korean firms to beat the quotas. Russian labor costs are less than half those in Guatemala, but comparable to China, which, for the time being, faces more stringent trade restrictions.

Sources: Kolko, 1988, pp. 278-296; Kagarlitsky, 1995; Working, 1999, pp. D1, 23.

The globalization project, then, began with market liberalization. The debt regime fostered this liberalization by forcing governments to downsize. It was a regime precisely because it established new rules to which indebted states conformed in order to sustain their flow of credit. In doing so, they surrendered their powers to manage their national economic growth. Sale of public enterprises and reduction of social subsidies effectively remade Third World states and restructured societies, placing the burden on lower classes, especially women in these lower classes. Scaling back public capacity transformed nation-states into states that administer global flows of money and goods alongside increasingly tenuous local economies in which states lack public capacity to pursue nationally coordinated development initiatives. The transformation is reflected in governments' greater dedication to market rather than social (welfare) principles in their growth strategy.

The Comparative Advantage Axiom

The development strategy of the globalization project depends on the world market rather than the domestic market for its stimulus. It is premised on English political economist David Ricardo's neoclassical concept of **comparative advantage**: that prosperity derives from national economic specialization and the exchange among countries of goods and services produced most efficiently, by the countries that have a comparative advantage in producing them.[12] This theorem obviously contradicts the development project's ideal of a series of integrated national economies, elevating the world market as the unit of development. This is why the restructurings during the 1980s were strategic in shifting the terms of development. The case study of Singapore that follows is a contemporary example of successful economic restructuring, although it comes at the cost of considerable political authoritarianism.

CASE STUDY

Restructuring in Singapore: A Successful Mini-Dragon

Singapore is an exceptional city-state that is highly dependent on foreign investment. It has experienced more than three decades of paternal rule under the People's Action Party (PAP) since gaining independence in 1959 from Britain and its subsequent expulsion from the Malaysian federation in 1965. Along with Hong Kong, Taiwan, and South Korea, Singapore is one of the four newly industrializing countries (NICs) of Pacific Asia known as the "mini-dragons." Its status as a NIC depended on centralized planning that brought together state bureaucracies, public enterprise, and transnational companies. It also rested on a corporatist (developmentalist) political system that silenced political opposition, turned labor unions into tools of the state, and elaborated a social discipline based on Confucian ethics of loyalty.

In 1985, at the height of a local recession and the reorganizations under way in the global economy, a government economic

committee recommended a new strategy to liberalize the economy. Beginning with Singapore Airlines, the government began
a gradual process to privatize its substantial public sector and to
foster local enterprise and high-tech foreign investment. The
recent technological upgrading in financial services and manufacturing is part of a strategy to position Singapore as the source
of specialized exports (including producer services such as computer technologies) to the fastest-growing region of the world
economy, the Pacific Asian region. Restructuring also involves
relocating lower-value and "dirty" pork production for the
Singapore consumer to agro-export platforms in nearby Indonesia and Malaysia, as well as developing high-value and "clean"
agro-technology parks within Singapore. Meanwhile, the PAP's
strategy of using social investments—in nearly universal public
housing, universal public health services and education, and
vocational retraining—allows it to coordinate wage levels with
economic strategies and, most important, to continue its tradition
of low unemployment levels and social cohesion.

Sources: Deyo, 1991; Ufkes, 1995.

Until now, "comparative advantage" represented a minority strand of
economic thought, partly because it was out of step with social history. In
particular, social movements such as organized labor demanded social
entitlements and protections from the free market, especially after the
Great Depression of the 1930s. Now, the globalization project fore-
grounds the notion that liberalization brings greater economic efficiency,
relegating to the background Keynesian ideas of state economic intervention and public investment. The evidence is all around us in various
guises—in welfare reform or reversal, in wage cutting, and in privatization schemes. It is a universal process, most dramatically played out in the
former Second World countries, where public resources have been sold at
rock-bottom prices to well-placed new capitalists (usually former state
officials) and markets have been released from government regulation.

Logically, as states open up and pursue global efficiency—with wage
cuts, for example—other states are compelled to follow or suffer off-
shoring of their capital to these cheaper zones. In these conditions, comparative advantage in cheap labor becomes significant. Under these

conditions, individual states may offer specific packages to attract foreign investment, but the *global* labor force finds its wages trending downward.

The globalization project includes an *explicit vision of global order*, which is quite distinct from that of the post–World War II modernization era. At that time, the slogan was "Learn from, and catch up with, the West." Now, under comparative advantage, the slogan is "Find your niche in the global marketplace." Whereas the first held out *replication* as the key to national development, the second presents *specialization* as the path to economic prosperity. But specialization in different commodity chains does not alter the reality that the mechanisms of specialization— wage cutting, foreign investment concessions, privatization, and reduction of social entitlements—are repeated everywhere, intensifying market competition and generating processes of economic marginalization.

Global Governance

In addition to restructuring their economies and societies to serve global priorities, states face a new world order in which global institutions have assumed a different governing role. This role is by no means absolute, and it requires compliance from the states themselves—particularly in pursuing efficiency in the world market.

Shifts in World Bank lending patterns illustrate the new forms of governance. Traditionally, the Bank focused on *project* loans for public infrastructure in Third World states. Project loans have continued into the present, but in the 1980s the Bank shifted its emphasis from projects to *policy* loans. It linked loans to policies that pursued market-oriented economic growth strategies, especially the structural adjustment loan (SAL). In 1983, World Bank President Clausen remarked: "The fundamental philosophy of our institution is to help countries diversify their exports . . . and to have an export orientation." From 1983 to 1985, concessional loans from the International Development Association (IDA) for the poorest countries were reduced about 15 percent, while there was a 35 percent rise in loans to private firms through the **International Finance Corporation (IFC),** a Bank affiliate. Most important, the IDA redirected its lending from the poorest countries (those with a per capita income of $400 or less) to those "making the greatest efforts to restructure their economies," according to President Clausen.[13] By reducing its global welfare function, the Bank reversed its 1970s basic needs policy. The priority had shifted to the stabilization of global, rather than local, organization.

The most immediate form of governance is the leverage gained through debt. Most people who own credit cards know of the discipline that debt can exert on their spending habits, especially now that credit ratings count. This is true for states as well: all states are now subject to universal credit ratings. Debt became a powerful form of political leverage under the debt regime when the multilateral financial agencies strengthened their control over national policy making by assuming the lending role.

During the 1980s, the composition of loans to the former Third World changed dramatically. In 1981, 42 percent of net loans came from commercial banks and 37 percent from the multilateral financial agencies; by 1988, the banks supplied only 6 percent and the multilaterals 88 percent of net loans.[14] In effect, during that decade the multilaterals loaned public funds to help indebted states repay the debt they owed private banks. The result was that the recomposition of the debt of the former Third World centralized financial power in official hands. Because this financial power extracted major political concessions from those states, it amounted to an informal practice of global governance.

By the 1990s, global debt management was firmly institutionalized in the World Bank and the IMF. Because these institutions were ultimately beholden to the so-called Group of 7 (G-7) "Northern" powers (the United States, Britain, France, Germany, Italy, Canada, and Japan), the newly formed South Commission made a provocative declaration in 1990:

> What is abundantly clear is that the North has used the plight of developing countries to strengthen its dominance and its influence over the development paths of the South. . . . While adjustment is pressed on them, countries in the North with massive payments imbalances are immune from any pressure to adjust, and free to follow policies that deepen the South's difficulties. The most powerful countries in the North have become a *de facto* board of management for the world economy, protecting their interests and imposing their will on the South. The governments of the South are then left to face the wrath, even the violence, of their own people, whose standards of living are being depressed for the sake of preserving the present patterns of operation of the world economy.[15]

This declaration continues the Third Worldist tradition of identifying the cause of underdevelopment in the North/South division. What it does not address in doing so is the decline of living standards in the so-called North. The South Commission's declaration also draws attention to a new dimension in development discourse: the priority given to managing the world economy as a *singular entity*.

During the next two decades, however, as the debt regime took over, international financial stability depended on preventing default by Third World states and restructuring national economies. The outcome, as we have seen, was a general reorganization of the international system in such a way that national currencies and national economic policies became thoroughly interdependent.

In these circumstances, ongoing management of global financial relations has become a practical necessity. For example, when the Mexican peso devalued by 30 percent in December 1994, Latin American stock and bond markets fell sharply. The international financial community hastily assembled a financial loan package of $18 billion to stabilize the peso. The United States committed $9 billion (and more), while the Bank for International Settlements in Switzerland, owned by the European central banks, provided $5 billion, Canada contributed $1 billion, and a dozen global banks, including Citibank, added a $3 billion line of credit. Finally, the International Monetary Fund was called in to lend both money *and* its stamp of approval to restore investor confidence in the Mexican economy.

The continuing lesson has been that the bailouts of Mexico (1982, 1995) were in fact necessary to restore confidence in the operation of the global economy. If Mexican financial instability was not resolved quickly, confidence in the functioning of the international financial system would decline. U.S. President Clinton remarked in 1995: "Mexico is sort of a bellwether for the rest of Latin America and developing countries throughout the world."[16]

Perhaps more important, confidence in the new North American Free Trade Agreement (NAFTA) was also at stake. If NAFTA were to unravel, a protectionist counter-move by governments around the world would follow. Needless to say, the condition of Mexico's more recent bailout was reminiscent of the conditions under the debt regime, though less drastic. Mexican wages (already devalued) and prices were frozen, and public spending was slashed. The optimism surrounding NAFTA and Mexico's recent entry into the Organization for Economic Cooperation and Development evaporated as President Ernesto Zedillo Ponce de León proclaimed: "The development of Mexico demands that we recognize with all realism that we do not constitute a rich country but a nation of grave needs and wants."[17] In other words, Mexican adjustment was the condition for stabilization of the global economy.

Concern with management of the global economy arises from several sources but converges as the globalization project. This is a *new threshold in world affairs*, and it has two essential and related aspects: (1) international financial stability has a higher priority than national development planning, and (2) national economies are so embedded (through debt, money, and stock market links) in the global system that financial stability considerations actually drive economic policy making. In other words, global governance is as much embedded in state policy as it is executed through multilateral interventions.

GATT: The Making of a Free Trade Regime

The debt regime elevated the Bretton Woods institutions to positions of global governance by way of economic management, with the former Third World as the target. By contrast, the whole world became the target of the Uruguay Round, begun in 1986 in Punte del Este, Uruguay, under the auspices of the GATT organization. The Uruguay Round attempted to establish a systematic set of world trade rules, including rules concerning freedom of investment and protection of intellectual property rights.

The General Agreement on Tariffs and Trade (GATT) was established in 1947 to reduce constraints on trade. From 1947 through 1980, GATT successfully reduced tariff rates on trade in manufactured goods by more than 75 percent.[18] In 1955, the United States insisted that agriculture be excluded from GATT considerations; it was concerned with protecting its farm supply policies, which used price supports and production controls to establish a floor for farm prices. The U.S. government removed these agricultural supply constraints for several years during the mid-1970s and adopted a green power strategy of agro-export expansion (see Chapter 2). Then, at the end of the 1970s, a world economic recession produced a rising tide of trade protectionism. At this time, more than 100 governments around the world signed on to a new "Uruguay Round" of GATT negotiations, which included reform of agricultural trade.

The United States initiated the Uruguay Round, because it wished to extend GATT liberalization measures to agriculture and other areas such as services (banking, insurance, telecommunications). First World countries recognized the advantages they had in these areas, but Third World countries were quite skeptical. In the early 1980s, many had been subjected to a range of "voluntary" export restraints (VERs) against their cheaper exports of steel products, footwear, electronic products, and agricultural products. India and Brazil, two of the largest Third World states, led the resistance to broadening GATT. First World pressure and the promise of open markets, including agricultural markets, won the day.[19] A GATT ministerial meeting recognized an "urgent need to bring more discipline and predictability to world agricultural trade by preventing restrictions and distortions, including those related to structural surpluses, so as to reduce the uncertainty, imbalances and instability in world markets."[20]

The liberalization movement was supported by an activist lobby of "free trader" agro-exporting states, called the Cairns Group: Argentina, Australia, Brazil, Canada, Chile, Colombia, Fiji, Hungary, Indonesia, Malaysia, the Philippines, New Zealand, Thailand, and Uruguay. The widespread belief was that free trade would enhance the farm commodity exports of the members of the Cairns Group and of the United States. The United States took the initiative also to consolidate its green power strategy in the belief that European Community farm exports would decline under a new trade regime. It also wanted further liberalization of markets to facilitate the freedom of enterprise that it had promoted under the development project.

Not surprisingly, the transnational corporations supported GATT-style liberalization. In fact, 14,000 firms—including General Motors, IBM, and American Express—formed a multinational trade negotiations coalition to lobby GATT member nations. It was in the interest of agribusinesses such as Cargill, Ralston-Purina, General Mills, Continental Grain, RJR Nabisco, and ConAgra to use GATT to challenge agricultural regulation. This regulation included national trade controls on import quantities, farm subsidies that inflate domestic prices for agricultural commodities, and supply-management policies that restrict the demand for farm inputs like fertilizer and chemicals. Such regulations all compromise the flexibility of transnationals to use the lower-priced products of their global sourcing operations as a competitive market weapon against high-priced producers.[21]

Free trade versus the less-protected farmer. The goal of the Uruguay Round was to establish new trade rules to regulate the global economy. Such rule making necessarily generates tension between global rules and national policies, that is, between global firms and national manufacturing and agricultural sectors—and their firms, farmers, and workers. The tension in agriculture is particularly salient because farming is associated with territory, and the Uruguay Round focused on agriculture. Global firms favor liberalization because it opens up global sourcing possibilities, especially desirable to the spatially mobile transnationals. They stand to gain if they can sell farm products all over the world; they benefit from seasonal differences, from different and shared diets, and from the opportunity to seek the lowest-cost producers.

Alternatively, commercial farmers are spatially fixed. They traditionally have depended on national farm policy—input and price subsidies, farm credit, and import controls—for their economic viability. They invariably oppose farm sector deregulation, which exposes them directly to world prices. Because of the inequality of land productivity and cost variation, not to mention export subsidization by wealthier governments, most farmers need protection from price competition. These factors are in addition to the normal price instability that attends the variabilities associated with farming, such as unpredictable weather and crop blight.

The *absence* of trade rules during the closing years of the development project showed in the widespread use of *export subsidies*. The impact of subsidized exports was especially clear in the 1980s, as the United States and the European Community (EC) farm blocs competed for market share with their agricultural surpluses. While First World farmers reaped the benefits of having powerful states behind them, Third World farmers faced falling agricultural commodity prices, especially since their governments had become used to importing food, as discussed in Chapter 2.

Farm subsidies quadrupled in the United States and doubled in the European Community in the early 1980s, generating ever larger surpluses to be dumped on the world market. These American and European surpluses substantially depressed world agricultural prices—from a mean of 100 in 1975 down to 61 in 1989, a decline of 39 percent. The relatively wealthy agro-exporter Argentina experienced a 40 percent fall in earnings from cereals and vegetable oil seeds in the 1980s—and these products accounted for 50 percent of its export earnings in 1980.[22] Many Third World farm sectors were adversely affected by such commercial dumping, which deepened food import dependency, especially in sub-Saharan Africa. In Zimbabwe, for example, U.S. corn dumping forced that country's grain marketing board to cut domestic producer prices almost in half in 1986 and to reduce its purchase quota from these producers.[23]

GATT-style liberalization of agricultural trade claims to stabilize commodity markets, but it does not guarantee survival of Third World farmers. Global firms monopolize trade in agricultural commodities; they market 70 percent to 80 percent of all global trade in primary commodities.[24] This share means they are in a position to manipulate prices to secure markets. Church leaders of the European Ecumenical Organization for Development, implicitly referring to global managerialism, claimed: "With four grain corporations controlling over 80% of world cereals trade . . . market liberalization would simply transfer authority from governments to corporate leaders whose activity is guided by the profit motive. We reject this starting point on ethical grounds."[25]

In addition, wealthier farm sectors have all kinds of infrastructural advantages (transport systems, subsidies for irrigation and other inputs) as well as related economies of scale (the larger the producer, the greater the cost spread). For example, the comparative advantage of U.S. corn producers over their considerably smaller counterparts in Mexico includes a productivity differential of 6.9 tons versus 1.7 tons per hectare. Under the NAFTA agreement, the Mexican government agreed to a phaseout of guaranteed prices for staples such as corn and beans.[26] The future of Mexican small producers is therefore in doubt. As Herman Daly, former World Bank senior economist, observed: "U.S. corn subsidized by depleting topsoil, aquifers, oil wells and the federal treasury can be freely imported [to Mexico, and] it is likely that NAFTA will ruin Mexican peasants."[27]

The Mexican agreement under NAFTA anticipates an ultimate goal of the free traders, which is to phase out special treatment for many of the farmers in the former Third World. In the rules established originally in GATT, Third World countries received special and differential treatment. That is, they were not required to match First World liberal trade reforms "inconsistent with their development, financial and trade needs." Although this position was reaffirmed at the opening of the GATT Uruguay Round (for the forty-seven least-developed countries), proposals have since been made to remove such special treatment except for the very poorest countries, mainly those in sub-Saharan Africa.[28]

CASE STUDY

GATT Institutionalizes Green Power in the Philippines

In the early 1990s, the U.S. Department of Agriculture estimated that Pacific Asia would absorb two-thirds of the more than $3 billion increase in global demand for farm exports by the year 2000. Pacific Asian imports would be assisted by $1 billion in U.S. Export Enhancement Program subsidies to American exporters. A portion of this lucrative market (much of which is tinned beef and processed foods sold in South Korea and Taiwan) would involve bulk wheat and corn imports by Indonesia, Malaysia, and the Philippines. The USDA predicted: "In the absence of sustained, aggressive investment in infrastructure and increased competitiveness for corn production, the Philippines could become a regular corn importer by the end of the decade. . . . US corn may be able to capture a large share of this growing market."

Given the 1994 agricultural agreement of the Uruguay Round, OECD projections predicted that U.S. corn exports would undercut local corn prices by 20 percent by the early twenty-first century, depressing domestic corn prices and threatening half a million peasant households with income declines of 15 percent. According to Kevin Watkins, this would result in high social costs such as reduced expenditure on education, increased reliance on child labor, nutritional decline, and the intensification of women's work outside the home to compensate. Comparatively speaking, the average subsidy to U.S. farmers and grain traders is roughly 100 times the income of a corn farmer in Mindanao. Watkins remarks, "In the real world, as distinct from the imaginary one inhabited by free traders, survival in agricultural markets depends less on comparative advantage than upon comparative access to subsidies."

Source: Watkins, 1996, pp. 245-250.

Trade liberalization is understood as an efficiency move on one hand and a leveling of the playing field on the other. The playing field looks quite different, however, depending on the vantage point from which you view it. The Jamaican government, for example, demanded that GATT distinguish between First World subsidies that may finance overproduction and dumping and Third World subsidies that may promote food self-reliance, rural employment, and sustainable agriculture.[29] The issue demonstrates the opposition between global and national goals, where global goals are largely those of the wealthier states and their firms.

Free trade versus food security. The opposition between global and national goals is particularly divisive around the question of *food security*. The goal of food security is to provide populations with sufficient and predictable food supplies. How to attain that goal varies, as food supplies are not always local—and how *local* is defined varies by regional ecology and economic organization. At its inception, GATT's Article XI included food security provisions that permitted member nations to implement "export prohibitions or restrictions temporarily applied to prevent or relieve critical shortages of foodstuffs or other products essential to the exporting contracting party."[30]

In the Uruguay Round, however, the United States challenged this provision on the grounds of the superior efficiency of free world markets in food:

> The U.S. has always maintained that self-sufficiency and food security are not one and the same. Food security—the ability to acquire the food you need when you need it—is best provided through a smooth-functioning world market. . . . In the food security context, we have also proposed that the permission to restrict or inhibit exports of agricultural food products to relieve critical food shortage be removed from Article XI.[31]

This global conception of food security stems from the superior position of U.S. farm exports in the world economy. But it is more than a market superiority; it is backed by the institutional legacies of the postwar international food regime and the green power strategy. The 1985 U.S. Farm Bill continued this goal of reorganizing the world food market by drastically cheapening prices of U.S. agro-exports. In 1986, Agricultural Secretary John Block remarked:

> The push by some developing countries to become more self-sufficient in food may be reminiscent of a bygone era. These countries could save money by importing food from the United States. . . . The U.S. has used the World Bank to back up this policy, going so far as making the dismantling of farmer support programs a condition for loans, as is the case for Morocco's support for their domestic cereal producers.[32]

This is a remarkably clear statement of the viewpoint, and practice, of global economic management. This view depends, of course, on the existence of breadbasket regions and/or the organization of global provisioning by transnational food companies. From a North/South perspective, global thinking such as this aims to subordinate Southern states to global/Northern institutions; indeed, some perceive globalism as a process of "recolonization."[33] To the extent that globalism demands universal trade liberalization, however, it goes beyond the North/South divide, which is no longer so clear-cut because the success of the globalization project was in part the result of its ability to divide the Third World, and new divisions cut across both sides of the old divide. Malaysia, the Philippines, and Thailand, for example, belong to the Cairns Group of agro-exporters in favor of free trade, because of their palm oil, coconut oil, and rice exports, respectively. Their governments subscribe to agricultural liberalization, while Northern countries such as Norway and France are more circumspect about its impact on their farm communities.

Since the mid-1980s, the goal of agricultural trade liberalization has driven U.S. trade policy, especially with South Korea and Japan, but also including Taiwan, Singapore, Hong Kong, Thailand, Indonesia, India, and Brazil. Deploying the Super-301 clause of the 1988 trade act, which allows the United States to retaliate against states it deems to be practicing unfair trade, the United States put tremendous trade pressure on South Korea and Japan to open up their heavily protected rice sectors. Rice protection created a price differential of roughly 1 to 7 between world market and domestic East Asian prices. To the free trader, this is economic inefficiency, but as we saw above, price differentials ignore additional inputs, or externalities, not to mention domestic food security. In general, small-farm agriculture is "multi-functional" in protecting biodiversity, enabling food security, anchoring rural social development, and preserving cultural heritage.[34]

In both Japan and South Korea, rice has traditionally been a sacred cultural symbol, and in the postwar era it has also symbolized national food security. The dilemma for them is that they are both super-exporters of manufactured goods. They need to optimize their access to world markets for these goods, so it was only a matter of time before the logic of liberalizing rice markets would triumph. This liberalization, however, requires dislocating both a long-standing self-sufficiency in rice and a form of paddy farming that is environmentally constructive.[35]

Freedom of enterprise under a GATT regime. Under the terms of the Uruguay Round, trade liberalization means more than the freer movement of goods, especially because much of this movement is intra-firm transfer. Liberalization includes three other key issues: (1) ensuring freedom of investments by reducing local regulation of foreign investment, such as specifications of local content and equity; (2) ensuring freedom of trade in services, a rapidly growing area of foreign investment where, for example, global banks purchase local banks; and (3) ensuring freedom of intellectual property rights—protection of technological licenses from imitation and protection of corporate patents across national borders.

All in all, the GATT regime codifies new spheres of global economic activity, with new regulations that would streamline the global economy largely for the benefit of global firms. For example, when global corporations extend patents over seeds, they potentially monopolize genetic resources developed by local communities of producers over centuries of cultural experimentation. It is not surprising that Indian farmers have strongly protested corporate intentions to use the GATT regime for seed patenting, which removes local control over genetic resources. As the case study suggests, the implementation of GATT accords is met with sustained resistance, which is a central part of the globalization process itself.

CASE STUDY

Indian Mobilization Against Bio-Piracy

In early 1993, the Karnataka Farmers Association (KRRS) in Bangalore (claiming a membership of 10 million) protested against the intentions of Cargill Seeds to patent germplasm, demanding preservation of the law against patents on all life forms in the Indian Patent Act (1970). This action has been followed by demonstrations in Delhi of 40,000 farmers, protesting against "gene theft" and the GATT proposals. In the later 1990s, the KRRS turned its attention to the biotechnology corporate giant Monsanto, which claims patent rights over thirty "new" crop varieties, including corn, rice, tomatoes, and potatoes, which have been genetically altered to resist one of Monsanto's herbicides. The KRRS has ripped up and burned genetically modified crops in Karnataka and Andrha Pradesh, and it encourages other grassroots organizations to resist the development of transgenic crops, which are legally protected under the new GATT agreements. One of the spokespersons of "Operation Cremate Monsanto," Professor Nanjundaswamy, stated to the Indian press: "We denounce the ignorance, incompetence and irresponsibility of the Union government to gamble with the future of Indian agriculture." On August 9, 1998, the anniversary of Gandhi's telling the British to quit India, a Monsanto Quit India campaign was launched by a group of nonfarm organizations that have been mailing Quit India postcards to Monsanto's headquarters in Illinois.

Sources: Lang & Hines, 1993, p. 55; Kingsnorth, 1999, pp. 9-10.

Grassroots resistance to bio-piracy is mirrored by African farmers' concern that if firms can patent traditional seed stock, farmers planting traditional crops that their families have cultivated for centuries may be liable for patent infringement.[36] Cause for this concern came as firms such as I.C. Industries and Pioneer Hi-bred sought licensing rights to use a gene from an African cowpea. When inserted into crops like corn and soybeans, this gene increases pest resistance. As the Rural Advancement Foundation International (RAFI) asked: "The question is, who are the inventors? [The scientists] who isolated the gene? Or West African farmers who identified the value of the plant holding the gene and then developed and protected it?"[37]

The World Trade Organization

A major outcome of the GATT Uruguay Round was the creation of the **World Trade Organization** (WTO) on January 1, 1995. This organization, with more than 130 voting members, assumes unprecedented power to enforce GATT provisions. The WTO has independent jurisdiction, like the United Nations, and oversees trade in manufactures, agriculture, services, investment, and intellectual property protection. The rules it administers reflect the power of the free market/transnational corporation lobby in the global economy. Whereas earlier any state could ignore a GATT ruling, the WTO's rules are binding on all members.[38] That is, it has global governing powers. The WTO is perhaps the first institution of truly global governance, even though its powers are far from absolute.

The WTO has an integrated dispute settlement mechanism. If a state is perceived to be violating free trade obligations in one area, such as curbing investments in timber cutting to protect a forest, it can be disciplined through the application of sanctions against another area of economic activity, such as some of its manufactured exports. Member states can lodge such complaints through the WTO, whose decision holds automatically unless every member of the WTO votes to reverse it.[39]

The WTO has the potential to overrule state and local powers in regulating environmental, product, and food safety. As an example of this potential of a WTO overruling, a GATT body ruled in 1991 that the U.S. Marine Mammal Protection Act of 1972, which prohibits imports of tuna caught in drift nets that kill large numbers of dolphins, was an "illegal trade barrier" and therefore should be reversed. Further, the international standards for food safety are set by Codex Alimentarius, a U.N. group with near majority representation from food, chemical, and agribusiness companies as well as representatives from consumer and health groups. One standard recommended by Codex was the use of chemicals long banned in the United States; in particular, it allows up to fifty times the residues of DDT permitted under U.S. laws in grains, meat, and dairy products.[40]

The WTO can require nations to alter such domestic laws to bring them in line with its provisions, overriding national regulatory powers. Furthermore, the WTO staff are unelected bureaucrats who answer to no constituency other than an abstract set of free trade rules. Their proceedings are secret, denying citizen participation. In other words, citizens are excluded from making and evaluating policy. In its confidential bureaucratic guise, such global authority displays a *clear preference for universal market rule over individual state rule*. This is a remarkable development: states, the historical site of democratic politics, potentially become the object of abstract rules.

In this sense, the WTO expresses the essence of the globalization project, even though its implementation is hardly complete. In this arrangement, global managers assume extraordinary powers to manage the web of global economic relations lying across nation-states, often at the expense of national and/or democratic process. What is so remarkable is that the reach of real economic globalization itself is so limited in terms of the populations it includes, yet its impact is so extensive. The impact is extensive precisely because states collaborate, or have no choice but to collaborate, in the project. Just as nation-states were the ideal vehicle of the development project, so restructured states convey the globalization project to their populations. Such restructuring of political authority is multilayered, however, as it includes a macro-regional dimension between states and global managers.

Regional Free Trade Agreements

The macro-regional dimension of the globalization project lies in the recent spread of **free trade agreements (FTAs)**. These are agreements among neighboring countries to reform trade and investment rules governing their economic intercourse. Free trade agreements range from the North American FTA (known as NAFTA and including originally Canada, the United States, and Mexico) through the Southern Cone of Latin America, where Brazil, Uruguay, Argentina, and Paraguay participate in the Mercosur Treaty, to the South African Development Community, including Angola, Botswana, Lesotho, Malawi, Mozambique, Namibia, South Africa, Swaziland, Zambia, and Zimbabwe. The emerging mega-regions are NAFTA, centered on the United States; the European Union (EU), centered on Germany; and the Asian Pacific Economic Community (APEC), centered on Japan. They are considered mega-regions because they currently produce about 62 percent of world manufacturing output

FIGURE 5.2

Major Free Trade Zones

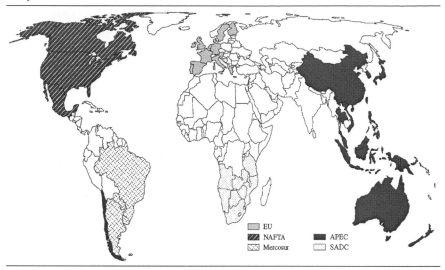

- ▨ EU
- ▨ NAFTA
- ▨ Mercosur
- ■ APEC
- ▨ SADC

and 77 percent of world exports. In fact, the market represented by the "Triad" countries belonging to these three mega-regions consists of more than 600 million middle-class consumers "whose academic backgrounds, income levels both discretionary and nondiscretionary, life-style, use of leisure time, and aspirations are quite similar."[41]

Regionalist groupings encourage liberal economic reform at an intermediate level within the nation-state system. They subscribe to the global principles of free trade but implement them among neighboring states as a logical, intermediate step. For example, NAFTA was logical for Canada and Mexico, which conduct 70 percent of their trade with the United States.[42] Such a grouping is considered an intermediate step for two reasons: first, because it anticipates globalism through the signing of regional FTAs; and second, because it is a competitive weapon against other regional groupings.

As regional integration occurs, states elsewhere may respond with local regional groupings, anticipating the possible exclusion of their exports from other trading blocs. In this sense, regionalism is a defensive, or preemptive, strategy. Much has been written, for example, about the threat to Japanese and U.S. producers of the European Community's attempts to establish a single currency and a European-wide common market, termed "Fortress Europe," and the resulting movement toward

The Region-State in the Borderless World

Japanese economist Kenichi Ohmae depicts the global economy as a "borderless world," rendering states "powerless." He argues that the "region-state" (e.g., the San Diego/Tijuana zone; the Growth Triangle of Singapore, Johore of southern Malaysia and the nearby Riau Islands of Indonesia; and the South China region, linking Taiwan, Hong Kong, and the Chinese province of Guandong) is the natural economic zone in a borderless world: "Because of the pressures operating on them, the predictable focus of nation states is on mechanisms for propping up troubled industries," whereas "Region states . . . are economic not political units, and they are anything but local in focus. They may lie with the borders of an established nation state, but they are such powerful engines of development because their primary orientation is toward—and their primary linkage is with—the global economy. They are, in fact, its most reliable ports of entry." In theory, Ohmae's perspective describes the purest form of "flow governance," where the region-state can ignore the pressures of legitimacy faced by states, individually or collectively in macroregional free trade agreements, in coauthoring market rule. In practice, however, states themselves coordinate such zones and administer to the populations and social conditions included in and exploited by the zones.

Source: Ohmae, 1990, pp. 80, 89, 99.

integration in the Asia-Pacific region and the Americas. The United States and Japan conduct 74 percent and 64 percent of their trade, respectively, *outside* their regions. Compare this with a figure of only 30 percent for the EC members and their European Free Trade Association.[43] It was therefore strategic in the early 1990s for the United States and Japan to embrace regional integration as a fallback, should the global free trade movement fracture into regional blocs. Also, with Japan running a persistent trade surplus with the United States and the EC, in the mid-1990s the possibility of forming an Atlantic free trade zone, linking North America with Europe, was under investigation.[44]

Regionalism embodies the tensions between global and national authority that exist in the globalization project. It just occurs at a more intermediate, and perhaps a more immediate, level. The European Community has revealed these tensions in its movement toward a common governance in the 1980s culminating in the 1992 Treaty of Maastricht, declaring the European Union (EU), which includes all Western European states, except Norway and Switzerland, and integrates 300 million consumers. When the secrecy of the technocratic decision making behind the formation of the EU was challenged in the European Court of Justice in Luxembourg, lawyers for the European Council of Ministers responded by stating that "there is no principle of community law which gives citizens the right to EU documents." As one observer argued: "The Treaty of Maastricht seeks to create a supranational, centralized, bureaucratic state—a homogenized union. It would destroy the pillars on which Europe was built—its nations. . . . The strength of the European Parliament and the [European] Commission is in inverse proportion to that of the national democratic institutions."[45] More recently, the European Monetary Union (EMU) movement for a single currency, the euro, has generated further tensions, with Britain, Denmark, and Sweden, opting out, Greece considered ineligible for now, and widespread opposition to the relocation of monetary policy from nations to the European Central Bank (Frankfurt), which has no democratic oversight and will focus on reducing inflation rather than unemployment (about 18 million at the turn of the century). The EMU performs the function of deferring the question of a Social Charter (labor protections) by focusing on financial disciplines and dismantling the so-called social market "to build Europe á l'americaine." One consequence of this was the highly publicized and effective strike of five million French public servants in 1995, protesting the prime minister's austerity plan to meet the budgetary conditions of the EMU.[46] The question of national sovereignty is explored in the following case study.

CASE STUDY

NAFTA and the Question of Sovereignty

The North American Free Trade Agreement (NAFTA), implemented in 1994, is an unelected and confidential bureaucratic entity that regulates flows of goods, services, and capital between the three member nations (Canada, the United States, and Mexico) according to abstract market rules. As in the WTO, national and local regulations regarding health, labor, and environmental standards are subjected to the rules of freedom of trade. For example, NAFTA rules proposed that the United States could not limit imports based on production methods (child or unprotected labor, or environmentally damaging practices such as drift netting for tuna).

NAFTA formalized a decade-long process of Mexican structural adjustment. In a World Bank/IMF–proclaimed model privatization, more than 80 percent of the 1,555 companies run by the government were sold or dissolved during the 1980s to pay the country's debt and satisfy the Bank that Mexico was committed to liberalization. Although many of these were inefficient, their sale enriched the fabled thirteen wealthy families of Mexico and eliminated employment and services for tens of thousands of other Mexicans. As Mexican export composition shifted from oil to manufactured goods, 85 percent of which crossed the northern border, the Mexican government secured this export relation by depressing wages further—a decline of 60 percent since 1976—and signing a series of agreements to preempt U.S. protectionism. In 1995 Mexican hourly labor costs were 9 percent of those in the United States. Average Mexican tariffs fell from 27 percent to 8 percent between 1982 and 1992, agricultural subsidies were reduced, infrastructural investments in rural areas were cut by 65 percent between 1981 and 1989, and regulations were relaxed on foreign ownership of land. In Judith Hellman's *Mexican Lives*, a domestic consumer electronics manufacturer, Bernardo, sold 49 percent of his firm to Japanese investors in 1986 and turned his firm into an assembly operation using global inputs. Meanwhile, the TNC electronics giant, Phillips, laid off its three thousand workers in Mexico City and established a *maquila* in the border region. Bernardo observed: "As I see it, we lost Phillips for Mexico, or at least we lost Phillips as part of the integrated industrial base of Mexico."

Preparation for NAFTA, then, was a decade-long process of establishing Mexico's liberal credentials at the expense of its national economic coherence and its poorer majority. NAFTA did not decree thoroughgoing opening of the Mexican economy. For example, Mexico agreed to allow foreign banks to enter the country gradually, permitting them to obtain up to a 15 percent share by 1999; it also reserved exemptions for several state enterprises, including railroads and satellite operations. The 1994 debt crisis, however, compelled the Mexican government to raise funds by allowing 100 percent ownership of Mexican financial institutions and selling off its railroads and its satellite operations.

In the debates over the signing of NAFTA, the opposition presidential candidate, Cuauhtémoc Cárdenas, argued that "exploitation of cheap labor, energy, and raw materials, technological dependency, and lax environmental protection should not be the premises upon which Mexico establishes links with the United States, Canada and the world economy." Alternatively, a GATT director endorsed Mexican progress since joining GATT in 1986: "Mexico is one of the new trading powers of the world that has helped to maintain the pace for bringing about an ambitious reform of the world trading system." In other words, Mexico has been a model state, anchoring the implementation of a free trade regime. The globalization project is deeply rooted in the Mexican reforms, and vice versa.

Sources: DePalma, 1993; Barkin, 1991, p. 35; Schwedel, 1991, p. 25; Schwedel & Haley, 1992, pp. 54-55; Fenley, 1991, p. 41; "Free Trade: The Ifs, Ands, and Buts," 1993, p. 32; Fidler & Bransten, 1995; Hellman, 1994, pp. 103-107; Moody, 1999, p. 133.

The Globalization Project as a Utopia

The development project was an ideal that some say was a confidence trick or an illusion because the world economy has always rested on an exploited base, or periphery;[47] others say it was a success because it was never intended to be absolute.

> Some critics make the mistake of proclaiming that development has failed. It hasn't. Development as historically conceived and officially practised has been a huge success. It sought to integrate the upper echelons, say ten to forty per cent, of a given third world population into the international, westernized, consuming classes and the global market economy. This it has accomplished brilliantly.[48]

Whatever the case, it is clear that the development project was a process wherein states *attempted* to manage national economic integration, but the integration was often incomplete. Not only did states have different points of departure and different resources with which to work, but in essence capitalist development is an unequal and uneven process. In addition, the fixation on industrialization marginalized rural communities and their redundant populations, who found their way into the shantytowns bordering cities. States often exploited weaker communities in their hinterlands (such as forest-dwellers or peasant villages), in order to build dams; to expand mines, plantations, and commercial farms for export revenues; or to relocate other displaced peasants, justifying this action in the name of national development. In short, large social segments of the Third World remained on the margins or experienced dislocation as the development project took hold. In fact, only about one-fifth of the world's almost 6 billion people participate in the cash or consumer credit economy. In many ways, development has been quite limited and often undemocratic, however inclusive its ideals. Even then the ideals derive from the Western market model, which is just one of a multiplicity of cultural frameworks.

The globalization project is analogous. Indeed, as our case studies have suggested, there appears to be a disintegrating trend at the national level under the globalization project because of an integrating trend at the global level. But global integration is neither homogenous nor stable. Although it is certainly true that more people across the world now consume standardized goods, it is also true that the conditions under which many of these goods are produced are quite diverse and uncertain. Any labor integration trends under twentieth-century forms of national capitalism appear to disintegrate as economic globalization deepens.

We know that the recent history of formation of Western welfare states rested on a common organizing drive by the working classes of those nations, demanding adequate wages, job and employment protections, the right to organize into unions, and a voice in national politics.[49] This trend has subsided recently as industrial restructuring, offshore investment, public works downsizing, labor demobilization, and rising unemployment have swept across the First World. On the other side of this process we have seen the incorporation of new labor forces across the world into commodity chains of global production. Peasant contractors, *maquila* workers, child labor, casual female and male labor, sweatshop work, plantation labor, homework, and even slave labor constitute a quite heterogeneous mix of labor in the global economy. With transnational corporations using global sourcing employment and countries trimming the national workforce, employment insecurity rises across the world. In short, the world market may standardize consumption, but it tends to fragment production and, in the process, disorganize producing communities.

If this is in fact the dominant scenario under the globalization project, likely to become more tenuous with further social and national disintegration, then the globalization project looks more and more like a utopia itself. The point of thinking about it this way is to emphasize that the globalization project, like the development project, is likely an unrealizable ideal on two counts:

- First, as suggested, the expectations do not square with the reality in which either project is pursued. Neither nation-states nor the world community are singularly composed of market-oriented individuals: there are class, gender, and ethnic relations that divide people to begin with. Some regions are historically more equal than others, and there are powerful institutional forces that actually organize and reorganize markets, with profits rather than social welfare in mind.

- Second, there are many social movements and state organizations that actively resist and/or qualify the globalization project. Many of these movements reject belief in the self-regulating global market as the most logical principle of social organization. Some movements aim to protect their communities by reregulating the market; others see withdrawing from the market as the most satisfactory form of resistance. Whatever the alternatives, the globalization project is only one way, albeit the most powerful we have seen, of reorganizing the world.

The globalization project is the most powerful force so far, in part because it has not had to confront its contradictory effects in any fundamental way. Some of these effects are spelled out in the following chapters. One effect is already causing alarm in the inner circles of global management: the fragility of the world monetary system. The United States is the most indebted state in the world, but because those debts are not denominated in other currencies (because trade partners accept dollars), to date it has avoided having to tighten its financial belt under the kinds of debt management conditions laid down by the International Monetary Fund. In 1994, a group called the Bretton Woods Commission, headed by former Federal Reserve Board chairman Paul Volcker, suggested that the world monetary system required overhauling to tame its unstable and speculative dynamic, and that this implied bringing all countries (including the United States) under IMF discipline.

Although the G-7 countries have attempted to stabilize the system, the Commission stated: "There has been no reliable long-term global approach to coordinating policy, stabilizing market expectations, and preventing extreme volatility and misalignments among the key currencies."[50] In 1995, the perception of a growing possibility that an international discipline might be imposed on the United States provoked a deadly bomb attack on a U.S. federal government office building in Oklahoma City, allegedly by a citizen militia group eager to stem such a challenge to U.S. sovereignty. The point of this story is that the globalization project contains some powerful tensions. National sovereignty may have a brittle shell in the United States, home of the ideal of national self-determination.

Whereas the United States may be in the driver's seat in the globalization project in general, as it was in the development project, its seating arrangement is only as good as the willingness of the world to use the dollar, or its own willingness to assert its military superiority globally. The existence of an alternative world currency, the euro, poses a potential threat to the dollar. Whereas the United States runs a persistent trade deficit in addition to its net debtor status, Europe runs a trade surplus with the rest of the world, which owes it about $1 trillion, establishing the possibility of substituting euros for dollars and obliging the United States to stop assuming that its deficits will continue to be financed because of the dollar's international reserve currency status to date.[51]

We can only speculate on how the globalization project, as a new organizing principle for the world, will play out. In the meantime, in June 1995 the G-7 powers created a worldwide emergency fund to bail out states on the verge of national bankruptcy. The United States, along with its European allies, pursued this initiative to stabilize the world monetary system. It had three essential aspects. The first was to shift the burden of such bailouts from the United States, which bore the brunt of the Mexican bailout of 1994. The second was an expectation that the prosperous Asian countries would underwrite the fund with their financial surpluses—in effect a way of redistributing the world's financial wealth so that money would continue to make the world go around. Finally, the third involved a plan to establish an "improved early warning system" based on comprehensive public disclosure by member states of financial information (such as foreign exchange reserves) hitherto confidential—using IMF leverage to deepen financial surveillance of the system at large.[52]

Ironically, East Asia experienced a dramatic financial collapse late in 1997, effectively putting the G-7 back to square one in preparing for financial crisis. The managing director of the IMF, Michel Camdessus, acknowledged in 1998 that the Asian crisis had revealed flaws in the liberalization of global capital flows, whereby unregulated it is potentially damaging to "emerging economies."[53] In October of that year, the G-7 came up with a proposed line of credit, making billions of dollars available to prevent attacks on currencies or markets that are spillovers from economic crises elsewhere. Global financiers like George Soros have argued for reform of the global economy along the lines of establishing an International Credit Insurance Corporation. Other proposals are for an international central bank to coordinate international private borrowing, a "Tobin tax" (named after Nobel laureate James Tobin) on international flows of capital as friction and revenue to reduce financial collapses, or the Chilean system of imposing a one-year moratorium on capital reflux, as constituting effective and sufficient control on the problem of capital flight. In April 1999, the G-7 established a Financial Stability Forum based in the Bank for International Settlements, designed to coordinate information, but with no powers of enforcement.[54]

There are three unresolved, and perhaps unresolvable, problems: first, nation-states in the North are unwilling to have global agencies regulating their financial markets; second, there is an estimated $500 billion in offshore bank accounts in the Cayman Islands alone—beyond any institutional regulation; and third, opinions are seriously divided on the degree of market rule, depending in part on one's position in the global political and currency hierarchies.[55] Meanwhile, the Chinese economy, which has been expanding while the rest of the East Asian economies have been collapsing or shrinking, exemplifies an alternative to market rule. China, of course, is perhaps exceptional in its resource base and its reservoir of cheap labor. It is also much more autonomous: "Its currency is not freely convertible, its financial system is owned and controlled by the state, and there is relatively little foreign ownership of equities. And it does not have to take orders from the IMF." But there are other countries, like Malaysia, Hong Kong, Chile, and Colombia that have instituted modest currency and/or capital controls to stabilize their national economies, and show the way towards reinstating national economic sovereignty. Indeed, the World Bank reversed its initial opposition to Malaysia's 1997 capital controls in September, 1999, on the grounds that the predicted adverse effects of such intervention did not occur.[56] The ultimate issue is whether and to what extent markets should be subordinated to political regulation. This will be resolved through the contradictory dynamics of the globalization project, which are the subjects of the following chapters: its structural instabilities and its countermovements.

Summary

This chapter has recounted how the development project incubated a new direction in the world capitalist order, which hatched during the 1980s debt crisis. This new direction is the globalization project, an alternative way of organizing economic growth that corresponds to the growing scale and power of the transnational banks and corporations. The increasing volume of economic exchanges and the greater mobility of money and firms require forms of regulation beyond the reach of the nation-state.

All markets have institutional supports; that is, they require certain kinds of political and social regulation to work. When monetary exchanges began to govern European productive activity in the nineteenth century and industrial labor markets emerged, central banks and state bureaucracies stepped in to regulate and protect the value and rights of these flows of money and labor, respectively. Markets in money and labor could not work automatically. Similarly, when global money markets became dominant in the 1970s and then the flows of credit needed to be protected in the 1980s, the International Monetary Fund stepped in to regulate the value of international currency.

The new global regulatory system subordinated states' labor protections to financial credit protection. This new balance of power marked the transition from the development project to the globalization project. Indebted states remained viable regulators of market exchanges, but only through agreeing to restructure their institutions and their priorities. They were turned inside out; that is, they downgraded their social functions of subsidizing education, health, food prices, producer credit, and other social services and beefed up their financial and commercial export ministries. Overall, with variation according to capacity and indebtedness, states became surrogate managers of the global economy. These tendencies are also replicated in regional free trade agreements, which express goals similar to those of the globalization project.

The imposition of austerity measures by indebted governments deepened inequalities within their societies. Their surrender of public capacity yielded power to global institutions. Economic liberalization and currency devaluation heightened competition among states for credit and investment, consolidating Third World disunity. Structural adjustment programs required the reduction of social infrastructure, privatization of public enterprise, and repeal of protective laws regarding foreign investment, national banking, and trade policy. So were laid the foundations for the new globalization project, the components of which are summarized in the following insert.

What Are the Elements of the Globalization Project?
The globalization project combines several strands: (1) a consensus among global managers/policymakers favoring market-based rather than state-managed development strategies; (2) centralized management of global market rules by the G-7 states; (3) implementation of these rules by the multilateral agencies: the World Bank, the IMF, and the WTO; (4) concentration of market power in the hands of transnational corporations and financial power in the hands of transnational banks; (5) subjection of all states to global forces (institutional or financial), but with considerable variation according to position in the state system (North/South/East), global currency hierarchy, debt load, resource endowments, and so forth; and (6) a counter-movement at all levels, from marginalized communities to state managers to factions within multilateral institutions, contesting and second-guessing unbridled market rule.

The standardized prescriptions for liberalization reorganize regions and locales: from the removal of Mexican *campesinos* from long-held public lands, through the rapid dismantling of public ownership of the economies of Eastern Europe, to the proliferation of export processing zones and agro-export platforms. Many of these mushrooming export sites suffer the instability of flexible strategies of "footloose" firms, as they pick and choose their way among global sourcing sites. Social protections decline as communities lose their resource bases (as forests dwindle) or their employment bases (as firms downsize or move offshore).

Under these conditions, globalization is everything but universalist in its consequences. It assigns communities, regions, and nation-states new niches or specialized roles (including marginalization) in the global economy. The development project proposed social integration through national economic growth under individual state supervision. Alternatively, the globalization project offers new forms of authority and discipline according to the laws of the market. Whether these forms of authority and discipline are based in global institutions like the World Trade Organization or in national institutions managing the global marketplace within their territories, they perform the governance functions of the globalization project.

6

The Globalization Project
Structural Instabilities

The next two chapters look behind the attempt to institute globalization as a project of world development, for while political and economic elites attempt to formulate new rules for the global market, the world attempts to carry on. Global integration is not a harmonious process, nor is it straightforward. It is, in some ways, a form of crisis management stemming from the demise of the development project.

The development crisis has two threads:

- *Structural instabilities* stemming from the transition from development to globalization projects. These include the casualization of labor, crises in political legitimacy of governments, financial market volatility, and a growing informal sector of great social significance, despite its "illegitimacy" in the eyes of the formal sector. This will be the subject of this chapter.

- *Counter-movements* within the globalization project across various social axes, including gender, religion, environmentalism, localism, social movement unionism, and indigenous and human rights movements. These will be addressed in the following chapter.

Although these threads are related, the most important point is that they express the different facets of a single process: the attempt to construct a liberal economic order as the new blueprint for development. That attempt generates its own tensions in the accumulating instabilities and resistances that define the world in the twenty-first century. Because of this, there is a profound debate among the global managers themselves as to the speed and direction of globalization, stimulated by the contagion of financial crisis as much as by organized opposition to, and silent rejection of, market rule. While the IMF is busy fighting financial fires around the world, corporate elites are busy fighting to control the discursive agenda associated with the globalization project—including such terms as "comparative advantage," "free/fair trade," "sustainable development," "organic farming," "food security," "**social capital**," and "best practice."

The existence of these tensions suggests that the globalization project, as such, does not have a lock on the future. Not only is it unstable, but it also has some of the qualities of the sorcerer's apprentice about it. It promises to intensify the transformation of social structures that we associate with the development project. Intensification does not just mean a quantitative increase; it also means qualitative changes that we can only speculate about at this point. What happens if 3 billion peasants leave the land because they cannot compete in the global grain market? Where do they go, and with what consequence? How will the "Nemesis Effect" (whereby corroding ecosystems interact; for example, climate changes affect forest fire cycles, feeding back on climate) fundamentally alter our material environment? And what new social arrangements might emerge via new techniques of bio-engineering of human and plant genetic makeup?

Proponents of globalization focus on its contributions to the material prosperity of global consumers, but it is by no means clear if this trend is sustainable over the long term. It is impossible to predict the social, ecological, and political impact of transformations induced or sped up by wholesale liberalization of the global economic and political order. The future is uncertain, and it is unlikely that current bureaucratic forms of global governance will suffice to "manage" the extraordinary social and ecological changes afoot. It is already clear that the globalization project includes alternative voices in the counter-movements that contest, and seek to shape, its discourse and direction—how effectively is anybody's guess. All we can do here is explore some of the central points of tension to understand the complexity of this new development.

In this chapter we consider some of the destabilizing effects of global integration. These are (1) the bifurcation of labor, including a process of labor casualization that generates labor surpluses across the world, expressed in new global circuits of migrating laborers; (2) intensified informalization of economic activity; (3) the legitimacy crisis of governance; and (4) the contagion of financial crisis. Some of these provide the stimulus to the oppositional social movements examined in Chapter 7.

Global Labor Force Bifurcation

Trends in labor relations across the world are as varied and numerous as countries and industries, but there is unity in the diversity. Perhaps the dominant trend is **labor force bifurcation**, whereby the global labor force polarizes into a core of relatively stable, well-paid workers and a periphery of casualized labor. Bifurcation is both an outcome and a relational process, where core and casual labor forces condition one another. For instance, as firms restructure and embrace "**lean production**," they may trim less skilled jobs and fulfill the tasks associated with them through subcontracting arrangements relying on casual labor, often overseas. The U.S. automobile sector outsourced so much of its components production beginning in the late 1970s that the percentage of its workforce belonging to unions fell from two-thirds to one-quarter by the mid-1990s. Not only did outsourcing bifurcate auto industry labor, but the expansion of this non-union workforce eroded wages, such that between 1975 and 1990 the low-wage workforce grew by 142 percent, from 17 to 40 percent of the automobile workforce. For the U.S. workforce as a whole, industrial restructuring reduced real average weekly earnings by 18 percent from the mid-1970s to the mid-1990s. Meanwhile, union density fell from about 25 percent in 1980 to 14.5 percent by 1995 (and, in the private sector, to 10.2 percent by 1996).[1]

While Northern firms restructure their workforce and relocate some semi-skilled and unskilled jobs overseas, the impact in the South varies considerably, where unionism (sometimes state-organized) is on the rise. NICs such as South Korea, Brazil, and South Africa have experienced growth in core industrial jobs, while other states such as Bangladesh, Thailand, Indonesia, the Philippines, and those in the Caribbean have seen expansion in low-tech, labor-intensive jobs in garment and electronics assembly, employing mainly women. In twenty years garment production has spawned 1.2 million jobs in Bangladesh, 80 percent of which are held by young women (with considerable impact on Islamic culture). Women tend to enter the new industrial jobs, such as in *maquiladoras* in Mexico, where they constitute two-thirds of the labor force, and in global factories in East Asia, where they average 42 percent of the workforce. In Latin America in particular, in the post-ISI phase, this trend of the *feminization of global labor* parallels the downgrading of male employment as many formal jobs are restructured and turned into casual employment. In either case, casualization of labor is the overwhelming outcome.[2]

In the shadow of globalization lurks a rising dilemma: the casualization and, indeed, the redundancy of labor. For example, in France the GNP grew by 80 percent between 1973 and 1993, but unemployment grew from 420,000 to 5.1 million.[3] Two major trends seem to contribute to labor casualization, one secular and the other cyclical.

The *secular* or linear trend is the ongoing process of "de-peasantization." Peasant expulsion from the land and migration to urban centers has, of course, been occurring for centuries, but it has accelerated outside the First World since the post–World War II era as more and more areas of land and forest are absorbed into the global marketplace. The resulting pools of labor create the low-cost and casual labor forces sought by firms in their global sourcing operations. Secular growth in labor productivity, without a matching reduction of the working day/week/year, also expels some workers from production. In 1995, for instance, the same sized labor force in U.S. manufacturing produced five times its output in 1950.[4]

The *cyclical* trend is the instability of employment under competitive capitalist production systems and competitive labor markets. As firms retool, restructure, or go out of business, they shed labor. Private enterprise systems do not guarantee alternative employment, although during the era of welfare capitalism governments established various safety nets. As the world moves (backward) to competitive capitalism, these safety nets are fraying.

Globalization combines these trends. As peasant farmers lose markets to cheaper imported foods or surrender their land to larger commercial agro-export operations, they flood the towns and cities looking for work. When barriers to trade and investment fall, the cheaper labor these peasants can provide attracts foreign investment as firms scour the world, or the region, to reduce production costs. The following case study of Mexican *campesinos* illustrates this trend.

CASE STUDY

The Mexican *Campesino* Shapes the Global Labor Force

Of the more than 500,000 workers in the Mexican *maquiladoras*, roughly 70 percent moved there from the countryside during the 1980s. The border region is a low-wage enclave; wages there were lower in 1993 than were Mexican industrial wages in 1981, even though productivity rose 41 percent during the same period. The implication is that the mere presence of such a labor pool depresses wages, and we know that the Mexican government enforced low wages in its preparation to join NAFTA. A further implication is that a low-wage enclave can have an eroding effect on a higher-wage system once firms are free to relocate. Harley Shaiken observed that "Mexican plants achieving U.S. productivity levels at one-seventh the wages offer a powerful incentive for many U.S. firms to relocate production or lower their labor costs by threatening to move or both." Once NAFTA passed, auto parts suppliers expanded from 192 to 210 plants within a year, increasing output in value from $6.4 to $9.5 billion.

The border region of Mexico, according to Shaiken, has become "almost a 51st state in terms of production" as the automation of *maquiladoras* has proceeded. In the state of Chihuahua in 1993, the Ford engine plant paid assemblers $1.55 an hour (compared with $17.38 in the United States) and skilled workers $2.87 an hour (compared with $20.21 across the border). The trend of substituting semi-automated assembly in Chihuahua for fully automated assembly in the American Midwest is illustrated by Ford's moving the manufacturing of dashboard gauges from a factory in Saline, Michigan, to a *maquiladora* in Chihuahua, which Ford named Altec. This *maquiladora* has a labor force of 3,000 producing radios and other car parts, with 700 people producing dashboard gauges, replacing 400 Michigan workers.

One consequence of this process is a stratification of Mexican industrial workers, as wages for some auto work on the border drift up with rising skill levels—on the order of a 40 percent increase in the first half of the 1990s, even though the pay differential across the border is still more than 6 to 1. While the border region acts as a magnet for U.S. jobs, the automation process south of the border has its own local job-displacing effect. The mayor of Chihuahua observed in 1993: "I would say that the unemployment rate in the city has risen to 8 percent or more, double what it was three years ago. This does not include housewives who worked and now don't. We don't count them as unemployed."

Sources: Shaiken, 1993; Uchitelle, 1993a; Harper, 1994; Moody, 1999, p. 71.

The Role of Free Trade Agreements in the Race to the Bottom

The free trade agreement (FTA) tends to merge national labor forces into a global labor force. Labor costs vary within and across national arenas, depending on local historical conditions. In the U.S./Mexican comparison, there is variation between an industrial or service-based post-industrial society and a semi-industrial society. Their unification into a single market includes mature labor forces and first-generation wage laborers from rural communities. The wage differential is enormous. On the other hand, between Canada and the United States, which signed an FTA in 1988, the differential is the social wage—the Canadian system having a more comprehensive social security system than the United States. In the United States, for example, approximately two-thirds of the more than 8 million unemployed in 1986 received no compensation.[5]

In both cases, United States/Mexico and Canada/United States, free trade is intended to harmonize policies regarding levels of wages and social services. "Harmonization" means reducing the differential in the direction of the minimal standard, given the competitive advantage of the lower-cost regions. This process is known as downward leveling, or "the race to the bottom."[6] It was clearly articulated by the former president of the Canadian Manufacturer's Association, J. Laurent Thibault:

> As we remove trade restrictions and move more and more towards an open flow of goods, it is obvious that we reduce the degree of political independence in Canada. There is nothing sinister in that. It is simply a fact that, as we ask our industries to compete toe to toe with American industry under a full free product flow basis, we in Canada are obviously forced to create the same conditions in Canada that exist in the US, whether it is the unemployment insurance scheme, Workmen's Compensation, the cost of government, the level of taxation, or whatever . . . and that means that we would have less freedom to create in Canada an environment that is very much different from that which exists in the United States.[7]

The harmonization process is also at work on the U.S. side. Although proponents of NAFTA claimed it would create 400,000 jobs in its first two years, at least that many jobs were lost. Real wages declined on both sides of the border, and the U.S. Department of Labor predicted that from the mid-1990s to the mid-2000s the top job-growth occupations would be cashiers, janitors, retail sales clerks, and waiters/waitresses. Industries that shift to Mexico are those in which women are disproportionately employed, such as apparel, consumer electronics, and food processing. Many of these North American women entered the workforce in the late 1970s and 1980s because families could no longer get by on a single wage. Once their already low-wage jobs move south, the possibility lessens for these women to find equivalent work. The pressure on family livelihood increases. The general downward pressure on the U.S. wage heightens as Mexico's cheaper labor comes on line.

Consequences within the United States include further declines in real wages (a clear trend since 1972), rising poverty rates, increased family stress and social disorder, and rising public health costs. The foundations of social cohesion crack. A study issued in 1995, titled *Families in Focus*, found that family decay is worldwide; this situation is attributed largely to the trend of women assuming a greater role as income earners. Their jobs are usually inferior, requiring longer hours of work than men's work and leading to new stresses in households.[8]

Proposed retraining schemes to help American workers adjust to a shifting employment scene are often ineffectual. Indeed, the United States Department Labor issued a report evaluating a long-standing $200 million annual program for retraining manufacturing workers who lost their jobs to foreign trade. It concluded

> that only 19 percent of the "retrained" workers found jobs that demanded their new skills and paid at least 80 percent of their former wages; 20 percent remained jobless; most of the rest sank into low-wage slots that they occupied for just eight months. In Buffalo [New York], once a manufacturing powerhouse, formerly unionized steel and auto workers now compete for openings in the top employment categories of retail salesperson, office clerk, waiter, janitor or maid, secretary and food-counter worker. More people have jobs than ever before in that region's history, but deskilling, not reskilling, is the trend, as 86 percent of all new jobs there are in services paying an average of $5.60 an hour.[9]

Retraining is likely to be ineffectual when Northern governments surrender the prerogative to regulate investment and labor markets to global market forces. In the global marketplace, product cycles are unstable, as consumer fashions and sourcing sites change relentlessly. The loss of jobs is not simply an economic transfer from one nation to another; more fundamentally, it represents the "hollowing-out" of a nation's economic base and the erosion of social institutions that stabilize the conditions of employment and habitat associated with those jobs. A century of institution building in labor markets, in corporate/union relations, and in communities can disappear overnight when the winds of the market are allowed to blow across uneven national boundaries. Those who have work find they are often working longer hours to make ends meet, despite remarkable technological advances.

CASE STUDY

Labor Organizing in the Globalization Project

One of the consequences of the globalization project is labor union decline associated with the restructuring of work and corporate downsizing, as firms and states pursue efficiency in the global economy. One of labor's responses is to forge new forms of organization, such as the new labor internationalism that has emerged to present a solid front to footloose firms that would divide national labor forces, and to states that enter free trade agreements that would undermine labor benefits. The new labor internationalism was a key part of the political debate surrounding NAFTA. American organized labor took a big step in distancing itself from U.S. national policy, arguing that NAFTA was not in the interests of U.S. labor. Led by the rank and file, organized labor joined a substantial national political coalition of consumers, environmentalists, and others in opposing the implementation of NAFTA, arguing especially that, because Mexican unions were organs of the state, which maintained a low minimum wage, NAFTA could not protect U.S. labor from unfair competition. Subsequently, cross-border unionism to protect labor on either side has taken off. The stranglehold of the Mexican government on union organization has begun to fray, evidenced by the formation of an independent union, the Authentic Labor Front, which formed an alliance with the U.S. United Electrical Workers, Teamsters, Steel Workers, and four other U.S. and Canadian unions in 1992. The U.S. AFL-CIO has also sought alliances with independent Mexican unions, including calling for independent labor organizing in the *maquiladoras*. On December 12, 1997, following a long struggle, the Korean-owned Han Young plant in Tijuana agreed to the formation of an independent union among its *maquila* factory workers, a 30 percent pay raise, and reinstatement of fired activists.

This development mirrors movements elsewhere in the South where nongovernment-controlled unions are springing up in the new environment of global integration. Organizations facilitating this development have included the revamped Transnationals Information Exchange (TIE), dedicated to forging networks of labor organization across the world, which it pioneered in connection with the "global factory" associated with the production of the "world car." A particularly innovative project was the

Cocoa-Chocolate Network, based in the "production chain" idea, whereby TIE linked European industrial workers with Asian and Latin American plantation workers and peasants, extending the production chain back from the chocolate factories to the cacao bean fields. Beyond the 1980s, TIE moved into social movement unionism, connecting casualized labor across national boundaries, organizing regionalized networks of labor, and addressing issues of racism and immigrant workers. It evolved a flexible, decentralized structure mirroring the age of lean production, on one hand, and empowering labor and its activists across the networks on the other. It modeled international social movement unionism within the globalization project.

Sources: Ross & Trachte, 1990; Brechere & Costello, 1994, pp. 153-154; Benería, 1995, p. 48; Calvo, 1997; Moody, 1999, pp. 255-262; Dillon, 1997, 1998.

Restructuring of Work in the Global Economy

Structural unemployment, in which redundant workers cease rotating into new jobs, has grown dramatically in the centers of the global economy since the 1960s. Three major sources of structural unemployment are

- *Automation*, a tactic of competitive advantage pursued by firms in the global marketplace. In the United States between 1980 and 1985, about 2.3 million manufacturing jobs disappeared as robotization spread.

- *Lean production* (see box, page 199), a related form of industrial restructuring, where economies of scope (product flexibility) combine with economies of scale and depend on casualization of labor, by which many employees are converted into "self-employed workers."

- *Global competition* from export processing zones. Offshore competition began in the late 1960s in unskilled industries such as textiles, apparel, furniture, rubber, and plastics, and then moved to more skilled industries such as shipbuilding, steel, machinery, and services by the 1980s.[10]

From 1970 to 1994, manufacturing employment fell 50 percent in Britain, 8 percent in the United States, 18 percent in France, and 17 percent in

Germany, although most of these jobs were in "low-tech" industries such as footwear, textiles, and metals. In 1995 alone, the U.S. apparel industry lost 10 percent of its jobs; that, along with jobs lost in the fabrics industry, accounted for 40 percent of manufacturing jobs lost that year. More than 50 percent of the U.S. clothing market is accounted for by cheap imports from Asia and Latin America, from which smaller manufacturers increasingly must source their materials to survive, while large, profitable textile manufacturers shift to high technology to trim their labor costs. Around 65,300 U.S. footwear jobs disappeared between 1982 and 1989. Associated with this was Nike's decision to stop making athletic shoes in the United States, relocating most of its production to South Korea and Indonesia. In the early 1990s, a worker, usually female, in the footwear industry in Indonesia earned $1.03 per day compared to an average wage in the U.S. footwear industry of $6.94 per *hour*.[11]

Under competition from cheap labor overseas, core industries in the United States and the United Kingdom had lost the power to set wages and stimulate local supplier industries by the late 1970s. By the mid-1980s, the same decline was occurring in Japan.[12] Some Japanese manufacturing had shifted offshore to Southeast Asia, as Japan increasingly supplied components and production machinery, such as robots, to other countries for use in final product assembly. Across the First World, service and information-based industries have increasingly overshadowed industrial manufacturing, confirming the rise of "postindustrialism."

Whether postindustrial services (retailing, health care, restaurants, finance, security) are the basis of future economic expansion is hotly debated. Some see many service jobs as inferior to manufacturing jobs, whereas others argue that service jobs such as design and sales are generated by manufacturing systems as they become more sophisticated.[13] Service employment is not, however, immune to downsizing or relocation. Many new jobs in the Caribbean, for example, are data processing jobs that large U.S. insurance, health industry, magazine subscription renewal, consumer credit, and retailing firms have shifted offshore at a lower cost. Swissair, British Airways, and Lufthansa relocated much of their reservations to Indian subcontractors in Bangalore, where the staff "are well educated at English-speaking universities yet cost only a fraction of what their counterparts are paid in the North." According to a spokesperson for Swissair: "We can hire three Indians for the price of one Swiss." The relocation of revenue accounts preparation saved 8 million francs and 120 jobs in Zurich. In addition, since 1990, Eastern Europe has become an increasingly competitive site (with India) for labor-intensive computer programming.[14]

What Is Lean Production?

Lean production is a mixed bag of information technologies, craft work, and archaic or repressive forms of work organization including self-employment, subcontracting, and piece-rate work. Responding to "just-in-time" supply patterns, it bifurcates labor forces between stable cores of full-time employment and unstable peripheries of "flexible," part-time or temporary, workers. It derives from the Toyota model of a subcontracting pyramid, where a base of insecure, low-paid, and labor-intensive jobs supports a stable core of blue-collar workers. The hierarchy provides production flexibility and management options to discipline core workers with the threat of outsourcing. At the turn of the twenty-first century, the U.S. economic boom was expressed in expanding high-end managerial and computer systems jobs, but temporary and part-time labor is a defining feature of the twenty-first-century labor market. By 1995, the largest employer in the United States was no longer General Motors but Manpower, Inc., a firm coordinating "temps." Thirty percent of the temporary workforce was located in manufacturing, construction, transportation, and utilities. The model of lean production is the U.S. labor market, where companies can hire part-time employees without traditional full benefits, creating millions of second-class jobs (most workers prefer full-time work). Women constitute 70-90 percent of the temps in the First World. The proportion of part-time workers in the workforce grew between 1979 and 1995 from 16.4 percent to 24.1 percent in the United Kingdom, from 8.1 percent to 15. 6 percent in France, from 11.4 percent to 16.3 percent in Germany, and from 13.8 percent to 18.6 percent in Canada. To meet European Monetary Union requirements, European governments are relaxing labor laws and generating new part-time jobs, at the rate of 10 percent a year, to improve the flexibility of European firms competing in the world market.

Sources: Cooper & Kuhn, 1998, p. A1; Moody, 1999, pp. 97-99.

Manufacturing labor has lost considerable organizational as well as numerical power to corporate strategies of restructuring, leading to the qualitative restructuring of work discussed in the insert on lean production. After a decade of conservative government restructuring of the

British labor force (weakening union rights, eliminating minimum wages, reducing jobless benefits), Britain in the 1990s became a new site for off-shore investment from Europe—mostly in part-time jobs (electronic assembly, apparel, clerical tasks) undertaken by women at considerably lower wages than would be paid in Europe.[15] Typically, "Third World" working conditions are just as likely to appear in the global centers under the policy of economic liberalism and the practice of lean production. Garment sweatshops are a recurring phenomenon, for example, in New York City, and a range of "Third World" jobs has spread in First World cities over the past two decades.[16]

Meanwhile, in the former Third World, more than half the labor force was unemployed or underemployed in the 1980s.[17] In the Organization for Economic Cooperation and Development (OECD) countries, approximately 35 million people were officially unemployed in 1993. In the formerly Communist countries of Eastern Europe, the proportion of unemployed was more than double that in the OECD countries. In 1996, according to estimates by the International Labor Organization, 1 billion were unemployed or underemployed across the world, with the figures inaccurate because of the rise of part-time or temporary work.[18]

CASE STUDY

The Hybridity of Lean Production in Agribusiness: Mexican Tomatoes

The global fruit and vegetable industry depends on flexible contract labor arrangements. Coordination of multiple production sites, for a year-round supply of fresh produce, is achieved through information technologies. Deborah Barndt's research retraces the journey of the tomato from Mexico to the ubiquitous McDonald's outlets in North America. Naming it "Tomasita" to foreground its labor origins in national and gendered terms, she describes the Sayula plant of one of Mexico's largest agro-exporters, Santa Anita Packers, where, in the peak season Sayula employs more than 2,000 pickers and 700 packers. The improved variety seeds used originate in Mexico but are developed and patented in Israel or the United States. Such seeds need heavy doses of pesticides, but

> the company did not provide any health and safety education or protective gear. Perhaps a more visually striking indicator of

monocultural production was the packing plant, employing hundreds of young women whom the company moved by season from one site to another as a kind of "mobile maquiladora." . . . [T]he only Mexican inputs are the land, the sun, and the workers. . . . The South has been the source of the seeds, while the North has the biotechnology to alter them. . . . [T]he workers who produce the tomatoes do not benefit. Their role in agro-export production also denies them participation in subsistence agriculture, especially since the peso crisis in 1995, which has forced migrant workers to move to even more scattered work sites. They now travel most of the year—with little time to grow food on their own plots in their home communities. . . . [W]ith this loss of control comes a spiritual loss, and a loss of a knowledge of seeds, of organic fertilizers and pesticides, of sustainable practices such as crop rotation or leaving the land fallow for a year—practices that had maintained the land for millennia.

Casualized *campesino* farm labor, producing slightly cheaper tomatoes to compete with Florida growers, is no substitute for stable peasant communities.

Source: Barndt, 1997, pp. 59-62.

The increasingly unregulated global economy habitually marginalizes people and their communities as jobs are automated, shed, or relocated under the competitive pressure of the global marketplace. Competition compels firms not only to go global but also to keep their sourcing flexible and, therefore, their suppliers—and their workers—guessing. The women's wear retailer Liz Claiborne, which divides its sources mainly among the United States, Hong Kong, South Korea, Taiwan, the Philippines, China, and Brazil, claims: "The Company does not own any manufacturing facilities: all of its products are manufactured through arrangements with independent suppliers. . . . The Company does not have any long-term, formal arrangements with any of the suppliers which manufacture its products."[19]

Legacies of First World Labor Importing

Labor redundancy on such a grand scale contributes to social disorder across the world, as restructuring and relocation of firms destabilize organized labor markets, industrial districts, and human habitats. The quickened movement of the global economy stratifies populations across, rather than simply within, national borders. With provocative imagery, Jacques Attali, former president of the European Bank for Reconstruction and Development, distinguishes *rich nomads* ("consumer-citizens of the world's privileged regions") from *poor nomads* ("boat people on a planetary scale"). In a gloomy projection in the wake of the "lost decade," Attali suggests:

> In restless despair, the hopeless masses of the periphery will witness the spectacle of another hemisphere's growth. Particularly in those regions of the South that are geographically contiguous and culturally linked to the North—places such as Mexico, Central America, or North Africa—millions of people will be tempted and enraged by the constant stimulation of wants that can't be satisfied. . . . With no future of their own in an age of air travel and telecommunications, the terminally impoverished will look for one in the North. . . . The movement of peoples has already begun; only the scale will grow: Turks in Berlin, Moroccans in Madrid, Indians in London, Mexicans in Los Angeles, Puerto Ricans and Haitians in New York, Vietnamese in Hong Kong.[20]

Such fears, founded in latent stereotypes, underlie the concern of the global managers and many First World "consumer citizens" with stemming the tide of global labor migration. During the NAFTA debate, one study claimed that failure to implement NAFTA would devastate the Mexican economy to the degree that "at least 500,000 extra migrants would sneak north each year throughout the next decade."[21] A year later, following sharp devaluation of the peso, the Clinton Administration argued that if the United States did not increase the Mexican bailout fund from $9 billion to $40 billion, an additional 430,000 Mexicans would cross the border into Texas and California.[22]

A cursory glance at the First World newspapers of the 1990s confirms the broad anxiety about the ethnic composition of the global labor force, often manifested in outbreaks of racist violence toward "guest workers." This attitude has been particularly manifest in Europe, where 20 million immigrants from other world zones live. It is worthwhile to remember that in the postwar development decades governments actively encouraged guest workers—when European firms needed a cheap labor force while basic industries were expanding, and when Southwestern U.S. industrial and agribusiness firms needed cheap Mexican labor under the *bracero* program, an official labor immigration policy. Continuing immigration is in the interests of firms needing cheap labor and of privileged people needing servants, even though it has become the focus of cultural backlash and political fear campaigns. The extent and content of global labor circulation are illustrated in the following case study.

CASE STUDY

Migrant Labor in the Global Economy: Economic and Environmental Refugees

In the early 1990s, as many as 80 million people were estimated to be living as expatriate laborers around the world. Asian women are the fastest-growing group of foreign workers, increasing by 800,000 each year. At the turn of the twenty-first century there were 20 million refugees and 100 million migrants, of whom 42 million are official guest workers, and 25 million are environmental migrants, deriving from the destruction of natural resources by unregulated economic growth. It is predicted that, at present rates, environmental migration will double by the year 2010. Likely sources include

- 135 million people whose land is being desertified
- 900 million of the world's poorest, existing on less than a dollar a day and living in areas vulnerable to soil erosion, droughts, desertification, and floods
- 200 million people who may face rising sea levels due to climate change
- 50 million people in famine-vulnerable areas subject to climate change
- 550 million people already suffering from chronic water shortage

Source: Montalbano, 1991, p. H1; New Internationalist, 305, 1998, p. 17.

Labor: The New Export

Just as money circulates the globe seeking investment opportunities, so labor increasingly circulates seeking employment opportunities. Migration is of course not new to the late twentieth century. The unrelenting separation of people from the land is etched into the making of the modern world. Colonialism propelled migrations of free and unfree people across the world. Between 1810 and 1921, 34 million people, mainly Europeans, emigrated to the United States alone.[23] The difference today is largely one of scale.

During the 1980s, spurred by debt regime restructurings, there was an internal migration in the former Third World of between 300 and 400 million people.[24] This pool of labor, then, contributes to current levels of global migration from overburdened cities to metropolitan regions as it seeks to earn money for families back home. Estimates suggest that roughly 100 million kinfolk depend on remittances of the global labor force. In the 1990s, for example, two-thirds of Turkey's trade deficit was financed by remittances from Turks working abroad. Also spurred by debt, labor export has become a significant foreign currency earner: Filipino overseas earnings are estimated to amount to $5.7 billion, for example. About 6 million Filipinos, increasingly rural, work overseas in 130 countries as contract workers (seamen, carpenters, masons, mechanics, or maids).[25]

The government of the Philippines has a de facto labor export policy that has become an important component of an export-led development strategy.[26] In addition to products, labor is exported, mainly to the oil-rich Middle East, where contractors organize the ebb and flow of foreign labor. One contractor, Northwest Placement, a privately run recruiting agency, receives 5,000 pesos ($181)—the maximum allowed by the Department of Labor—from Filipino applicants on assurance of a job; this covers the costs of a medical check, visas, and government clearance fees. Not surprisingly, there are plenty of unlicensed agencies operating as well.[27]

CASE STUDY

Trafficking in Women: The Global Sex Industry vs. Human Rights

Exploitation of migrant labor, lacking legal status and language skills, is easy and widespread. This is particularly so for women, who constitute the majority of migrant labor from Asia today. In Thailand, female emigration took off in the 1980s as the East Asian boom consolidated, disrupting cultural traditions and family livelihoods. It drew on the young women flooding into Bangkok from the Thai countryside, looking for income to remit to their villages. Many of these women would end up in Europe, Southeast Asia, the United States, Australia, South Africa, or the Arabian Gulf, in the burgeoning sex industry by deceit or by choice (being a relatively high-income trade open to uneducated women). Evidence suggests that sex tourism to Thailand contributed to the demand for Thai women overseas, and trafficking in women is more profitable than either illegal gambling or drugs and arms trafficking. By 1993 there were almost 100,000 Thai women working in the Japanese sex industry, and 5,000 in Berlin alone. Research in northern Thailand has shown that about 28 percent of household income was remitted by absent daughters. A common motive is relieving poverty and debt (especially in the wake of the Asian financial crisis), and often parents sell their daughters to agents for a cash advance to be paid off by work in the global sex industry. Alternatively, individual women pay an agent's fee of around $500. From then on, women are devoid of human rights: they work as bonded labor, are subject to arrest for illicit work and illegal residence, have no rights to medical or social services overseas, are forced to sell sex with no power to choose their customers or service, remain at high risk of contracting HIV, and are targets of racial discrimination and public humiliation if arrested. Action against trafficking is difficult because of the collusion between families who benefit materially from absent daughters and agents of the trade; because of the underground lifestyle of the women, trapped by underground employers; and because of governments interested in suppressing information about the sex trade to avoid adverse publicity.

Source: Skrobanek, Boonpakdi, & Janthakeero, 1997, pp. 13, 23, 24, 31, 68, 103.

International labor circulation combines formal policies with decidedly informal working conditions. Migrant workers routinely lack human rights. Workers in the Gulf states, for example, are indentured, with no civic rights, no choice of alternative jobs, and no recourse against poor employment conditions and low wages—which are determined by the income levels of the country of origin. Migrant workers must surrender their passports on arrival; they reportedly work twelve to sixteen hours a day, seven days a week. Governments in the migrant workers' home countries in Asia, dependent on foreign currency earnings, are reportedly resigned to the exploitation of their nationals. International labor union organizations have been ineffectual, especially as Middle Eastern states have united to suppress discussion in international forums of working conditions inside their countries.[28]

The Politics of Global Labor Circulation

In the United States, labor comes from all over the world, principally Mexico (around 60 percent in 1990), Asia (22.1 percent), Europe (7.3 percent), South America (5.6 percent), and Africa (2.3 percent). About 33 percent of the population of Los Angeles County is foreign-born, a number that has tripled since 1970. "Latinos, now 28 percent of California's population, will likely be the majority by 2040."[29] The scale is large enough that immigrants retain their cultural and linguistic traditions rather than assimilate, as they did earlier in the formation of U.S. society. Robert Reich has commented that "the old American 'melting pot' is now cooking a variegated stew, each of whose ingredients maintains a singular taste."[30]

The juxtaposing of distinct cultures in countries to which labor migrates creates this *multicultural* effect. The United States took a turn in this direction in 1965, when the Immigration and Nationality Act Amendments abolished the previous policy of organizing immigration according to the already established patterns of cultural origin. "During the 1950s there were nine times as many European immigrants as there were Asians. Following the passage of the new Immigration Act, the proportions were sharply reversed."[31] In the context of economic restructuring in the United States, however, a heightened "nativism" is appearing—a local backlash in response to the economic, social, and cultural uncertainties associated with this trend. Since 1965, the polled percentage of Americans objecting to immigration has almost doubled—from 33 percent to 60 percent.[32] The following case study examines varying responses to immigration in Europe.

Increasingly, given the scale of labor migration, minority cultures are forming identifiable communities in their new labor sites, maintaining a certain distance from the local culture. The inhabitants of these "transnational communities" have regular contact with their sending countries and other migrant communities through modern electronic communication (e-mail, fax), transportation, and media developments; they establish their own cultural beachhead within the host society. Such communities may engage in what Benedict Anderson has referred to as "long-distance nationalism"; they are activists residing in an immigrant community but involved politically in their country of origin.[33] Such offshore activities distort politics in the countries of origin.

The circulation of cultures of labor binds the world through multiculturalism; however, the conditions in which labor circulation has intensified have made multiculturalism a fragile ideal. Labor export arrangements deny rights and representation to the migrant workforce.

CASE STUDY

Migrant Workers and European Xenophobia

In France, the question of multiculturalism has been tested recently with the growing presence of the more than 3.5 million Muslims living in that country. Muslims constitute a quarter of the total immigrant population (mostly from European countries). Their presence stems from French policy to import large numbers of North African men for factory and construction work from the 1960s through 1974, after which families were allowed to join the men. Arab and African immigrants and their French-born children form an increasingly distinct suburban underclass in French society. A principal of a Parisian school with a considerable immigrant population remarked in 1993: "In the 1970s and 1980s, we promoted multiculturalism. We had a day of couscous, a day of paella, it was 'vive la différence' much of the time. Now the pendulum is going the other way."

In Spain, by contrast, when a fascist group, Falange-Española-Frente Nacional Sindicalista (FE-FNS), obtained permission in June, 1997, to protest against North African immigrants in Valencia, a local agency of a European anti-racism organization, SOS Racismo, overwhelmed the protest. The Spanish people, as well as trade unions, have a relatively high tolerance level toward migrants, partly because many Spaniards worked abroad in the 1970s. This may be just as well because of forecasts of African immigration (from as far south as Rwanda and Somalia) to Southern Europe surpassing recent immigration waves from Turkey and Eastern Europe as a result of the marginalization of Africa in the global economy today.

Source: Riding, 1993; Qassim, 1998, pp. 28-30.

Deteriorating economies and communities in the centers of the global economy spark exclusionist politics that scapegoat cultural minorities. In the days of the development project, a more inclusive attitude prevailed, rooted in broad-based class movements and political coalitions committed to cultural integration and the redistribution of resources. In the present context, inclusion is threatened by separatist politics. The race to the bottom has profound destabilizing tendencies.

Informal Activity

The globalization project is Janus-faced. It exaggerates the contradictory tendency within the former development project, intensifying the market culture at the same time as it intensifies its opposite—a growing culture of informal, or marginal, activity. This culture involves people working on the fringes of the market, performing casual and unregulated labor, working in cooperative arrangements, street vending, engaging in criminal activities, or pursuing what are deemed illegal economic activities. This culture did not just appear, however. With the rise of market societies, the boundaries of the formal economy were identified and regulated by the state for tax purposes, but they have always been incomplete and fluid, often by design and certainly by custom. An army of servants and housecleaners, for example, routinely works "off the books." Casual labor has always accompanied small-scale enterprise and even large-scale harvesting operations where labor use is cyclical. Also, a substantial portion of labor performed across the world every day is unpaid labor—such as housework and family farm labor.

It is somewhat artificial, then, to distinguish between a formal economy with its legal/moral connotations and an informal sector with its illegal/immoral connotations. They are often intimately connected and mutually conditioning. The distinction is made by economists concerned with models of economic activity that can be measured, and the measurement is done by governments that are concerned with their records and their tax base. We continue to make the distinction here because it helps to illuminate the limits of official, formal development strategy, on one hand, and to identify alternative, informal livelihood strategies on the other.

Our point is that those who are bypassed or marginalized by development often form a culture parallel to the market culture. There is, of course, a question as to whether this informal culture is a real alternative or simply an impoverished margin of the formal culture. This may be an issue of scale, or it may depend on the context. For example, withdrawal from the formal economy in the countryside may revive subsistence farming that represents an improvement in living standards over working as a rural laborer or existing on the urban fringe, as long as land is available. The scale of marginalized populations grows with de-peasantization and the labor redundancy discussed in the previous section. That is, these trends are often connected, so that informalization is a direct outgrowth of expanded formal economic activity or the concentration of resources in fewer corporate hands.

One source of the quite dramatic expansion of the informal sector has been the hyper-urbanization in former Third World countries. Agricultural modernization routinely expelled peasants and rural labor from secure rural livelihoods; they migrated to the urban centers where, as they had heard on the radio and through the migrant labor networks, jobs and amenities were available. One vivid account of this trend is given by Hernando De Soto, a libertarian critic of developmentalism:

> Quite simply, Peru's legal institutions had been developed over the years to meet the needs and bolster the privileges of certain dominant groups in the cities and to isolate the peasants geographically in rural areas. As long as this system worked, the implicit legal discrimination was not apparent. Once the peasants settled in the cities, however, the law began to lose social relevance. The migrants discovered that their numbers were considerable, that the system was not prepared to accept them, that more and more barriers were being erected against them, that they had to fight to extract every right from an unwilling establishment, that they were excluded from the facilities and benefits offered by the law. . . . In short, they discovered that they must compete not only against people but also against the system. Thus it was, that in order to survive, the migrants became informals.[34]

In effect, then, development engendered a growing marginal population. Of course, these *peri-urban communities*, as they are known, expanded throughout the twentieth century: the urban South grew from 90 million in 1900 to nearly 1 billion in 1985, with an increase of more than 40 million a year. Its share of world urban population increased from 39 percent to 63 percent between 1950 and 1990. Between 1990 and 1995, Southern urban populations grew by 263 million—the equivalent of a Shanghai or a Los Angeles every month. By United Nations estimates, in 2000 there were 2 billion urban dwellers in the South, with increases since 1990 of 109 percent in Africa, 50 percent in Latin America, and 65 percent in Asia.[35]

With global integration, the lines are drawn even more clearly, on a larger scale, and possibly more rapidly. There are professional and managerial classes who participate within global circuits (involved with products, money, electronic communications, high-speed transport) linking enclaves of producers/consumers across state borders. Many of these people increasingly live and work within corporate domains. For the United States, Robert Reich termed this the "secession of the successful," meaning the top fifth of income earners in America, who "now inhabit a different economy from other Americans. The new, *Fast World* elite is linked by jet, modem, fax, satellite and fiber-optic cable to the great commercial and recreational centers of the world, but it is not particularly connected to the rest of the nation."[36] There are those whom these circuits bypass, or indeed displace. These are the redundant labor forces, the structurally unemployed, and the marginals, who live in shantytowns and urban ghettos across the world. Some join the global labor force as migrants and/or refugees, and others enter the informal, or underground, economy.

Informalization is not new, but under economic globalization it has some different facets. One facet is the industrial decay or downsizing that occurs as the global labor market comes into play. The labor expelled in this process is quite distinct from first-generation peasants forced to leave the land. Middle-class people are now entering the ranks of the structurally unemployed daily across the First World, and the phenomenon of self-employment attests to this social transformation.

Projections abound concerning the impact of a GATT/WTO "free trade" regime. Only time will tell how accurate they are, because the free trade regime is in its infancy. In the year prior to the formation of the WTO, the former chair of the Group of 77, Luis Fernando Jaramillo, predicted that "the industrialized countries, which make up only 20% of the membership of GATT, will appropriate 70% of the additional income to be generated by the implementation of the Uruguay Round."[37] According to a GATT report released nine months later, the big winners would be the United States and the European Union, and these predictions still stand. It stands to reason that the "level playing field" under a free trade regime would privilege the strongest markets, but it is by no means clear that there will be a rising tide of global economic activity. The OECD predicts that after a decade of a GATT regime, Africa will lose an additional $3 billion of trade income annually; wheat and corn prices will rise, while cocoa and coffee prices will continue to fall.[38] Finally, former European Member of Parliament James Goldsmith reported in a U.S. Senate inquiry that with 4 billion people joining the world economy at the end of the Cold War, which had confined them to the Second World,

> The application of GATT will also cause a great tragedy in the third world. Modern economists believe that an efficient agriculture is one that produces the maximum amount of food for the minimum cost, using the least number of people. . . . It is estimated that there are still 3.1 billion people in the

world who live from the land. If GATT manages to impose worldwide the sort of productivity achieved by the intensive agriculture of nations such as Australia, then it is easy to calculate that about 2 billion of these people will become redundant. Some of these GATT refugees will move to urban slums. But a large number of them will be forced into mass migration. . . . We will have profoundly and tragically destabilized the world's population.[39]

Informalization

Economic and environmental refugees will enlarge the social weight of informal activities across the world. That is, with an enlarging mass of people existing on the fringes of the formal economy, informalization will rise. *Informalization involves two related processes: the casualization of labor via corporate restructuring and the generation of new forms of individual and collective livelihood strategies.* The latter have recently become the target of World Bank and NGO-driven schemes, which view such informal networking as social capital to be "developed." Informalization (understood as a *social movement*) reputedly first defined the consolidation of informal activity in Africa in the 1970s, a trend that grew out of successive development failures.[40]

Informal activity can be viewed as an alternative society or set of social institutions, rather than simply as an invisible economic reality that is negative or anti-state. The state view of informals is negative by definition. Informals—for example, women performing unwaged work—are perceived by planners as beyond the formal realm of official statistics, and, by definition, unproductive. Such a negative description parallels common First World perceptions of Third World people. According to Arturo Escobar, non-European people often tend to be perceived by what they lack—capital, entrepreneurship, organization and political conscience, education, political participation, infrastructure, and rationality.[41] This perception underlay the assumptions of the development project, and it continues to prejudice our understanding of this exploding other world. The positive description of the informal economy transcends the notion that informalization represents an anti-state movement. For Fantu Cheru, the withdrawal of African peasants from a failing formal economy, including paying taxes, represents a "silent revolution." Exiting was the choice for producers and workers consistently bypassed by state policies. Self-defense "has required the resuscitation of rural co-operatives, traditional caravan trade across borders, catering services and other activities that had once fallen into disuse, depriving the state of the revenue that traditionally financed its anti-people and anti-peasant development policies."[42]

Informalization vs. the African State: The Other Side of "Globalization"

Aili Mari Tripp views the elaboration of new rules of the game in the burgeoning informal sector across Africa as a form of resistance. Viewing informalization as more than a passive outcome of state/corporate restructuring, she focuses on the creative ways in which African populations have responded to the failure of development states, exacerbated by more than a decade of structural adjustment. Urban farming has proliferated in the absence of food subsidies, such that 68 percent of families in Dar es Salaam, Tanzania, now grow their own vegetables and raise livestock. Noncompliance with the state has generated new institutional resources in Tanzania:

> Hometown development associations became visible in the late 1980s as urban dwellers sought to provide assistance to the rural towns from which they originated. They used these associations to build schools, orphanages, libraries, roads, and clinics; to establish projects to conserve the environment; to provide solar electricity and water; to disburse soft loans to women's groups engaged in business; and to raise funds for flood relief and other such causes. These new associations resemble the early, ethnically based welfare and burial societies that formed in Dar es Salaam in the early 1900s to help new migrants adjust to city life, except that their focus today is to assist people in their rural towns and villages.

In addition to these new resources, traditional resources such as midwifery and craftwork are revived, often undertaken by women, and new activities, from street vending, pastry selling, and hair braiding to exporting seaweed have sprung up. In some cases informal businesses have become so successful in monetary terms that they have moved into the formal sector—for example, in flour milling, dry cleaning, and prawn farming. The phenomenon of informalization combines individualistic market-economy behavior with "moral-economy," where community interests, rather than markets, define the values shaping economic activity.

In Tanzania, the cultural weight of informalization led to the 1991 Zanzibar Declaration, acknowledging the legitimacy and social necessity of informal activities, outside official corruption. In this way, informalization not only conditions some aspects of the formal economy but also reshapes the state.

Source: Tripp, 1997, pp. 13, 127, 188; O'Meara, 1999, p. 34.

In many ways, informalization has become more and more prominent because more and more people are disenchanted with the economic models associated with the development and globalization projects. The discovery of survival strategies among the poor and dispossessed has thus become an academic industry. Activists are finding these communities to be sources of hope rather than despair. Ivan Illich, for example, notes that "up to now, economic development has always meant that people, instead of doing something, are instead enabled to buy it."[43] In this parable he finds that the "development castaways" constitute a proliferating culture of alternatives.

Serge LaTouche views informal activity as

comprehensive strategies of response to the challenges that life poses for displaced and uprooted populations in peri-urban areas. These are people torn between lost tradition and impossible modernity. The sphere of the informal has, incontestably, a major economic significance. It is characterised by a neo-artisanal activity that generates a lot of employment and produces incomes comparable to those of the modern sector. . . . Resolving practical problems of living spaces and daily life has all sorts of economic ramifications, so much so that the practical importance of the "informal economy" is no longer a matter of debate. Some 50-80% of the population in the urban areas of these countries live in and from the informal, one way or another. Moreover, the "informal economy" and more generally the "informal society" do not constitute a closed world. There are all sorts of bridges and ties into "formal" national and international structures.[44]

The "lost decade" intensified pressures to consolidate new livelihood strategies in already overburdened cities. In Latin America, whereas formal employment rose by 3.2 percent annually in the 1980s, informal jobs rose at more than twice that rate. Presently about a third of urban jobs in Asia and Latin America and more than half in Africa are estimated to be informal.[45] It is estimated that 90 percent of Eastern European computer software is illegally produced.[46] Among the poor in urban Mexico, collective pooling of resources to acquire land, shelter, and basic public services (water, electricity) was one widespread strategy for establishing networks among friends and neighbors to build their own cheap housing.[47]

Many different strategies contribute to the *culture of the new commons*, a social inventiveness arising on the fringes of industrial society and drawing on traditional collective interaction to allow people to make ends meet. Mexican intellectual Gustavo Esteva observes:

> Peasants and grassroots groups in the cities are now sharing with people forced to leave the economic centre the ten thousand tricks they have learned to limit the economy, to mock the economic creed, or to refunctionalize and reformulate modern technology. The "crisis" of the 1980s removed from the payroll people already educated in dependency on incomes and the market people lacking the social setting enabling them to survive by themselves. Now the margins are coping with the difficult task of relocating these people. The process poses great challenges and tensions for everyone, but it also offers a creative opportunity for regeneration.[48]

Growth and Marginalization

The globalization project involves a growth/marginalization dynamic, so the culture of the new commons may spread, as more and more regions across the world decay from neglect. The neglect has two sources. The first is the incapacity of debt-stressed state organizations to support regions that do not contribute to the global project. For example, in the poorer states, with borrowed funds earmarked to promote export production to service debt, little remains to subsidize sectors and communities on the margins. In sub-Saharan Africa, where total external debt represented 78.7 percent of GNP in 1994, total debt servicing amounts to $10 billion annually, four times the amount spent on health and education.[49] The First World is not immune to this fiscal stress—the United States continues to confront its rising debt burden by cutting social services, and the European states have been shrinking their social contract in preparing for monetary union.

Second, the hallmark of a market regime is inequality—the reinforcing of growth poles and the neglect of the remainder. We already can see this in practice:

- During the 1980s, the North/South gap widened such that the differential in average living standards was 10 to 1. The *Human Development Report 1996* documented an enlarged gap between the world's (and the United States') rich and poor, with eighty-nine states being worse off than they were a decade or more ago, but worldwide, 358 billionaires controlling assets greater than the combined annual incomes of countries containing 45 percent of the world's population. Ankie Hoogvelt observes that contemporary globalization is characterized by financial implosion, concentrating global financial wealth.[50]

- Cross-border investment continues to concentrate in the markets of the three super-regions—the United States, Europe, and Japan (the "Triad")—accounting for more than one-third of such investment worldwide. "In terms of trade, interactions within the Triad have outpaced both interactions in the rest of the world, and interactions between the Triad and the rest of the world, indicating a faster rate of integration within the Triad than between the Triad and the rest of the world."[51]

- In the first half of the 1990s, foreign direct investment (FDI) in the former Third World nearly tripled, but 60 percent of it was concentrated in Asia (China, Singapore, Malaysia, Thailand, Hong Kong, Taiwan, and Indonesia). In 1995, 2 percent of total private investment flowed into the Middle East and North Africa, and 5 percent flowed into sub-Saharan Africa, compared with 16 percent into Eastern Europe, 29 percent into Latin America, and 49 percent into Asia.[52]

- Between 1990 and 1997, Africa's share of the cumulative flow of FDI to the South was less than one-half of a percent (and 70 percent of that flowed to oil producers Angola and Nigeria, and to Ghana, Uganda, and South Africa). The African share of world exports is now about 1.3 percent, whereas Latin America's is around 4.3 percent. African exports remain overwhelmingly in agricultural and natural resources, with agricultural exports accounting for 76 percent of earnings, and terms of trade deteriorating substantially for many African countries between 1985 and 1994.[53]

- Bleak images of "Europe's periphery, Africa, [as] a lost continent" abound: "Since 1970, Africa's share of the world markets has been reduced by half; its debt has been multiplied by twenty and now equals its total gross product; and income per capita in sub-Saharan Africa has fallen by one-quarter since 1987."[54]

- Of the forty-five countries at the bottom of the Human Development Index, thirty-five are sub-Saharan African. On average, less than 50 percent of the people have access to health care and clean water, and the daily caloric intake is below that of Mexico or China

FIGURE 6.1

Global Patterns of Foreign Direct Investment, 1995

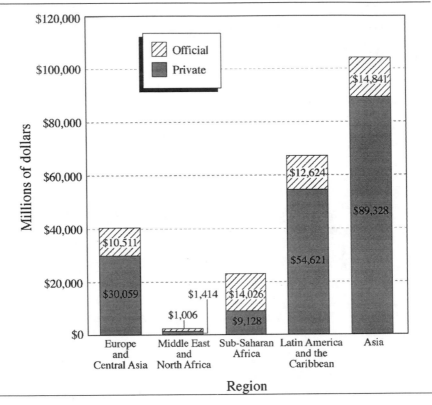

SOURCE: World Bank, 1997.

by a third or more. Child mortality below age five is 174 in 1,000, compared with a world average of 89 in 1,000, and the survivors confront pneumonia, tuberculosis, malaria, and now an exploding AIDS epidemic that is devastating the continent's financial resources and the people's lives.[55]

The globalization project is likely to be considerably more selective in its reach. Just because its progenitors speak of globalization does not mean there is universal and homogeneous development. Weaker regions of the world have no real channels of representation. They can attract attention from investors only by making themselves weaker through further structural adjustment. Even then, with less public spending, labor forces lack education (Africa is the only continent where school absenteeism is increasing), and attractive markets are lacking. The selectivity of the globalization project distinguishes it from the direct interventions in the non-European world under colonialism and from the aid and geopolitics of the development project. The globalization project appears to be a recipe for considerable marginalization.

CASE STUDY

Africa in the Globalization Project

The record of the globalization project in Africa is largely one of failure. Many African countries have submitted to structural adjustment programs over the last two decades, with comparatively little financial aid. The Heavily Indebted Poor Countries (HIPC) debt relief package, instituted by the IMF and the World Bank in 1996, targeted about forty countries, thirty-two of which are African. Conditionality included demonstrating six years of prudent fiscal management. Failure of this initiative to spur growth or relieve poverty led, in 1999, to the G-8 countries shortening this time period and requiring that aid be spent on education and health. There was, however, no mechanism to ensure compliance.

Meanwhile, in response to complaints by African politicians that relatively large amounts of multilateral aid flowed quickly into Asia, following the financial crisis of 1997, the IMF and World Bank have argued that their assistance to Asia reflects the greater significance of that region to the global financial system. Multilaterals' claims of African foot-dragging on economic liberalization ring hollow to critics who point out that countries such as Rwanda, Zimbabwe, and Ghana, presented as World Bank success stories in the 1980s and early 1990s, have not lived up to the promise. By 1997, the World Bank's *Development Report* was highlighting the decay of the African state, even though multilateral policies arguably contribute to this outcome through state-shrinking conditions that lead to neglect of education, erosion of infrastructure and institutional capacity, and rising unemployment, promoting informalization. This is likely to be the outcome of the contemporary U.S. Congress's Africa Trade Bill, unofficially termed "NAFTA for Africa." Although the aim of the bill is to liberalize trade and investment flows between the United

States and Africa, it comes with the usual conditions: reducing social spending, corporate taxes and agricultural subsidies, opening all sectors to foreign investment, emphasizing export crops over local production of staple foods, and privatization of public assets. Many African countries have chosen not to join the WTO, but this bill requires participating countries to join. It does not incorporate policies requested by the Africans: debt relief, sovereignty in determining economic and social policies, and financial compensation for historic exploitation of Africa.

Sources: French, 1998, p. A3; Hawkins, 1998, p. I; Herbert, 1998, p. A15; "How to Make Aid Work," 1999.

As noted in the development literature, conditions in sub-Saharan Africa are expected to deteriorate further, and some note that the reconstruction of Eastern Europe is drawing assistance monies away from the African continent. According to Brown and Tiffen, "Africa is being marginalised as never before, as the single European market, the American continental trade bloc and the Japanese Pacific Rim—the 'triad'—become the foci for capital investment and the target markets for the products of that investment." Over and above the neglect, there are the maturing industrial and biotechnological substitutes for tropical exports (such as sugar, rubber, oils, fish protein, and cocoa). Robert Schaeffer terms this scenario indifferent **imperialism**, where the wealthy countries "have so greatly increased their technological advantages that they do not *need* to exploit the whole world, just some of it."[56]

Informalization is one consequence of marginalization. Another is the loss of governmental legitimacy. In the kind of transition through which we are living, the erosion of national capacities expresses itself in the erosion of representative politics. No one votes for global management systems, yet, as governments undertake such managerial functions for the global economy, they compromise their sovereignty and their representative role, and their citizens lose faith—as we see in the following section.

Legitimacy Crisis

An increasingly pressing social impact of the globalization project is a growing **legitimacy crisis** of government. This means that citizens lose faith in their government or its policies. We have already seen that global managerialism generates new forms of governance—either multilateral regulation of government policies or surrogate "global" management by individual states themselves. Both of these new forms of governance pose problems for national governments in relation to their citizens, because both erode national sovereignty, and hence government legitimacy. Erosion takes many forms—from foreign ownership of essential national resources (banking and energy infrastructures), through the undoing of political coalitions formed around national development projects, to the dismantling of social services provided by governments to their needier populations. All these trends erode government capacity or social responsibility. With the disappearance of social protections, described in the following insert, the government's legitimacy becomes more fragile.

What Are Social Protections?

When capitalist economies came into being, they undid the tight-knit, sometimes oppressive, community relationships of the premarket society. Peasants, expelled from the land to work as wage laborers in the cities, found that they were in a fiercely competitive labor market and at the mercy of their employers. Over time, the new working classes banded together and fought for their right to organize in unions, and then they demanded the right to vote. Once able to exercise some power through the electoral systems, they were in a position to demand social rights— that is, entitlements to unemployment protection, health and welfare benefits, work safety laws, and other safeguards. They had the power to get their way in the early twentieth century because governments needed their loyalty for military and taxing purposes. Also, as industry grew, labor held increasing power with its threat of a strike. The politics of social protection is of course more complex than this, but it does involve these various kinds of economic, political, and social relationships. By the mid-twentieth century, the welfare state was quite well established, at least for a time.

Of course legitimacy problems are not the creation solely of the globalization project. They have profound historical roots, beginning with the disorganizing legacy of colonialism, carried into the postcolonial era when independent states struggled to develop coherent societies and economies in a global order dependent on sustaining natural resource exports to the First World. Military aid protected this order, and governments embracing the development project privileged urban-industrial sectors.

Development Project Legacies

Two ingredients of the development project typically compromised Third World states in their pursuit of modernity: the network of military alliances in the Cold War and the urban bias of economic growth strategies. In Africa, for example, *urban bias* channeled wealth away from the rural sector, inflating public works in the cities at the expense of the agricultural sector. While urban bias was common across the Third World, it was amplified in Africa by state patronage systems constructed during colonialism on the basis of artificial tribal hierarchies.[57] This structure of power facilitated the exploitation of rural areas by urban elites enriched by resource exploitation financed by foreign interests. For example, Kinshasa, the capital of Zaire, a "giant spider at the hub of a subcontinental web, acted as an 'overwhelming suction pump' absorbing all attainable rural resources as well as whatever might be milked from foreign donors and investors."[58] Citizens disengaged from the formal economy, pursuing activities such as hoarding, currency exchanging, smuggling, and bartering. Ghana's head of state, Jerry Rawlings, referred to the "culture of silence,"[59] and in the 1980s African scholar Fantu Cheru documented African states' weakened capacity to regulate and stimulate national economies under the pressures of the debt regime in *The Silent Revolution in Africa* (1989).

Militarization, through aid packages from the Cold War superpowers and through choices made by military or authoritarian regimes, diverted scarce funds from developmental programs. Between 1960 and 1987, military spending in the Third World rose almost three times as fast as in the First World, as the Third World more than doubled its share of global military spending—from 7 percent to 15 percent. Meanwhile, the Third World's share of global income stayed below 5 percent. In 1992, eighteen former Third World countries devoted more to military spending than to their education and health budgets, and eight of these were among the world's poorest nations.[60]

These spending decisions, however, reflect far more than simply the diversion of resources. The militarization of governments and societies carries vast consequences. Basic human rights and potential civil rights suffer in states whose regimes hold power through terror and intimidation of their subject populations. Legitimacy is always compromised in states that rule through coercion rather than consent. It is true that certain states like South Korea managed to establish some legitimacy by providing material benefits to the population while suppressing their political rights. Having North Korea as a neighbor, of course, helped, and this proximity explains why the Cold War was so critical to the implementation of the development project. If governments were balancing their developmental needs with security needs in a hostile world, then coercion (and military aid) was more readily justified.

Development and Democracy?

Even in circumstances where militarization compromised or slowed political development, the expectation was that economic growth eventually would lead to political democratization. This was the model held out to the Third World. But it was controversial, because many newly industrializing countries and middle-income states grew economically while their governments remained bureaucratic, authoritarian, and militaristic. The term **bureaucratic-authoritarian industrializing regimes (BAIRs)** was coined to describe this type of government.[61] The former prime minister of Singapore, Lee Kuan Yew, justified authoritarianism in his characteristic paternalist way: "I do not believe that democracy necessarily leads to development. I believe that what a country needs to develop is discipline more than democracy. The exuberance of democracy leads to indiscipline and disorderly conduct which are inimical to development."[62] Lee Kuan Yew may have meant that when different classes put conflicting demands on the state—industrial-capitalists seeking propitious business conditions, workers asking for higher wages, farmers requesting subsidies—the bureaucratic elites have less flexibility. In addition, a docile labor force is a strong incentive for foreign investment. Economic change and the restructuring of economic opportunity do alter a country's social structure, which in turn changes the balance of social and political forces.

South Korea is a case in point. It appeared to confirm the dictum that development does bring about democracy. During the 1980s, as it modernized on an expanding base of heavy industry, the South Korean state experienced a sequence of political challenges. The national economy was experiencing stress, as rising labor costs were affecting the competitiveness of South Korean export manufacturing. Powerful industrialists, a burgeoning middle class, and a mobilized working class all put pressure on the state to adjust the economic system to improve their respective conditions. Hagen Koo observed at the time:

> The capitalist class has grown too strong to be easily dominated by the state, and workers are not as docile and quiescent as they once were. At the same time the presence of a relatively large, well-educated middle class exerts pressure on the state for political democratization.[63]

In 1987, a political explosion occurred, as labor unrest and broad demonstrations directly challenged the paternalism of the South Korean
regime, starting a movement for greater democracy in the electoral system.[64] During this strike wave, Korean unions doubled their numbers and
consolidated the democratic labor movement, laying the foundations for
the new Korean Confederation of Trade Unions, formed in 1995. The
KCTU represents the new **social movement unionism**, based in new strategic global industries (versus traditional industrial areas dominated by
government unionism in the Third World), espousing a politics of grassroots organizing directed at authoritarian rule. In 1997, following Korea's
admission into the OECD, the KCTU struck powerfully against an
attempt by a conservative alliance of its powerful *chaebol* (global firms)
and the New Korea Party to strengthen the chaebols' and the state's hands
in restructuring the labor force to improve global competitiveness. Later
that year, the Asian financial crisis forced Korean labor into concessions,
but the democratic movement survives.[65]

The relationship between development and democracy is always complex, depending at a minimum on the mix of local conditions and the
global position of states and economic actors. The development project
was always infused with the expectation that development would lead to
democracy. As the globalization project takes shape, expressed in political-economic restructuring, declining state legitimacy *also* encourages
movements for democracy. The shrinking of the state can open space for
political activism as patronage systems lose their funds. It can also stimulate political upheaval when urban communities lose resources as their
states restructure. These complex relationships are illustrated in the following case study of Brazil.

CASE STUDY

Development, Class, and Democracy in Brazil

The relationship between development and democracy is often
mediated by class politics. Middle-income states (such as the
NICs) typically have substantial domestic economies and therefore quite mature industrial structures in which class politics
features centrally. These circumstances came together in Brazil.

The Brazilian economic "miracle" followed the 1964 military
coup, which had dismantled the previous government's development alliance. Although it encouraged foreign investment in the
auto and auto parts, electrical goods, and capital goods sectors,

the military junta squeezed wages, demobilized labor unions, and repressed political rights. The new working class that emerged in this private industrial sector erupted in the late 1970s, demanding improved wages and working conditions and forming a Workers Party, followed by a new national trade union organization. These workers were a different breed from the public-sector workers the junta had demobilized in the 1960s. The earlier workforce was politically incorporated into the state's development alliance; the new labor force had direct class concerns—for economic rights (improved working conditions) and political rights (to organize independently of the state). Also, these workers came from communities denied social resources by the dismantling of the development alliance. Labor activism included demands for community resources, known as *social-movement unionism*. These demands spread to other classes, and in the 1980s the military government was brought down by a broad new coalition of social forces demanding a democratized political system.

Gay Seidman's comparative study of Brazil and South Africa shows that in such industrializing middle-income countries, democratization requires specific conditions—primarily, a show of real power by the new industrial working class at a moment when there is conflict between industrialists and the state. In Brazil, relatively skilled labor forces had to deploy factory-based organizations to disrupt production before the state or large employers would consider extending them political rights or economic benefits. The opportune moment came when Brazilian industrialists found that the international business climate had moved against them, pushing them into a confrontation with industrial policy makers in the state. At that moment, in the 1970s and 1980s, labor had its way and established a new democratic beachhead.

Sources: Hewitt, 1992, pp. 86-89; Seidman, 1994, pp. 260-263.

The democratic impulse spread throughout the Second and Third Worlds in the 1980s, albeit unevenly. It was often based in relatively new industrial working classes. They tended to focus on their falling living standards; that is, they were not following a sequence of democratization on a wave of development. This was particularly true in Eastern Europe.

Mass resistance built on growing dissatisfaction throughout the Soviet bloc. The focus was on both the inability of the centrally planned regimes to raise living standards as they had promised and the continued repression of political rights. The Polish Solidarity movement began the challenge to the communist political system in the early 1980s. Indebted states submitted to the conditions of loans from the International Monetary Fund, but rather than saving these regimes, the conditions sank them. Privatization posed new problems because "the state could no longer compensate itself for its expenses out of the profits of enterprises" as it had done under the central planning system, and so it went deeper into debt, bringing ever-declining living conditions. These regimes had crumbled from within by the end of the decade.[66]

As citizenship demands have mushroomed in Eastern Europe, the instant markets promoted by the global managers encouraged Mafia-like activity, the formation of private militias, and self-enrichment for the former members of the party-states, as well as a general social disintegration. The tidy link between democracy and development no longer appears to hold in this region of the global economy. It seems that under a restructuring global system, the politics of economic change no longer follow a clear formula.

The collapse of the Second World coincided with the collapse of the Third World. This was a major threshold, marking the end of the development project and the simultaneous incorporation of all regions into the liberalizing thrust of the globalization project. This thrust came in the form of loan conditions laid down by the debt managers. It occurred in a period of heightened tensions. Across the former Second and Third Worlds, so-called *IMF riots*, described in the following case study, marked the end of the development era. These large-scale, sometimes coordinated urban uprisings protested the austerity measures of their governments, with the rioters often breaking into food banks to help themselves. Between 1976 and 1992, some 146 riots occurred in thirty-nine of the approximately eighty debtor countries (including Romania, Yugoslavia, Poland, and Hungary).[67]

CASE STUDY

The IMF Food Riots

Food riots, associated with the historic transition to market society, reemerged on a broad, global scale around the mid-1970s, coinciding with the erosion of the development project. The target of these uprisings was the continuing austerity measures meted out in Latin America, Eastern Europe, and Africa. Walton and Seddon define these austerity protests as "large-scale collective actions including political demonstrations, general strikes, and riots, which are animated by grievances over state policies of economic liberalization implemented in response to the debt crisis and market reforms urged by international agencies." The authors documented 146 incidents of protest between 1976 and 1992, noting that protests within each country were characteristically well-organized movements that spread simultaneously across several urban centers.

These austerity protests addressed the unequal distribution of the means of livelihood, targeting policies that eroded urban dwellers' social supports. The collapsing social supports included a range of subsidized items or services necessary to members of hyper-urbanized environments, including food, health care, education, transportation, housing, and others. The supports were the elements of the social pact made between the developmentalist state and its urban population during the period of industrialization by way of import substitution; the services were to be delivered in return for the people's political loyalty.

The *classical* food riot, which signaled the destabilization of traditional food markets during the transition from customary to market society, occurred during the era of European state-building in the eighteenth and nineteenth centuries. By contrast, the *contemporary* food riot signals a new transition, occurring across a world experiencing the hollowing-out of the national economic project. The conception of the public household—a state-underwritten program of public welfare—arose in the First World as states replaced communities. This conception also shaped Second and Third World state policies as these governments supervised national economic development. It is now undergoing a dramatic reversal as structural adjustment policies universally enforce austerity. The consequences are more drastic outside the First World, where social security nets are thinner. Austerity protests seek to restore lost social rights within the national project. At the same time, they bear witness to and in some cases identify global restructuring as the driving force behind the shrinking of the public household.

Source: Walton & Seddon, 1994.

FIGURE 6.2

Locations of Riots Against Austerity Programs

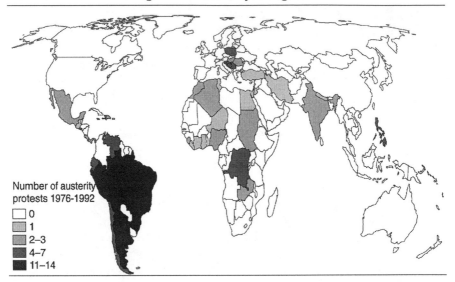

Number of austerity protests 1976-1992
- ☐ 0
- 1
- 2–3
- 4–7
- 11–14

SOURCE: Walton and Seddon, 1994.

The IMF riots symbolized the link made by protesters between IMF conditions and the loss of capacity and legitimacy of governments, especially as "developers." One scholar has observed that the logic of the structural adjustment program "is to further weaken the motivation of the state to respond to the popular demands that have been built into the process of postcolonial state formation."[68] The protests were not simply indicators of a linear decline in states' power; they also were a recognition of the restructuring of states according to reformist criteria imposed and adopted by the global managers. This restructuring exacerbated the sense of a declining government legitimacy.

Political Reforms

Political reform is a key element of structural adjustment. This prescription was articulated in the World Bank's influential report in 1989, *Sub-Saharan Africa From Crisis to Sustainable Growth* "Africa needs not just less government but better government—government that concentrates its efforts less on direct [economic] interventions and more on enabling others to be productive."[69] The goal was to encourage liberal democracy to replace the one-party state, in conjunction with releasing entrepreneurial forces at all levels of society. This is the political side of the globalization project. This view, of course, was dominant in the development establishment in the 1980s. Subsequently, the World Bank discovered the importance of the strong, development state as the secret of the East Asian "miracle" and titled its World Development Report for 1997 *The State in a Changing World*.[70] In that report, the decaying African state was identified as a problem given the Asian experience. Of course, Africa is not Asia, and development discourse routinely forgets that cultural and historical circumstances make a world of difference, so to speak. East Asian development states, for one thing, rested on a reciprocal authoritarianism, embedded in the norms of Confucianism, that sustained capitalist development in this strategic region. African geopolitics and historical cultures differ markedly.

African states inherited complex power structures from the colonial experience. European colonization combined forms of urban power directly excluding natives from civil freedoms on racial grounds, with forms of rule in the countryside via a reconstruction of tribal authority in order to rule natives indirectly. With decolonization, independence abolished racial discrimination and affirmed civil freedoms, but it also divided power within the new nation-states according to the artificial tribal constructs (ethnic, religious, regional) established during colonial rule.[71] The vulnerability of African politics stems from inheriting a centralized state and its patronage networks (common to all states), as well as a "tribalization" of politics—which we have seen reassert itself with a vengeance in the 1990s.

When African governments were compelled to shrink the state, under the dictates of the global managers, the growing scarcity of resources became the pivot on which ethnicized political conflict turned. This is not to say that beneath the veneer of the African nation-state lies a primordial tribalism, which is how the tragedy of African politics is often presented. It is to say, however, that the historical legacy has segmented African states in tribal terms, sometimes by invention. When resources disappear, contestants exploit ethnicity because preexisting social and political hierarchies are structured in ethnic terms. In this way, ethnic identity organizes political conflict and undermines a politics of inclusion that is associated with Western liberal democracy, as the following case study suggests.

CASE STUDY

Identity Politics and the Fracturing and Underdevelopment of Nigeria

Nigeria, with more than 250 ethnic groups, has three dominant ethnicities—the Hausa-Fulani, the Yoruba, and the Ibo—each of which has quite distinct political practices. The Hausa-Fulani, in the north, have roots in autocratic, bureaucratic, and hierarchical precolonial states; the Yoruba, in the west, have a tradition of loose confederation among centralized kingdoms where monarchs were elected by, and shared power with, a council of chiefs; and the Ibo, in the south, practiced decentralized and egalitarian forms of social organization. In short, not only is cultural and political unity within the nation-state compromised by inter-ethnic competition, but in addition the political values brought to the table are often irreconcilable, to the extent that a politics of ethnic identity governs negotiations. Related to these historically constructed fracture lines is an elemental division of Nigeria into a Muslim north and a Christian south, exacerbated by the exploitation of the south's oil resources by the north, where oil rents have financed a string of corrupt generals since Nigeria's independence in 1960. Per capita income is now one-quarter of what it was in the 1980s. These generals have not reinvested profits in the Niger Delta (population of 7 million) on the grounds that a developing south could attempt to secede, like the then-Republic of Biafra did in 1967. In an internationally condemned incident in 1995, when Nigerian writer Ken Saro-Wiwa protested southern underdevelopment, linking it to exploitation by the northern-dominated government and foreign oil interests, and demanding compensation for the region and his Ogoni people, he was executed by the regime. Mobil, Shell, Texaco, Chevron, and other Western oil companies extract oil from the Delta, and, for example, Chevron's worldwide revenues of $30.6 billion in 1998 matched Nigeria's GNP of $30.7 billion (one of Africa's biggest) in 1997. Mobil, Shell, and Chevron, at least, now play a de facto government role in the absence of state investment. Local movements demanding compensation from these firms have managed to involve them in financing basic forms of community development such as running water, electricity, hospitals, and roads.

Sources: Sandbrook, 1995, pp. 93-94; Onishi, 1998, pp. A1, A6; Roger Cohen, 1998, p. A1; Onishi, 1999, pp. 28-29.

The stereotypical African one-party state arose out of the difficulties in securing power in, and administering, nation-states with artificial political boundaries drawn up in the Berlin Conference of 1885, and then reaffirmed in 1963 by the **Organization of African Unity** (OAU). At that time, early "African socialist" Presidents Léopold Senghor (Senegal) and Julius Nyrere (Tanzania) argued that the Western multiparty system would be ethnically divisive and inappropriate to the consensual African context, which lacked Western class divisions. Nyrere's attempt to base Tanzanian socialism on a collectivist ethic of self-reliant development at the village level (*ujaama*) overreached itself in rural resettlement and underestimated the corrosive individualism of agricultural modernization. The fate of this one-party state was different from that of the Western-oriented states that had no such rural-community based vision, and ruled by force.[72]

Uganda's Museveni, who took power at the end of decades of bloody civil war in 1986, "for many years succeeded in defying international pressure that makes aid contingent on democratization efforts."[73] Reportedly, he also rejected multiparty systems, viewing them as products of Western industrial societies with fluid class divisions, while African societies are divided vertically, along fixed tribal lines. He argued that a multiparty system may, therefore, divide along tribal lines, leading to ethnic conflict. Museveni's solution, of "national resistance councils," organized locally to bring local concerns into the national arena, was viewed by critics as a one-party state by another name.[74] In fact, the one-party state with its rule through patronage degenerated in the lost decade of the 1980s into what is termed "**predatory rule**," where the state becomes informalized and power is personalized in a dictatorship built on systematic extraction of resources from the society for enrichment of the ruler. President Mobutu, of Zaire (now the Congo), was the archetypal predatory ruler, amassing $4 billion (the equivalent of Zaire's foreign debt at the time) in foreign bank accounts.[75] Mobutu was overthrown in 1996 by a Zairian Tutsi rebellion led by Laurent Kabila, supported by surrounding states of Rwanda, Uganda, and Angola, among others.

As the twenty-first century arrived, sub-Saharan African states experienced destabilizing forces from within and without. From *within*, as economic conditions deteriorated with little relief from structural adjustment, democratizing trends spread, drawing inspiration and example from the collapse of the Eastern European one-party states and responding to governance pressures from the global managers. With the demise of one-party rule and in the context of declining economic opportunity, however, democratizing trends are complicated by internal conflict along protective ethnic lines. These lines often become the pretext for and vehicle of civil wars and ethnicized struggles for control over national resources—as evidenced in the implosion of Rwanda and Somalia and the breakup of Ethiopia in the mid-1990s.

From *without*, African states have broken with their initial (OAU) non-interference agreement and entered into a pattern of intervention in neighboring states. Conflicts between the Tutsi and Hutu groups in Rwanda escalated with the intervention of Uganda on the side of the former ethnic group in 1994. In 1996, Rwanda, Uganda, and Angola intervened in Zaire, which became the Congo; in 1997, Angola participated in a civil war in the Republic of Congo; and Ethiopia, Eritrea, and Uganda have assisted rebels in the Sudan fighting a civil war against the Islamic regime. Congo was again the site of intervention from six neighboring states at the turn of the century, with President Kabila allied with Zimbabwe, Angola, Namibia, and Chad, against eastern rebels supported by Uganda and Rwanda.[76] African scholar Basil Davidson refers to Zaire/Congo as a myth created originally at King Leopold of Belgium's convenience, and then, at independence in 1960, under Mobutu: "outside its coercions and corruptions the country was left to survive as it might, or else to rot."[77] The point is that there are substantial indications that African boundaries are no longer sacred, and that intervention in states like Congo, with its wealth of natural resources and its implications for geopolitical security, may be drawing Africa into an extended military contest over boundaries.

These instances suggest that sub-Saharan Africa struggles with enormous dilemmas, in which economic adjustment often fans social and geopolitical divisions over dwindling resources. The divisions often express themselves in ethnic conflict, supported from outside, as economies stagnate and political reforms destabilize one-party states. Spreading civil war signals the inability of some states to maintain any internal authority, especially in a world where global forces are now considerably more selective. The characteristic export dependency of many African states handicaps their ability to maneuver in a technologically changing world economy. The legitimacy crises of these states have deep roots.

One dramatic manifestation of the loss of political cohesion of some African states is an exploding refugee population. The United Nations makes a distinction between "international refugees" and "internally displaced persons." The latter category, generated through ethnopolitical conflict (such as that in Somalia, Rwanda, Sudan, and Liberia), soared in sub-Saharan Africa in the late 1980s and early 1990s, affecting about 16 million, or 60 percent of the world total of displaced persons. In addition, there are more than 6 million international refugees out of a total regional population of 600 million. Africa now leads the world in both categories.[78]

Loss of cohesion is not confined to Africa, however. On a world scale, the number of international refugees mushroomed from 10.5 million in 1984 to close to 23 million in 1994, in addition to the 26 million internally displaced persons—from places as far apart as Bosnia and Burma, Iraq and Sri Lanka.[79] Although economic and political power has been centralizing in the hands of transnational institutions, military power has remained at the state level—whether held as a monopoly of the state itself or subdivided between warring factions within the state.

With these destabilizing movements, further global governance mechanisms have come into play. The United Nations is assuming an expanding role in policing the world. Policing the world has an air of recolonization about it. In 1993, U.S. Marines landed in Somalia. In the absence of a functioning government, they were uninvited, but the U.N. Security Council approved the action on humanitarian grounds, in order to stem the destruction of civil war. This reappearance of "trusteeship," historically associated with colonialism, generated a provocative observation by Paul Johnson, a U.S. historian:

> We are witnessing today a revival of colonialism, albeit in a new form. It is a trend that should be encouraged, it seems to me, on practical as well as moral grounds. There simply is no alternative in nations where governments have crumbled and the most basic conditions for civilized life have disappeared, as is now the case in a great many third-world countries. . . . The appeals for help come not so much from Africa's political elites, who are anxious to cling to the trappings of power, as from ordinary, desperate citizens, who carry the burden of misrule.[80]

In 1999, the Balkans conflict, culminating in the massive "ethnic cleansing" by Serbs of Kosovian Albanians, saw NATO take matters into its own hands (without consulting the U.N. Security Council) and organize a bombing intervention against Serbian leader President Milosevic on the grounds of human rights protection. In the absence of using the same interventionist logic on behalf of the Kurds in Turkey, the East Timorese in Indonesia, and the Tibetans in China, critics argue the Kosovian conflict was a threshold in constructing the discourse and military actions underlying a new world order. In this order, "human rights imperialism" is deployed to bring rogue states under control, or to assert geopolitical power in specific regions, such as Yugoslavia, one of the few remaining spheres of influence of Russia.[81]

Financial Crisis

In a world in which US$2 trillion circulates daily, the total value of financial transactions is double that of production, and 97.5 percent of foreign exchange transactions are speculative, it is not surprising that financial crisis has become part of the landscape.[82] One could almost say that management of financial crisis has become routine, but its gravity outweighs its frequency. The debt regime of the 1980s was a series of multilaterally organized bailouts of banks as a result of a crisis of *government borrowing* in the then Second and Third Worlds. The structural adjustment of scores of states was to be a proving ground for crisis management on a broad scale. In the 1990s, debt crises were triggered by *private borrowing* via capital account liberalization, which encouraged closer financial integration of money markets. The Mexican (1994) and Asian (1997) crises revealed the instability of short-term lending from portfolio investors looking to profit from the ebullience associated with NAFTA and the East Asian miracle, respectively. In each case, the attraction of funds *followed* financial liberalization.

The recent Asian crisis "marks the unraveling of a model of development," of "fast-track capitalism." Walden Bello observes:

> This model was one of high-speed growth fuelled, not principally by domestic savings and investment, as in the case of Taiwan and Korea, the classical NICs or newly industrializing countries, but mainly by huge infusions of foreign capital. The mechanism to achieve this was to liberalize the capital account as fully as possible, achieving very considerable interaction between the domestic financial market and global financial markets. The illusion that propelled the advocates of this model was that countries could . . . leapfrog the normally long arduous course to advanced country status simply by maximizing their access to foreign capital inflows.[83]

In the Asian case, fast-track capitalism worked for a time because of the stabilizing effect of massive inflows of Japanese capital into the region, following yen revaluation in 1985, and a demonstration effect, attracting capital from the regional NICs, the United States, and Australia. By the 1990s, structural changes in global markets (privatization, financial liberalization, economic integration) encouraged institutional investors to target the Southeast Asian markets and their high interest rates as sources of quick yields on huge savings, pension, mutual, government, and corporate funds that they managed. The tolerance shown by the Bretton Woods institutions toward the accelerating foreign debt was, arguably, because it was privately financed.

As soon as currencies tumbled late in 1997, the IMF stepped in, as in Mexico, because the crisis implicated broad segments of the G-7 citizenry's savings. Again, the crisis was managed to recover the debt of the banks and institutional investors. In likening the Asian crisis to the Mexican crisis, neoliberal economist Jeffrey Sachs observed: "The IMF didn't really understand the Mexican crisis, and treated it incorrectly as a typical case of a profligate government rather than a crisis in the private capital markets."[84] This perhaps obscures a deeper reality: the role of vulnerable states (with weakened currencies) in absorbing the crisis.

CASE STUDY

Indonesian Democratization as a Condition of the Globalization Project

Restructuring may unmask patronage in development states, releasing democratic forces. For instance, at the turn of the twenty-first century the Indonesian state experienced a dramatic democratization as a mass movement successfully challenged the military regime and its equation of development with privatization and cronyism. This seismic shift in the domestic balance of political forces expressed the development crisis. First, structural adjustment intensified cronyism, as an estimated 80 percent of privatization contracts went to the president's children or friends. Second, the 1997 Asian regional financial crisis brought IMF reforms, challenging President Suharto's patronage networks, along with a drastic reduction in living standards, as the rupiah (national currency) lost three-quarters of its value. This episode suggests that the power negotiation between state and global managers has unintended consequences. It may be that the IMF gained more power to shape Indonesian economic policy, through debt restructuring over time. As the IMF actually admitted, however, its role in the negotiations may have worsened the financial crisis because speculators' fears—of the IMF withholding funds, and of domestic social instability—undermined the value of the rupiah. A political countermovement resulted, ending the military regime. This episode also revealed that global (financial) integration is unstable because it is politically negotiated. Changing balances of political forces affect stability and perceptions of stability when currency traders conduct a continual global plebiscite on national policies. They do this in real time, so the possibility of financial crisis is ever present.

Sources: Erlanger, 1998, p. A9; Sanger, 1998b, pp. A1, D11.

By integrating money markets, financial liberalization rendered the global financial system more vulnerable to financial/currency speculation. In the Asian case, states allowed their currencies to float with the dollar as a device to attract foreign capital but exercised no control over the disposition of the capital inflow, which found its way into property development, real estate schemes, tourism, golf courses, speculative mergers, and intensified natural resource extraction.[85] The increasing fragility of Southeast Asian debt eventually unnerved the currency traders, whose subsequent massive currency sales precipitated a rapid withdrawal of capital by global investors.

The IMF-supervised devaluation of Asian currencies, in the name of financial orthodoxy, shifted the burden of capital loss onto the citizens of the adjusted states, who experienced a dramatic reversal of living standards as a consequence of financial transactions and speculations against their national currency for which they were not responsible. On June 17, 1998, the World Bank vice-president for the Asia Pacific, Jean-Michel Severino, observed:

> The first point is to say that this depression is unavoidable. Since the beginning of this crisis, about $115 billion have fled out of the five major crisis countries—Korea, Thailand, Indonesia, Malaysia, Philippines. This is about 10 percent of the GDP of these countries. In addition to that, banking credits have also been reduced by about $88 billion, which is approximately another 8 percent of the GDP. It means that about 18 percent of the GDP of these countries has just vanished.[86]

The larger point is that while all states surrender power to unregulated global financial markets, some states must pay for the casino-like movement of short-term funds among national markets in search of quick profits. Market rule, via financial liberalization, obscures power relations in the "currency pyramid," where some currencies (e.g., the U.S. dollar) are more equal than others.[87] Further, the notion of national responsibility for sound currencies is contradicted or undermined by unregulated currency speculation, but then invoked in crisis management. Of course, such a global "protection racket" is not foolproof, and it is clear that even establishment voices acknowledge the risks of this operation. Thus, Jeffrey Sachs, a proponent of free-market "shock treatment" in post–Cold War Eastern Europe, commented on the IMF's Asian bailout:

> The IMF deepened the sense of panic not only because of its dire public pronouncements, but also because its proposed medicine—high interest rates, budget cuts, and immediate bank closures—convinced the markets that Asia indeed was about to enter a severe contraction (as had happened ear-

lier in Argentina, Bulgaria, and Mexico). Instead of dousing the fire, the IMF in effect screamed fire in the theatre.[88]

Former U.S. Secretary of State George Shultz former U.S. Secretary of the Treasury William Simon, and former Citicorp Chairman Walter Wriston, in an article titled "Who Needs the IMF?," observed somewhat self-servingly:

> IMF-prescribed tax increases and austerity will cause pain for the people of these nations, producing a backlash against the West. There is a conspiracy to beat down Asian asset values in order to provide bargains and control for Western investors. . . . The IMF interferes with this fundamental market mechanism by encouraging investors to seek out risky markets on the assumption that if their investments turn sour, they still stand a good chance of getting their money back through IMF bailouts. This kind of interference will only encourage more crises.[89]

Market rule is imposed through the financial markets, via structural adjustment conditions, and the internal management of national macroeconomic policy under IMF "trusteeship." Jeffrey Sachs observed:

> Not unlike the days when the British Empire placed senior officials directly into the Egyptian and Ottoman finance ministries, the IMF is insinuated into the inner sanctums of nearly 75 developing-country governments around the world—countries with a combined population of some 1.4 billion. These governments rarely move without consulting the IMF staff, and when they do, they risk their lifelines to capital markets, foreign aid, and international respectability.[90]

CASE STUDY

South Korea in Crisis: Running Down the Showcase

The crisis of the South Korean "miracle" is perhaps the marker of the "new world order." In the development era, South Korea was the showcase of successful development. Then, during the 1980s, South Korea was the subject of World Bank shifts of perspective on the question of managed capitalism versus free market policies. By the 1990s the Bank was presenting Korea as a successful case of managed capitalism, but in 1995, South Korea entered into a "Faustian bargain" with the United States, in which it accepted wholesale liberalization of its financial institutions in exchange for membership in the OECD. When the crisis hit Korea in 1997, official rhetoric about its origins in "crony capitalism" exploded the Korean model once and for all. In fact, in the post–Cold War/Third World era, there is no more need for a showcase of development. The severe adjustment of South Korea left the Koreans stunned—particularly given their recent admission to the OECD (cf. Mexico's admission in 1994, prior to the peso collapse), which conferred upon them First World status. The moral of the story is that market rule (i.e., crisis management) appears to take no prisoners. South Korea is no longer so much an example of successful development as it was *made example of*, through adjustment, in order to manage the global financial crisis.

Sources: Evans, 1995; Grosfoguel, 1996; Amsden & Euh, 1997.

Summary

The globalization project has many social and political consequences and implications for the future of the world. We have examined just four phenomena: the bifurcation of global labor, informalization, the legitimacy crisis of state organizations, and financial instability. None of these is unique to the global project. They have all appeared in previous eras, but possibly not on the scale found today. They are linked; indeed, they are mutually conditioning processes, being four dimensions of a single process of global restructuring affecting all states, although with local variation.

As the world market becomes more consequential, competition among firms heats up. It takes the form of technical upgrading, movement to cheaper labor zones, and constant product innovation. All three competitive strategies, in an era of lean production, undermine the stability of labor markets. Labor redundancy rises. This, in combination with the growing international migration of labor forces, generates political intolerance where ethnic hierarchies (constructed historically) are used to fuel tensions between culturally different labor forces. In this way, labor is even more divided and distracted from addressing the root cause of its insecurity: global restructuring. Labor organization on a world scale is still very much in its infancy, partly because of the divisive role of ethnic politics, and partly because of fast-changing market and working conditions.

The technological shedding of labor and the downsizing and stagnation produced by structural adjustment programs extend informalization. Indeed, the institution of wage labor is undergoing substantial change across the world. Not only is wage employment contracting, but wage labor is also displaying a *casualizing* trend, where jobs become part-time and impermanent. The strategies of flexibility embraced by firms contribute to this informalization as much as does the growing surplus of populations severed from their land and livelihood. Some observers see in informalization a counter-movement to the official economy and to state regulation—the new commons. Whether informalization is the source of future alternatives to the formal market economy, there is no doubt that it is the site of a diverse array of livelihood strategies, some of which are embedded in community or personal relations.

State legitimacy crisis is substantial under the globalization project because of the relative indifference or incapacity of states in a market regime to resolve the breakdown of social institutions. The breakdown marks the crossing of a threshold from the national-development era to a new era in which international competition and global efficiency increasingly govern, and privatize, national policy and growth strategies. In such a breakdown there are signs of a renewal, as people across the world push for democratic participation. Movements for democracy have emerged in the moment at which already overextended states, sometimes riddled with unproductive cronyism, are under pressure to end the pretense of development and repay the debts built up over two decades of development financing. This is exacerbated by the recent recurrence of financial crisis, from Mexico, to Asia, to Brazil, and to Russia. The emperor really doesn't have on any clothes, and disillusioned citizens, repressed workers, and neglected rural communities have demanded the opening of their political systems. This demand coincides with the reorganization of states as surrogate global managers. It also coincides with the growing realization by the global managers themselves that the suppositions of financial orthodoxy no longer can be taken for granted, leading to an unusually urgent "soul searching" by the financial and political elites regarding the rule of the market as the twenty-first century dawned. This chapter has suggested that the globalization project amplifies the contradictory features of developmentalism on the national and the global scale.

PART IV

Rethinking Development

7

The Globalization Project
and Its Counter-movements

The globalization project is a relatively coherent perspective and has a powerful set of agencies working on its behalf, but its discourse and the process of instituting its rules are in continuous contention. Like the development project, the globalization project is an attempt to fashion the world around a central principle through powerful political and financial institutions. Because the principle of market rule is framed in the liberal discourse of freedom, its power depends significantly on consent.

Counter-movements are not simply coincidental alternatives to the globalization project and its market regime. They *constitute* it because they express the material and discursive conditions that its corporate agents actively seek to appropriate. For example, the global managers and the biotechnology corporations impose a singular and abstracted logic on a culturally, ecologically, and politically diverse world. Thus, seed patenting reduces biodiversity to monoculture under the guise of addressing the world's food needs, and the concept of comparative advantage presents itself as an efficient allocation of global resources and benefits based on ecological and cultural endowments, but it is in reality a corporate, rather than a geographical, property. In other words, the discourse and practices of the market regime assert and manage globalization as the path to prosperity and, in doing so, limit cultural diversity, small producer and consumer rights, and biodiversity as alternative forms of sustainable development.

Most governments feel pressure to play by the new and emerging global rules, but their citizens do not always share their outlook. Where global restructuring weakens nation-states (by eroding their public welfare function, increasing social and regional polarization, and reducing state patronage systems), citizens have fresh opportunities to renew the political process. This chapter surveys some of these counter-movements, exploring their origins and goals and highlighting the range of opposition. Examining each movement offers a particular angle on the dilemmas associated with reformulating development in the globalization project. Although the various counter-movements have emerged in different ways and places and at different overlapping times, there is a sense in which they converge. This may be represented as an escalating tension between global (or universal) and local (or particular) understandings of how humanity should proceed as the globalization project subsumes the development project. We consider the following social counter-movements and assess their impact in the development debate: fundamentalism, environmentalism, **feminism**, human rights, and **cosmopolitan localism**.

Fundamentalism

Fundamentalism usually expresses a desire to return to the simplicity and security of traditional codes of behavior, but it is never quite so simple. First, who decides what is traditional? There may be sacred texts, but they are open to interpretation, and fundamentalist movements are usually split by factional differences and power struggles. Second, what are the conditions in which fundamentalism comes to the fore? These conditions are likely to shape the leadership and the interpretation of tradition. In the United States at present, the broad-based fundamentalism espousing family values, among other things, can be understood only in the context of a significant decline in the proportion of the population that is actually a part of the traditional nuclear family structure. Even then, the nuclear family is not exactly traditional; the extended family is the more traditional structure. What may be traditional is the unquestioned power of the family patriarch.

In uncertain times, fundamentalism often moves to the front burner. People gravitate to fundamentalism for protection and security. We have seen a variant of this in the rising use of ethnic politics as competition for jobs grows while the economy shrinks. Nothing is absolute or definite about the content of fundamentalism or about the elevation of ethnic identity as a way of drawing boundaries between people. The interpretation of ethnicity is quite plastic and depends very much on the historical and social context in which people reconstruct ethnic divisions. Nevertheless, in an increasingly confused and uncertain world, the presumed essentialism of ethnic identity either comforts people or allows them to identify scapegoats. The current challenge to affirmative action in the United States represents one such reaction. In whatever form, fundamentalist politics has become a powerful weapon for mobilizing people as the political and class coalitions of the development era crumble.

The Iranian case discussed in Chapter 5 illustrates religious fundamentalism presented as a cultural alternative to developmentalism. It also shows how developmentalism, whether based in oil wealth or not, fuels fundamentalist opposition in overcrowded cities. In Turkey, for example, Istanbul's population has doubled every fifteen years. When the modern Turkish Republic was created in 1923, only 15 percent of its population of 13 million was urban. Now two-thirds of Turkey's 60 million people live in urban areas. These city dwellers offer fertile ground for an Islamic revival challenging Kemalism, the secular, developmentalist politics associated with the founder of the early-twentieth-century Turkish republic, Kemal Ataturk.[1] Anti-Westernism challenges global developmentalism and will be a major fracture line in the future.

In Egypt, a legitimacy crisis stemming from economic stagnation and political corruption in the government has emboldened Islamic fundamentalism. Its ranks have expanded among the urban poor, partly because Islam offers community and basic services in the midst of the disorder of huge, sprawling cities such as Cairo. Fundamentalists have mounted a cultural offensive against Egyptian secular institutions (education, media, courts, and the arts). In 1994, a fundamentalist member of the Egyptian parliament, Galal Gharib, accused the minister of culture, Fariq Husni, of promoting Western pornography to "demolish Islamic religious and moral values." He condemned specifically a Gustav Klimt painting of Adam and Eve, an Egyptian adaptation of a Bertolt Brecht play, and government sponsorship of ballet schools, movie festivals, and translations of foreign literature. In southern Egypt's public schools, fundamentalist teachers reimpose the veil on girls as young as six and revise schoolbooks to emphasize Islamic teachings. They argue that secularization has suppressed Egypt's deep Islamic and Arab roots in the pursuit of a communion with Western culture.[2]

Opposition to the cultural implications of development is perhaps amplified by the terms of the globalization project. India, a leader of the Non-Aligned Movement, was perhaps the last significant holdout among former Third World states against IMF-style economic liberalization. In 1991, the Indian Finance Ministry acceded to the borrowing conditions set out by the International Monetary Fund, and India joined the "structural adjustment" club. Right-wing Hindu groups, once advocates of economic liberalism, then organized a "Buy Indian" campaign against imports and the efforts to "globalize" the Indian economy on the part of Prime Minister P. V. Narasimha Rao. The Swadeshi Jagran Manch (SJM), an organization promoted by a Hindu revivalist group (Rashtriya Swayamsewak Sangh), urges Indians to boycott foreign-made goods such as toothpaste, shaving cream, soaps, detergents, cosmetics, soft drinks, paint, canned food, and even crayons. The convener of the SJM, S. Gurmurthy, wore homespun cotton clothes to invoke the economic nationalism of India's beloved anticolonial leader Mahatma Gandhi. Gurmurthy declared:

> We want to create a nationalist feeling that every nation has to evolve a mind of its own in economics. The integration of India with the rest of the world will be restricted to just one percent of our population. . . . A nation should largely live within its means and produce for its own market with trans-country commerce restricted to its needs.[3]

In sum, the fundamentalist movements springing up around the world have two main features. First, they articulate the uncertainties and distress brought about by the social decay that populations experience as a result of the limits of developmentalism and the increasing selectivity of globalization. Second, they often take the form of a nationalist resurgence against perceived threats to their culture. The combination frequently involves contesting the universalist assumptions of global development along with presenting alternative ways of organizing social life on a national or local level.

Environmentalism

Environmentalism as a counter-movement involves questioning modern assumptions that nature and its bounty are infinite. It has two main strands. One derives from growing environmental awareness in the West, initially inspired by the publication of Rachel Carson's *Silent Spring* in 1962. This path-breaking book documented the disruption in the earth's ecosystems that was being caused by modern economic practices such as the use of agricultural chemicals. Its title refers to the absence of bird songs in the spring. Carson's metaphor dramatized the dependence of life on sustainable ecological systems. It also emphasized the shortcomings of Western rationalism insofar as it perceives nature as "external" to society. This perception encourages the belief that nature is an infinitely exploitable domain.[4]

A range of "green" movements has mushroomed throughout the First World as the simple truths revealed by Carson's study have gained an audience. First World "greens" typically challenge the assumptions and practices of unbridled economic growth, arguing for scaling back to a renewable economic system of resource use. One of their foci is agricultural sustainability—that is, reversing the environmental stress associated with capital- and chemical-intensive agriculture. A key goal is maintaining a natural aesthetic to complement the consumer lifestyle, the emphasis being on preserving human health on one hand and enhancing leisure activities on the other.

The second strand of environmentalism appears in active movements to protect particular bioregions from environmentally damaging practices. Across the world, rural populations depend greatly on the viability of regional ecologies for their livelihood. Such movements are therefore often distinguished by their attempts to protect existing cultural practices. In contrast to First World environmentalism, which attempts to regulate the environmental implications of the market economy, Southern environmentalism questions the benefits of market forces. This is especially true where states and firms seek to "monetize" and harvest natural resources on which human communities depend.

Local communities have always challenged environmentally damaging practices where natural conservation is integral to local culture. Opposition has run from the protests of eighteenth-century English peasants at the enclosure of the commons, through the resistance of nineteenth-century Native Americans to the takeover of their lands and the elimination of the buffalo, to Indian struggles against British colonial forestry practices.

In the late twentieth century, forest-dwellers across the tropics grabbed the world's attention as they attempted to preserve tropical rain forests from the extensive timber cutting associated with commercial logging. Timbering and the pasturing of beef cattle in degraded forest areas intensified with the agro-export boom of the 1980s, spawning Southern environmentalism. Demands for First World–style environmental regulation gathered momentum as a means of addressing environmental stresses from overuse of natural resources associated with the green revolution, which had resulted in desertification, excessive water salinity, and chemical contamination.

The common denominator of most environmental movements is the belief that natural resources are not infinitely renewable. The finiteness of nature has been a global preoccupation, from the neo-Malthusian specter of population growth overwhelming available supplies of land and the food grown on it to anxiety about the dwindling supplies of raw materials, such as fossil fuels and timber, that sustain modern economies.

Lately, however, this rather linear perspective has yielded to a more dynamic one that sees a serious threat to essential natural elements such as the atmosphere, climates, and biodiversity. Trees may be renewable through replanting schemes, but the atmospheric conditions that nurture them may not be so easily replenished. As Paul Harrison implies, the world has moved to a new threshold of risk to its sustainability:

It used to be feared that we would run out of non-renewable resources—
things like oil, or gold. Yet these, it seems, are the ones we need worry least
about. It is the renewables—the ones we thought would last forever—that
are being destroyed at an accelerating rate. They are all living things, or
dynamic parts of living ecosystems.[5]

Furthermore, the very survival of the human species is increasingly at risk
as pollution and environmental degradation lead to public health epi-
demics. These include lead poisoning, new strains of cancer, cataracts
from ozone destruction, immune suppression by ultraviolet radiation,
and loss of genetic and biological resources for producing food and medicines.[6]

Destruction of renewable resources is understood increasingly as
undermining the sustainability of formal economic activity. Although a
tree plantation may provide timber products, it cannot perform the regen-
erative function that natural systems perform because it is a monoculture
and lacks natural diversity. Robert Repetto of the World Resources Institute articulated the shortcomings of conventional economic notions of
value:

> Under the current system of national accounting, a country could exhaust
> its mineral resources, cut down its forests, erode its soils, pollute its aqui-
> fers, and hunt its wildlife and fisheries to extinction, but measured income
> would not be affected as these assets disappeared. . . . [The] difference in the
> treatment of natural resources and other tangible assets confuse the deple-
> tion of valuable assets with the generation of income. . . . The result can be
> illusory gains in income and permanent losses in wealth.[7]

As a consequence of the appreciation of "nature's services," a form of
ecological accounting is emerging. For example, it was recently estimated
that the economic value of the world's ecosystem services is currently
around $33 trillion a year, exceeding the global GNP of $25 trillion.
Whether or not it is appropriate to value nature in this way, this trend is an
antidote to traditional economics reasoning that externalizes environmental impact.[8]

The change in thinking has been stimulated from several quarters. In
the first place, there are the **new social movements** (conceptualized in
the following insert), some of which are the subject of this chapter.
Their appearance on the historical stage reflects the demise of developmentalism and the search for new directions of social and political
action.[9]

What Are the New Social Movements?

The new social movements, such as the greens, feminism, participatory action research, and grassroots or *basismo* politics, share criticism of developmentalism. Where developmentalism advocates state economic management (of national/global dimensions), the new movements tend to reject centralism and stress community empowerment instead. Where developmentalism emphasizes industrialism and material abundance, the new movements tend to seek post- or preindustrial values of decentralization, flexibility, and simplicity; and where developmentalism champions state and market institutions, the new social movements seek grassroots autonomy and the reassertion of cultural values over those of the market. In short, the new social movements are distinguished by their expressive politics and their challenge to the economism and instrumental politics of the "developed society" model. They have grown as the institutions of the welfare state (including labor organizations) have receded, and they contribute to the declining legitimacy of developmentalism and its new vehicle, globalism.

Sources: Buttel, 1992; Lehman, 1990.

The second indication of a change in thinking is a growing awareness of the limits of "spaceship earth." From the late 1960s, space photographs of planet Earth dramatized the biophysical finiteness of our world. The dangerous synergies arising from global economic intercourse and ecology were driven home by the Brundtland Commission's declaration in 1987: "The Earth is one but the world is not. We all depend on one biosphere for sustaining our lives." In 1997 the Environmental Defense Fund warned that the burning of the Amazon forests would have "potentially enormous global consequences."[10]

Third, various grassroots movements focus attention on the growing conflict on the margins between local cultures and the global market. For example, the Kayapo Indians of the Amazon strengthened their demands by appealing to the global community regarding defense of their forest habitat from logging, cattle pasturing, and extraction of genetic resources. One response by the Brazilian government to this kind of demand was the creation of self-managing **extractive reserves** for native tribes and rubber tappers to protect them from encroaching ranchers and colonists. These reserves are relatively large areas of forest land set aside, with government protection, for extractive activities by forest-dwellers.[11]

Finally, from the 1970s on, the pressure on natural resources from the rural poor has intensified. This pressure stems from the long-term impoverishment of rural populations forced to overwork their land and fuel sources to eke out a subsistence. As land and forest were increasingly devoted to export production in the 1980s, millions of rural poor were pushed into occupying marginal tropical forest ecosystems. Environmental degradation, including deforestation, resulted. Environmental movements have proposed both local and global solutions under the mantle of "sustainable development." The following case study illustrates opposition to a massive development project in India.

CASE STUDY

Resistance to the Narmada Dam Project in India

Since the 1980s, the Indian government has been implementing a huge dam project in the Narmada River valley, with financial assistance from the World Bank. This massive development project involves 30 large and more than 3,000 medium and small dams on the Narmada River, expected eventually to displace more than 2 million people and their culture. In 1992, at the time of the Earth Summit, there was an embarrassing simultaneous release of an independent review (the first ever) of the Bank's Sardar Sarovar dam project in India. Commissioned by the Bank president, the review claimed "gross delinquency" on the part of the Bank and the Indian government in both the engineering and the forcible resettlement of displaced peasants. These revelations, and the growing resistance movement, the *Narmada Bachao Andolan* (Movement to Save the Narmada), had considerable success in forcing the Bank to withdraw its support for this project. Members of the grassroots opposition to the dam argue that the resistance "articulates . . . the critical legacy of Mahatma Gandhi . . . of the struggles all over the country that continue to challenge both the growing centralization and authoritarianism of the state and the extractive character of the dominant economic process—a process which not only erodes and destroys the subsistence economies of these areas, but also the diversity of their systems. . . . The movement is therefore representative of growing assertions of marginal populations for greater economic and political control over their lives."

Sources: Kothari & Parajuli, 1993, p. 233.

Sustainable Development

The concept of **sustainable development** gained currency as a result of the 1987 Brundtland report, entitled *Our Common Future*. The report defined sustainable development as "meet[ing] the needs of the present without compromising the ability of future generations to meet their own needs."[12] How to achieve this remains a puzzle. The Brundtland Commission suggested steps such as conserving and enhancing natural resources, encouraging grassroots involvement in development, and adopting appropriate technologies (smaller scale, energy conserving). While acknowledging that "an additional person in an industrial country consumes far more and places far greater pressure on natural resources than an additional person in the Third World," the Commission nevertheless recommended continued emphasis on economic growth to reduce the pressure of the poor on the environment.[13]

The report did not resolve the interpretive debate over the root cause of environmental deterioration. This is the debate over whether the threat to our common future stems from poverty or from affluence. Those who argue the poverty cause consider the gravest stress on the environment to be impoverished masses pressing on resources. Population control and economic growth are the suggested solutions. Those who identify affluence as the problem believe the gravest stress on the environment comes from global inequality and the consumption of resources to support affluent lifestyles. Measures of this effect abound, one of the more provocative being the claim that each U.S. citizen contributes 60 times more to global warming than each Mexican and that a Canadian's contribution equals that of 190 Indonesians.[14] This perspective has generated the "impossibility theorem" of former World Bank economist Herman E. Daly that "a U.S.-style high-resource consumption standard for a world of 4 billion people is impossible."[15]

The Earth Summit

The terms of this debate infused the 1992 **United Nations Conference on Environment and Development (UNCED)**. Popularized as the Rio de Janeiro "Earth Summit," it was the largest diplomatic gathering ever held. The United Nations Environment Program (UNEP) organized the conference to review progress on the Brundtland report. Conference preparations resulted in a document, known as Agenda 21, detailing a global program for the twenty-first century and implicitly addressing all sides of the debate, which continued through the 1990s.

The South, for instance, recognizes that the First World has an interest in reducing carbon dioxide emissions and preserving biodiversity and the tropical rain forests for planetary survival. It has agreed to participate in the global program in return for financial assistance, arguing that "poverty is the greatest polluter," a phrase once used by the now deceased Indian president Indira Gandhi. Accordingly, it has called for massive investment by the First World in sustainable development measures in the South, including health, sanitation, education, technical assistance, and conservation.[16]

In the end, UNCED detoured from the question of global inequities, stressing that environmental protection should be a development priority, but "without distorting international trade and investment."[17] The outcome was a shift in emphasis from the Brundtland report in two senses: (1) privileging *global* management of the environment over local/national concerns and (2) maintaining the viability of the global economy rather than addressing deteriorating economic conditions in the South. The globalization project was alive and well.

CASE STUDY

Deforestation Under the Globalization Project, Post–Earth Summit

Since Rio, forest destruction has continued unabated, and in fact has intensified. The United States has suspended all laws on national forests to facilitate logging; the Siberian and Eastern Russian boreal forests have been plundered; the rate of Amazonian deforestation has risen by one-third, and burning has tripled; and, after destroying more than 50 percent of Southeast Asian forests, logging companies from Burma, Indonesia, Malaysia, the Philippines, and South Korea have moved on to Amazonia. There, they now receive the blessing of the Brazilian government (once they have submitted an environmental impact study and become licensed), although government studies estimate that 60 to 70 percent of licensees operate illegally, and President Cardoso's hands are tied because he declared a ten-year moratorium on penalties for environmental crimes in order to attract $50 million in foreign investment in 1999. In fact, *Brazil* moved expeditiously to situate Amazonia as the logging frontier of the twenty-first century—allowing private interests to legally challenge indigenous land titles, building a huge transport infrastructure as a subsidy to private investment in Brazilian natural resources, implementing plans to resettle thousands of Brazilians under pressure from the Sem Terra landless movement, and privatizing thirty-nine of its national forests to attract foreign loggers. Meanwhile, under the terms of the IMF bailout of *Indonesia* in the 1997 crisis, that country's forests (the products of which rank third among Indonesian foreign exchange earning sectors) will be opened to foreign ownership. In *Mexico*, NAFTA has no provision for protecting forests. Following the peso crash in 1994, the International Paper Corporation leveraged reform of Mexican laws regarding forest exploitation, removing protections for biodiversity and for soil and water quality, and acquired generous federal subsidies. A new Forest Reform Law legalized private industrial tree plantations in the indigenous reserves and *ejido* lands, where 80 percent of Mexican forests are located. International Paper plans a 100,000 hectare eucalyptus and pine plantation in Chiapas. Meanwhile, the WTO is preparing a National Treatment code requiring foreign investors to claim the same rights as domestic ones, which threatens to institutionalize "cut and run" logging around the world.

Sources: Tautz, 1997, pp. 1-2; Menotti, 1998, pp. 352-362; Menotti, 1999, p. 181.

Managing the Global Commons

Environmental management is as old as the need for human communities to ensure material and cultural survival. *Global* environmental management seeks to preserve planetary resources, but there is no resolution as yet as to what end will be served. This question is posed and resolved on a continuing basis by struggles between communities and counter-movements, on one hand, and private interests, states, and global institutions on the other. Within the terms of the globalization project, it is not difficult to see that states, strapped for foreign exchange and sometimes required to undergo reform to earn foreign exchange, are beholden to wealthy corporations that want to exploit natural resources and/or secure control over their supply in the future. In many cases it is left up to local inhabitants, and their NGO supporters, to question the commercialization and degradation of environments to which they are historically and spiritually attached. Southern grassroots movements in particular regard global environmental managers and their powerful state allies as focused on managing the global environment to ensure the profitability of global economic activity. This includes regulating the use of planetary resources and global waste sinks such as forests, wetlands, and bodies of water. Instead of linking environmental concerns to issues of social justice and resource distribution, the new "global ecology" has converged on four priorities: reducing greenhouse gas emissions, primarily from automobiles and burning forests; protecting biodiversity, mainly in tropical forests; reducing pollution in international waters; and curbing ozone-layer depletion.

The institutional fallout from UNCED strengthened global economic management. A **Global Environmental Facility (GEF)** was installed, geared to funding global ecology initiatives. The World Bank initiated the establishment of the GEF to channel monies into global environmental projects, especially in the four areas identified above; 50 percent of the projects approved in the GEF's first tranche were for biodiversity protection. Additionally, UNCED, via the **Food and Agricultural Organization (FAO),** planned to zone Southern land for cash cropping with the assistance of national governments. Under this facility, subsistence farming would be allowed only where "natural resource limitations" or "environmental or socioeconomic constraints" prevent intensification. Where governments deem marginal land to be overpopulated, the inhabitants would be forced into transmigration or resettlement programs.

The logic of this scenario is that of managing the "global commons" and viewing surplus populations and their relation to scarce natural resources as the immediate problem, rather than situating the problem of *surplus* population in a broader framework that accounts for extreme inequality of access to resources. In Brazil, for example, less than 1 percent of the population owns about 44 percent of the fertile agricultural land, and 32 million people are officially considered destitute. SAPs, grain imports, and expansion of soy export production have led to the expropriation of the small peasants. Under conditions where Brazilian social ministries have been gutted, those landless peasants who do not join the mass migration to the towns or the frontier are incorporated into NGO-organized "poverty management" programs, constituting a cheap labor force for wealthy landowners.[18]

Global ecology, geared to environmental management on a large scale, has priorities for sustainability that often differ from those of the remaining local environmental managers. It is estimated that there are 200-300 million forest-dwellers in South and Southeast Asia, distinct from lowland communities dependent on irrigated agriculture. Some of these peo-

CASE STUDY

Managing the Global Commons: The GEF and Nicaraguan Biosphere Reserves

In 1997, the Global Environmental Facility (GEF) developed a strategy for protection of the Bosawas rain forest region in Nicaragua, on the grounds that it is globally significant biodiversity under threat of *campesino* colonization and unregulated logging by transnational firms attracted to the abundant timber, cheap labor, and relatively lawless conditions. The GEF strategy proposed "institutional strengthening," "participation of local stakeholders," and "decentralized management of protected areas." A GEF grant of $7.1 million, combined with European aid of $12.8 million, was promised the Nicaraguan government in return for brokering this strategy of biospheric reserve management on behalf of the indigenous communities of Mayangna Indians. The GEF views the Indians as guards and guardians of the high biodiversity areas: "by strengthening and reinforcing land and natural resource rights of indigenous communities . . . when indigenous communities have fairly secure tenure of their land, they can represent formidable barriers to the expansion of the agricultural frontier." The GEF pledged money for demarcation and titling of indigenous lands. Instituting this plan ran into formidable obstacles, because the Nicaraguan government was juggling the GEF "sustainable development" program and a program of broad logging concessions. These are contested through physical demonstrations and challenge in the courts (including the Inter-American Commission on Human Rights) by the Indians. They claim use of two-thirds of the land, conceded by the state to a subsidiary of a Korean clothing TNC, for hunting, burial sites, and areas of spiritual significance. The sticking point is that *indigenas* are not inclined to accept land parcels that fragment collectively used forests, to complement private logging concessions, and the state is caught between its international image as embracing "sustainable development" and its revenue-enhancing relationship to the logging firms.

Source: Weinberg, 1998.

ple have been given official group names assigning them a special—and usually second-class—status in their national society: India's "scheduled tribes" (*adivasis*), Thailand's "hill tribes," China's "minority nationalities," the Philippines's "cultural minorities," Indonesia's "isolated and alien peoples," Taiwan's "aboriginal tribes," and Malaysia's "aborigines." Challenging their national status and elevating their internationally common bonds, these groups have recently redefined themselves as "indigenous."[19]

Indigenous and tribal people around the world have had their rights to land and self-determination enshrined in the International Labor Organization Convention. Nevertheless, they are routinely viewed from afar as marginal. The World Bank, in adopting the term *indigenous* in its documents, stated in 1990: "The term indigenous covers indigenous, tribal, low caste and ethnic minority groups. Despite their historical and cultural differences, they often have a limited capacity to participate in the national development process because of cultural barriers or low social and political status."[20]

Viewed through the development lens, this is a predictable perspective, and it carries a significant implication. On one hand, it perpetuates the often unexamined assumption that these cultural minorities need guidance. On the other, it often subordinates minorities to national development initiatives, such as commercial logging or government forestry projects involving tree plantations. More often than not, such indigenous peoples find themselves on the receiving end of large-scale resettlement programs justified by the belief that forest destruction is a consequence of their poverty. This has been the case recently on the Indonesian island of Kalimantan, where the state has been actively encouraging commercial logging at the expense of a sophisticated and centuries-old rattan culture practiced by the Dayak Indians. They have formed their own resistance, documenting their ownership of cultivars in the forest.[21]

The focus on poverty as the destroyer of forests guided the establishment of the Tropical Forest Action Plan (TFAP) in the 1980s by a global management group consisting of the World Bank, the Food and Agricultural Organization, the **United Nations Development Program (UNDP)**, and the World Resources Institute. The TFAP was designed to pool funds to provide alternative fuel-wood sources, strengthen forestry and environmental institutions, conserve protected areas and watersheds, and promote social forestry. It became the "most ambitious environmental aid program ever conceived" and, as such, attracted requests for aid from sixty-two Southern states looking for new, seemingly "green," sources of funds for extraction of forest products for export. TFAP projects were completed in Peru, Guyana, Cameroon, Ghana, Tanzania, Papua New Guinea, Nepal, Colombia, and the Philippines. Seeing their effects, however, and charging that the TFAP projects furthered deforestation through intervention and zoning, a worldwide rain forest movement mobilized sufficient criticism (including that of Britain's Prince Charles) that the TFAP initiative ended. Forestry loans, however, continued through the World Bank.[22]

CASE STUDY

Chico Mendes, Brazilian Environmentalist by Default

As the leader of Brazil's National Council of Rubber Tappers, Chico Mendes concerned himself with the safety of his tappers as ranchers tried to force them off their land. By the Catholic Church's reckoning, between 1964 and 1988, 982 murders over land disputes in the Amazon occurred, largely by ranchers' hired guns. Under these circumstances, the Brazilian government obtained a forestry loan from the World Bank for "agro-ecological zoning" in the Brazilian Polonoroeste area of Rondônia and Mato Grosso to set aside land for farmers, provide for extractive reserves for the rubber tappers (so they could supplement their tapping wages with sales of other forest products), and protect Indian reserves in addition to national parks, forest reserves, and other protected forest areas. The minorities affected were not consulted, even though Mendes lobbied the World Bank in Washington on behalf of the rubber tappers in 1988. He feared a repetition of the mistakes made during the 1980s, when Rondônia was occupied by impoverished settlers who burned the Amazonian jungle in vain hopes of farming. He observed:

> We think that the extractive reserves included in Polonoroeste II only serve to lend the Government's project proposal to the World Bank an ecological tone—which has been very fashionable lately— in order to secure this huge loan. . . . What will be created will not be extractive reserves, but colonization settlements with the same mistakes that have led to the present disaster of Polonoroeste. In other words, a lot of money will be spent on infrastructures which do not mean anything to the peoples of the forest and the maintenance of which will not be sustainable.

Mendes was later murdered by a hired gun for his part in championing the rubber tappers' cause to secure their land.

While he was a forest worker, he left an environmentalist's legacy in the idea of the extractive reserve, which is still taking root.
At the very moment that the Rondônian Natural Resources Management Project loan was approved in 1992, the Brazilian land
agency, INCRA, "was proceeding with plans to settle some
50,000 new colonists a year in areas that were supposed to be set
aside as protected forests and extractive reserves for rubber
tappers under the Bank project."

Sources: Rich, 1994, pp. 167-169; Schemo, 1998, p. A3.

On the other side of the world, a similar resettlement project was
under way in Indonesia. In this transmigration project, millions of poor
peasants were moved from densely populated inner islands of Indonesia,
notably Java, to the outer islands of Kalimantan, Irian Jaya, and Sumatra
to settle and cultivate cash crops for export, such as cacao, coffee, and
palm oil. The outer islands were inhabited by non-Javanese indigenous
tribes and contained 10 percent of the world's remaining rain forests.
Critics saw this project as both a money-spinner for the Indonesian government and a security project against non-Javanese people who desired
autonomy from the military government.

Building on the Indonesian government's initial resettlement of more
than half a million people since 1950, the World Bank assisted a further
resettlement of 3.5 million people between 1974 and 1990, with that many
again moving to the outer islands as private colonizers. The project, by the
Bank's own accounting, simply redistributed poverty spatially, from the
inner to the outer islands; additionally, it eliminated roughly 4 percent of
the Indonesian forests.[23]

Environmental Resistance Movements

In all these cases, there is a discernible pattern of collaboration between
the multilateral financiers and governments concerned with securing territory and foreign exchange. Indigenous cultures, on the other hand, are
typically marginalized. Indonesia's Forestry Department controls 74 percent of the national territory, and the minister for forestry claimed in 1989
that, "In Indonesia, the forest belongs to the state and not to the people. . . .
[T]hey have no right of compensation" when their habitats fall to logging
concessions.[24]

Under these conditions, grassroots environmental movements proliferate. They take two forms: active resistance, which seeks to curb invasion
of habitats by states and markets; and adaptation to environmental depre-
dation, which exemplifies the centuries-old practice of renewing habitats
in the face of environmental deterioration. In the latter practice lie some of
the answers to current problems.

Perhaps the most dramatic form of resistance was undertaken by the
Chipko movement in the Central Himalaya region of India. Renewing an
ancient tradition of peasant resistance in 1973, the Chipko adopted a
Gandhian strategy of nonviolence, symbolized in tree-hugging protests
led primarily by women against commercial logging. Similar protests
spread across northern India in a move to protect forest habitats for tribal
peoples. Emulating the Chipko practice of tree planting to restore forests
and soils, the movement developed a "pluck and plant" tactic. Its members uprooted eucalyptus seedlings—the tree of choice in official social
forestry, even though it does not provide shade and does ravish aquifers—and replaced them with indigenous species of trees that yield products useful to the locals. Success of these movements has been measured
primarily in two ways: by withdrawal of Bank involvement and the redefinition of forestry management by the Indian government, and by the
flowering of new political associations, sometimes called "user groups,"
that are democratic and dedicated to reclaiming lands and redefining
grassroots development.[25]

Environmental activism like this is paralleled across the South. In
Thailand, where the state has promoted eucalyptus plantations that
threaten massive displacement of forest-dwellers, there has been

> an explosion of rural activism. . . . Small farmers are standing up to assassi-
> nation threats; weathering the contempt of bureaucrats; petitioning cabinet
> officials; arranging strategy meetings with other villagers; calling on
> reserves of political experience going back decades; marching; rallying;
> blocking roads; ripping out seedlings; chopping down eucalyptus trees;
> burning nurseries; planting fruit, rubber and forest trees in order to demon-
> strate their own conservationist awareness. . . . Their message is simple.
> They want individual land rights. They want community rights to local for-
> ests which they will conserve themselves. They want a reconsideration of all
> existing eucalyptus projects. And they want the right to veto any commer-
> cial plantation scheme in their locality.[26]

In the Philippines, a successful reforestation program undertaken by
the Ikalahan of the eastern Cordillera followed the decentralization of
resource control from the Department of Energy and Natural Resources to

management by the local community in the 1980s. The state in effect transferred ancestral land back to the community. On the island of Mindanao, indigenous communities have reclaimed state and pastoral lands for subsistence farming, organizing themselves democratically along Chipko lines.[27]

As grassroots environmentalism mushrooms across the South, community control gains credibility by example. At the same time, the institutional aspects of technology transfer associated with the development project come under question. A former director of forestry at the Food and Agricultural Organization commented in 1987:

> Only very much later did it dawn on the development establishment that the very act of establishing new institutions often meant the weakening, even the destruction of existing indigenous institutions which ought to have served as the basis for sane and durable development: the family, the clans, the tribe, the village, sundry mutual aid organizations, peasant associations, rural trade unions, marketing and distribution systems and so on.[28]

Of course, the point is that forest-dwellers have always managed their environment. From the perspective of colonial rule and the developers, these communities did not appear to be involved in management because their practices were alien to the rational, specialized pursuit of commercial wealth characterizing Western ways beginning under colonialism. Local practices were therefore either suppressed or ignored.

Now, where colonial forestry practices erased local knowledge and eroded natural resources, recent grassroots mobilization, such as the Green Belt Movement in Kenya, organized by women, has reestablished inter-cropping to replenish soils and tree planting to sustain forests. Where development agencies and planners have attempted to impose irrigated cash cropping, such as in eastern Senegal, movements like the Senegalese Federation of Sarakolle Villages have collectively resisted in the interests of sustainable peasant farming (sustainable in the social as well as the ecological sense).[29]

CASE STUDY

Local Environmental Managers in Ghana

Hundreds of local communities have evolved new resource management practices as livelihood strategies, often with the aid of **nongovernmental organizations (NGOs)**. A case in point is the revival of local environmental management in the Manya Krobo area of southeastern Ghana, in the wake of environmental deterioration visited on the forest land by cash cropping. British colonialism promoted the production of palm oil, followed by cocoa cultivation, for export. The displacement of forest cover by monocultural cocoa crops led to severe degradation of the soils. With cocoa prices falling in the second half of the twentieth century, local farmers shifted to growing cassava and corn for local food markets; they also cultivated oil palms and activated a local crafts industry (distilling) used for subsistence rather than for export. Forest restoration technologies, combined with food crops, have emerged as a viable adaptation. These restoration methods are based on the preservation of pioneer forest species rather than the fast-growing exotics promoted by development agencies as fuel-wood supplies and short-term forest cover. The lesson is that the community of cultivators is "an originator of technology, rather than a consumer of technology packages."

Source: Amanor, 1994, p. 64.

The challenge for grassroots environmental movements in the former Third World is twofold: (1) to create alternatives to the capital- and energy-intensive forms of specialized agriculture and agro-forestry that are appropriate to the goal of restoring and sustaining local ecologies, and (2) to build alternative models to the bureaucratic, top-down development plans that have typically subordinated natural resource use to commercial rather than to sustainable, social ends. Perhaps the fundamental challenge to Southern environmental movements is the perspective stated in the Bank's *World Development Report* for 1992: "Promoting development is the best way to protect the environment."[30] Whether development, understood from the Bank's perspective, is a source of sustainability is the question. Thus, alternative methods of environmental management and development, as ideas and practices, underlie the growing conflict between local and global forces.

Feminism

Where Southern grassroots movements entail protection of local resources and community, women typically play a defining role. This has always been so, but one consequence of colonialism is that this activity has become almost exclusively a women's preserve. As private property in land emerged, women's work tended to specialize in use of the commons for livestock grazing, firewood collection, game hunting, and seed gathering for medicinal purposes. These activities allowed women to supplement the incomes earned by men in the commercial sector. Women assumed a role as environmental managers, often forced to adapt to deteriorating conditions as commercial extractions increased over time.

The establishment of individual rights to property under colonialism typically privileged men. The result was the fragmentation of social systems built on the complementarity of male and female work. Men's work became specialized; in national economic statistics, it is routinely counted as contributing to the commercial sector. Conversely, the specialization of women's labor as "non-income-earning" work remains outside the commercial sector. Oppositions such as waged and non-waged work or productive and nonproductive work emerged. In modern national accounting systems, only "productive" work is counted or valued, leaving much of women's work invisible. The domain of invisible work in many cases involves the work of maintaining the commons.

When we trace the development of feminism, we find that it has circled back toward recovery of this sense of the commons. The journey has been both practical and theoretical—moving from bringing women into development to an alternative conception of the relationship of women to development. It began with the movement to integrate women into development in the early 1970s. The first U.N. world conference on women was held in Mexico City in 1975 and concentrated on extending existing development programs to include women. This movement was known as *Women in Development* (WID). Since then, the movement has changed gears, shifting from what Rounaq Jahan terms an "integrationist" to an "agenda-setting" approach, which challenges the existing development system of thought with a feminist perspective.[31] The goal includes involving women as decision makers concerned with empowering all women in their various life situations.

Feminist Formulations

The shift from integration to transformation of the development model has involved a redefinition of feminism from WID to *women, environment, and alternative development* (WED). The redefinition symbolizes a movement from remedies to alternatives.[32] There are two aspects to this shift. First, the WID position emerged to redress the absence of gender issues in development theory and practice. The arguments are familiar: women's contributions were made invisible by economic statistics that measured only the contributions to development of income-earning units (waged labor and commercial enterprises). *WID feminists* have identified problems and formulated remedies in the following ways:

- Women have always been de facto producers, but because of their invisibility, their technological and vocational supports have been minimal. Planners should therefore recognize women's contributions, especially as food producers for rural households and even urban markets, where males labor when not migrating to the agro-export or cash-crop sector.

- Women also bear children, and a more robust understanding of development would include education, health care, family planning, and nutrition as social supports.

- Finally, because of patriarchal expectations that women perform unpaid household/farm labor in addition to any paid labor, development planners should pursue ameliorative measures. Findings reveal that where women can be incorporated into income-earning activities, a net benefit accrues to community welfare because male income is often dissipated in consumer/ urban markets.

By contrast, the *WED feminist* position includes critiques and remedies as follow:

- Conventional economics is hierarchical and male-oriented in its assumptions about development strategy. It excludes the contributions of women and nature from its models.

- Development practices, where informed by economic theory, reveal a predatory relationship, in which women are exploited and socially and economically marginalized, and nature is plundered. The human future is therefore depleted.

- In developing an alternative understanding of the world and its need for renewal, "the task is not simply to add women into the known equation but to establish a new development paradigm."[33] Economic theory is incapable of reform because its rationalist (Eurocentric) approach abstracts knowledge from practice and history and presumes its universal application. An alternative form of knowledge is practical and rooted in cultural traditions.

- Western traditions of rational science have devalued and displaced practical knowledge through colonialism and the development project.[34] That is, local cultures in both the European and the non-European worlds have submitted to the rationality of the marketplace. For example, craft traditions have been mechanized; multiple cropping and animal husbandry combinations have been separated, specialized, and infused with chemical inputs; and traditional health practices have been overridden by Western medical science.

- Finally, "the work of caring for the environment, and women's role as nurturers, are also undervalued in the logic of development."[35]

The difference between WID and WED feminism is further explored in the following insert.

What Is the Difference Between WID and WED Feminism?

The difference in the two perspectives is not just one of emphasis. It involves how we look at the world, including what we take account of. WID feminism tends to accept the developmentalist framework and look for ways within development programs to improve the position of women. For example, the impetus for pushing for new jobs for women in the paid workforce was that women's unpaid work was implicitly devalued and removed from consideration as activity contributing to livelihoods. The movement from WID to WED follows a conceptual shift from a universalist (rational) toward a diverse (expressive) understanding of the world. It is a shift from a linear, to an inter-relational, view of social change. Thus WED feminists question the separation in Western thought between nature and culture, where nature is viewed as separate from and acted on by culture rather than each shaping the other. In the WED view, stewardship of nature is understood as integral to the renewal of culture rather than being constructed as a program per se.

The WED position argues that, within the WID paradigm, women are presumed to be universally subordinate to men. Further, development is redefined as a mechanism of emancipation of women. But this perspective is flawed insofar as it tends to judge Third World women's position against the ideal of the emancipated (economically independent) woman of the First World.[36]

In making this comparison, WED feminism stresses that development is a relative, not a universal, process and that we should be aware of how our ideals shape our assumptions about other societies. Concerns for the empowerment of women in Third World settings should refer to those circumstances, not to abstract ideals of individual emancipation. In other words, women's role in sustaining cultural and ecological relations is complex, place specific, and incapable of being reduced to universal formulas.

CASE STUDY

Human Rights vs. Cultural Rights: The Ritual of Female Genital Mutilation

Genital cutting, formerly known as female circumcision, retains prominence in some cultures today as a rite of passage for young females. Global opposition to the ritual, in the name of human rights, is met by defense of it as a valued cultural ritual. In Sudan, where 89 percent of women are circumcised, justifications for the ritual include a custom originating in religious practice (sanctioned, if not required, by Islamic law), the clitoris's "evil" properties, enhanced fertility, and enhancement of male sexual pleasure. Subtler cultural functions associated with patriarchal valuation of women, including the necessity of virginity at marriage, also contribute to this ritual. Human rights activists view female genital mutilation as a violation of the rights of women and children across the globe, claiming that its pain and harm to women's sexual pleasure and physical and psychological health is cruel and unnecessary. The United Nations and NGOs pressure governments to stop the ritual, but often such pressure, including advocating education (which has been shown to change women's attitudes toward circumcision), is experienced as *cultural imperialism*. To validate cultures and their practitioners, alternative ceremonies have evolved, such as in Kenya where the ritual is changed into a rite of passage through a week-long program of counseling. In eastern Uganda, the Sabiny people use a symbolic ritual pioneered by the Elders Association, who also counsel parents about the medical risks of cutting, in terms of exposing females to HIV and AIDS and compromising childbirth later on.

Sources: Crossette, 1998a, p. A8; Kohli & Webster, 1999; Sobieszczyk & Williams, 1997.

Women and the Environment

At the practical level, women engage in multifaceted activity. Across the world, women's organizations have mobilized to manage local resources, to empower poor women and communities, and to pressure governments and international agencies on behalf of women's rights. Countless activities of resource management undertaken by women form the basis of these practices. Perhaps most basic is the preservation of biodiversity in market and kitchen gardens. In Peru, the Aguarunu Jivaro women nurture more than 100 varieties of manioc, the local staple root crop. Women have devised ingenious ways of household provisioning beside and within the cash-cropping systems managed by men. Hedgerows and wastelands become sites of local food crops.[37] Forest products (game, medicinal plants, condiments) are cultivated and harvested routinely by women. In rural Laos, more than 100 different forest products are collected chiefly by women for home use or sale. Women in Ghana process, distribute, and market game. Indian women anchor household income—with an array of nontimber forest products amounting to 40 percent of total Forest Department revenues—as do Brazilian women in Acre, working by the side of the male rubber tappers.[38] A particular success from Kenya is reported in the following case study.

CASE STUDY

The Kikuyu Cooperative in Kenya

In Kenya, the Kikuyu women in Laikipia have formed 354 women's groups to help them coordinate community decisions about access to and use of resources. Groups vary in size from 20 to 100 neighbors, both squatters and peasants; members contribute cash, products, and/or labor to the group, which in turn distributes resources equally among them. The groups have been able to pool funds to purchase land and establish small enterprises for the members. One such group, the Mwenda-Niire, formed in 1963 among landless squatters on the margins of a large commercial estate. Twenty years later, through saving funds, by growing maize and potatoes among the owner's crops, and through political negotiation, the group purchased the 567-hectare farm, allowing 130 landless families to become farmers. Group dynamics continue through labor-sharing schemes, collective infrastructure projects, and collective marketing. Collective movements such as this go beyond remedying development failures. They restore women's access to resources removed from them under colonial and postcolonial developments.

Source: Wacker, 1994, pp. 135-139.

Women, Poverty, and Fertility

Women's resource management is often ingenious, but often poverty subverts their ingenuity. For example, where women have no secure rights to land, they are less able to engage in sustainable resource extraction. Environmental deterioration may follow. When we see women stripping forests and overworking fragile land, we are often seeing just the tip of the iceberg. Many of these women have been displaced from lands converted for export cropping, or they have lost common land on which to subsist.

Environmental damage stemming from poverty has fueled the debate surrounding population growth in the former Third World. Population control has typically been directed at women—ranging from female infanticide through forced sterilization (as in India) to family planning interventions by development agencies. In Peru, government agencies have seized the initiative from women and founding NGOs in deploying a women's health program to perform 80 percent of sterilizations in a broad sterilization campaign that has cut Peru's fertility rate almost in half since 1961.[39] Feminists have entered this debate to protect women from such manipulation of their social and biological contributions.

Feminists demand the enabling of women to take control of their fertility without targeting women as the source of the population problem. On a global scale, the current world population of almost 6 billion is expected to double by 2050, according to U.N. projections, unless more aggressive intervention occurs. Studies suggest that female education and health services reduce birthrates. The 1992 World Bank report pointed out that women without secondary education on average have seven children; if almost half these women receive secondary education, the average declines to three children per woman.[40]

In addition, recent evidence based on the results of contraceptive use in Bangladesh has been cited as superseding conventional theories of "demographic transition." Demographic theory extrapolates from the Western experience a pattern of demographic transition whereby birthrates decline significantly as economic growth proceeds. The threshold is the shift from preindustrial to industrial society, in which education and health technologies spread. This is expected to cause families to view children increasingly as an economic liability rather than as necessary hands in the household economy or as a response to high childhood mortality rates.

Evidence from Bangladesh, one of the twenty poorest countries of the world, shows a 21 percent decline in fertility rates during the decade and a half (1975-1991) in which a national family planning program was in effect. The study's authors claimed these findings "dispute the notion that 'development is the best contraceptive,' " adding that "contraceptives are the best contraceptive."[41]

Feminist groups argue that family planning and contraception need to be rooted in the broader context of women's rights. Presently, almost twice as many women as men are illiterate, and that difference is growing. Poor women with no education often do not understand their rights or contraceptive choices. The International Women's Health Coalition identified the Bangladesh Women's Health Coalition, serving 110,000 women at ten clinics around the country, as a model for future United Nations planning. This group began in 1980, offering abortions. With suggestions from the women it served, the Coalition has expanded into family planning, basic health care services, child immunizations, legal aid, and training in literacy and employment skills.[42] Similar success stories are presented in the following case study.

CASE STUDY

Women's Rights and Fertility

The correlation between women's rights and low fertility rates has ample confirmation. In Tunisia, the 1956 Code of Individual Rights guaranteed women political equality, backed with family planning and other social programs that included free, legal abortions. Tunisia is a leader in family planning in Africa, with a population growth rate of only 1.9 percent. The director general of Tunisia's National Office of Family and Population, Nebiha

Gueddana, claims that successful family planning can occur in a Muslim society: "We have thirty years of experience with the equality of women and . . . none of it has come at the expense of family values."

In Kerala, where the literacy rate for women is two and a half times the average for India, and where the status of women was high throughout the twentieth century relative to the rest of the country, land reforms and comprehensive social welfare programs were instrumental in achieving a 40 percent reduction in the fertility rate between 1960 and 1985, reducing the population growth rate to 1.8 percent in the 1980s.

Sources: Crossette, 1994, p. A8; Bello, 1992-1993, p. 5.

With supportive social conditions, fertility decisions by women can have both individual and social benefits. Fertility decisions by individual women usually occur within patriarchal settings—households or societies—as well as within definite livelihood situations. It is these conditions that the feminist movements and women's groups have identified as necessary to the calculus in fertility decisions. Recently, the population issue has incorporated elements of the feminist perspective, which emphasizes women's reproductive rights and health, in the context of their need for secure livelihoods and political participation.[43] This view was embedded in the 1994 U.N. Conference on Population and Development document. The document, contested by the Vatican and some Muslim nations (particularly Iran), states that women have the right to reproductive and sexual health, defined as "a state of complete physical, mental and social well-being" in all matters relating to reproduction.[44]

Women's Rights

Feminism has clearly made an impact on the development agenda since the days of WID's inception. The improvement of women's material condition and social status across the world has not, however, followed in step, even if the statistical reporting of women's work in subsistence production has improved.[45] In 1989, at the end of a decade of structural adjustment, the United Nations made the following report in its World Survey on the Role of Women in Development:

The bottom line shows that, despite economic progress measured in growth rates, at least for the majority of developing countries, economic progress for women has virtually stopped, social progress has slowed, and social well-being in many cases has deteriorated, and because of the importance of women's social and economic roles, the aspirations for them in current development strategies will not be met.[46]

Five years later, the United Nations's *Human Development Report 1994* found that "despite advances in labor-force participation, education and health, women still constitute about two-thirds of the world's illiterates, hold fewer than half of the jobs on the market and are paid half as much as men for work of equal value."[47] Even so, feminism has put its stamp on the reformulations of development, as the 1994 U.N. report declared in response to the crisis in the former Third World:

> It requires a long, quiet process of sustainable human development . . . [a] development that not only generates economic growth but distributes its benefits equitably, that regenerates the environment rather than destroying it; that empowers people rather than marginalizing them. It is development that gives priority to the poor, enlarging their choices and opportunities and providing for their participation in decisions that affect their lives. It is development that is pro-people, pro-nature, pro-jobs and pro-women.[48]

In Muslim cultures, with considerable variation, women's rights remain subordinated to Islamic law, or, as Muslim feminists claim, to male interpretation of the Koran. In Morocco, for example, women require permission of male relatives to marry, name their children, or work. Sisters inherit half that of brothers, and male coercion in marriage is customary. Islamic women's groups across the Muslim world are mobilizing against what they term Muslim apartheid, especially since the United Nations Fourth World Conference on Women in Beijing in 1995. In the Mediterranean region, rapid urbanization has produced more educated and professional women, who are now focusing on changing secular laws to make an end run around Islamic law.[49]

Finally, in an evaluation of the Beijing Conference entitled *Mapping Progress: Assessing Implementation of the Beijing Platform 1998,* the Women's Environment and Development Organization reported that 70 percent of 187 national governments had laid plans to improve women's rights, sixty-six countries have offices for women's affairs, and thirty-four of these have legislative input. Pressure from local and international women's organizations since Beijing in countries as different as Mexico, Germany, New Zealand, and China has made some gains, such as instituting laws against domestic violence.[50]

Cosmopolitan Localism

Perhaps the litmus test of the globalization project is that as global integration intensifies, the currents of multiculturalism swirl faster. Fractious mobilizations of communities—urban, rural, class/ethnic—across the world threaten national and regional orders. The politics of identity substitutes for the politics of nation-building. Regions and communities see self-determination as more than a political goal. It now includes the idea of cultural renewal, expressed in the recovery of local knowledge. Wolfgang Sachs remarks:

> Today, more than ever, universalism is under siege. To be sure, the victorious march of science, state and market has not come to a stop, but the enthusiasm of the onlookers is flagging. . . . The globe is not any longer imagined as a homogeneous space where contrasts ought to be levelled out, but as a discontinuous space where differences flourish in a multiplicity of places.[51]

The new forms of imagination embody what Sachs terms **cosmopolitan localism**, that is, the assertion of diversity as a universal right, and the identification of locality as globally formed. Cosmopolitan localism questions the assumption of uniformity in the global development project, redefining global relations as heterogeneous. This is a protective response, insofar as communities seek to avoid the marginalization or disruption of unpredictable global markets. Such questioning also asserts the need to respect alternative cultural traditions as a matter of global survival. Finally, it is a question of preserving or asserting human and democratic rights within broader settings, whether a world community or individual national arenas.

CASE STUDY

Andean Counter-development, or "Cultural Affirmation"

Cosmopolitan localism takes a variety of forms. One that is spreading across the world is a dialogical method of privileging the local worldview, including an evaluation of modern Western knowledge from the local standpoint. This means learning to value local culture and developing a contextualized understanding of foreign knowledges, so that they do not assume some universal truth and inevitability, as sometimes claimed by Western knowledge and its officialdom. In this sense modernity is understood as a peculiarly Western cosmology arising from European culture and history, which includes universalist claims legitimizing imperial expansion across the world. In the Peruvian Andes, indigenous writers and activists formed an NGO in 1987 called PRATEC (Proyecto Andino de Tecnologias Campesinas), which is concerned with recovering and implementing traditional Andean peasant culture and technologies, via education of would-be rural developers. PRATEC links the Andean cosmology to its particular history and local ecology. It does not see itself as a political movement, but rather as a form of cultural politics dedicated to revaluing Andean culture and affirming local diversity over abstract homogenizing knowledges associated with modernity. One PRATEC peasant explained:

> We have great faith in what nature transmits to us. These indicators are neither the result of the science of humans, nor the invention of people with great experience. Rather, it is the voice of nature itself which announces to us the manner in which we must plant our crops.

Andean peasants grow and know some 1,500 varieties of quinoa, 330 of kaniwa, 228 of tarwi, 3,500 of potatoes, 610 of oca (another tuber), and so on. In situating this cultural affirmation, a core founding member of PRATEC explained that "to decolonize ourselves is to break with the global enterprise of development." In the context of the collapse of Peru's formal economy, the delegitimization of government development initiatives, and environmental deterioration, PRATEC is the vehicle of a dynamic alternative, rooted in indigenous ecology, and a participatory culture which puts the particularity of the Western project in perspective.

Source: Apffel-Marglin, 1997.

The most potent example of cosmopolitan localism was the peasant revolt in Mexico's southern state of Chiapas, a region in which small peasant farms are surrounded by huge cattle ranches and coffee plantations. About one-third of the unresolved land reforms in the Mexican agrarian reform department, going back more than half a century, are in Chiapas. The government's solution over the years has been to allow landless *campesinos* to colonize the Lacandon jungle and produce subsistence crops, coffee, and cattle. During the 1980s, coffee, cattle, and corn prices all fell, and *campesinos* were prohibited from logging—even though timber companies continued the practice.[52] The revolt had these deepening classical class inequities as its foundation, but the source of the inequities transcended the region.

On New Year's Day, 1994, hundreds of impoverished peasants rose up against what they perceived to be the Mexican state's continued violation of local rights. Not coincidentally, the revolt fell on the day the North American Free Trade Agreement (NAFTA) was implemented. To the Chiapas rebels, NAFTA symbolized the undermining of the revolutionary heritage in the Mexican Constitution of 1917, by which communal lands were protected from alienation. In 1992, under the pretext of structural adjustment policies and the promise of NAFTA, the Mexican government opened these lands for sale to Mexican and foreign agribusinesses. In addition, NAFTA included a provision to deregulate commodity markets—especially the market for corn, the staple peasant food.

The Chiapas revolt illustrates cosmopolitan localism well because it linked the struggle for local rights to a political and historical context. That is, the *Zapatistas* (as the rebels call themselves, after Mexican revolutionary Emilano Zapata) perceive the Mexican state as the chief agent of exploitation of the region's cultural and natural wealth. In one of many communiqués aimed at the global community, Subcomandante Marcos, the *Zapatista* spokesperson, characterized the Chiapas condition:

> Oil, electric energy, cattle, money, coffee, bananas, honey, corn, cocoa, tobacco, sugar, soy, melons, sorghum, mamey, mangos, tamarind, avocados, and Chiapan blood flow out through a thousand and one fangs sunk into the neck of Southeastern Mexico. Billions of tons of natural resources go through Mexican ports, railway stations, airports, and road systems to various destinations: the United States, Canada, Holland, Germany, Italy, Japan—but all with the same destiny: to feed the empire. . . . The jungle is opened with machetes, wielded by the same campesinos whose land has been taken away by the insatiable beast. . . . Poor people can not cut down trees, but the oil company, more and more in the hands of foreigners, can. . . . Why does the federal government take the question of national politics off the proposed agenda of the dialogue for peace? Are the indigenous Chiapan people only Mexican enough to be exploited, but not Mexican enough to be allowed an opinion on national politics? . . . What kind of citizens are the indigenous people of Chiapas? "Citizens in formation?"[53]

In these communiqués the *Ejército Zapatista de Liberación Nacional* (EZLN) movement addresses processes of both decline and renewal in Mexican civil society. The process of decline refers to the dismantling of the communal tradition of the Mexican national state symbolized in the infamous reform of Article 27 of the Constitution. The Article now privileges private (foreign) investment in land over the traditional rights of *campesinos* to petition for land redistribution within the *ejido* (Indian community land held in common) framework. The *Zapatistas* argue that this reform, in conjunction with the new liberalization under NAFTA, will undermine the Mexican smallholder and the basic grains sector. Since the Article 27 reform, followed by an abrupt withdrawal of public support for agriculture, "new investment is flowing disproportionately to commercially lucrative *ejidos* with the greatest potential for expanding export performance."[54] Further, the Zapatistas understand that the U.S. "comparative advantage" in corn production (6.9 U.S. tons versus 1.7 Mexican tons per hectare, including infrastructure disparities) seriously threatens Mexican maize producers, especially because under NAFTA the Mexican government has agreed to phase out guaranteed prices for staples such as maize and beans.[55] With an estimated 200 percent rise in corn imports under NAFTA's full implementation by 2008, it is expected that more than two-thirds of Mexican maize production will not survive the competition.[56] Global Food Watch, an NGO, estimates that 1.8 million Mexican maize farmers have been undermined recently by heavily subsidized corn imports from the United States.[57]

The renewal side involves the renewal of "citizenship" demands by the Chiapas movement. This directly addresses the need for free and fair elections in Chiapas (and elsewhere in Mexico), adequate political representation of *campesino* interests (as against those of Chiapas planters and ranchers), and the elimination of violence and authoritarianism in local government. The EZLN's demands included a formal challenge to a centuries-old pattern of *caciquismo* (local strongman tradition) in which federal government initiatives have been routinely thwarted by local political and economic interests. A case in point has been in the patronage system, whereby the governor of Chiapas state has channeled federal government welfare funds (*Solidaridad* loans) to local political allies.[58]

The renewal side also includes the demonstration effect of the Chiapas revolt, because communities throughout Mexico have since mobilized around similar demands—especially because local communities face common pressures, such as market reforms. In challenging local patronage politics, the *Zapatistas* elevated demands nationally for inclusion of *campesino* organizations in political decisions regarding rural reforms, including equity demands for small farmers as well as farm workers. They also advanced the cause of local and/or indigenous development projects that sustain local ecologies and cultures.[59] Chiapas is a region with considerable inter-ethnic mixing (*mestizo*), although Tzoltal is the local language along with Spanish. The rebellion has a pan-Mayan identity rather than a specific ethnic character with ethnic demands, other than the demand for indigenous co-governors.

Arguably, the Chiapas rebellion is a model for the postnational developmental era. This model has several elements, many of which have been associated with the so-called new social movements that have sprung up across the world. These movements mark the demise of classical liberal politics—the framing ideology of modern national political-economic institutions.[60] Classical liberalism addressed issues of political representation, not to be confused with contemporary neo-liberalism, which espouses private market initiatives. It nurtured the rise in the West of the labor movement, citizenship politics, and the notion of social entitlement; its demise now coincides with the dismantling of the welfare state. As discussed earlier in this chapter, the new social movements tend to reject the interest-group politics of liberalism and espouse a more associative politics, connecting a diverse range of social causes.

What is distinctive about the Chiapas rebellion is the *texture* of its political action. Timed to coincide with the implementation of NAFTA, it wove together a powerful and symbolic critique of the politics of globalization. This critique had two goals. First, it opposed the involvement of national elites and governments in implementing neo-liberal economic reforms on a global or regional scale, reforms that undo the institutionalized social entitlements associated with political liberalism. Second, it asserted a new agenda of renewal involving a politics of rights that goes beyond individual or property rights to human, and therefore community, rights. The push for regional autonomy challenged local class inequalities and demanded the empowerment of *campesino* communities. It also asserted the associative political style of the EZLN, composed of a coalition of *campesino* and women's organizations. This form of politics addressed conditions elsewhere in Mexico and the world, demonstrating the power of cosmopolitan localism.

The Mexican government responded to the rebellion by creating the "National Commission for Integral Development and Social Justice for Indigenous People" and promised more monies by way of the government's national solidarity program. The *Zapatistas* rejected these proposals, however, as "just another step in their cultural assimilation and economic annihilation."[61] The EZLN program rejects integration into outside development projects, outlining a plan for land restoration, abolition of peasant debts, and reparations to be paid to the Indians of Chiapas by those who have exploited their human and natural resources. Self-determination involves the development of new organizational forms of cooperation among different groups in the region. These have evolved over time into a "fabric of cooperation" woven from the various threads of local groupings. They substitute fluid organizational patterns for the bureaucratic organizational forms associated with modernist politics—such as political parties, trade unions, and hierarchical state structures.[62] In these senses, whether the *Zapatistas* survive the Mexican army's continuing siege of Chiapas, the movement they have quickened will intensify the unresolved tension between globalism and localism and between global managerialism and political representation.

Summary

We have toured some of the world's hot spots in this chapter, noting the particular forms in which social movements respond to the failures of developmentalism and the further disorganizing impact of globalism. Responses range from withdrawal into alternative projects (for example, Islamic revival, feminist cooperatives, recovery of noncapitalist agroecological practices) to attempts to reframe development as a question of rights and basic social protections (such as the feminist movement as opposed to developmentalism, social-environmentalism, local rebellions like the one in Chiapas, and right-wing fundamentalism). All these responses express the uncertainties of social arrangements under globalizing tendencies. Many express a fundamental desire to break out of the homogenizing and disempowering dynamics of the globalization project and to establish a sustainable form of social life based on new forms of associative politics.

Other forms of resistance to the globalization project include mushrooming consumer advocacy, community supported agriculture, organic food systems, and fair trade groups. One of the most effective has been the United Students Against Sweatshops (SWAS), formed in 1998 after several years of campus organizing against the link between U.S. universities and offshore sweatshops producing logo-emblazoned clothing. Approximately 160 colleges support an antisweatshop code proposed by the Collegiate Licensing Company, which purchases apparel from the manufacturers. Continuing contention about the stringency of the code has led to building occupations and mass meetings at a number of campuses including Duke, Wisconsin, Georgetown, Stanford, and Cornell. Nike has since raised wages for its workers in Indonesia, even though the financial crisis undermined their real purchasing power.[63] In related human rights areas, consumer movements have successfully focused attention on child labor stitching soccer balls in Pakistan, although monitoring remains incomplete.

In sum, the road to the political future has several forks. Across the world, counter-movements form in regional cereal banks in Zimbabwe, ecological campaigns by women's groups in West Bengal, *campesino* credit unions in Mexico, the emergence of solidarity networks among labor forces, food safety campaigns in Europe, and the defense of forest-dwellers throughout the tropics. How effectively these movements will interconnect politically—at the national, regional, and global levels—is an open question. Another question is how these movements will negotiate with existing states over the terms of local and/or cultural sustenance. Potentially, the new movements breathe new life into politics. They transcend the centralizing thrust of the development states of the postwar era and present models for the recovery of local forms of social organization and for the extension of the meaning of civil society. Overriding questions include how new political movements will articulate with states and whether they will replenish nation-states. Many of the people and communities left behind by the development and globalization projects look to nongovernmental organizations (NGOs), rather than to states or international agencies, to represent them and to meet their needs. Indeed, we are currently in a phase of "NGOization," in that national governments and international institutions have lost much of their legitimacy, and NGOs take considerable initiative in guiding grassroots development activities.

As a consequence of these counter-movements, the global market is revealed to be a social invention with decidedly antisocial tendencies. Even the global managers recognize this. In 1996, the World Economic Forum, an organization of executives from the top 1,000 global corporations that meets annually in Davos, Switzerland, produced an article entitled "Start Taking the Backlash to Globalization Seriously." The article states that "a mounting backlash to economic globalization is threatening a very disruptive impact on the economic activity and social stability in many countries" and that globalization "leads to winner-take-all situations; those who come out on top win big, and the losers lose even bigger."[64] Although "a very disruptive impact" can be taken both ways, there is no doubt that the battle lines regarding the assumptions and content of the global development project are being drawn and redrawn daily. In the following (and concluding) chapter we examine how our future and the future of development are shaping up.

8

Whither Development?

Development was perhaps the "master" concept of the social sciences, but it is no longer clear if this continues to be the case, because the concept now appears to be in crisis. The nineteenth-century European social thinkers, who gave us our theories of development, saw social development evolving along rational industrial lines. Eventually the European colonies were expected to make the same journey. Development spoke to the human condition, with a universal expectation. This expectation was formalized in the development project, but it proved to be an unrealizable ideal. It has been replaced with another unrealizable ideal, the globalization project, which speaks a similar language about the centrality of economic growth, but with different means. It is old wine in a new bottle. In this chapter, we review the implications of this reformulation of development and the contention that it has generated across the world.

Legacies of the Development Project

Three observations can be made about the development project and its underlying message. First, it represented a fork in the historical road, favoring the Western model over alternative models in the non-Western world. Second, this fork included a strong dose of economistic thinking, which threatens to overpower all other conceptions of social organization. Third, because of the combined impact of these two forces, the world faces an uncertain future, and development itself is under serious question.

Historical Choices

Historical choices were made in the 1940s, but they grew out of previous historical relationships. Development is a long-standing European idea, woven from two related strands of thought. One is the Promethean self-conception of European civilization, stemming from a combination of the

Aristotelian association of change with a theory of nature, St. Augustine's projection of the Christian theology of salvation as a historical necessity, and the Enlightenment belief in unlimited progress.[1] This progressivism evolved as the core ideal parallel to Europe's emergence as a world power and was expressed in the capitalist ethos of the endless accumulation of wealth as a rational economic activity. The second strand took root in this global endeavor. The inevitable, and unreflective, comparison Europeans made between their civilization and the apparently backward culture of their colonial subjects produced a particularistic conception of modernity that they universalized as human destiny. It was this conception that governed the choice to institutionalize development on a world scale.

We have focused on the political and economic dynamics involved in instituting the development project and on the shortcomings of these institutional dynamics. These were accompanied by a broad range of rationalistic technical and cultural education missions, whose shortcomings are exposed today to the glare of postmodern and pluri-cultural thinking, which questions the inevitability and necessity of monocultures of industrialism and postindustrialism. For instance, the initiative "Education for Nation-Building" was part of the goals of the United Nations Educational, Scientific, and Cultural Organization (UNESCO): promoting scientific humanism as the basis for a development society. This goal energized planners and political elites alike. Education became a vehicle for introducing politics and bringing the advantages of political patronage down to the village level. As Eric Hobsbawm remarked: "In a literal sense, knowledge meant power, most obviously in countries where the state appeared to its subjects to be a machine that extracted their resources and then distributed these resources to state employees."[2] Although some benefits were recorded—fewer for women than for men—education has been routinely framed within the expectations of the development project. Critics have argued that formal schooling has encouraged economic rationalism and a consumer mentality at the expense of deepening pupils' understanding and appreciation of their own cultures and local ecologies. **Participatory action research (PAR)** has become a preferred form of dialogical education, as illustrated in the last case study in the previous chapter.

The development project took the fork that led toward a common future, defined by the standards of the Western experience and bundled up in the idea of national economic growth. It rejected the other fork, the one of empowering local cultures—or at least allowing them to be replenished after the ravages of colonialism. Truly multilateral institutions would have been required to rebuild a world order that emphasized empowerment of local social needs rather than what were presumed to be common economic needs.

How these social needs would be politically implemented is an open question, because there may have been alternatives to the national form of political organization. Certainly advocates of the pan-African movement in the 1950s understood that the national form was not appropriate to African needs at that time. It also appears that the nation-state may not have been appropriate to Central Europe forty years earlier, and recently we have seen the violent implosion of Yugoslavia, Somalia, Rwanda, and Colombia, to name a few examples. Indeed, as a consequence a growing proportion of the world's population is "chronically mobile and routinely displaced," such that identification with place is far more complex now than a conventional sociology of national territorialized populations (and their identity) would allow.[3] At the same time, macro-regions super-imposed on neighboring nation-states are forming tentatively. In other words, the national form of political and economic organization may become only a moment in the longer sweep of history. Whether its democratic legacy will infuse future social organization, and how, is an open question.

Economism

Our second observation about the development project is that its fundamental economism has borne fruit, but not necessarily of a kind expected by some at its inception. Certainly, the capitalist form of economy has prospered, but its wealth and promise of technological abundance are quite unequally distributed. The development project brought all nations into line with the idea of national economic growth, even across the Cold War divide. The pursuit of economic growth within the terms of the development project, however, led to these terms being undercut by global economic relations, especially global money circuits, and the management of these circuits has come to erode national sovereignty.

The globalization project has given *neoclassical economic thought* renewed prominence. Proponents of neoclassical economics perceive national management and public expenditure as interfering with market efficiencies. They believe nationally managed economic growth is anachronistic in an era of global communications, corporate organization, and global freedom for goods and money—but not labor. It is these ideas that underlay the debt management program in the 1980s and still inform global management notions today. More significantly, these ideas guide national political elites on both the right and the left as nations scramble to survive in the global economy, triggering what some refer to as the race to the bottom. This scramble, of course, puts increasing distance between where the world is now and the relatively tidy national framework of the development project previously envisioned.

The scramble reveals itself most dramatically in the *global reorganization of labor*. We examined this in Chapter 6, pointing out that as barriers to investment and trade fall, labor forces across the world become cost competitors with one another. Employment security has declined as firms have either downsized to remain competitive in a global market or relocated production to lower rungs on the global wage ladder. These changes have been in part responsible for the declining living standards in the North. More and more of the labor force finds itself in part-time, low-skill, and low-paying jobs as lean production generates a labor force of self-employed workers with diminishing guarantees of benefits. In the United States, one-third of jobs are estimated to be at risk to the growing productivity of low-wage labor in China, India, Mexico, and Latin America.[4]

There are three important consequences of these changes. One is that the organization of Northern societies around stable employment patterns associated with the expectations of the development project is in serious flux. Another is that, no matter how much automation and postindustrialism may be celebrated as further economic progress, there is still the problem of stable employment—and this dilemma will occupy political elites and labor organizations for decades to come. A third consequence is that, as social entitlements for labor dwindle, antagonism toward immigrant and refugee labor groups intensifies. Current management of labor markets invokes racist divisions among segments of national populations, unraveling the inclusive politics of citizenship that matured within the framework of the metropolitan nation-state. In short, all these changes have profound political consequences because they threaten the liberal underpinnings of Western democracy.

If employment patterns and living standards have become tenuous in the First World, their status is even more fragile in the former Second and Third Worlds. No country is immune to the vicissitudes of a global labor market. Export zones may attract jobs, but can they survive when other zones come on line? In order to compete, some of these zones, noted for their absence of labor protections, include child labor.

Ultimately, the fortunes of labor across the world are intertwined. The development project promised a parallel national movement toward First World–style regulation of national wage levels in an increasingly prosperous consumer society. It now appears that as the project has unraveled, with governments surrendering the social achievements of labor in the name of efficiency, the very institution of wage labor—its organization, its rights, and its social entitlements—is also being transformed. The process is truly global.

Under these circumstances, where the future is unpredictable, development itself is becoming an uncertain paradigm. It is not surprising to find the opposing sides of the development debate reformulating the meaning of development. One example is the common use of the term *sustainable development*, although it has different meanings on each side. These unintended fruits of the development project are another reason to put it in historical context.

Environmental Deterioration

The third observation has to do with the deterioration of the environment. Not only is the future unpredictable, but to a growing number of people around the world it is becoming increasingly uncertain. If the unraveling of the development project has unleashed expressions of diverse identities and local needs, it has at the same time confronted us with the certainty of global environmental degradation. We do have a common future in that we all face growing environmental limits.

In Chapter 7 we saw the wide differences that exist in strategies of sustainability, distribution, and democracy, dividing along global and local lines. Of course, there is a need to attend to global *and* local questions of sustainability, given that diverse cultures inhabit a single planet. The pressing issue now is whether the social and physical world can sustain current economic growth trends with current forms of energy. This problem must be addressed at all levels of organization, under conditions of adequate political representation.

Cumulative deterioration. We can examine the issue from two angles. The first is *cumulative.* We face astounding problems in the depletion of our physical environment. In the United States, for example, 1 million acres disappear annually to urbanization, industrial development, and road building. About 2 million acres of farmland are lost annually to erosion, soil salinization, and flooding or soil saturation, much of which is caused by intensive agriculture. Agriculture is also responsible for serious depletion of groundwater reserves; this water is being consumed up to 160 percent as fast as it can be replenished. By 2050, according to some estimates, the United States will be able to supply only the domestic market with food crops.[5]

From a global perspective, estimates of this type cause deep concern. The United States currently provides 50 percent of the world's grain exports, but overall the world has crossed the threshold to declining rates of agricultural productivity. In 1990, less food was produced per person globally than in 1970, and during the 1980s food production lagged behind population growth in seventy-five poor countries. Plant breeders, addressing these trends, are hard at work developing new seed varieties, such as superhigh-yield rice, blight-resistant potatoes, higher-yielding cassava varieties, and tropical corn, but they are in a race against social trends stemming from the development project.

Looking across the Pacific Ocean to China, we find a veritable economic revolution under way that has serious long-term implications. Factories spring up overnight in the roughly 3,000 development zones displacing rice paddies and farmlands.[6] Foreign investors have been taking advantage of the $2- to $4-a-day wage rates for literate, healthy employees, and automobile producers such as Volkswagen and Ford Motor Company expect huge market growth.[7] Despite China's remarkable gains in industrial efficiency since the early 1980s, however, it also ranks third in carbon dioxide emissions, behind the United States and the former Soviet Union. By some predictions, China could pass the United States in carbon dioxide emissions by 2025.

Meanwhile, intensive agriculture has accelerated since 1949, when the Chinese Communist party assumed state power. Chinese soils are deteriorating from reduced crop rotation, erosion, over-fertilization, and the loss of organic content of soils once nourished by manure-based farming. In 1993 alone, 50 million Chinese farmers abandoned farming for higher-paying urban jobs.[8] Cropland is shrinking at the rate of 1 percent a year, and slowing farm productivity rates suggest a potential 20 percent decline in China's grain production between 1990 and 2030. Even if consumption of animal protein holds constant, China will probably experience a shortfall in grain supplies *in excess of* current world grain exports. Officials at the Chinese National People's Congress in March 1995 acknowledged China's looming grain crisis. Given the projections for shrinking American grain exports, Lester Brown concludes that "the vast deficit projected for China will set up a fierce competition for limited exportable supplies, driving world grain prices far above familiar levels."[9] This is one cumulative scenario—using China as the "wild card" given its sheer size, a population increase of 14 million a year, and its evident industrial trajectory.

Another cumulative scenario is the unpredictability associated with global environmental changes. The United Nations World Commission on Environment and Development noted in 1987 that "major, unintended changes are occurring in the atmosphere, in soils, in waters, among plants and animals, and in relationships among these. . . . The rate of change is outstripping the ability of scientific disciplines and our capabilities to assess and advise." According to epidemiologist A. J. McMichael, these changes foretell threats to global public health arising from "planetary overload, entailing circumstances that are qualitatively different from the familiar, localised problem of environmental pollution." McMichael identifies threats such as immune suppression from ultraviolet radiation, indirect health consequences of climate change on food production and the spread of infections, and loss of biological and genetic resources for producing medicines. He observes:

> This is not to deny the health gains associated with agrarian and industrial settlement, but it emphasizes that human cultural evolution has produced distortions of ecological relationships, causing four main types of health hazard. First came infectious diseases. Then came diseases of industrialisation and environmental pollution by toxic chemicals. Simultaneously, in rich populations, various "lifestyle" diseases of affluence (heart disease, assorted cancers, diabetes, etc.) emerged. Today we face the health consequences of disruption of the world's natural systems.[10]

We cannot pin these cumulative trends on the development project itself; they have had a longer cultural gestation stemming from a long-held belief in the West in the subordination of the natural world to human progress. Industrial development hastened these changes, and the development project acted as midwife to their universalization.

Maldistribution of wealth. The other angle on the sustainability question is a *relational* one, concerning the distribution of global wealth. About 80 percent of the world's income is produced and consumed by 15 percent of the world's population. Meanwhile, despite positive indices of economic growth, the World Bank has estimated that 200 million more people were living in abject poverty at the end of the 1990s than at their beginning. The World Bank's *World Development Report 1999/2000: Entering the 21st Century* notes that "the average per capita income of the poorest and middle thirds of all countries has lost ground steadily over the last several decades compared with the average income of the richest third . . . [and predicts that] the absolute number of those living on $1 per day or less continues to increase" from 1.2 billion in 1987 compared to close to 2 billion by 2015.[11]

Global resources are disproportionately controlled and consumed by a small minority of the world's population, residing mainly in the First

World. For example, grains fed to U.S. livestock equal as much food as is consumed by the combined populations of India and China.[12] Northern nations account for 75 percent of the world's energy use and have produced two-thirds of the greenhouse gases altering the earth's climate. Since 1950, the world's population has consumed as many goods and services, and the U.S. population has used as many mineral resources, as those consumed by all previous generations of people.[13] In short, the practice of development has brought us up sharply against growing environmental, resource, and health limits. It is too early to know whether humans are the ultimate "endangered species."

Rethinking Development

The world appears to be at an important crossroads regarding development. A number of paradoxes have crystallized as the twenty-first century gets under way. These concern the apparent incompatibility of various development initiatives, suggesting that development indeed is in crisis, as an idea and as a practice.

Paradoxes in the Global Development Project

One paradox is *the dilemma of Southern countries aspiring to the Western lifestyle*, at the risk of undermining it. Northern attempts to regulate the burning of the Amazon in the interests of biospheric health have been met with frosty responses on the part of the Brazilian government. Southern elites insist that their countries should have the same right to develop as the First World had historically. Despite withdrawal of support from the World Bank and the U.S. government, the Chinese ruling elite is pursuing the giant Three Gorges Dam project for electric power and flood control, in the name of socialist modernization but with huge costs: $25 billion, environmental damage, the resettlement of 1.3 million people, and a (gradually unraveling) ban on public debate regarding the wisdom of damming the Yangtze River.[14] Malaysian Prime Minister Mahathir Mohamad has planned to catch up to the North by 2020. Part of his plan includes a hydroelectric dam in Sarawak that requires clearing tens of thousands of acres of rain forest and displacing native populations. Mahathir claims that it is inappropriate for the West, which long ago cut down its own forests and subdued native populations, to protest a repetition in Malaysia now.[15] Advocates of this position suggest in addition that the First World offer compensatory financial assistance for the implementation of environmental protections.

This argument reveals another paradox of development. First, the new industrializers want to realize the terms of the development project and its promise that all countries should have the same opportunity. We have seen that these terms apply less and less in a global marketplace, where impermanence of production complexes, markets, and social entitlements is a governing principle. The terms of the globalization project appear to be that *equal opportunity is no longer a national property in a global market*, if it ever was. The globalization project does not promote the same kind of universalism proclaimed by the development project. The development project proposed *replication* of the model of national economic growth across the system of states. By contrast, the globalization project intensifies the differentiation of states and their producing regions (e.g., see Figure 8.1). It assigns communities, regions, and states new niches or specialized roles—including marginalization—in the global economy. Repetition of the Western experience appears to be unrealizable.

A third paradox concerns interpretations of *sustainable development*. As we saw in the previous chapter, this term is part of the discourse of the global managers and the counter-movements alike. Ultimately the difference in interpretation turns on the understanding of what is to be sustained. On the global managers' part, sustainable development is usually interpreted in terms of the viability of the global development project in the face of environmental stress—in other words, regulating the access to and use of natural resources in such a way as to not compromise the accumulation of economic wealth. Where corporations control resources, they are likely to determine the distributional outcome of this form of development. This is particularly so now that the United Nations appears to have bought into the notion of a corporate regime of free trade. In 1999, U.N. Secretary-General Kofi Annan appealed to the corporate world to build a "global compact" with the U.N. to give "a human face to the global market," by consulting about universal labor, environmental, and human rights principles, in return for U.N. support of global free trade. In turn the U.N. Development Program (UNDP) plans to take $50,000 subventions from twenty corporations to sponsor a new program: the Global Sustainable Development Facility. With the expressed goal of encouraging corporate investment in impoverished areas of the world, the U.N. plans to lease access to its networks and its prestigious image to the TNCs. Whether global firms like Dow Chemical, Royal Dutch/Shell, and British mining colossus Rio Tinto can address the needs of the poor for basic

FIGURE 8.1

Resource Use in Selected Countries

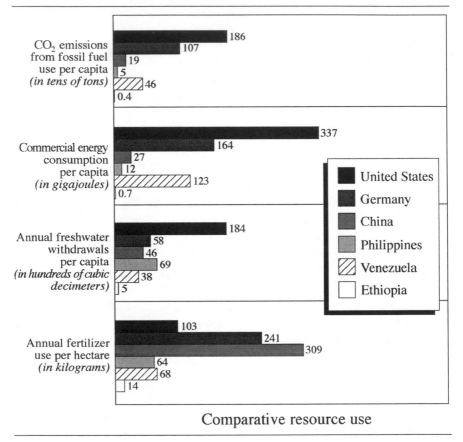

Comparative resource use

SOURCE: World Resource Institute, 1998.

health, education, and food is a reasonable question posed by human rights and environmental groups concerned that U.N.-sanctioned corporations will improve their ability to "greenwash" their global activities.[16] Alternatively, as we saw in Chapter 7, where local communities or counter-movements embrace the ideal of sustainable development, it is more likely to be of a participatory nature, valuing local cultural and ecological diversity. Of course, these initiatives are not without their own dilemmas of inequality within communities and of overzealous NGOs and lack of control over the impact of states and global forces, including external sources of pollution. The social, political, and epistemological distance between advocates of global corporate development and practitioners of "sustainable development" represents a considerable paradox, especially where the global logic is at odds with local biodiversity (as illustrated in the following case study).

CASE STUDY

Indian Community Resistance to Corporate Development

The "blue revolution" in shrimp farming for export to supply affluent consumers has been at considerable social and environmental cost, from the mangroves of Thailand to Ecuadoran aquaculture regions. A significant legal setback to the farmed shrimp industry came in December of 1996, when the Indian Supreme Court ruled that shrimp farms were detrimental to the environment and that farms in the Coastal Regulation Zone of the state of Orissa were to be demolished. Activists and coastal residents celebrated this success in a long campaign against corporate attempts to "greenwash" the shrimp industry, a campaign that was supported by the Food and Agriculture Organization and the World Bank, on the grounds of food security and market expansion, respectively. The campaign included numerous local meetings to disseminate information about the impact on the coasts and local fishing communities of Orissa, Tamil Nadu, and Andhra Pradesh, as well as a gathering of concerned scholars from other regions in India and overseas to collect evidence of the negative social and ecological effects of shrimp farming across the world, including its negative impact on local food security.

Also in 1996, the small Indian village of Pattuvam, in the southern state of Kerala, declared its absolute ownership over all genetic resources within its jurisdiction. This move to preempt corporate genetic prospecting is protected by the 73rd amendment to the Indian Constitution, which mandates decentralization of powers to village-level institutions (the *panchayat* system). The initiative stemmed from a group of young villages, disaffected with the Indian party system and committed to sustainable development. They came up with the idea of having the village youth document local plant species and crop cultivars growing within the village's boundaries. By registering its biodiversity, in local names, the village has moved to claim own-

ership of local genetic materials and deny the possibility of corporate patents applying to these materials. Indian scientist
Vandana Shiva observed: "The declaration gives recognition to
community rights to the intellectual and biological commons and
provides a new interpretation to the *sui generis* option of TRIPS"
(the Trade-Related Intellectual Property Rights provision of the
World Trade Organization charter).

Sources: Goss, 1997, pp. 2-3; Shiva, quoted in Alvares, 1997, pp. 11-12.

A fourth paradox concerns the *politics of food security*. Biotechnology
firms are engaged in a massive campaign to advocate their potential to
feed an increasingly hungry, or food-deficient, world. Monsanto Corporation's home Web page has proclaimed: "Guess Who's Coming to
Dinner? 10 billion by 2030." It warns that low-tech agriculture "will not
produce sufficient crop yield increases and improvements to feed the
world's burgeoning population" and declares that "biotechnology inno-
vations will triple crop yields without requiring any additional farmland,
saving valuable rainforests and animal habitats" and that "biotechnology
can feed the world . . . let the harvest begin." Corporate claims regarding
the potential of genetic engineering in increasing food supplies of a certain kind may not be at issue. Rather, to avoid compounding the problem
of hunger, the issue is to understand its context: For example, 78 percent
of all malnourished children under five years of age in the South live in
countries with food surpluses.[17]

Not only do half a billion rural people lack access to land to grow their
own food, largely because of agro-export bias, but also, and related, a substantial proportion of commercial food production supplies affluent diets
that are unsustainable. As Frances Moore Lappé pointed out in her *Diet
for a Small Planet*, a quarter of a century ago, the mass production of animal
protein is an inefficient *and* inequitable use of world grain supplies. Marc
Lappé and Britt Bailey observe:

> The U.S. beef industry . . . generate(s) close to $40 billion per year, [but]
> leaves less than 10% of planted forage crops to feed people in the U.S. and
> elsewhere. Chemical companies also benefit greatly by having land farmed
> to feed animals, since animal feed carries far less stringent pesticide toler-
> ances than does feed intended for human consumption. The net result of
> using transgenic crops to feed animals is that more chemicals can be used.[18]

It appears that most of the food products (milk, soybeans, animal feed,
canola, sugar beets, corn, and potatoes) targeted by Monsanto for trans-

genic development enhance their chemical business rather than addressing the issue of supplying food to the world's hungry.[19]

Monsanto's CEO, Robert Shapiro, has stated that "Sustainable development will be a primary emphasis in everything we do," but the meaning of sustainable development here is open to question.[20] Arguably, the
embrace of transgenic technology threatens not only sustainable development but sustainability in general, by substituting monopoly for diversity. In describing the "commercial enclosure of the world's seeds,"
Jeremy Rifkin notes that just a century ago hundreds of millions of farmers across the world controlled their seed stocks, and their reproduction,
whereas today "much of the seed stock has been bought up, engineered,
and patented by global companies and kept in the form of intellectual
property," with farmers becoming simply a new market for genetically
altered seeds, under an arrangement termed "bioserfdom."[21] Further, the
large-scale introduction of transgenic crops could contaminate remaining
centers of crop diversity through gene drift from transgenic plants to
landraces—gene complexes with multiple forms of resistance to disease.

Where does this leave "development," then? Its status as an *organizing
myth* has perhaps become clearer. My concepts of the development and
globalization projects are designed to emphasize that development ultimately is a strategy of organizing social change. Development occurs
within a field of power—national, international, or both. Development
also occurs within a cultural field, where local/national cultures adopt,
and are incorporated into, the Western enterprise of endless wealth creation as measured by capital accumulation or an infinite array of commodities. As an organizing myth, development mobilized all societies,
justifying the cultural frame in appeals to universalistic economic rationality. In the post–World War II world, this appeal was anchored in the
substantive idea of national self-determination. It was a powerful idea,
with some tangible benefits across the world, and in retrospect it seems
progressive compared to the globalization project. But listen to the words
of the South Commission, a think tank of Southern intellectuals and political leaders. In their 1990 report, *The Challenge to the South*, they wrote:

> In the period following the end of the Second World War until the end of
> the 1970s, a great many of the countries of the South registered impressive
> social and economic gains. This gave rise to the expectation that the North-
> South divide in wealth and power could be bridged. The 1980s belied that ex-
> pectation. They have been rightly described as a lost decade for development.[22]

This clearly expressed the crisis of development in the decade of structural adjustment, which has continued as states remain in debt and are

adjusted in response to financial crises following unpredictable movements of hot money.

Public disillusionment with development echoes across the world. The Alternative Forum: The Other Voices of the Planet is a group representing the growing networks of nongovernmental organizations (NGOs) that now challenge the global development project. Its 1994 proclamation is worth quoting at length because of how it is framed:

> To overcome the myth of development, to develop more locally self-sufficient economic systems and to disassociate from traditional techno-cratic and economic indicators, does not imply perpetuating the status quo between the supposedly developed North and the supposedly under-developed South. Obviously, the production of goods and services in the South has to increase and must be directed primarily towards meeting the enormous number of basic needs that are not being covered. With or without the permission of the North, the countries of the South have to use up the world natural resources needed for this increase in production. However, out of pure self interest they should try to adapt their productive systems as far as possible to local ecological conditions, rather than copying the irresponsible and unsustainable models of the North. This, above all, means generating and using as much of production locally as possible because this is the level at which real human needs are most clearly expressed. . . . The end of the Development Era will be harder for the North than for the South. In fact, if we take the level of social conflict, the fear of the future and the social fulfillment of people, as general indicators, the North is probably already starting to experience this process.[23]

The sentiments expressed here speak to several issues in the process by which development is being reconceived. The essential point is that groups with this perspective are proposing a departure from the Western model and a reinvigoration of alternative and/or local systems. Of course, local systems do not have a monopoly on virtue—they are often the site of patriarchy and authoritarianism undiluted by individual rights. But human and individual rights are a fundamental part of the new equation. They constitute the discourse of a potential world civil society.

CASE STUDY

The Civil Side of Globalization

Although the globalization project concerns the attempt to impose market rule on the world, this does not mean that there are no other forms of global integration and global connection taking place. One such movement is the rapid proliferation of nongovernmental organizations (NGOs), often as a response to government shortcomings and corporate power and privilege. In the early 1990s there were more than 100,000 NGOs working on environmental issues; their activities included pressuring the World Bank and the U.S. government to withdraw support for the Three Gorges Dam in China. By 2000, there were about 2 million NGOs in the United States alone and more than 20,000 international NGOs in the world. As middle classes have expanded in countries such as Brazil, Mexico, South Korea, the Philippines, and Indonesia, and as governments have contracted, NGOs concerned with human rights, women's rights, environment, and democracy have matured. The globalization project directly engenders much of this counter-movement organization, as evidenced in the massive presence of activist coalitions at the World Trade Organization Ministerial Meeting in Seattle in November 1999. The rise of these groups and coalitions reflects the historical context of corporate globalization as well as the computer and telecommunication revolution, which enables a global exchange and democratization of information. The potential power of such organizations is illustrated in the following story, which demonstrates the countervailing role of information in the discursive confrontation between global corporations and international activism.

On July 30, 1999, *The Wall Street Journal* reported that a Greenpeace member faxed a questionnaire to the Gerber Corporation including a question regarding what steps Gerber had taken to ensure that it was not using genetically modified ingredients in its baby food products. The fax was passed up the corporate hierarchy to the CEO of Novartis, Gerber's Swiss-based parent company. Sensitive to the example of European consumer concerns over the safety of bio-engineered foods, the Novartis Corporation moved decisively to preempt the spread of such concerns in the United States, announcing in a return fax that it would disengage from suppliers of genetically modified corn and soybeans. Some of the most effective NGOs are the following.

- U.S. Grassroots Land Trusts that have purchased roughly 5 million acres of set-aside land to protect open spaces

- The Green Belt Movement in Kenya that has planted more than 20 million trees in a reforestation effort to counter desertification and promote sustainable use of fuel wood for rural communities

- The San Francisco–based Rainforest Action Network

- The Grameen Bank (see case study, page 295)

- The Rural Advancement Foundation International, which has opposed genetically modified crops across the world and successfully challenged the genetic technology that would render harvested seed infertile and farmers dependent on the purchase of new seeds, by naming it the "terminator gene"

- Grupo Ecologico Sierra Gorda, which has obtained official preservation of the diverse but fragile Sierra Gorda mountains of central Mexico by organizing local communities of 100,000 *campesinos* into tree planting groups and establishing small-scale enterprise for impoverished women.

The direction of the development debate will surely depend on the growing presence of such organizations and their ability to mobilize populations and to pressure and shape the political discourse and action of national governments and multilateral institutions. Such engagement constitutes the essence of a global civil society in formation.

Source: Runyan, 1999, pp. 12-21.

The shift in thinking expressed by the Alternative Forum is not simply of scale—from global to local—but also of substance. It speaks to reversing the view of the market as the key instrument of social organization and as subordinating the economy to community and ecological requirements. Once we address the issue of why we presently surrender our social and natural resources to market disciplines, we can raise the question of who benefits. If countries are indeed racing to the bottom by submitting to the logic of lower labor costs and stripping away social protections, where is this taking us, and who stands to gain?

It is interesting to observe that the members of the Alternative Forum perceive Westerners as being at a comparative disadvantage because they are much more thoroughly incorporated into, and therefore more thoroughly affected by the reversals of, the development myth. One reversal that is currently redefining First World politics is the perceived threat of

formerly colonized peoples migrating into the First World. This movement has the air of historical chickens coming home to roost:

> For the first time the Northern countries themselves are exposed to the bit-
> ter results of Westernizing the world. Immigration, population pressure,
> tribalism with mega-arms, and above all, the environmental consequences
> of worldwide industrialization threaten to destabilize the Northern way of
> life. It is as if the cycle which had been opened by Columbus is about to be
> closed at the end of this century.[24]

These are admittedly alarming notions, but it is necessary to remember that the first rule in responding to gloomy predictions is to recognize
that the more we can understand the process, the better we can respond
to it. Most important, understanding the process allows us to see that the
history of development wove together the fate of people on opposite
sides of the world.

Development and Governance

Meanwhile, the institutions of the original development project will continue devising measures to improve or ameliorate the conditions of the
world's populations. In an idea resembling the 1980s debt-for-nature
swap, the suggestion was made at the U.N. Social Summit in 1995 to insist
that every dollar of canceled debt should be spent on social services, and
forgiven debt should be matched by reductions in arms expenditure. Sub-
Saharan Africa was named as the major development challenge.[25] In an
era when foreign aid faces growing skepticism, the prime minister of Denmark, Poul Nyrup Rasmussen, explained the rationale for continuing aid:
"We have a good argument now, a very concrete one, for ordinary people,
which is, if you don't help the third world, if you don't help northern
Africa, if you don't help eastern and central Europe with a little part of
your welfare, then you will have these poor people in our society."[26]

If the globalization project has any appeal to people in the North beyond the idea of rising prosperity—which is credible only to a minority—
it is the notion of *Northern security*. In this scenario, attending to Southern
needs is a prerequisite to stemming the tide of migration. Because economic conditions are hardly robust across the First World, freedom of
movement for labor is an unlikely political platform—even though under
the terms of the globalization project freedom is extended to money, capital, and goods. The security question, then, compels the global managers
to focus on a *new form of loan conditionality*: assistance when governments
attend to stabilizing their populations. This factor has been included in

the World Bank's new lending criteria, concerned with "state effectiveness." It is part of a broad strategy of stabilization to sustain the idea of "globalization" as the path to economic well-being. Thus the Bank stated in its *World Development Report 1997*:

> The cost of not opening up will be a widening gap in living standards between those countries that have integrated and those that remain outside. For lagging countries the route to higher incomes will lie in pursuing sound domestic policies and building the capability of the state. Integration gives powerful support to such policies—and increases the benefits from them—but it cannot substitute for them. *In that sense, globalization begins at home. But multilateral institutions such as the World Trade Organization have an important role to play in providing countries with the incentive to make the leap.* [italics added][27]

The leap may be a leap of faith: faith in institutions created to sponsor privatization. The Asian financial crisis of the late 1990s weakened faith in privatization, emphasizing that one consequence of financial deregulation is that speculation rather than social investment drives the restless movement of money across national boundaries. The World Bank became more circumspect in the light of Malaysia's relative success in implementing capital controls in defiance of the financial orthodoxy of the development establishment in 1997 (see Chapter 5). In the meantime, the emphasis on governance includes a strong dose of decentralization to partner private entrepreneurship and the release of "social capital." This new emphasis on alternative scales of governance (sub-national and supranational) has several interpretations. First, it occurs in an ideological context where national governments have been perceived to be either bureaucratically top-heavy or too interventionist in the market. Second, and related, it occurs in a historical context where state organizations have lost power and capacity as a result of the deregulation of banking and financial markets in the post–Bretton Woods era. Loss of control over national currency values and over national macroeconomic policy under the debt regime has weakened the power of central governments and devolved some fiscal powers to sub-national authorities. Third, state shrinking has enabled and encouraged a proliferation of sub-national NGO activity and a growing awareness that good governance involves mutual negotiation between NGOs and the state. In fact, the World Bank's *World Development Report 1999/2000* urges participatory policy making, observing that "Institutions of good governance that embody such processes are critical for development and should encompass partnerships among all elements of civil society."[28] Fourth, the reformulation of governance expresses the redistribution of state power upward and downward, as a consequence of the globalization project of globally instituted liberalization of social and economic policies. Fifth, the decentralization of governance is at one and the same time an attempt to stabilize communities ravaged by structural adjustment. One of the most palpable indicators of this latter interpretation is the mushrooming micro-credit business, illustrated in the following case study.

CASE STUDY

Global Meets Local: The Micro-Credit Business

Micro-credit is one of the fastest growing world industries today. Its popularity stems from the model of the Grameen Bank, begun by Muhammad Yunus in 1976 in a village near Chittagong, Bangladesh, to assist impoverished villagers. With a high rate of payback of 90+ percent and a loan volume of $500 million in 1995, this bank has rapidly become known as the champion of poor women across the South. It extends small amounts of commercial credit for micro-enterprise to cells of five women, each of whom receives a loan and guarantees that all members of the cell will repay their own loans, at an interest rate of about 20 percent. Grameen has been so successful that it no longer requires subsidies from donor governments or the International Fund for Agricultural Development.

Micro-credit has mushroomed, with liberal assistance from international donor agencies such as the Ford Foundation, UNDP, and the Swiss Agency for Development and Cooperation. Interest rates for micro-credit range between 20 to 100 percent, so multilateral development banks embrace micro-credit as an opportunity to replace capital-intensive "development as charity" with the more profitable "development as business." The business is shared around. In India, for example, banks lend to NGOs at 9 percent, NGOs are allowed to lend to self-help groups (SHGs) at rates up to 15 percent, and SHGs in turn charge up to 30 percent to individual borrowers. The expectation is that the poor will use the credit for commercial purposes, but the loans are largely used to meet daily consumption needs. Nonetheless, the development community is riding the micro-credit bandwagon given that it is consistent with the dominant paradigm of self-help, decentralization, and stimulating "social capital" at the local level to promote community-based entrepreneurship, and given that structural adjustment programs have forced the poor into self-employment. The World Bank established a microlending arm, the Consultative Group to Assist the Poorest (CGAP) at the Fourth World Conference on Women in Beijing, in 1995, with the goal of "systematically increasing resources in microfinance." Although the CGAP program comes with conditions governed by profitability considerations, such as countries privatizing their microlending institutions and strengthening their debt collection laws, there are other micro-credit operations like the Self-Employed Women's Association (SEWA) of Ahmedabad, India, that focus on empowering women with practical support programs like labor advocacy, provision of health care, and training.

Sources: Tyler, 1995, p. A6; Kane, 1996; Singh & Wysham, 1997.

Unthinking Development

Where does this leave development theory, then? Let us retrace its steps. Initially, development theory was formalized as part of the foundation of the development project. It took its cues from nineteenth-century European social thought, which was concerned primarily with different aspects of the rise of capitalism and industrialism. The grand sociological trio—Karl Marx, Max Weber, and Emile Durkheim—addressed quite distinct problems, respectively: How can we account for the transition between distinct forms of social organization (feudalism, capitalism, and socialism)? How can we account for the fact that capitalism developed in the West and not the Orient? And how is it possible to retain social cohesion as the division of labor advances?

If there was any common ground among these theorists and others, it was in their identification of *contradictions* attending development in the capitalist era. Marx saw class inequality as the major contradiction and the market as a new religion that obscures inequality. Weber distrusted the rationalizing thrust that displaced wonder and cultural myth-making. Durkheim worried about social disorder as the scale and complexity of society grew. These social theorists have recently been criticized as proclaiming a Eurocentric "grand narrative" of history and social change. Whether they did or not, their interpreters in the earlier part of the twentieth century reproduced the progressivism of the Eurocentric narrative.

Such progressivism in turn shaped and formalized development theory in the mid-twentieth century, giving rise to the development project.

The most powerful theoretical critique of developmentalism came in Immanuel Wallerstein's formulation of **world system analysis** in the early 1970s. The argument he made was twofold. First, since the rise of the sixteenth-century European capitalist world economy under colonialism, the world has been hierarchically organized as a systemic whole divided into unequal zones of specialization—with Europe in the center, and the colonial and postcolonial world in the periphery. Like the middle classes of industrial society, there is also a buffer zone between the poles: the semi-periphery, comprising the middle-income states. In the postwar world, the newly industrializing countries joined other semi-peripheral states like Australia, New Zealand, and Canada; the Southern European states; and the Soviet bloc countries. Second, Wallerstein has produced a sustained critique of the character of developmentalism as an organizing myth, both because of its misapplication as a national strategy in a hierarchical world where only some states can "succeed" and because it has displaced other, more equitable, notions of social organization.[29]

As the development project proceeded, we have seen that revised conceptions of development emerged in response to changing conditions. Growing Third World poverty provoked the "basic needs" approach, new socialist/**dependency** interpretations of underdevelopment as a historical condition, and redefinitions of human development indexes.[30] The phenomenon of the newly industrializing countries in the 1970s produced the World Bank's notion of development as participation in the world market.

The debt crisis of the 1980s punctured illusions of development, and debt management became the new orthodoxy. The debt regime was a dress rehearsal for a reformulation of the development enterprise as a global project. This project seeks to embed regulatory mechanisms in global institutions as well as in restructured states acting on behalf of global economic management. Accompanying and shaping these developments, counter-movements have emerged with alternatives that we have identified as characteristically expressive (noneconomistic) and often rooted in notions of reducing the scale of resource use and stabilizing and revitalizing communities. It is interesting to note that in its turn-of-the-century *World Development Report*, the World Bank redefines development holistically, in part as a response to the groundswell of civil opposition to the centralizing implications of the original model. The Bank's contribution to the twenty-first century development debates is to have formulated what it calls the Comprehensive Development Framework

(CDF), which it terms a "compass, not a blueprint." Although the goals remain "to fight poverty and encourage growth," the Bank stresses that the new strategy "would involve consulting with and winning the support of actors in civil society, as well as NGOs, donor groups, and the private sector" to articulate a "long-term, collective vision of needs and solutions" capable of drawing "sustained national support," and including equal treatment of structural and social concerns, within a context of a "stable macroeconomy, shaped by prudent fiscal and monetary policies."[31] In short, the process of redefining development through appropriating ideas and language stems from the counter-movements, and the acknowledgment of previous shortcomings continues.

Redefining development is a healthy process as long as it goes beyond rhetoric. Even healthier, perhaps, would be a fundamental "unthinking" of development as a linear process and a rethinking of social and ecological priorities to sustain human existence in the long run. This would involve "de-colonizing" the future from singular, scientistic predictions, enabling an "ecological, multifarious and just future" that recognizes and realizes cultural pluralism and biodiversity.[32]

If one were to offer a comparative sketch of the two sides of the development debate, it would look something like this. Advocates of the project of globalization believe in the rationality of an open world economy, but the level playing field that is supposed to drive this operation is a fiction at best and an assertion of power at worst. Globalists deploy free trade arguments to "open" national economies to privileged investors and transnational corporations; they propose deregulated money markets that encourage financial speculation and huge, destabilizing capital flight as wealthy nationals shift their—and sometimes the public's—money to more inviting regions of the global economy. By contrast, opponents of the project of globalization begin from the position that the logic of market rule is at odds with the sustainability of local knowledges, cultures, and biodiversity, and with the ideal of social equality. Two examples will suffice. First, UNICEF reported in September 1999 that the status of women in Eastern Europe has eroded significantly since the introduction of market rule. More than half of the 25 million jobs lost over the past decade were held by women, and women and girls have been disproportionately affected by deteriorating social services and rising patterns of abuse. Positive responses have emerged through increasing numbers of female entrepreneurs and grassroots organizations addressing domestic violence.[33] Second, in August 1999, French farmers led a protest, supported by labor unions, ecologists, and leftist organizations, against a nearly completed McDonald's restaurant in the town of Millau. The leader of the protest declared the struggle to be against globalization and for people's right to choose how to feed themselves, targeting McDonald's as the symbol of "the multinationals of foul food." A French political analyst observed that Europeans have had an "allergy" to the accumulation of American power since the end of the Cold War, the most virulent expression of that power being imported food or food culture.[34]

Opposition to the globalization project sometimes situates resistance in relation to a universal process like cultural imperialism (echoing across cultures to generate transnational movements) and sometimes anchors its resistance in local communities. In the latter instance, the growing participatory action research movement is a key example of this kind of localism, where communities seek self-empowerment through active participation in self-knowledge. At its best, this process combines the recovery of local ways of interpreting and being in the world with an attempt to understand local ways as having been formed through relations with other cultural and social processes over time. This is the meaning of cosmopolitan localism (as discussed in Chapter 7). The cosmopolitan sensibility reduces the tendency toward the "metaphysical sedentarism" that assigns people, and culture, to physical places at the risk of privileging and/or romanticizing territorialized ("national") cultures and denying identity (and rights) to displaced or minority populations.[35] Thus communities are historical products and must come to terms with the national states and market institutions within which they currently exist, and sometimes this process brings their claims to the global arena.

A dramatic and successful example of empowerment through combined political, legal, and cultural activism was the victory for all aboriginal people in Australia that was won by the Murray Islander people of the Torres Strait in June 1992. The High Court of Australia, after years of pressure from aboriginal people, discarded the legal fiction of Australia as *terra nullius* (land belonging to no one) established at the moment of British colonization in 1788. Aboriginal negotiators must now clarify "the indissoluble tie of Aboriginal and Islander people to their land in contrast to the conception of land as a tradeable item."[36] The problem in drawing distinctions is that there are two basic languages in this case—one economic and one cultural. To the extent that the cultural language succeeds, it subverts the discourse of development. Elsewhere, in Ecuador, after years of pressure and an uprising in 1990, the indigenous rights movement won a significant voice, whereby the constitution has been revised to recognize Ecuador as a pluri-national state, providing legal recognition for indigenous community governments and bilingual, bicultural education in indigenous areas of Ecuador.[37] In April 1999, the Inuit of Northern

Canada obtained self-determination in a new territory called Nunavut, on the strength of their oral history–based claims to land occupied by white settlement.[38] The phenomenon of indigenous claims being taken seriously is perhaps a measure of both the growing power of transnational movements and the unraveling of the certitude of Western developmentalism. It is also a powerful symbol of the challenge to the cultural nationalism of majority rule inscribed in the development of the system of nation-states.

Elsewhere, communities must negotiate the complexity of class, gender, and cultural relations that shape those communities and connect them to their broader national and global contexts. Whether or not it endures as a grassroots initiative, the Chiapas revolt addresses this complexity in signaling a new form of political action. It powerfully linked the struggle for local rights to history—history in the long term in the sense that this region of Mayan ancestry has experienced waves of foreign intervention and exploitation of its natural and human resources, and history in the present in the sense that in pursuing structural adjustment, the Mexican state threatened all such communities (rural and urban) by steadily withdrawing social subsidies and was on the brink of withdrawing final protections from overwhelming global forces with the implementation of the North American Free Trade Agreement. The Chiapas revolt was rooted in local empowerment demands, but it resonated across communities in similar predicaments in Mexico, and indeed across the world.

From this perspective, the question "Whither development?" finds an answer in a basic idea: the idea of re-embedding the market in society. Market rule privileges abstract economic laws and profits over people and their relationship to the environment. There is a growing recognition of the costs of market rule, not the least being the imploding "Washington consensus." For instance, on October 6, 1998, the World Bank president publicly dissociated his institution from the U.S. president and the IMF managing director's position in managing the global financial crisis, remarking that global financial management was distracting attention from the expanding ranks of the global unemployed and the growing risk of political instability.[39] Further, different voices from within the G-7/multilateral institutional establishment are calling for attention to labor rights and environmental safety, as well as new controls on global markets, especially with recurring financial crises. In 1998, British Prime Minister Tony Blair called for a new Bretton Woods, and others talk of a new global financial architecture.

At the same time there is a *market disembedding* initiative under way in negotiations around an (OECD-based) Multilateral Agreement on Investment (MAI), to formulate global investment rules. While the WTO is as yet empowered to rule only on "trade-related investments" (TRIMS), an MAI would relax restrictions on foreign investment in any member state and grant the legal right for foreigners to invest and operate competitively in all sectors of the economy.[40] The initial proposal, entitled "A Level Playing Field for Direct Investment Worldwide," argued that foreign investment is essential to today's corporate strategies, with global communications creating a global marketplace. Further, it argued that multilateral rules should go beyond right of entry provisions to allow "accompanying measures" such as freedom to make financial transfers, rendering domestic regulations transparent.[41] Viewed as an open door for unregulated financial flows, privileging capital over citizenship, this initiative was stalled by (Internet) organized opposition in 1998, in part because of its discovery by national governments that moved immediately for exemptions, and in part because of the discovery by citizens and NGOs that it would lock in market rule for twenty years at a minimum. It is clear that citizens are not quite ready to completely surrender authority to the market, and there are active transnational movements, like the People's Global Action, organizing resistance to these measures across national boundaries. At the same time other initiatives, such as fair trade coalitions flourish. These are networks dedicated to empowering all social groups involved in these alternative commodity networks, so that trading relations are non-hierarchical, non-exploitative, and informed by considerations of social and environmental sustainability.

Second, there is the notion of *cosmopolitan localism*. To be sustainable, the global community faces a double challenge. The first is to regain popular control over market institutions, including money, so as to recover and rediscover social priorities. Counter-movements—transnational, national, and local—address this challenge, from the PGA through national NGOs to local alternative currency movements. Market re-embedding is a multilevel task, and regaining control over money means ending the current dynamic wherein money reproduces itself (and its culture of social polarization and resource abuse) through credit and other fictitious and speculative forms. The second challenge is to recognize that the global community, in integrating, does not have to choose the path of homogeneity. It means realizing constituent communities' needs by situating them within their world-historical context. In other words, the community comes to understand how it came to be within the context of global processes, and also how its members can empower themselves through that context. That includes ensuring that community empowerment means also empowering the individuals and minorities in those communities. It also means realizing that there are other communities with similar needs, precisely because they are woven from similar world-historical threads. It was the genius of the Chiapas rebels to articulate this (even though Chiapas state is under Mexican military occupation). It is also the mark of our times that these historical connections are now being made as the currency of development is devalued.

Conclusion

This concluding chapter brings some closure to the story of the rise and demise of the development project. Development was a powerful organizing ideal that was institutionalized on a world scale. In this text, we focused on the changing patterns of development as a world-historical project, citing individual case histories as instances of global trends. We examined developmentalist assumptions, practices, and social legacies. These legacies continue, even as global development overwhelms the historic project of national development. While states endure, their public capacities—those geared to comprehensive citizenship—are under threat across the world in varying degrees. Many international agencies, governments, nongovernmental organizations, and populations still pursue national development despite its reformulation and its eroding infrastructures. Development strategies, however, tend to privilege global rather than national economic forces. A protective global countermovement (as a combined movement) is imminent, evidenced in the proliferation of resistance movements among citizens, workers, consumers, landless peasants, indigenous peoples, and so forth.

Human sustainability, however, will depend on more than environmental conservation and less on economic growth. It requires preservation of community in inclusive terms rather than the exclusive or specialized terms of economic globalization. The moral of this story—of the development project's demise—is that the world is at a critical juncture in these respects. A powerful reorganizing myth of globalization would further weaken social protections in the name of economic efficiency. Public capacity to care for disadvantaged populations and to protect human and environmental futures is threatened. The globalization project is not just a successor to the development project. Its prescriptions are double edged because its conception of the future erases the past—a past created by movements for social protection. As the development project has subsided, a *general* reversal of thinking has emerged. The present is no longer the logical development of the past; rather, it is increasingly the hostage of the future. Those who define the future will frame this new post-developmentalist debate. At present, as we have seen, debate pivots on the adequacy of the market as a guardian of social and environmental sustainability. But this is a prelude to a broader, historical set of questions concerning the scale of human community and governance and the growing tension between material affluence and survival of the human species.

Endnotes

Development and the Global Marketplace

1. Crossette, 1997.
2. Hellman, 1994, p. 157.
3. Norberg-Hodge, 1992, pp. 95, 97-98.
4. Jose Maria Arguedes, "A Call to Certain Academics," translated from the Quechua by William Rowe.
5. Ruggiero, 1996, 1998.
6. Neville, 1997, pp. 48-49.
7. "Coffee Drinkers: Where Are Your Beans Grown?," 1999, p. 3B.
8. Rosenberg, 1998, p. A38.
9. Norberg-Hodge, 1994-1995, p. 2.
10. Hedland and Sundstrom, 1996, p. 889.
11. Crossette, 1997.
12. Korzeniewicz, 1994.
13. Collins, 1995.
14. Barnet & Cavanagh, 1994, p. 383.

Chapter 1: Instituting the Development Project

1. *Human Development Report*, quoted in Rist, 1997, p. 9.
2. Davidson, 1992, pp. 83, 99-101.
3. Quoted in Rist, 1997, p. 58.
4. Bujra, 1992, p. 147.
5. Bujra, 1992, p. 146.
6. Quoted in Stavrianos, 1981, p. 247.
7. Chirot, 1977, p. 124.
8. Wolf, 1982, pp. 369, 377.
9. Wacker, 1994, pp. 132-134.
10. James, 1963.
11. Quoted in Davidson, 1992, p. 164.

12. Memmi, 1967, p. 74.

13. Fanon, 1967, pp. 254-255.

14. Cooper, 1997, pp. 66-67.

15. Stavrianos, 1981, p. 624.

16. Adams, 1993, pp. 2-3, 6-7.

17. Quoted in Esteva, 1992, p. 6.

18. Quoted in Davidson, 1992, p. 167.

19. Cooper, 1997, p. 64.

20. Esteva, 1992, p. 7.

21. Rist, 1997, p. 79.

22. Cited in Cooper, 1997, p. 79.

23. Quoted in Davidson, 1992, p. 203.

24. Davidson, 1992, pp. 183-184.

25. Dube, 1988, p. 1.

26. Rostow, 1960.

27. Quoted in Hettne, 1990, p. 53.

28. LaTouche, 1993, p. 201.

29. Shiva, 1991, p. 215.

30. Quoted in Hettne, 1990, p. 3.

31. Kaldor, 1990, pp. 62, 67.

32. Quoted in Dube, 1988, p. 16.

33. Bose, 1997, p. 153.

34. Lehman, 1990, pp. 5-6.

35. Lehman, 1990, pp. 5-6.

36. Harris, 1987, p. 17.

37. Cardoso & Faletto, 1979, pp. 129-131.

38. Kemp, 1989, pp. 162-165.

Chapter 2: The Development Project in Global Context

1. Block, 1977, pp. 76-77.

2. Quoted in Brett, 1985, pp. 106-107.

3. Quoted in Kolko, 1988, p. 17.

4. Cleaver, 1977, p. 16.

5. Wood, 1986, pp. 38-61.

6. Ideas and quotations from Rich, 1994, pp. 55, 56.

7. Quoted in Adams, 1993, p. 32.

8. Rich, 1994, p. 72.

9. Rich, 1994, p. 58; George & Sabelli, 1994, p. 15.

10. Rich, 1994, p. 73.

11. The examples in the next four paragraphs are from Rich, 1994, pp. 10-13, 39, 41, and 94.

12. Rich, 1994, p. 75.

13. Adams, 1993, pp. 68-69.

14. Quoted in Magdoff, 1969, p. 54.

15. Magdoff, 1969, p. 124; Chirot, 1977, pp. 164-165.

16. Quoted in Williams, 1981, pp. 56-57.

17. Brett, 1985, p. 209; Wood, 1986, p. 73; Rist, 1997, p. 88.

18. Brett, 1985, p. 209; Wood, 1986, p. 73.

19. Adams, 1993, p. 73.

20. Rich, 1994, p. 84.

21. Harris, 1987, p. 28.

22. Harris, 1987, p. 102.

23. Grigg, 1993, p. 251.

24. Revel & Riboud, 1986, pp. 43-44.

25. Grigg, 1993, pp. 243-244; Bradley & Carter, 1989, p. 104. Self-sufficiency measures do not necessarily reveal the state of nutrition in a country or region, because a country—for example, Japan—may have a low self-sufficiency because its population eats an affluent diet, which depends on imports.

26. Hoogvelt, 1997, p. 31.

27. For an extended discussion of food regimes, see Friedmann, 1990; for a discussion of the international monetary regime associated with Bretton Woods, see Ruggie, 1982.

28. Quoted in Magdoff, 1969, p. 135.

29. Quoted in George, 1977, p. 170.

30. Raikes, 1988, pp. 175, 178.

31. Harriet Friedmann, 1992, p. 373.

32. Wessel, 1983, p. 173.

33. Chung, 1990, p. 143.

34. To be sure, Korean farmers protested and in the 1970s the state modernized rice-farming regions to raise rural incomes, but this policy ran out of steam as rice consumption continued to decline with the changing Korean diet (McMichael & Kim, 1994).

35. Dudley & Sandilands, 1975; Friedmann, 1990, p. 20.

36. Morgan, 1980, p. 301.

37. Quoted in George, 1977, p. 170.

38. Friedmann, 1990, p. 20.

39. Harriet Friedmann, 1992, p. 373.

40. McMichael & Raynolds, 1994, p. 322. The terms *peasant foods* and *wage foods* are from de Janvry, 1981.

41. Hathaway, 1987, p. 13.

42. Revel & Riboud, 1986, p. 62.

43. de Janvry, 1981, p. 179.

44. Middleton, O'Keefe, & Moyo, 1993, p. 129.

45. Wessel, 1983, p. 158.

46. Berlan, 1991, pp. 126-127.

47. Burbach & Flynn, 1980, p. 66; George, 1977, p. 171.

48. Quoted in George, 1977, pp. 171-172.

49. Harriet Friedmann, 1992, p. 377.

50. Dalrymple, 1985, p. 1069; Andrae & Beckman, 1985; Raikes, 1988.

51. George, 1977, pp. 174-175.

52. Agarwal, 1994, p. 312.

53. Griffin, 1974; Pearse, 1980; Byres, 1981; Sanderson, 1986b; Dhanagare, 1988; Raikes, 1988; Llambi, 1990.

54. Griffin, 1974; Athreya, Djurfeldt, & Lindberg, 1990.

55. Shiva, 1991, pp. 175-176.

56. Lipton, 1977.

57. McMichael & Kim, 1994; Araghi, 1995.

58. Grigg, 1993, pp. 103-104, 185; Araghi, 1995.

59. Rich, 1994, pp. 95, 155.

60. Rich, 1994, pp. 91, 97; Feder, 1983, p. 222.

61. de Janvry, 1981; Araghi, 1995.

Chapter 3: The Global Economy Reborn

1. Arrighi, 1994, p. 68.

2. Bello, Cunningham, & Rau, 1994, p. 7.

3. Hoogvelt, 1987, pp. 43-45.

4. Harris, 1987, p. 75.

5. Hoogvelt, 1987, p. 40.

6. Knox & Agnew, 1994, p. 340.

7. The term *newly industrializing countries* (NICs) was coined by the Organization for Economic Cooperation and Development in 1979 and included four other Southern European countries: Spain, Portugal, Yugoslavia, and Greece. The common attributes of NICs were (1) rapid penetration of the world market with manufactured exports, (2) a rising share of industrial

employment, and (3) an increase in real GDP per capita relative to the First World (Hoogvelt, 1987, p. 25).

8. Brett, 1985, pp. 185-186.

9. Hoogvelt, 1987, p. 28.

10. Brett, 1985, p. 188.

11. Knox & Agnew, 1994, p. 347.

12. Hoogvelt, 1987, p. 64.

13. Knox & Agnew, 1994, p. 331. (Between 1975. and 1989, this group enlarged to include China, South Africa, Thailand, and Taiwan; Argentina dropped out.)

14. Martin & Schumann, 1997, pp. 100-101.

15. Quoted in Brett, 1985, p. 188.

16. The following two paragraphs draw on Gereffi, 1989.

17. McMichael, 1987.

18. Nayyar, 1976, p. 25.

19. Hoogvelt, 1987, pp. 26-31. At the same time, as a consequence of import-substitution industrialization and the buoyancy of the export-oriented industrialization strategy in the 1970s, the composition of imports, mainly from the First World, moved from manufactured consumer goods to capital goods.

20. Landsberg, 1979, pp. 52, 54.

21. See Gereffi, 1994.

22. Quoted in Baird & McCaughan, 1979, p. 130.

23. Baird & McCaughan, 1979, pp. 130-132; Bernard, 1996. For an excellent and detailed study of the *maquiladora* industry, see Sklair, 1989.

24. Henderson, 1991, p. 3.

25. Reich, 1992, pp. 81, 113.

26. Sivanandan, 1989, pp. 2, 8; Strom, 1999, p. A3; Stimson, 1999, p. A1.

27. See Harris, 1987. See also Gereffi, 1994, for an alternative formulation of the world product as a series of commodity chains.

28. Brown, 1993, p. 46.

29. Barnet & Cavanagh, 1994, p. 300; Dicken, 1998, p. 131.

30. For an extended account of the gendered restructuring of the world labor force, see Mies, 1991, and Benería & Feldman, 1992.

31. Baird & McCaughan, 1979, pp. 135-136.

32. Baird & McCaughan, 1979, p. 135.

33. Brown, 1993, p. 47.

34. Ellwood, 1993, p. 5; Korten, 1995, p. 323; Karliner, 1997, p. 5.

35. Daly & Logan, 1989, p. 67; Martin & Schumann, 1997, p. 112.

36. *The Economist*, July 16, 1994, p. 56; Beams, 1999.

37. *The New Internationalist*, August 1993, p. 18.

38. Hobsbawm, 1992, p. 56; Araghi, 1999.

39. Henderson, 1991.

40. *Pacific Basin Reports*, August 1973, p. 171.

41. Fröbel, Heinrichs, & Kreye, 1979, pp. 34-36.

42. Henderson, 1991, p. 54.

43. Henderson, 1991, pp. 57-58, 61.

44. Korzeniewicz, 1994, p. 261.

45. *The Economist*, June 3, 1995, p. 59.

46. Heffernan & Constance, 1994, pp. 42-45; Kneen 1990, p. 10; Heffernan, 1999, p. 4.

47. Friedmann, 1991.

48. Sanderson, 1986a; Raynolds, Myhre, McMichael, Carro-Figueroa, & Buttel, 1993; Raynolds, 1994.

49. DeWalt, 1985.

50. DeWalt, 1985.

51. Friedland, 1994.

52. Rama, 1992, p. 269.

53. Schoenberger, 1994, p. 59.

54. Quoted in Appelbaum & Gereffi, 1994, p. 54.

55. Daly & Logan, 1989, p. 13; Schoenberger, 1994, pp. 59-61; Chossudovsky, 1997, pp. 87-88; Herbert, 1996.

56. Templin, 1994, p. A10; Meredith, 1997.

57. Schwedel & Haley, 1992, p. 49; Kuenzler, 1992, p. 47.

58. Carlsen, 1991, pp. 20-23.

59. Crook, 1993, p. 16.

60. Uchitelle, 1994, p. D2; Barboza, 1999.

Chapter 4: International Finance and the Rise of Global Managerialism

1. Hoogvelt, 1987, p. 58.

2. Strange, 1994, p. 112.

3. Crook, 1992, p. 10.

4. Helleiner, 1996, pp. 111-119.

5. Strange, 1994, p. 107.

6. Quoted in Brecher & Costello, 1994, p. 30.

7. *The New Internationalist*, August 1993, p. 18; Kolko, 1988, p. 24.

8. *Debt Crisis Network*, 1986, p. 25.

9. Kolko, 1988, p. 26.
10. Lissakers, 1993, p. 59; Arruda, 1994, p. 44.
11. George, 1988, p. 36.
12. George, 1988, p. 33.
13. Lissakers, 1993, p. 66.
14. Lissakers, 1993, p. 56.
15. Lissakers, 1993, pp. 69-73.
16. Wood, 1986, pp. 247, 253, 255; Evans, 1979.
17. George, 1988, p. 6.
18. Amin, 1997, p. 28.
19. Quoted in Wood, 1986, p. 197.
20. Hoogvelt, 1987, p. 77.
21. Seers, 1979, p. 12.
22. Rich, 1994, p. 84.
23. Rich, 1994, p. 85.
24. Wood, 1986, pp. 210-212; Hoogvelt, 1987, p. 102.
25. Quoted in Adams, 1993, p. 123.
26. Hoogvelt, 1987, pp. 80-87.
27. Rist, 1997, pp. 152-153.
28. Schaeffer, 1997, p. 49; Helleiner, 1996, pp. 171-175.
29. Adams, 1993, p. 127.
30. Hoogvelt, 1987, pp. 87-95.
31. George, 1988, p. 6.
32. Walton & Seddon, 1994, pp. 13-14.
33. George, 1988, pp. 28-29.
34. Lissakers, 1993, p. 67.
35. Singh, 1992, p. 141.
36. George, 1988, pp. 12, 73.
37. Singh, 1992, p. 144.
38. George, 1988, p. 60.
39. Economic Commission for Latin America and the Caribbean, 1989, p. 123.
40. Quoted in Helleiner, 1996, p. 177.
41. George, 1988, pp. 41, 49.
42. Barkin, 1990, pp. 104-105.
43. Cheru, 1989, pp. 24, 27-28, 41-42.
44. Cited in George, 1988, p. 95.
45. Rich, 1994, pp. 186-187.
46. Singh, 1992, pp. 138-139, 147-148.

47. Bello, Cunningham, & Rau, 1994.

48. George, 1992, p. xvi.

49. George, 1992, p. 97.

50. Cox, 1987, p. 301.

51. Corbridge, 1993, pp. 129, 131-132.

52. Calculated from Crook, 1993, p. 16; Avery, 1994, p. 95; Hoogvelt, 1997, p. 138.

53. George, 1988, p. 97.

54. Crook, 1992, p. 9.

55. Crook, 1993, p. 16.

56. Arrighi, 1990; Khor, quoted in Danaher & Yunus, 1994, p. 28.

57. Payer, 1974.

58. Canak, 1989.

59. Bangura & Gibbon, 1992, p. 19; World Bank, 1981.

60. Gibbon, 1992, p. 137.

61. Bernstein, 1990, p. 17.

62. Beckman, 1992, p. 99.

63. Gibbon, 1992, p. 141.

64. Stephany Griffith-Jones, quoted in Crook, 1991, p. 19.

65. Cahn, 1993, p. 179.

66. Quoted in Cahn, 1993, p. 180.

67. Cahn, 1993, pp. 161, 163; Rich, 1994; Corbridge, 1993, p. 127.

68. Cahn, 1993, pp. 168, 172.

69. Gill, 1992.

70. World Bank, 1990, pp. 10-11.

Chapter 5: Instituting the Globalization Project

1. Giddens, 1990, p. 65.

2. Quoted in Bello, Cunningham, & Rau, 1994, p. 72.

3. Bello et al., 1994, p. 35.

4. Acharya, 1995, p. 22.

5. George, 1992, p. 11.

6. Nash, 1994, p. C4.

7. Bello et al., 1994, p. 59.

8. Rich, 1994, p. 188.

9. Quoted in Bello et al., 1994, p. 63.

10. Rich, 1994, p. 188.

11. Hathaway, 1987, pp. 40-41. World Bank, 2000, pp. 14, 25.

12. Ricardo, 1821/1951.

13. Kolko, 1988, pp. 271-272.

14. Bello et al., 1994, p. 68.

15. The South Centre, 1993, p. 13.

16. Quoted in Bradsher, 1995, p. D6.

17. Quoted in Golden, 1995, p. 5.

18. McMichael, 1993b.

19. Adams, 1993, pp. 196-197.

20. Quoted in Watkins, 1991, p. 44.

21. McMichael, 1993b.

22. Middleton, O'Keefe, & Moyo, 1993, pp. 127-129.

23. Watkins, 1991, p. 43.

24. Kolko, 1988, p. 215.

25. Quoted in Ritchie, 1994.

26. Harvey, 1994, p. 14.

27. Quoted in Chomsky, 1994, p. 180.

28. Watkins, 1991, p. 47.

29. Watkins, 1991, p. 50.

30. Quoted in Ritchie, 1993, p. 11.

31. Quoted in Ritchie, 1993, footnote 25.

32. Quoted in Schaeffer, 1995, p. 268.

33. See Raghavan, 1990.

34. Bello, 1999.

35. McMichael & Kim, 1994.

36. Madden & Madeley, 1993, p. 17.

37. Quoted in Weissman, 1991, p. 337.

38. Brecher & Costello, 1994, p. 59.

39. Brecher & Costello, 1994, p. 59.

40. *NAFTA Fact Sheet*, September 23, 1993. Retrieved from the World Wide Web: trade-news@igc.apc.org

41. Ohmae, 1985, pp. xvi-xvii.

42. Baer, 1991, p. 132.

43. Baer, 1991, p. 146.

44. Drozdiak, 1995.

45. Goldsmith, 1994, pp. 66, 67, 77.

46. Moody, 1999, pp. 181, 125-126.

47. See, for example, Wallerstein, 1983; Arrighi, 1990.

48. George & Sabelli, 1994, p. 147.

49. Rueschemeyer, Stephens, & Stephens, 1992.

50. Bacon, 1994, p. A1.

51. Thurow, 1999, pp. 22-23; Cohen, 1999b.

52. Sanger, 1995.

53. Dwyer, 1998, p. 4.

54. Eatwell & Taylor, 1999, p. 7.

55. Morgenthau, 1998, p. A25.

56. Weisbrot, 1999, p. 20; Global Intelligence Update, 1999.

Chapter 6: The Globalization Project: Structural Instabilities

1. Moody, 1999, pp. 183, 188.

2. Silver, 1985; Moody, 1999, pp. 202-204; Seabrook, 1996, pp. 115-116; Vilas, 1995, p. 149.

3. Goldsmith, 1994, p. 18. (The official French figure for current unemployment is 3.3 million, but according to Goldsmith, the government's own statistics show the omission of categories consisting of an additional 1.8 million people.)

4. Moody, 1999, p. 186.

5. Kolko, 1988, p. 339.

6. See, for example, Brecher & Costello, 1994.

7. Quoted in Rocher, 1993, p. 143.

8. Cited in Lewin, 1995, p. A5.

9. *The Nation*, November 8, 1993, p. 3.

10. Kolko, 1988, pp. 337-338; Moody, 1999, p. 86; Martin & Schumann, 1997, p. 119.

11. Lang & Hines, 1993, p. 81; Holusha, 1996.

12. Sassen, 1991, p. 219.

13. "The Manufacturing Myth," p. 92.

14. Woodall, 1994, p. 24; Martin & Schumann, 1997, pp. 100-101.

15. Milbank, 1994, pp. A1, A6.

16. Sassen, 1991.

17. Kolko, 1988, p. 341.

18. Brecher & Costello, 1994, p. 27; Moody, 1999, p. 41.

19. Quoted in Bonacich & Waller, 1994, p. 90.

20. Attali, 1991, pp. 5, 14.

21. Cited in Keatley, 1993.

22. Sanger, 1994, p. A3.

23. Enzenburger, 1994, p. 112.

24. Montalbano, 1991, p. H7; Graw, 1999; Ride, 1998, p. 9.

25. Montalbano, 1991, p. F1; Tan, 1991b.

26. Ball, 1990.

27. Tan, 1991a.

28. MacShane, 1991.

29. Andreas, 1994, p. 53.

30. Andreas, 1994, p. 52.

31. Goldsmith, 1994, pp. 64-65.

32. Andreas, 1994, p. 45.

33. Anderson, 1994.

34. De Soto, 1990, p. 11.

35. King & Schneider, 1991, p. 164; Harrison, 1993, p. 170; O'Meara, 1999, p. 15.

36. Reich, 1991, p. 42.

37. Quoted in Ritchie, 1994.

38. Cited in Ritchie, 1994.

39. Goldsmith, 1994, pp. 38-39.

40. LaTouche, 1993, p. 130.

41. Escobar, 1995, chap. 2.

42. Cheru, 1989, pp. 8, 19.

43. Quoted in LaTouche, 1993, p. 158.

44. LaTouche, 1993, pp. 133-134.

45. Harrison, 1993, p. 174.

46. Ayres, 1996, p. 12.

47. De la Rocha, 1994.

48. Esteva, 1992, p. 21.

49. Darnton, 1994c, p. A8; Castells, 1998, pp. 83-85.

50. Bello, Cunningham, & Rau, 1994, p. 52; United Nations Development Program, 1996, pp. 2-3; Hoogvelt, 1997, p. 129.

51. Quoted in Lang & Hines, 1993, p. 84.

52. Woodall, 1994, p. 24; World Bank, 1997.

53. Enzenburger, 1994, p. 35; Castells, 1998, pp. 83, 85; Hawkins, 1998, p. I.

54. Attali, 1991, p. 73.

55. Crossette, 1998b, p. 1.

56. Brown & Tiffen, 1992, p. 140; Schaeffer, 1995, p. 267.

57. Davidson, 1992, pp. 206, 257.

58. Mamdani, 1996, pp. 17-20.

59. Rothchild & Lawson, 1994, pp. 257-258.

60. Ul Haq, 1995, p. 9.

61. Cumings, 1987.

62. *The Economist*, August 27, 1995, p. 15.

63. Koo, 1987, p. 33.

64. Edwards, 1992, pp. 123-124.

65. Moody, 1999, pp. 14, 213-215.

66. Kagarlitsky, 1995, p. 217.

67. Walton & Seddon, 1994, p. 42.

68. Beckman, 1992, p. 97.

69. World Bank, 1989, p. 5.

70. World Bank, 1997; Berger & Beeson, 1998.

71. Mamdani, 1996, pp. 17-20.

72. Sandbrook, 1995, p. 92; Rist, 1997, pp. 130-132.

73. Lorch, 1995, p. A3.

74. Darnton, 1994a, p. A8.

75. Castells, 1998, pp. 96-98.

76. Fisher & Onishi, 1999, pp. A1, A9; French, 1997, p. A1.

77. Davidson, 1992, p. 257.

78. Darnton, 1994b, p. A1.

79. Darnton, 1994d, p. A1.

80. Johnson, 1993, p. 22.

81. Wood, 1999, p. 1.

82. Korten, 1995; Lietaer, 1997, p. 7.

83. Bello, 1998.

84. Sachs, 1998, p. 20.

85. Bernard, 1999.

86. *Sydney Morning Herald*, June 17, 1998.

87. Benjamin Cohen, 1998, p. 129.

88. Sachs, 1998, p. 17.

89. Shultz, Simon, & Wriston, 1998.

90. Sachs, 1998, p. 17.

Chapter 7: The Globalization Project and Its Counter-movements

1. Cowell, 1994, p. A14.

2. Ibrahim, 1994, pp. A1, 10.

3. Swamy, 1995.

4. A. J. McMichael, 1993, p. 51.

5. Harrison, 1993, p. 54.

6. See A. J. McMichael, 1993.

7. Quoted in Abramovitz, 1999, p. 12.

8. Abramovitz, 1999, pp. 18-19.

9. Amin, Arrighi, Frank, & Wallerstein, 1990.

10. Quoted in Sachs, 1992, p. 107; Schemo, 1997, p. 3.

11. Stewart, 1994, pp. 108-109.

12. Quoted in Rich, 1994, p. 197.

13. Quoted in Middleton, O'Keefe, & Moyo, et al., 1993, p. 19.

14. Agarwal & Nurain, cited in Rich, 1994, p. 262.

15. Quoted in John Friedmann, 1992, p. 123.

16. Rich, 1994, pp. 244-245.

17. Middleton et al., 1993, p. 25.

18. Hildyard, 1993, pp. 32-34; Chossudovsky, 1997, pp. 187-188.

19. Colchester, 1994, pp. 71-72.

20. Quoted in Colchester, 1994, p. 72.

21. Fried, forthcoming.

22. Rich, 1994, pp. 160-165.

23. Rich, 1994, pp. 34-37.

24. Quoted in Colchester, 1994, p. 78.

25. Colchester, 1994, pp. 83, 88.

26. Lohmann, 1993, p. 10.

27. Colchester, 1994, p. 88.

28. Quoted in Colchester, 1994, p. 89.

29. Rau, 1991, pp. 156-157, 160.

30. Quoted in George & Sabelli, 1994, p. 170.

31. Jahan, 1995, p. 13.

32. Harcourt, 1994, p. 4.

33. Harcourt, 1994, p. 5.

34. Apffel-Marglin & Simon, 1994.

35. Harcourt, 1994, p. 19.

36. Apffel-Marglin & Simon, 1994, p. 33.

37. Rocheleau, 1991.

38. Abramovitz, 1994, p. 201.

39. Boyd, 1998.

40. "Battle of the Bulge," 1994, p. 25.

41. Bryant Robey, Shea O. Rutstein, & Leo Morris, quoted in Stevens, 1994, p. A8.

42. Chira, 1994, p. A12.

43. Sen, 1994, p. 221.

44. Quoted in Hedges, 1994, p. A10.

45. Benería, 1992.

46. Quoted in Jahan, 1995, p. 77.

47. Quoted in Jahan, 1995, p. 109.

48. Quoted in Jahan, 1995, p. 109.

49. Simons, 1999, p. A1, A6.

50. Crossette, 1998c, p. A14.

51. Sachs, 1992, p. 112.

52. Fox, 1994.

53. Communiqués No. 1, 22, quoted in *AVA* 42, 31, 1994, p. 1.

54. Cornelius & Myhre, 1998, p. 16.

55. Harvey, 1994, p. 14.

56. Watkins, 1996, p. 253.

57. Mittal, 1998, p. 101.

58. Hernández, 1994, p. 51; Harvey, 1994, p. 20.

59. Harvey, 1994, pp. 36-37; Fox, 1994, p. 18.

60. Wallerstein, 1992.

61. Cleaver, 1994, p. 150.

62. Cleaver, 1994, pp. 154-155.

63. Cooper, 1999, pp. 12, 14; Moberg, 1999, p. 16.

64. Quoted in Menotti, 1996, p. 1.

Chapter 8: Whither Development?

1. Rist, 1997.

2. Hobsbawm, 1994, p. 353.

3. Davidson, 1992; Malkki, 1997, p. 52.

4. Uchitelle, 1993b; Chase, 1995, p. 16.

5. Segelken, 1995, p. 5.

6. Lappin, 1994, p. 193.

7. WuDunn, 1993.

8. Tyler, 1994, p. D8.

9. Brown, 1994, p. 19.

10. A. J. McMichael, 1993, p. 336.

11. Ihonvbere, 1993-1994, p. 8; Borosage, 1999, p. 19.

12. Hildyard, 1993, p. 30.

13. Durning, 1993, pp. 14-15.

14. Faison, 1997; Eckholm, 1999.

15. *The Economist*, April 8, 1995, p. 34.

16. Karliner, 1999.

17. Lappé, Collins, Rosset, & Esparza, 1998, pp. 8-11; World Bank, 2000, pp. 14, 25.

18. Lappé & Bailey, 1998, p. 87.

19. Bruno, 1998, p. 293.

20. Quoted in Bruno, 1998, p. 292.

21. Rifkin, 1998, p. 114.

22. Quoted in The South Centre, 1993, p. 3.

23. The Alternative Forum (of NGOs), "Borrador Conclusiones," Global Forum, Madrid, May 1994.

24. Sachs, 1993, p. 20.

25. Crossette, 1995b.

26. Quoted in Crossette, 1995a.

27. World Bank, 1997, p. 12.

28. World Bank, 2000, p. 3.

29. Wallerstein, 1983. See also Sklair, 1991, for a global sociology of the current world economy.

30. Frank, 1967; Cardoso & Faletto, 1979.

31. World Bank, 2000, p. 21.

32. Lal, 1999, p. 220.

33. Olson, 1999, p. A6.

34. Cohen, 1999a, sec. 4, p. 1.

35. Malkki, 1997.

36. Sharp, 1994, pp. 116, 126.

37. Heurich, 1999; Selverston, 1998.

38. Levey, 1999, p. A11; Mukhopadhyay, 1999; DePalma, 1998, p. A1.

39. Sanger, 1998a, p. A6.

40. Clarke & Barlow, 1997.

41. Khor, 1995.

References

Abramovitz, Janet N. 1994. "Biodiversity and Gender Issues." In Wendy Harcourt (Ed.), *Feminist Perspectives on Sustainable Development.* London: Zed Books.

Abramovitz, Janet N. 1999. "Nature's Hidden Economy." *World Watch,* 11, 1:10, 19.

Acharya, Anjali. 1995. "Plundering the Boreal Forests." *World Watch* 8, 3:2-29.

Adams, Nassau A. 1993. *Worlds Apart: The North-South Divide and the International System.* London: Zed Books.

Africa Information Service (Ed.). 1973. *Return to the Source: Selected Speeches by Amilcar Cabral.* New York: Author.

Agarwal, Bina. 1994. *A Field of One's Own: Gender and Land Rights in South Asia.* Cambridge: Cambridge University Press.

Alvares, Claude. 1997. "An Indian Village Bucks GATT Over Control of Genetic Resources." *Resurgence,* 84:11-12.

Amanor, Kojo. 1994. "Ecological Knowledge and the Regional Economy: Environmental Management in the Asesewa District of Ghana." In Dharam Ghai (Ed.), *Environment & Development: Sustaining People and Nature.* Oxford: Blackwell.

Amin, Samir. 1997. *Capitalism in the Age of Globalization.* London: Zed Books.

Amin, Samir, Giovanni Arrighi, Andre Gunder Frank, and Immanuel Wallerstein. 1990. *Transforming the Revolution: Social Movements and the World System.* New York: Monthly Review Press.

Amsden, Alice, and Yoon-Dae Euh. 1997. "Behind Korea's Plunge." *The New York Times,* November 27:D1.

Anderson, Benedict. 1994. "Exodus." *Critical Inquiry,* Winter.

Andrae, Gunilla, and Björn Beckman. 1985. *The Wheat Trap.* London: Zed Books.

Andreas, Peter. 1994. "The Making of Amerexico." *World Policy Journal,* Summer:45-56.

Apffel-Marglin, Frédérique. 1997. "Counter-Development in the Andes." *The Ecologist,* 27, 6: 221-224.

Apffel-Marglin, Frédérique, and Suzanne L. Simon. 1994. "Feminist Orientalism and Development." In Wendy Harcourt (Ed.), *Feminist Perspectives on Sustainable Development.* London: Zed Books.

Appelbaum, Richard P., and Gary Gereffi. 1994. "Power and Profits in the Apparel Commodity Chain." In Edna Bonacich, Lucie Cheng, Norma Chinchilla, Nora Hamilton, and Paul Ong (Eds.), *Global Production: The Apparel Industry in the Pacific Rim*. Philadelphia: Temple University Press.

Araghi, Farshad. 1989. "Land Reform Policies in Iran: A Comment." *American Journal of Agricultural Economics* 74, 4:1046-1049.

———. 1995. "Global Depeasantization, 1945-1990." *The Sociological Quarterly* 36, 2:337-368.

———. 1999. *The Great Enclosure of Our Times*. Unpublished manuscript, Florida State University.

Arrighi, Giovanni. 1990. "The Developmentalist Illusion: A Reconceptualization of the Semiperiphery." In William G. Martin (Ed.), *Semiperipheral States in the World Economy*. Westport, CT: Greenwood.

———. 1994. *The Long Twentieth Century: Money, Power, and the Origins of Our Times*. London: Verso.

Arruda, Marcos. 1994. "Brazil: Drowning in Debt." In Kevin Danaher and Muhammad Yunus (Eds.), *50 Years Is Enough: The Case Against the World Bank and the IMF*. Boston: South End Press.

Athreya, Venkatesh B., Göran Djurfeldt, and Staffan Lindberg. 1990. *Barriers Broken: Production Relations and Agrarian Change in Tamil Nadu*. Newbury Park, CA: Sage.

Attali, Jacques. 1991. *Millennium: Winners and Losers in the Coming World Order*. New York: Times Books.

Avery, Natalie. 1994. "Stealing from the State." In Kevin Danaher and Muhammad Yunus (Eds.), *50 Years Is Enough: The Case Against the World Bank and the IMF*. Boston: South End Press.

Ayres, Ed. 1996. "The Shadow Economy." *World Watch* 9, 4:10-23.

Bacon, Kenneth M. 1994. "Politics Could Doom a New Currency Plan." *The Wall Street Journal*, May 9:A1.

Baer, M. Delal. 1991. "North American Free Trade." *Foreign Affairs* 70, 4:132-149.

Baird, Peter, and Ed McCaughan. 1979. *Beyond the Border: Mexico & the U.S. Today*. New York: North American Congress on Latin America.

Ball, Rochelle. 1990. *The Process of International Contract Labor Migration from the Philippines: The Case of Filipino Nurses*. Unpublished doctoral dissertation. Sydney: Department of Geography, University of Sydney.

Bangura, Yusuf, and Peter Gibbon. 1992. "Adjustment, Authoritarianism and Democracy in Sub-Saharan Africa: An Introduction to Some Conceptual and Empirical Issues." In Peter Gibbon, Yusuf Bangura, and Arve Ofstad (Eds.), *Authoritarianism, Democracy and Adjustment: The Politics of Economic Reform in Africa*. Uppsala: Nordiska Afrikainstitutet.

Barboza, David. 1999. "Pluralism Under Golden Arches." *The New York Times*, February 12:D1, 7.

Barkin, David. 1990. *Distorted Development: Mexico in the World Economy*. Boulder, CO: Westview Press.

———. 1991. "About Face." *North American Congress on Latin America (NACLA)* 24, 6:35.

Barndt, Deborah. 1997. "Bio/cultural Diversity and Equity in Post-NAFTA Mexico (or: Tomasita Comes North While Big Mac Goes South)." In Jay Drydyk and Peter Penz (Eds.), *Global Justice, Global Democracy*. Winnipeg: Fernwood Publishing.

Barnet, Richard J., and John Cavanagh. 1994. *Global Dreams: Imperial Corporations and the New World Order*. New York: Touchstone.

Barry, Tom. 1995. *Zapata's Revenge: Free Trade and the Farm Crisis in Mexico*. Boston: South End Press.

"Battle of the Bulge." 1994. *The Economist*, September 3:25.

Beams, Nick. 1999. *UN Figures Show: International Production System Developing*. Retrieved from the World Wide Web: http://www.wsws.org/articles/1999/Oct1999/un-o09.html

Beckman, Björn. 1992. "Empowerment or Repression? The World Bank and the Politics of African Adjustment." In Peter Gibbon, Yusuf Bangura, and Arve Ofstad (Eds.), *Authoritarianism, Democracy and Adjustment: The Politics of Economic Reform in Sub-Saharan Africa*. Uppsala: Nordiska Afrikainstitutet.

Bello, Walden. 1992-1993. "Population and the Environment." *Food First Action Alert*, Winter:5.

———. 1998. "Addicted to Capital: The Ten-Year High and Present-Day Withdrawal Trauma of Southeast Asia's Economies." In *FOCUS on the Global South*. Chulalongkorn University, Bangkok.

———. 1999. "The WTO's Big Losers." *Far Eastern Economic Review* (Interactive Edition E-Newsletter), June 24, 25.

Bello, Walden, with Shea Cunningham and Bill Rau. 1994. *Dark Victory: The United States, Structural Adjustment and Global Poverty*. London: Pluto Press, with Food First and Transnational Institute.

Benería, Lourdes. 1992. "Accounting for Women's Work: The Progress of Two Decades." *World Development* 20, 11:1547-1560.

———. 1995. "Response: The Dynamics of Globalization" (Scholarly Controversy: Global Flows of Labor and Capital). *International Labor and Working-Class History* 47:45-52.

Benería, Lourdes, and Shelley Feldman (Eds.). 1992. *Unequal Burden: Economic Crises, Persistent Poverty, and Women's Work*. Boulder, CO: Westview Press.

Berger, Mark T., and Mark Beeson. 1998. "Lineages of Liberalism and Miracles of Modernisation: The World Bank, the East Asian Trajectory and the International Development Debate." *Third World Quarterly* 19, 3:487-504.

Berlan, Jean-Pierre. 1991. "The Historical Roots of the Present Agricultural Crisis." In W. Friedland, L. Busch, F. Buttel, and A. Rudy (Eds.), *Towards a New Political Economy of Agriculture*. Boulder, CO: Westview Press.

Bernard, Mitchell. 1996. "Beyond the Local-Global Divide in the Formation of the Eastern Asian Region." *New Political Economy* 1, 3:335-353.

———. 1999. "East Asia's Tumbling Dominoes: Financial Crises and the Myth of the Regional Model." In Leo Panitch and Colin Leys (Eds.), *Global Capitalism Versus Democracy: Socialist Register 1999*. London: Merlin Press.

Bernstein, Henry. 1990. "Agricultural 'Modernization' and the Era of Structural Adjustment: Observations on Sub-Saharan Africa." *Journal of Peasant Studies* 18, 1:3-35.

Block, Fred L. 1977. *The Origins of International Economic Disorder: A Study of United States International Monetary Policy from World War II to the Present.* Berkeley: University of California Press.

Bonacich, Edna, and David V. Waller. 1994. "The Role of U.S. Apparel Manufacturers in the Globalization of the Industry in the Pacific Rim." In Edna Bonacich, Lucie Cheng, Norma Chinchilla, Nora Hamilton, and Paul Ong (Eds.), *Global Production: The Apparel Industry in the Pacific Rim.* Philadelphia: Temple University Press.

Borosage, Robert L. 1999. "The Global Turning." *The Nation*, July 19:19-22.

Borthwick, Mark. 1992. *Pacific Century: The Emergence of Modern Pacific Asia.* Boulder, CO: Westview Press.

Bose, Sugata. 1997. "Instruments and Idioms of Colonial and National Development: India's Historical Experience in Comparative Perspective." In Frederick Cooper and Randall Packard (Eds.), *International Development and the Social Sciences.* Berkeley: University of California Press.

Boyd, Stephanie. 1998. "Secrets and Lies." *The New Internationalist* 303:16-17.

Bradley, P. N., and S. E. Carter. 1989. "Food Production and Distribution—and Hunger." In R. J. Johnston and P. J. Taylor (Eds.), *A World in Crisis? Geographical Perspectives.* Oxford: Blackwell.

Bradsher, Keith. 1995. "White House Moves to Increase Aid to Mexico." *The New York Times*, January 12:D6.

Brandt Commission (Independent Commission on International Development Issues). 1983. *Common Crisis: North, South & Cooperation for World Recovery.* London: Pan Books.

Brecher, Jeremy, and Tim Costello. 1994. *Global Village or Global Pillage? Economic Reconstruction from the Bottom Up.* Boston: South End Press.

Brett, E. A. 1985. *The World Economy Since the War: The Politics of Uneven Development.* London: Macmillan.

Brown, Lester R. 1994. "Who Will Feed China?" *World Watch* 7, 5:10-19.

———. 1995. "China's Food Problem: The Massive Imports Begin." *World Watch* 8, 5:38.

Brown, Michael Barratt. 1993. *Fair Trade.* London: Zed Books.

Brown, Michael Barratt, and Pauline Tiffen. 1992. *Short Changed: Africa and World Trade.* Boulder, CO: Pluto Press with the Transnational Institute.

Bruno, Kenny. 1998. "Monsanto's Failing PR Strategy." *The Ecologist* 28, 5:287-293.

Bujra, Janet. 1992. "Diversity in Pre-capitalist Societies." In Tim Allen and Allan Thomas (Eds.), *Poverty and Development in the 1990s.* Oxford: Oxford University Press.

Burbach, Roger, and Patricia Flynn. 1980. *Agribusiness in the Americas.* New York: Monthly Review Press.

Buttel, Frederick H. 1992. "Environmentalization: Origins, Processes, and Implications for Rural Social Change." *Rural Sociology* 57, 1:1-28.

Byres, Terry J. 1981. "The New Technology, Class Formation and Class Action in the Indian Countryside." *Journal of Peasant Studies* 8, 4:405-454.

Cahn, Jonathan. 1993. "Challenging the New Imperial Authority: The World Bank and the Democratization of Development." *Harvard Human Rights Journal* 6:159-194.

Calvo, Dana. 1997. "Tijuana Workers Win Labor Battle." Retrieved December 1997 from the World Wide Web: tw-list@essential.org

Canak, William L. 1989. "Debt, Austerity, and Latin America in the New International Division of Labor." In William L. Canak (Ed.), *Lost Promises: Debt, Austerity, and Development in Latin America.* Boulder, CO: Westview Press.

Cardoso, Fernando H., and Enzo Faletto. 1979. *Dependency and Development in Latin America.* Berkeley: University of California Press.

Carlsen, L. 1991. "Reaping Winter's Harvest." *Business Mexico*, May:20-23.

Carson, Rachel. 1962. *Silent Spring.* New York: Houghton Mifflin.

Castells, Manuel. 1996. *The Rise of the Network Society.* Oxford: Blackwell.

———. 1998. *End of Millennium.* Oxford: Blackwell.

Chaliand, Gerard. 1969. *Armed Struggle in Africa: With the Guerillas in "Portuguese" Guinea.* New York: Monthly Review Press.

Chan, Anita. 1996. "Boot Camp at the Shoe Factory." *Washington Post*, November 17:20-21.

Chase, Edward T. 1995. "Down and Out in London, Paris and New York." *The Bookpress* (Ithaca), March:16.

Cheru, Fantu. 1989. *The Silent Revolution in Africa: Debt, Development and Democracy.* London: Zed Books.

Chira, Susan. 1994. "Women Campaign for New Plan to Curb the World's Population." *The New York Times*, April 13:A12.

Chirot, Daniel. 1977. *Social Change in the Twentieth Century.* New York: Harcourt Brace Jovanovich.

Chomsky, Noam. 1994. *World Orders Old and New.* New York: Columbia University Press.

Chossudovsky, Michel. 1997. *The Globalisation of Poverty: Impacts of IMF and World Bank Reforms.* Penang, Malaysia: Third World Network.

Chung, Youg-Il. 1990. "The Agricultural Foundation for Korean Industrial Development." In Chung Lee and Ippei Yamazawa (Eds.), *The Economic Development of Japan and Korea*. New York: Praeger.

Clarke, T., and M. Barlow. 1997. *MAI: The Multilateral Agreement on Investment and the Threat to Canadian Sovereignty*. Toronto: Stoddart.

Cleaver, Harry. 1977. "Food, Famine and the International Crisis." *Zerowork* 2:7-70.

———. 1994. "The Chiapas Uprising." *Studies in Political Economy* 44:141-157.

"Coffee Drinkers: Where Are Your Beans Grown?" 1999. *The Ithaca Journal*, January 5:3B. (Originally published in *The Washington Post*)

Cohen, Benjamin J. 1998. *The Geography of Money*. Ithaca, NY: Cornell University Press.

Cohen, Roger. 1998. "High Claims in Spill Betray Depth of Nigerian Poverty." *The New York Times*, September 20:A1, 6.

———. 1999a. "Fearful Over the Future, Europe Seizes on Food." *The New York Times*, August 29: Sec. 4, p. 1.

———. 1999b. "Shiny, Prosperous 'Euroland' Has Some Cracks in Façade." *The New York Times*, January 3:A1, 6.

Colchester, Marcus. 1994. "Sustaining the Forests: The Community-based Approach in South and Southeast Asia." In Dharam Ghai (Ed.), *Development & Environment: Sustaining People and Nature*. Oxford: Blackwell.

Collins, Jane. 1995. "Gender and Cheap Labor in Agriculture." In Philip McMichael (Ed.), *Food and Agrarian Orders in the World-Economy*. Westport, CT: Praeger.

Collins, Joseph, and John Lear. 1996. *Chile's Free Market Miracle: A Second Look*. Oakland, CA: Food First Books.

Cooper, Frederick. 1997. "Modernizing Bureaucrats, Backward Africans, and the Development Concept." In Frederick Cooper and Randall Packard (Eds.), *International Development and the Social Sciences*. Berkeley: University of California Press.

Cooper, Helene, and Thomas Kuhn. 1998. "Much of Europe Eases Its Rigid Labor Laws and Temps Proliferate." *The Wall Street Journal*, June 4:A1, 5.

Cooper, Marc. 1999. "No Sweat." *The Nation*, June 7:11-14.

Corbridge, Stuart. 1993. "Ethics in Development Studies: The Example of Debt." In Frans J. Schuurman (Ed.), *Beyond the Impasse: New Directions in Development Theory*. London: Zed Books.

Cornelius, Wayne A., and David Myhre. 1998. "Introduction." In Wayne A. Cornelius and David Myhre (Eds.), *The Transformation of Rural Mexico*. La Jolla: Center for U.S.-Mexican Studies, UCSD.

Cowell, Alan. 1994. "Muslim Party Threatens Turk's Secular Heritage." *The New York Times*, November 30:A14.

Cox, Robert W. 1987. *Production, Power, and World Order: Social Forces in the Making of History*. New York: Columbia University Press.

Crook, Clive. 1991. "Sisters in the Wood: A Survey of the IMF and the World Bank." *The Economist*, Special Supplement, October 12.

———. 1992. "Fear of Finance: A Survey of the World Economy." *The Economist*, Special Supplement, September 19.

———. 1993. "New Ways to Grow: A Survey of World Finance." *The Economist*, Special Supplement, September 25.

Crossette, Barbara. 1994. "A Third-World Effort on Family Planning." *The New York Times*, September 7:A8.

———. 1995a. "Talks in Denmark Redefine 'Foreign Aid' in Post-Cold-War Era." *The New York Times*, March 10:A5.

———. 1995b. "U.N. Parley Puts Focus on Africa." *The New York Times*, March 9:A10.

———. 1997. "Kofi Annan's Astonishing Facts!" In United Nations Development Programme, *Human Development Report 1997*. New York, UNDP.

———. 1998a. "A Uganda Tribe Fights Genital Cutting." *The New York Times*, July 16:A8.

———. 1998b. "Where the Hunger Season Is Part of Life." *The New York Times*, Week in Review, August 16:1, 5.

———. 1998c. "Women See Key Gains Since Talks in Beijing." *The New York Times*, March 8:A14.

Cumings, Bruce. 1987. "The Origin and Development of the Northeast Asian Political Economy: Industrial Sectors, Product Cycles, and Political Consequences." In Frederic C. Deyo (Ed.), *The Political Economy of the New Asian Industrialism*. Ithaca, NY: Cornell University Press.

Dalrymple, D. 1985. "The Development and Adoption of High-Yielding Varieties of Wheat and Rice in Developing Countries." *American Journal of Agricultural Economics* 67:1067-1073.

Daly, M. T., and M. I. Logan. 1989. *The Brittle Rim: Finance, Business and the Pacific Region*. Ringwood, Victoria, Australia: Penguin.

Danaher, Kevin, and Muhammad Yunus (Eds.). 1994. *50 Years Is Enough: The Case Against the World Bank and the International Monetary Fund*. Boston: South End Press.

Darnton, John. 1994a. "Africa Tries Democracy, Finding Hope and Peril." *The New York Times*, June 21:A8.

———. 1994b. "Crisis-torn Africa Becomes Continent of Refugees." *The New York Times*, May 23:A1.

———. 1994c. "In Poor, Decolonized Africa Bankers Are New Overlords." *The New York Times*, June 20:A1, A8.

———. 1994d. "U.N. Faces Refugee Crisis That Never Ends." *The New York Times*, August 8:A1.

Davidson, Basil. 1992. *The Black Man's Burden: Africa and the Curse of the Nation-State*. New York: Times Books.

de Castro, Josué. 1969. "Introduction: Not One Latin America." In Irving Louis Horowitz, Josué de Castro, and John Gerassi (Eds.), *Latin American Radicalism*. New York: Vintage Press.

de Janvry, Alain. 1981. *The Agrarian Question and Reformism in Latin America.* Baltimore: Johns Hopkins University Press.

de la Rocha, Mercedes González. 1994. *The Resources of Poverty: Women and Survival in a Mexican City.* Cambridge, MA: Blackwell.

DePalma, Anthony. 1993. "Mexico Unloads State Companies, Pocketing Billions, but Hits Snags." *The New York Times*, October 27:A1, 8.

———. 1998. "Canadian Indians Win a Ruling Vindicating Their Oral History." *The New York Times*, February 9:A1, A8.

De Soto, Hernando. 1990. *The Other Path: The Invisible Revolution in the Third World.* New York: Harper & Row.

DeWalt, Billie. 1985. "Mexico's Second Green Revolution: Food for Feed." *Mexican Studies/Estudios Mexicanos* 1:29-60.

Deyo, Frederic C. 1991. "Singapore: Developmental Paternalism." In Steven M. Goldstein (Ed.), *Mini-Dragons: Fragile Economic Miracles in the Pacific.* Boulder, CO: Westview Press.

Dhanagare, D. N. 1988. "The Green Revolution and Social Inequalities in Rural India." *Bulletin of Concerned Asian Scholars* 20, 2:2-13.

Dicken, Peter. 1992. "International Production in a Volatile Regulatory Environment: The Influence of National Regulatory Policies on the Spatial Strategies of Transnational Corporations." *Geoforum* 23:303-316.

———. 1998. *Global Shift: Transforming the World Economy.* New York: Guilford Press.

Dillon, Sam. 1997. "After 4 Years of Nafta, Labor Is Forging Cross-Border Ties." *The New York Times*, December 20:A1, 7.

———. 1998. "U.S. Labor Leader Seeks Union Support in Mexico." *The New York Times*, January 23:A3.

Drozdiak, William. 1995. "Trade Zone Plan Intrigues Leaders on Both Sides of Atlantic." *The Washington Post*, May 28:A39.

Dube, S. C. 1988. *Modernization and Development—The Search for Alternative Paradigms.* London: Zed Books.

Dudley, Leonard, and Roger Sandilands. 1975. "The Side Effects of Foreign Aid: The Case of Public Law 480 Wheat in Colombia." *Economic Development and Cultural Change* 23, 2:325-336.

Durning, Alan Thein. 1993. "Supporting Indigenous Peoples." In Lester Brown (Ed.), *State of the World.* New York: Norton.

Dwyer, Michael. 1998. "IMF Starts to Query Its Own Ideology." *The Australian Financial Review*, November 30:4.

Eatwell, John, and Lance Taylor. 1999. "Bankers Without Borders." *The Nation*, April 26:7.

Eckholm, Erik. 1999. "China Shifts on How to Resettle Million People for Giant Dam." *The New York Times*, May 25:A3.

Economic Commission for Latin America and the Caribbean (ECLAC). 1989. *Transnational Bank Behaviour and the International Debt Crisis*. Santiago, Chile: ECLAC/UN Center on Transnational Corporations.

Edwards, Chris. 1992. "Industrialization in South Korea." In Tom Hewitt, Hazel Johnson, and Dave Wield (Eds.), *Industrialization and Development*. Oxford: Oxford University Press.

Ellwood, Wayne. 1993. "Multinationals and the Subversion of Sovereignty." *New Internationalist* 246:4-7.

Enzenburger, Hans Magnus. 1994. *Civil Wars: From L.A. to Bosnia*. New York: The New Press.

Erlanger, Steven. 1998. "Suharto Fostered Rapid Economic Growth, and Staggering Graft." *The New York Times*, May 22:A9.

Escobar, Arturo. 1995. *Encountering Development: The Making and Unmaking of the Third World*. Princeton, NJ: Princeton University Press.

Esteva, Gustavo. 1992. "Development." In Wolfgang Sachs (Ed.), *The Development Dictionary*. London: Zed Books.

Evans, Peter. 1979. *Dependent Development*. Princeton, NJ: Princeton University Press.

———. 1995. *Embedded Autonomy: States and Industrial Transformation*. Princeton, NJ: Princeton University Press.

Faison, Seth. 1997a. "Detours Behind It, the Giant Follows Asian's Growth Path." *The New York Times*, March 4:A1, D4.

Faison, Seth. 1997b. "Set to Build Dam, China Diverts Yangtze While Crowing About It." *The New York Times*, November 9:A1, A14.

Fanon, Frantz. 1967. *The Wretched of the Earth*. Harmondsworth: Penguin.

Feder, Ernst. 1983. *Perverse Development*. Quezon City, Philippines: Foundation for Nationalist Studies.

Fenley, Lindajoy. 1991. "Promoting the Pacific Rim." *Business Mexico*, June:41.

Fidler, Stephen, and Lisa Bransten. 1995. "Mexican Sell-Offs to Help Solve the Debt Crisis." *Financial Times*, August 1:1.

Fisher, Ian, and Norimitsu Onishi. 1999. "Congo's Struggle May Unleash Broad Strife to Redraw Africa." *The New York Times*, January 12:A1, A9.

Fox, Jonathan. 1994. "The Challenge of Democracy: Rebellion as Catalyst." *Akwe:kon* 11, 2:13-19.

Frank, Andre Gunder. 1967. *Capitalism and Underdevelopment in Latin America*. New York: Monthly Review Press.

"Free Trade: The Ifs, Ands and Buts." 1993. *Resource Center Bulletin*: 31-32.

French, Howard W. 1997. "A Century Later, Letting Africans Draw Their Own Map." *The New York Times*, Week in Review, November 23:A1.

————. 1998. "Africans Resentful as Asia Rakes in Aid." *The New York Times*, March 8:A3.

Fried, Stephanie. Forthcoming. "Writing for Their Lives: Bentian Authors and Indonesian Development Discourse." In C. Zerner (Ed.), *Forests, Coasts, and Seas: Culture and the Question of Rights to Southeast Asian Environmental Resources.* Durham, NC: Duke University Press.

Friedland, William H. 1994. "The Global Fresh Fruit and Vegetable System: An Industrial Organization Analysis." In Philip McMichael (Ed.), *The Global Restructuring of Agro-Food Systems.* Ithaca, NY: Cornell University Press.

Friedmann, Harriet. 1990. "The Origins of Third World Food Dependence." In Henry Bernstein, Ben Crow, Maureen Mackintosh, and Charlotte Martin (Eds.), *The Food Question: Profits Versus People?* New York: Monthly Review Press.

————. 1991. "Changes in the International Division of Labor: Agri-food Complexes and Export Agriculture." In William Friedland, Lawrence Busch, Frederick H. Buttel, and Alan P. Rudy (Eds.), *Towards a New Political Economy of Agriculture.* Boulder, CO: Westview Press.

————. 1992. "Distance and Durability: Shaky Foundations of the World Food Economy." *Third World Quarterly* 13, 2:371-383.

Friedmann, Harriet, and Philip McMichael. 1989. "Agriculture and the State System: The Rise and Fall of National Agricultures, 1870 to the Present." *Sociologia Ruralis* 29, 2:93-117.

Friedmann, John. 1992. *Empowerment: The Politics of Alternative Development.* Cambridge, MA: Blackwell.

Fröbel, Folker, Jürgen Heinrichs, and Otto Kreye. 1979. *The New International Division of Labor.* New York: Cambridge University Press.

Fujita, Kuniko, and Richard Child Hill. 1995. "Global Toyotaism and Local Development." *International Journal of Urban & Regional Research* 19, 1:7-22.

George, Susan. 1977. *How the Other Half Dies: The Real Reasons for World Hunger.* Montclair, NJ: Allenheld, Osmun and Co.

————. 1988. *A Fate Worse than Debt: The World Financial Crisis and the Poor.* New York: Grove Press.

————. 1992. *The Debt Boomerang: How Third World Debt Harms Us All.* Boulder, CO: Westview Press.

George, Susan, and Fabrizio Sabelli. 1994. *Faith and Credit: The World Bank's Secular Empire.* Boulder, CO: Westview Press.

Gereffi, Gary. 1989. "Rethinking Development Theory: Insights from East Asia and Latin America." *Sociological Forum* 4, 4:505-533.

————. 1994. "The Organization of Buyer-Driven Global Commodity Chains: How U.S. Retailers Shape Overseas Production Networks." In Gary Gereffi and Miguel Korzeniewicz (Eds.), *Commodity Chains and Global Capitalism.* Westport, CT: Praeger.

Gibbon, Peter. 1992. "Structural Adjustment and Pressures Toward Multipartyism in Sub-Saharan Africa." In Peter Gibbon, Yusuf Bangura, and Arve Ofstad (Eds.), *Authoritarianism, Democracy and Adjustment: The Politics of Economic Reform in Sub-Saharan Africa.* Uppsala: Nordiska Afrikainstitutet.

Giddens, Anthony. 1990. *The Consequences of Modernity.* Stanford, CA: Stanford University Press.

Gill, Stephen. 1992. "Economic Globalization and the Internationalization of Authority: Limits and Contradictions." *Geoforum* 23, 3:269-283.

Global Intelligence Update. 1999. *World Bank Reverses Position on Financial Controls and on Malaysia.* Retrieved from the World Wide Web: www.stratfor.com

Golden, Tim. 1995. "Mexicans Find Dream Devalued." *The New York Times,* Week in Review, January 8:5.

Goldsmith, James. 1994. *The Trap.* New York: Carroll & Graf.

Goss, Jasper. 1997. "Conflict and Resistance in Indian Shrimp Aquaculture." *Resurgence,* 84:2-3.

Goss, Jasper, David Burch, and Roy E. Rickson. In press. "Agri-Food Restructuring and Third World Transnationals: Thailand, the CP Group and the Global Shrimp Industry." *World Development* 28, 3.

Graw, Stephen. 1999. "Overseas Labor Remittances: Spare Change or New Changes?" Paper presented at the annual meeting of the Association for Asian Studies, Boston, March.

Griffin, K. B. 1974. *The Political Economy of Agrarian Change: An Essay on the Green Revolution.* Cambridge: Harvard University Press.

Grigg, David. 1993. *The World Food Problem.* Oxford: Blackwell.

Grosfoguel, Ramon. 1996. "From Cepalismo to Neoliberalism: A World-Systems Approach to Conceptual Shifts in Latin America." *Review* 19:131-154.

Gupta, Akhil. 1997. "Agrarian Populism in the Development of a Modern Nation (India)." In Frederick Cooper and Randall Packard (Eds.), *International Development and the Social Sciences.* Berkeley: University of California Press.

Harcourt, Wendy. 1994. "Introduction." In Wendy Harcourt (Ed.), *Feminist Perspectives on Sustainable Development.* London: Zed Books.

Harper, Doug. 1994. "Auto Imports Jump in Mexico." *The New York Times,* July 7:D1.

Harris, Nigel. 1987. *The End of the Third World: Newly Industrializing Countries and the Decline of an Ideology.* Harmondsworth: Penguin.

Harrison, Paul. 1993. *The Third Revolution: Population, Environment and a Sustainable World.* Harmondsworth: Penguin.

Harvey, Neil. 1994. *Rebellion in Chiapas: Rural Reforms, Campesino Radicalism, and the Limits to Salinismo.* San Diego: Center for U.S.-Mexican Studies.

Hathaway, Dale E. 1987. *Agriculture and the GATT: Rewriting the Rules.* Washington, DC: Institute for International Economics.

Hawkins, Tony. 1998. "At the Heart of Further Progress." *Financial Times*, Survey on African Banking and Development, June 2:I-VI.

Hedges, Chris. 1994. "Key Panel at Cairo Talks Agrees on Population Plan." *The New York Times*, September 13:A10.

Hedland, Stefan, and Niclas Sundstrom. 1996. "The Russian Economy After Systemic Change." *Europe-Asia Studies* 48, 6:889.

Heffernan, William D. 1999. *Consolidation in the Food and Agriculture System.* Report to the National Farmers Union. Washington, DC: National Farmers Union.

Heffernan, William D., and Douglas H. Constance. 1994. "Transnational Corporations and the Globalization of the Food System." In Alessandro Bonanno, Lawrence Busch, William Friedland, Lourdes Gouveia, and Enzo Mingione (Eds.), *From Columbus to ConAgra: The Globalization of Agriculture and Food.* Lawrence: University Press of Kansas.

Helleiner, Eric. 1996. *States and the Reemergence of Global Finance: From Bretton Woods to the 1990s.* Ithaca, NY: Cornell University Press.

Hellman, Judith Adler. 1994. *Mexican Lives.* New York: Free Press.

Henderson, Jeffrey. 1991. *The Globalisation of High Technology Production.* London: Routledge.

Herbert, Bob. 1996. "Nike's Pyramid Scheme." *The New York Times*, June 10:33.

———. 1998. "At What Cost?" *The New York Times*, June 7:A15.

Hernández, Luis Navarro. 1994. "The Chiapas Uprising." In Neil Harvey (Ed.), *Rebellion in Chiapas.* University of California, San Diego: Center for U.S.-Mexican Studies.

Hettne, Björn. 1990. *Development Theory and the Three Worlds.* White Plains, NY: Longman.

Heurich, Tanya. 1999. *Rethinking the Nation/State: Developmentalism and Indigenous Activism in Ecuador.* Unpublished master's thesis, Rural Sociology, Cornell University.

Hewitt, Tom. 1992. "Brazilian Industrialization." In Tom Hewitt, Hazel Johnson, and Dave Wield (Eds.), *Industrialization and Development.* Oxford: Oxford University Press.

Hildyard, Nicholas. 1993. "Foxes in Charge of Chickens." In Wolfgang Sachs (Ed.), *Global Ecology: A New Arena of Political Conflict.* London: Zed Books.

Hobsbawm, Eric J. 1992. "The Crisis of Today's Ideologies." *New Left Review* 192:55-64.

———.1994. *The Age of Extremes: A History of the World from 1914 to 1991.* New York: Pantheon.

Holusha, John. 1996. "Squeezing the Textile Workers." *The New York Times*, February 21:D1, 20.

Hoogvelt, Ankie M. M. 1987. *The Third World in Global Development.* London: Macmillan.

———. 1997. *Globalization and the Postcolonial World: The New Political Economy of Development.* London: Macmillan.

"How to Make Aid Work." 1999. *The Economist,* June 26:23-25.

Ibrahim, Youssef M. 1994. "Fundamentalists Impose Culture on Egypt." *The New York Times,* February 3:A1, 10.

Ihonvbere, Julius O. 1993-1994. "The Third World and the New World Order in the 1990s." In Robert J. Griffiths (Ed.), *Third World 94/95: Annual Editions.* Guilford, CT: Dushkin.

Jahan, Rounaq. 1995. *The Elusive Agenda: Mainstreaming Women in Development.* London: Zed Books.

James, C. L. R. 1963. *The Black Jacobins: Toussaint L'Ouverture and the San Domingo Revolution.* New York: Vintage Press.

Jenkins, Rhys. 1992. "Industrialization and the Global Economy." In Tom Hewitt, Hazel Johnson, and Dave Wield (Eds.), *Industrialization and Development.* Oxford: Oxford University Press.

Johnson, Paul. 1993. "Colonialism's Back—and Not a Moment Too Soon." *The New York Times Magazine,* April 18:22.

Kagarlitsky, Boris 1995. *The Mirage of Modernization.* New York: Monthly Review Press.

Kaldor, Mary. 1990. *The Imaginary War: Understanding the East West Conflict.* Oxford: Blackwell.

Kane, Hal. 1996. "Micro-enterprise." *World Watch* 9, 2:11-19.

Karliner, Joshua. 1997. *The Corporate Planet: Ecology and Politics in the Age of Globalization.* San Francisco: Sierra Club Books.

———. 1999. "U.N. Enters a Perilous Partnership with Corporations." Bridge New Markets Roundup (New York): Knight Ridder/Tribune Business News. Retrieved from the World Wide Web: tw-list@essential.org

Keatley, Robert. 1993. "If Free-Trade Accord Fails, the Impact on Mexico Could Quickly Spread North." *The Wall Street Journal,* May 28:A1.

Kemp, Tom. 1989. *Industrialization in the Non-Western World.* London: Longman.

Khor, Martin. 1995. "Countering the North's New Trade Agenda." *Third World Network.* Retrieved November 9 from the World Wide Web: tw-list@essential.org

Kidrow, Michael, and Ronald Segal. 1981. *The State of the World Atlas.* London: Pan Books.

King, Alexander, and Bertrand Schneider. 1991. *The First Global Revolution: A Report by the Council to the Club of Rome.* New York: Pantheon.

Kingsnorth, Paul. 1999. "India Cheers While Monsanto Burns." *The Ecologist* 29, 1:9-11.

Kneen, Brewster. 1990. *Trading Up: How Cargill, the World's largest Grain Company, Is Changing World Agriculture.* Toronto: N.C. Press.

Knox, Paul, and John Agnew. 1994. *The Geography of the World Economy.* London: Edward Arnold.

Kohli, Geeta, and Kim Webster. 1999. *Female Circumcision: A Ritual Worth Continuing?* Unpublished term paper, Rural Sociology, Cornell University.

Kolko, Joyce. 1988. *Restructuring the World Economy.* New York: Pantheon.

Koo, Hagen. 1987. "The Interplay of State, Class, and World System in East Asian Development: The Cases of South Korea and Taiwan." In Frederic C. Deyo (Ed.), *The Political Economy of the New Asian Industrialism.* Ithaca, NY: Cornell University Press.

Korzeniewicz, Miguel. 1994. "Commodity Chains and Marketing Strategies: Nike and the Global Athletic Footwear Industry." In Gary Gereffi and Miguel Korzeniewicz (Eds.), *Commodity Chains and Global Capitalism.* Westport, CT: Praeger.

Korten, David. 1995. *When Corporations Rule the World.* New York: Kumarian.

Kothari, Smitu, and Pramod Parajuli. 1993. "No Nature Without Social Justice: A Plea for Cultural and Ecological Pluralism in India." In Wolfgang Sachs (Ed.), *Global Ecology: A New Arena of Political Conflict.* London: Zed Books.

Kuenzler, L. T. 1992. "Foreign Investment Opportunities in the Mexican Agricultural Sector." *Business Mexico*, Special Edition:44-47.

Lal, Vinay. 1999. "Futures and Knowledge." In Ziauddin Sardar (Ed.), *Rescuing All Our Futures: The Future of Futures Studies.* Westport, CT: Praeger.

Landsberg, Martin. 1979. "Export-led Industrialization in the Third World: Manufacturing Imperialism." *Review of Radical Political Economics* 2, 4:50-63.

Lang, Tim, and Colin Hines. 1993. *The New Protectionism: Protecting the Future Against Free Trade.* New York: The New Press.

Lappé, Frances Moore. 1982. *Diet for a Small Planet.* New York: Ballantine.

Lappé, Frances Moore, Joseph Collins, and Peter Rosset, with Luis Esparza. 1998. *World Hunger: Twelve Myths.* 2d ed. New York: Grove Press.

Lappé, Marc, and Britt Bailey. 1998. *Against the Grain: Biotechnology and the Corporate Takeover of Your Food.* Monroe, ME: Common Courage Press.

Lappin, Todd. 1994. "Can Green Mix with Red?" *The Nation*, February 14:193.

LaTouche, Serge. 1993. *In the Wake of the Affluent Society: An Exploration of Post-Development.* London: Zed Books.

Lehman, David. 1990. *Democracy and Development in Latin America.* Philadelphia: Temple University Press.

Levey, Collin. 1999. "Canada Gives the Inuits a Homeland, but No Malls Please." *The Wall Street Journal*, April 2:A11.

Lewin, Tamar. 1995. "Family Decay Global, Study Says." *The New York Times,* May 30:A5.

Lietaer, Bernard. 1997. "From the Real Economy to the Speculative." *International Forum on Globalization News,* 2:7-10.

Lipton, Michael. 1977. *Why Poor People Stay Poor: Urban Bias in World Development.* London: Temple Smith.

Lissakers, Karin. 1993. *Banks, Borrowers, and the Establishment: A Revisionist Account of the International Debt Crisis.* New York: Basic Books.

Llambi, Luis. 1990. "Transitions to and Within Capitalism: Agrarian Transitions in Latin America." *Sociologia Ruralis* 30, 2:174-196.

Lohmann, Larry. 1993. "Resisting Green Globalism." In Wolfgang Sachs (Ed.), *Global Ecology: A New Arena of Political Conflict.* London: Zed Books.

London, Christopher. 1993. *The Cultural Policies of Technical Change in Colombian Coffee Production.* Unpublished master's thesis, Development Sociology, Cornell University.

———. 1997. "Class Relations and Capitalist Development: Subsumption in the Colombian Coffee Industry." *Journal of Peasant Studies,* 24, 4: 269-295.

Lorch, Donatella. 1995. "Ugandan Strongman a Favorite of World Lenders." *The New York Times,* January 29:A3.

MacShane, Denis. 1991. "Working in Virtual Slavery: Gulf Migrant Labor." *The Nation,* March 18:325, 343-344.

Madden, Peter, and John Madeley. 1993. "Winners and Losers: The Impact of the GATT Uruguay Round in Developing Countries." *Christian Aid,* December:17.

Magdoff, Harry. 1969. *The Age of Imperialism.* New York: Monthly Review Press.

Malkki, Liisa. 1997. "National Geographic: The Rooting of Peoples and the Territorialization of National Identity Among Scholars and Refugees." In Akhil Gupta and James Ferguson (Eds.), *Culture, Power, Place: Explorations in Critical Anthropology.* Durham, NC: Duke University Press.

Mamdani, Mahmood. 1996. *Citizen and Subject: Contemporary Africa and the Legacy of Late Colonialism.* Princeton, NJ: Princeton University Press.

"The Manufacturing Myth." 1994. *The Economist,* March 19:91-92.

Martin, Hans-Peter, and Harold Schumann. 1997. *The Global Trap: Globalisation and the Assault on Democracy and Prosperity.* London: Zed Books.

McMichael, A. J. 1993. *Planetary Overload: Global Environmental Change and the Health of the Human Species.* Cambridge: Cambridge University Press.

McMichael, Philip. 1987. "Foundations of U.S./Japanese World-Economic Rivalry in the 'Pacific Rim.' " *Journal of Developing Societies* 3, 1:62-77.

———. 1993a. "Agro-Food Restructuring in the Pacific Rim: A Comparative-International Perspective on Japan, South Korea, the United States, Australia, and Thailand." In Ravi Palat (Ed.), *Pacific-Asia and the Future of the World-System*. Westport, CT: Greenwood.

———. 1993b. "World Food System Restructuring Under a GATT Regime." *Political Geography* 12, 3:198-214.

McMichael, Philip, and Chul-Kyoo Kim. 1994. "Japanese and South Korean Agricultural Restructuring in Comparative and Global Perspective." In Philip McMichael (Ed.), *The Global Restructuring of Agro-Food Systems*. Ithaca, NY: Cornell University Press.

McMichael, Philip, and David Myhre. 1991. "Global Regulation Versus the Nation-State: Agro-Food Systems and the New Politics of Capital." *Capital & Class* 43, 2:83-106.

McMichael, Philip, and Laura T. Raynolds. 1994. "Capitalism, Agriculture, and World Economy." In Leslie Sklair (Ed.), *Capitalism and Development*. London: Routledge.

Memmi, Albert. 1967. *The Colonizer and the Colonized*. Boston: Beacon Press.

Menotti, Victor. 1996. "World Leaders Warn of 'Backlash to Globalization.' " *International Forum on Globalization News*, Fall:1, 7.

Menotti, Victor. 1998. "Globalization and the Acceleration of Forest Destruction Since Rio." *The Ecologist*, 28, 6:354-362.

Menotti, Victor. 1999. "Forest Destruction and Globalisation." *The Ecologist*, 29, 3:180-181.

Meredith, Robyn. 1997. "Auto Giants Build a Glut of Asian Plants, Just as Demand Falls." *The New York Times*, November 5:D1, 8.

Middleton, Neil, Phil O'Keefe, and Sam Moyo. 1993. *Tears of the Crocodile: From Rio to Reality in the Developing World*. Boulder, CO: Pluto.

Mies, Maria. 1991. *Patriarchy and Accumulation on a World Scale: Women in the International Division of Labor*. London: Zed Books.

Milbank, Dana. 1994. "Unlike Rest of Europe, Britain Is Creating Jobs but They Pay Poorly." *The Wall Street Journal*. March 28:A1, A6.

Mittal, Anuradha. 1998. "Freedom to Trade vs. Freedom from Hunger: Food Security in the Age of Economic Globalization." In Eva Harton and Claes Olsson (Eds.), *WTO as a Conceptual Framework for Globalization*. Uppsala: Global Publications Foundation.

Moberg, David. 1999. "Bringing Down Niketown." *The Nation*, June 7:15-18.

Montalbano, William L. 1991. "A Global Pursuit of Happiness." *Los Angeles Times*, October 1:H1, H7.

Moody, Kim. 1999. *Workers in a Lean World: Unions in the International Economy*. London: Verso.

Morgan, Dan. 1980. *Merchants of Grain*. Harmondsworth: Penguin.

Morgenthau, Robert M. 1998. "On the Trail of Global Capital." *The New York Times*, November 9:A25.

Mukhopadhyay, Baijayanta. 1999. *Inuit Women and the Road to Nunavut.* Unpublished term paper, International Development course, Rural Sociology, Cornell University.

Myers, Norman. 1981. "The Hamburger Connection: How Central America's Forests Became North America's Hamburgers." *Ambio* 10, 1:3-8.

Myhre, David. 1994. "The Politics of Globalization in Rural Mexico: Campesino Initiatives to Restructure the Agricultural Credit System." In Philip McMichael (Ed.), *The Global Restructuring of Agro-Food Systems.* Ithaca, NY: Cornell University Press.

Nash, Nathaniel C. 1994. "Vast Areas of Rain Forest Are Being Destroyed in Chile." *The New York Times*, May 31:C4.

Nayyar, D. 1976. "Transnational Corporations and Manufactured Exports from Poor Countries." *University of Sussex Economic Seminar Paper Series* 76.

Neville, Richard. 1997. "The Business of Being Human." *The Age* (Melbourne), August 23:48-50.

Norberg-Hodge, Helena. 1992. *Ancient Futures: Learning from Ladakh.* San Francisco: Sierra Club.

———. 1994-1995. "Globalization Versus Community." *ISEC/Ladakh Project* 14:1-2.

Ohmae, Kenichi. 1985. *Triad Power: The Coming Shape of Global Competition.* New York: Free Press.

———. 1990. *The End of the Nation-State: The Rise of Regional Economies.* New York: Free Press.

Olson, Elizabeth. 1999. "Free Markets Leave Women Worse Off, Unicef Says." *The New York Times*, September 23:16.

O'Meara, Molly. 1999. *Reinventing Cities for People and the Planet* (Worldwatch Papers 147). Washington, DC: Worldwatch Papers.

Onishi, Norimitsu. 1998. "Nigeria Combustible as South's Oil Enriches North." *The New York Times*, November 22:A1, A6.

———. 1999. "Deep in the Republic of Chevron." *The New York Times Magazine*, July 4:26-31.

Payer, Cheryl. 1974. *The Debt Trap.* New York: Monthly Review Press.

Pearse, A. 1980. *Seeds of Plenty, Seeds of Want.* Oxford: Clarendon Press.

Place, Susan E. 1985. "Export Beef Production and Development Contradictions in Costa Rica." *Tijdschrift voor Econ. en Soc. Geografie* 76, 4:288-297.

Qassim, Ali. 1998. "Turning the Tide." *The New Internationalist* 305:28-30.

Raghavan, Chakravarthi. 1990. *Recolonization: GATT, the Uruguay Round and the Third World.* Penang, Malaysia: Third World Network.

Raikes, Philip. 1988. *Modernising Hunger: Famine, Food Surplus & Farm Policy in the EC and Africa.* London: Catholic Institute for International Affairs.

Rama, Ruth. 1992. *Investing in Food.* Paris: Organization for Economic Cooperation and Development.

Rau, Bill. 1991. *From Feast to Famine: Official Cures and Grassroots Remedies to Africa's Food Crisis.* London: Zed Books.

Raynolds, Laura T. 1994. "The Restructuring of Export Agriculture in the Dominican Republic: Changing Agrarian Relations and the State." In Philip McMichael (Ed.), *The Global Restructuring of Agro-Food Systems.* Ithaca, NY: Cornell University Press.

Raynolds, Laura T., David Myhre, Philip McMichael, Viviana Carro-Figueroa, and Frederick H. Buttel. 1993. "The 'New' Internationalization of Agriculture: A Reformulation." *World Development* 21, 7:1101-1121.

Reich, Robert B. 1991. "Secession of the Successful." *The New York Times Magazine,* January 20:42.

————. 1992. *The Work of Nations: Preparing Ourselves for 21st Century Capitalism.* New York: Vintage Press.

Revel, Alain, and Christophe Riboud. 1986. *American Green Power.* Baltimore: Johns Hopkins University Press.

Ricardo, David. 1951. *On the Principles of Political Economy and Taxation.* 3d ed. Reprinted in P. Sraffe and M. M. Dobb (Eds.), *The Works and Correspondence of David Ricardo,* Vol. 1. Cambridge: Cambridge University Press. (Original work published 1821)

Rich, Bruce. 1994. *Mortgaging the Earth: The World Bank, Environmental Impoverishment and the Crisis of Development.* Boston: Beacon Press.

Ride, Anouk. 1998. "Maps, Myths and Migrants." *The New Internationalist* 305:9.

Riding, Alan. 1993. "France, Reversing Course, Fights Immigrants' Refusal to Be French." *The New York Times,* December 5:A1, 14.

Rifkin, Jeremy. 1992. *Beyond Beef: The Rise and Fall of the Cattle Culture.* New York: Penguin.

————. 1998. *The Biotech Century: Harnessing the Gene and Remaking the World.* New York: Tarcher/Putnam.

Rist, Gilbert. 1997. *The History of Development: From Western Origins to Global Faith.* London: Zed Books.

Ritchie, Mark. 1993. *Breaking the Deadlock: The United States and Agriculture Policy in the Uruguay Round.* Minneapolis: Institute for Agriculture and Trade Policy.

————. 1994. *GATT Facts: Africa Loses Under GATT.* Working paper. Minneapolis: Institute for Agriculture and Trade Policy.

Rocheleau, Dianne E. 1991. "Gender, Ecology, and the Science of Survival: Stories and Lessons from Kenya." In Wendy Harcourt (Ed.), *Feminist Perspectives on Sustainable Development.* London: Zed Books.

Rocher, Francis. 1993. "Canadian Business, Free Trade and the Rhetoric of Economic Continentalization." *Studies in Political Economy* 35:136-152.

Rosenberg, Tina. 1998. "Trees and the Roots of a Storm's Destruction." *The New York Times*, November 26:A38.

Ross, Robert J. S., and Kent C. Trachte. 1990. *Global Capitalism: The New Leviathan*. Albany: State University of New York Press.

Rostow, Walt W. 1960. *The Stages of Economic Growth: A Non-Communist Manifesto*. Cambridge: Cambridge University Press.

Rothchild, Donald, and Letitia Lawson. 1994. "The Interactions Between State and Civil Society in Africa: From Deadlock to New Routines." In John W. Harbeson, Donald Rothchild, and Naomi Chazan (Eds.), *Civil Society and the State in Africa*. Boulder, CO: Lynne Reinner.

Rowley, C. D. 1974. *The Destruction of Aboriginal Society*. Ringwood, Victoria, Australia: Penguin.

Rueschemeyer, Dietrich, Evelyne Huber Stephens, and John Stephens. 1992. *Capitalist Development and Democracy*. Chicago: University of Chicago Press.

Ruggie, John G. 1982. "International Regimes, Transactions and Change: Embedded Liberalism in the Postwar Economic Order." *International Organization* 36:397-415.

Ruggiero, Renato. 1996. *Trading Towards Peace?* Address presented to the MENA II Conference, Cairo.

———. 1998. *From Vision to Reality: The Multilateral Trading System at Fifty*. Address presented to the Brookings Institution Forum, Washington, DC, December 4.

Runyan, Curtis. 1999. "Action on the Front Lines." *World Watch*, 12(6):12-21.

Sachs, Jeffrey,. 1998. "The IMF and the Asian Flu." *The American Prospect*, March-April:16-21.

Sachs, Wolfgang. 1992. "One World." In Wolfgang Sachs (Ed.), *The Development Dictionary*. London: Zed Books.

———. 1993. "Global Ecology and the Shadow of 'Development.' " In Wolfgang Sachs (Ed.), *Global Ecology: A New Arena of Political Conflict*. London: Zed Books.

Salinger, Lynn, and Jean-Jacques Dethier. 1989. *Policy-Based Lending in Agriculture: Agricultural Sector Adjustment in Mexico*. Paper presented at World Bank Seminar on Policy-Based Lending in Agriculture, Baltimore, May 17-19.

Sandbrook, Richard. 1995. *The Politics of Africa's Economic Recovery*. Cambridge: Cambridge University Press.

Sanderson, Steven. 1986a. "The Emergence of the 'World Steer': Internationalization and Foreign Domination in Latin American Cattle Production." In F. L. Tullis and W. L. Hollist (Eds.), *Food, the State and International Political Economy*. Lincoln: University of Nebraska Press.

———. 1986b. *The Transformation of Mexican Agriculture: International Structure and the Politics of Rural Change*. Princeton, NJ: Princeton University Press.

Sanger, David E. 1994. "Mexico Crisis Seen Spurring Flow of Aliens." *The New York Times*, January 18:A3.

————. 1995. "Big Powers Plan a World Economic Bailout Fund." *The New York Times*, June 8:A1, D8.

————. 1998a. "Dissension Erupts at Talks on World Financial Crisis." *The New York Times*, October 7:A6.

————. 1998b. "IMF Now Admits Tactics in Indonesia Deepened the Crisis." *The New York Times*, January 14:A1, D11.

Sassen, Saskia. 1991. *The Global City*. Princeton, NJ: Princeton University Press.

Schaeffer, Robert. 1995. "Free Trade Agreements: Their Impact on Agriculture and the Environment." In Philip McMichael (Ed.), *Food and Agrarian Orders in the World-Economy*. Westport, CT: Praeger.

————. 1997. *Understanding Globalization: The Social Consequences of Political, Economic, and Environmental Change*. New York: Rowman & Littlefield.

Schemo, Diana Jean. 1997. "Rising Fires Renew Threat to Amazon." *The New York Times*, November 2:6.

————. 1998. "Data Show Recent Burning of Amazon Is Worst Ever." *The New York Times*, January 27:A4.

Schneider, Cathy Lisa. 1995. *Shantytown Protest in Pinochet's Chile*. Philadelphia: Temple University Press.

Schoenberger, Erica. 1994. "Competition, Time, and Space in Industrial Change." In Gary Gereffi and Miguel Korzeniewicz (Eds.), *Commodity Chains and Global Capitalism*. Westport, CT: Praeger.

Schwedel, Kenneth. 1991. "Will the Countryside Modernize?" *Business Mexico*, July:25.

Schwedel, S., and K. Haley. 1992. "Foreign Investment in the Mexican Food System." *Business Mexico*, Special Edition:48-55.

Seabrook, Jeremy. 1996. *In the Cities of the South: Scenes from a Development World*. London: Verso.

Seers, Dudley. 1979. "The Meaning of Development." In David Lehman (Ed.), *Development Theory: Four Critical Studies*. London: Frank Cass.

Segelken, Roger. 1995. "Fewer Foods Predicted for Crowded Future Meals." *Cornell Chronicle*, February 23:5.

Seidman, Gay. 1994. *Manufacturing Militance: Workers' Movements in Brazil and South Africa, 1970-1985*. Berkeley: University of California Press.

Selverston, Melina H. 1998. "Pachacutik: Indigenous People and Democracy in Ecuador," *Native Americas* 15, 2:12-21.

Sen, Gita. 1994. "Women, Poverty, and Population: Issues for the Concerned Environmentalist." In Wendy Harcourt (Ed.), *Feminist Perspectives on Sustainable Development*. London: Zed Books.

Shaiken, Harley. 1993. "Two Myths About Mexico." *The New York Times*, August 22:A25.

Sharp, Nonie. 1994. "Native Title in the Reshaping of Australian Identity." *Arena Journal* 3:115-148.

Shenon, Philip. 1993. "Saipan Sweatshops Are No American Dream." *The New York Times*, July 18:A1, 10.

Shiva, Vandana. 1991. *The Violence of the Green Revolution.* London: Zed Books.

Shultz, George, P., William E. Simon, and Walter B. Wriston. 1998. "Who Needs the IMF?" Retrieved February 4 from the World Wide Web: tw-list@essential.org

Silver, Beverly. 1995. "World-Scale Patterns of Labor-Capital Conflict." *Review* 18, 1:155-192.

Simons, Marlise. 1999. "Cry of Muslim Women for Equal Rights Is Rising." *The New York Times*, February 24:A1, A6.

Singh, Ajit. 1992. "The Lost Decade: The Economic Crisis of the Third World in the 1980s: How the North Caused the South's Crisis." *Contention* 2:136-158.

Singh, Kavaljit, and Daphne Wysham. 1997. "Micro-Credit: Band-Aid or Wound?" *The Ecologist* 27, 2:42-43.

Sivanandan, A. 1989. "New Circuits of Imperialism." *Race & Class* 30, 4:1-19.

Sklair, Leslie. 1989. *Assembling for Development: The Maquila Industry in Mexico and the United States.* Boston: Unwin Hyman.

———. 1991. *The Sociology of the Global System.* Baltimore: Johns Hopkins University Press.

Skrobanek, Siripan, Nattaya Boonpakdi, and Chutina Janthakeero. 1997. *The Human Realities of Traffic in International Women.* London: Zed Books.

Sobieszczyk, Teresa, and Lindy Williams. 1997. "Attitudes Surrounding the Continuation of Female Circumcision in the Sudan: Passing the Tradition to the Next Generation." *Journal of Marriage and the Family* 59:966-981.

The South Centre. 1993. *Facing the Challenge: Responses to the Report of the South Commission.* London: Zed Books.

Stavrianos, L. S. 1981. *Global Rift: The Third World Comes of Age.* New York: William Morrow & Co.

Stevens, William K. 1994. "Poor Lands' Success in Cutting Birth Rate Upsets Old Theories." *The New York Times*, January 2:A8.

Stevenson, Richard W. 1993. "Ford Sets Its Sights on a 'World Car.' " *The New York Times*, October 27:D1, 4.

Stewart, Douglas Ian. 1994. *After the Trees: Living on the Amazon Highway.* Austin: University of Texas Press.

Stimson, Robert L. 1999. "General Motors Drives Some Hard Bargains with Asian Suppliers." *The Wall Street Journal*, April 2:A1, 6.

Strange, Susan. 1994. *States and Markets.* London: Pinter.

Strom, Stephanie. 1999. "In Renault-Nissan Deal, Big Risks and Big Opportunities." *The New York Times*, March 28:A3.

Swamy, M. R. Narayan. 1995. "Hindu Groups Step Up 'Buy Indian' Campaign." *IA News*, January 10. Retrieved February 4 from the World Wide Web: tw-list@essential.org

Tan, Abby. 1991a. "The Labor Brokers: For a Price, There's a Job Abroad—Maybe." *Los Angeles Times*, October 1:H1.

———. 1991b. "Paychecks Sent Home May Not Cover Human Losses." *Los Angeles Times*, October 1:H2-3.

Tautz, Carlos Sergio Figueiredo. 1997. "The Asian Invasion: Asian Multinationals Come to the Amazon." *Multinational Monitor*, 18, 9:1-5.

Templin, Neal. 1994. "Mexican Industrial Belt Is Beginning to Form as Car Makers Expand." *The Wall Street Journal*, June 29:A1, 10.

Thomas, Alan, Ben Crow, Paul Franz, Tom Hewitt, Sabrina Kassam, and Steven Treagust. 1994. *Third World Atlas* (2d ed.). Washington, DC: Taylor & Francis.

Thurow, Lester C. 1999. "The Dollar's Day of Reckoning." *The Nation*, January 11:22-24.

Tripp, Aili Mari. 1997. *Changing the Rules: The Politics of Liberalization and the Urban Informal Economy in Tanzania*. Berkeley: University of California Press.

Tyler, Patrick E. 1994. "China Planning People's Car to Put Masses Behind Wheel." *The New York Times*, September 22:A1, D8.

———. 1995. "Star at Conference on Women: Banker Who Lends to the Poor." *The New York Times*, September 14:A6.

Uchitelle, Louis. 1993a. "America's Newest Industrial Belt." *The New York Times*, March 21, Business Section:1.

———. 1993b. "Stanching the Loss of Good Jobs." *The New York Times*, January 31, Section 3:1, 6.

———. 1994. "U.S. Corporations Expanding Abroad at a Quicker Pace." *The New York Times*, July 25:A1, D2.

Udesky, Laurie. 1994. "Sweatshops Behind the Labels." *The Nation*, May 16:665-668.

Ufkes, Fran. 1995. "Industrial Restructuring and Agrarian Change: The Greening of Singapore." In Philip McMichael (Ed.), *Food and Agrarian Orders in the World Economy*. Westport, CT: Praeger.

Ul Haq, Mahbub. 1995. "Whatever Happened to the Peace Dividend?" *Our Planet 7*, 1:8-10.

United Nations Development Programme (UNDP). 1996. *Human Development Report 1996*. New York: Oxford University Press.

———. 1997. *Human Development Report 1997*. New York: Oxford University Press.

Vilas, Carlos. 1995. "Economic Restructuring, Neoliberal Reforms, and the Working Class in Latin America." In Sandor Halebsky and Richard L. Harris (Eds.), *Capital, Power, and Inequality in Latin America*. Boulder, CO: Westview Press.

Wacker, Corinne. 1994. "Sustainable Development Through Women's Groups: A Cultural Approach to Sustainable Development." In Wendy Harcourt (Ed.), *Feminist Perspectives on Sustainable Development*. London: Zed Books.

Wallerstein, Immanuel. 1983. *Historical Capitalism*. London: Verso.

————. 1992. "The Collapse of Liberalism." In Ralph Miliband and Leo Panitch (Eds.), *Socialist Register*. London: Merlin.

Walton, John, and David Seddon. 1994. *Free Markets and Food Riots: The Politics of Global Adjustment*. Oxford: Blackwell.

Watkins, Kevin. 1991. "Agriculture and Food Security in the GATT Uruguay Round." *Review of African Political Economy* 50:38-50.

————. 1996. "Free Trade and Farm Fallacies: From the Uruguay Round to the World Food Summit." *The Ecologist* 26, 6:244- 255.

Watts, Michael. 1992. "The Shock of Modernity: Petroleum, Protest, and Fast Capitalism in an Industrializing Society." In Allan Pred and Michael Watts (Eds.), *Reworking Modernity*. New Brunswick, NJ: Rutgers University Press.

————. 1994. "Life Under Contract: Contract Farming, Agrarian Restructuring and Flexible Accumulation." In Peter D. Little and Michael J. Watts (Eds.), *Living Under Contract: Contract Farming and Agrarian Transformation in Sub-Saharan Africa*. Madison: University of Wisconsin Press.

Weinberg, Bill. 1998. "La Miskitia Rears Up: Industrial Recolonization Threatens the Nicaraguan Rainforests—An Indigenous Response." *Native Americas* 15, 2:22-33.

Weisbrot, Mark. 1999. "How to Say No to the IMF." *The Nation*, June 21:20-21.

Weissman, Robert. 1991. "Prelude to a New Colonialism: The Real Purpose of GATT." *The Nation*, March 18:337.

Wessel, James. 1983. *Trading the Future: Farm Exports and the Concentration of Economic Power in Our Food System*. San Francisco: Institute for Food and Development Policy.

Williams, Gwyneth. 1981. *Third-World Political Organizations. A Review of Developments*. Montclair, NJ: Allenheld, Osmun & Co.

Williams, Robert G. 1986. *Export Agriculture and the Crisis in Central America*. Chapel Hill: University of North Carolina Press.

Wolf, Eric. 1982. *Europe and the People Without History*. Berkeley: University of California Press.

Wood, Ellen Meiksins. 1999. "Kosovo and the New Imperialism." *Monthly Review* 51, 2:1-8.

Wood, Robert E. 1986. *From Marshall Plan to Debt Crisis: Foreign Aid and Development Choices in the World Economy*. Berkeley: University of California Press.

Woodall, Pam. 1994. "War of the Worlds: A Survey of the Global Economy." *The Economist*, Special Supplement, October 1:24.

Working, Russell. 1999. "Russia's Patchwork Economy: Korean Companies, Chinese Workers and U.S. Entree." *The New York Times*, March 18:D1, D23.

World Bank. 1974. *Redistribution With Growth*. Washington, DC: World Bank.

————. 1981. *Accelerated Development in Sub-Saharan Africa: An Agenda to Action*. Washington, DC: World Bank.

————. 1989. *Sub-Saharan Africa From Crisis to Sustainable Growth: A Long Term Perspective Study*. Washington, DC: World Bank.

————. 1990. *World Development Report*. Washington, DC: World Bank.

————. 1997. *World Development Report: The State in a Changing World*. New York: Oxford University Press.

————. 1999. *World Development Report 1998/99: Knowledge for Development*. New York: Oxford University Press.

————. 2000. *World Development Report 1999/2000: Entering the 21st Century*. New York: Oxford University Press.

World Resource Institute. 1998. *World Resources 1998-99*. New York: Oxford University Press.

World Commission on Environment and Development. 1987. *Our Common Future*. Oxford: Oxford University Press.

WuDunn, Sheryl. 1993. "Booming China Is Dream Market for West." *The New York Times*, February 15:A1-6.

Recommended Supplements to This Text

Detailed case studies can usefully complement this globally oriented text. I particularly recommend Helena Norberg-Hodge's text *Ancient Futures: Learning from Ladakh* (Sierra Club Books, 1992) and its companion film *Ancient Futures*, distributed by The Ladakh Project/International Society for Ecology and Culture, Box 9475, Berkeley, CA 94709. This study presents strikingly clear and comprehensive images of life in Ladakh before and after its very recent modernization, and it evaluates our assumptions about development and raises questions about global social trends. It offers a human-scale version of development to complement the global story of the development project. Other case studies include a proliferating literature on grassroots projects (see the references in this book) and various communities, such as Borneo's forest-dwellers depicted in Wade Davis et al., *Nomads of the Dawn* (Pomegranate Artbooks, 1995). Additional case studies include various treatments of the debt crisis, studies of the international financial world such as Bruce Rich's *Mortgaging the Earth*, and studies of transnational firms such as Dan Morgan's *Merchants of Grain*, Richard Barnet and John Cavanagh's *Global Dreams* (see the references in this book), Brewster Kneen's study of Cargill, *Invisible Giant* (Pluto, 1995), and Judith Adler Hellman's *Mexican Lives* (New Press, 1995), an excellent ethnography of contemporary Mexican society in the aftermath of the political and economic restructuring associated with the passage of NAFTA.

Films that depicts aspects of developmentalism and globalism addressed in this text include PBS documentaries such as *The Politics of Food* (global agribusiness and food aid programs); *Local Heroes: Global Change* (case studies introduced by Southern intellectuals of structural adjustment programs, export processing zones, and so forth); series such as *The Africans*, narrated by Ali Mazrui, and East Asia's *Minidragons*; *The Global Economy: Four Weeks in the Life of the Earth* (global corporate and communication networks and the dilemma of unemployment); and *The Decade of Destruction* (of the Amazon forest in the 1980s). *Jungleburger*

(Filmkraft Production, 1986) is a graphic portrayal of the U.S./Costa Rica hamburger connection.

Publications such as the U.N. Development Program's (UNDP) annual *Human Development Report* and the World Bank's annual *Development Report* are useful databases, with up-to-date development agency interpretation. Visually striking geopolitical data sources are Alan Thomas's *Third World Atlas* (Taylor & Francis) and Michael Kidron and Ronald Segal's *The State of the World Atlas* (Penguin), both of which are updated periodically. Finally, the annual *State of the World* (Norton) volume, edited by the Worldwatch Institute, is an invaluable source of information and ideas concerning environmental dilemmas we face.

Glossary/Index

A

Aboriginals, 299

Africa
  agricultural self-sufficiency, 56
  civil war, 26
  crisis of state, 220
  debt crisis, 126-127, 132-133
  food dependency, 169
  gene patenting, 174-175
  informalization, 211-213
  labor, 8, 10, 13
  marginalization, 215
  one-party states, 227, 229
  precolonial, 6, 10
  refugees, 230-231
  structural adjustment, 132-133, 142-144, 226-227
  world export share, 215

Agribusiness
  concessions to, 139
  global spread of, 66, 100-103, 105-106, 108-109
  inequality, 71
  nontraditional exports, 103-104
  Public-Law 480 program, 70

Agriculture
  Chinese, 282
  food regime, 59-64
  global location, 56, 59
  green power strategy, 64
  green revolution, 68-70
  intensive, 69
  Third World, 56, 65
  traditional vs. modern, 69

Agro-ecological zoning, 225

Agro-export
  coalition, Latin American, 18-19
  development, Colombian, 19-20
  feed-grain supply zones, 66-68
  Malaysian, 51
  nontraditional, 103-104
  platforms, 158

Agro-industrialization, 102-105
  Chinese, 282
  Iranian, 151
  Thai, 103-104

Aguarunu Jivaro women, 264

Allende, President Salvador, 155

Alliance for Progress counter-insurgency organization formed by Latin American states with U.S. support, designed to redistribute resources, especially land, for development, 72, 101

Alternative Forum, 290

Anderson, Benedict, 206

Animal protein diets, xxxviii-xxxix, 66, 80, 288

Anticolonial movements, 5, 7
  Pan-Africanism, 25-26

Appropriate technology, 247

Argentina, 68

Asia
  foreign investment, 215
  NICs, 81-84, 86

Asia-Pacific Economic Conference (APEC) conference founded in 1989 on the initiative of Australia; comprises the United States, Canada, Japan, South Korea, Australia, New Zealand, Mexico, and the six ASEAN

designingborders

Noël Kingsbury

CASSELL
ILLUSTRATED

Contents

Introduction

Choosing and combining plants for borders is an art, a creative activity that for many people is the heart of gardening and the source of their passion for plants. Whereas lawns, hedges and vegetable patches are primarily functional, borders are about growing plants for the sheer enjoyment of gardening.

The 24 border plans created specially for this book show how today's leading professional designers use plants in different combinations, employing a wide range of styles for different situations. Some of the designs use plants as a means to an artistic end, while others are based on a love of the plants themselves. All take note, and this is a key point, of the conditions required by the plants.

Creating a beautiful border that will grow and change over time is, for many gardeners, a daunting prospect. The best way to start is by seeing how the experts do it, picking up tips and ideas, seeing how they arrange colours and leaf shapes, tall and small plants, and those with different textures. This book is an anthology of border schemes that show how successful and experienced designers use plants, and the kinds of plants they choose for particular situations. The plans demonstrate plant combinations for creating a particular effect, in a variety of styles and for different garden situations. Each is by a professional designer who is well known as a practising gardener.

John Brookes

is a prolific writer on garden design and is highly involved in the professional training of designers. He is associated with a contemporary approach to gardens, one that stresses the 'architecture' of plants chosen to fit his artistic vision.

Rupert Golby

is a busy practising garden designer whose approach is relatively traditional and plant orientated, showing sensitivity to surroundings and to his many clients.

Penelope Hobhouse

is known for her writings on colour scheming and garden history and for her association with high-profile garden designs and restorations. Her work involves meticulous research and a keen awareness of historical issues in gardening.

Noël Kingsbury

I am a writer and designer who advocates radical, ecologically based planting schemes. I have a passionate belief in the value of public space, for which nature-inspired plantings are often particularly effective.

Piet Oudolf

is a plantsman who brings a contemporary stance to the relationship between formality and lush planting. He runs a design practice and, with his wife Anja, a very successful nursery in Holland, specialising in grasses and perennials.

Nori and Sandra Pope

Today's colour gurus are a husband and wife team, who are gardeners and plantsmen rather than designers, and who have achieved recognition through the garden they have transformed and look after on a full-time basis at Hadspen House in Somerset, England.

[Left] Late season grasses and perennials are the high point of the year in Piet Oudolf's work: *Stipa calamagrostis*, *Achillea* 'Hella Glashof', *Astrantia* 'Ruby Wedding', *Monarda* 'Camanche' [rear right], *Persicaria amplexicaulis* 'Firedance' [front right]

[Right] At John Brookes' garden at Denmans, thistle-like *Eryngium giganteum* and other structural plants make for much visual stimulation

What was the brief?

The designers were asked to submit plans for four borders or plantings in a medium-sized garden. Beyond this there was no specification, though it was crucial that no one submitted anything too similar. The opportunity of designing a hypothetical scheme was meant to liberate the designers from the constraints within which they often have to work, helping them create designs that reflect their key interests and passions.

Such designs can sometimes be transferred direct from the page to a garden, but how often does that work? In established gardens there are many constraints or existing ingredients that have to be taken into account, ranging from the shape and style of the house and adjoining buildings, to features such as beautiful old trees that may be in the neighbouring garden. That is why it is dangerous to fall in love with a show garden at a horticultural exhibition, and imagine it can be installed without any modifications at home. By itself, it is fine, but how will it link up with the site?

Inspirational ideas, therefore, must be combined with practical needs. If a particular design in the book does inspire you, and actually fits a site in your own garden, it is imperative that you do some preliminary homework. First, make sure that its style blends, and does not jar, with the style of your surroundings. And second, check that the plants suit your garden's aspect, soil and climate by looking them up in a plant encyclopaedia (and if you can not provide their needs, find alternative plants that will be happy there). If, though, the plan is too large for your small garden, scale down and modify the design while making sure that you provide all-year interest using either evergreens or a seasonal succession of flowering plants. Alternatively, use one of these plans as a starting point for your own design, choosing your own colour scheme and plants with attractive shapes and textures.

The designers have submitted carefully thought out drawings as they might for a client. These designs are for medium-sized gardens with neutral soil and normal conditions, unless stipulated otherwise. An estimated number of plants required has also been supplied as a rough guideline.

The changing look of border styles

Before looking at the following designs, and examining the key criteria in creating a border, it helps if we have a quick look at how borders have developed over the years, giving the 24 designs a context.

There have been borders of some kind ever since people started growing plants for pleasure, but it was not until the late 19th century that they really began to acquire a life of their own. Complex shapes and patterns were developed, often incorporating displays of exotic and tender bedding plants. The early years of the 20th century saw an increasing interest in hardy plants rather than tender ones and, in Britain and central Europe especially, the border became a focus for herbaceous perennials. The herbaceous border reached its apogee in Edwardian England as a majestic spectacle (orchestrated by armies of gardeners), putting on its grand finale in late summer.

Since this high point early in the 20th century, the trend has been towards a more relaxed garden style. In England, Gertrude Jekyll created borders that played with sophisticated colour schemes; she often worked to architectural garden layouts designed in conjunction with her collaborator, the architect Edwin Lutyens. Later, the writer Vita Sackville-West brought a sense of cottage-like informality to her highly influential garden at Sissinghurst, in Kent, keeping her readers up to date of her progress in her newspaper articles.

Meanwhile, in central Europe, gardening was dominated more by perennials than shrubs. This was because many of the shrubs that are hardy in Britain or France were likely to be killed, or cut back to ground level, by their intensely cold winters. The leading figure in gardening with perennials and grasses at this time was the highly influential German garden designer (and possibly most influential of all time), Karl Foerster. A nurseryman and prolific writer, in the 1930s and 1950s he began to promote a naturalistic style using grasses and natural species perennials. While Foerster's work has been little recognized in Britain, his legacy has been immensely important in central Europe and the USA. Wolfgang Oehme, of the American Oehme Van Sweden design partnership, was trained in the Foerster tradition, while Piet Oudolf also regards him as a major contemporary influence. (This influence is discussed on page 150.)

If there has been an 'end result' over the last century of innovation and experimentation, it has been the mixed border. Since few amateur gardeners have ever had the space for borders devoted entirely to perennials or summer annuals, there has always been a tendency to combine these different plants within one border. The mixed border therefore fulfils a variety of different functions: the shrubs provide spring flowers, structure and screening; bulbs create spring displays; perennials bring

summer and autumn colour; and annuals make an appearance in odd gaps for extra summer interest.

Recent developments have seen a much greater use of climbers in borders, clambering up supports such as obelisks, wigwams of canes and other purpose-built structures, and the introduction of vegetables, exploiting the intense colours of, for example, ruby chard, red cabbage and red lettuce. And while the archetypal borders of the Edwardian era were very neat, with a careful gradient from the tallest plants at the back to the shortest at the front, there has since been a tendency towards a more informal structuring of heights. The apparently artless jumble of the cottage garden style has been a considerable influence in this respect. Yet planting styles still heavily relied on a backdrop – a hedge, wall or fence – which meant that the plants could be seen from a limited range of viewpoints.

A major breakthrough came in the 1960s with the popularization of 'island beds' by nurseryman Alan Bloom. Surrounded by oceans of lawn, they incorporated shrubs and perennials, usually built around a 'hill' of taller plants in the centre. The island beds injected greater flexibility into mixed borders by allowing plant combinations to be appreciated from a variety of angles. Beth Chatto's garden,

in Essex, in the UK, also became highly influential from this time on, with its informal, fluid layout, and plants usually chosen to match the prevailing conditions.

The most recent changes to the border have come from an awareness of how plants grow in nature, often in distinct groups. German public landscapes, with their marked, naturalistic style, have been a particular focus of interest. These plantings lie somewhere between a conventional herbaceous border and a wildflower meadow. They are open, with narrow paths winding through perennials and ornamental grasses arranged in romantic drifts. Dutch designers, such as Mien Ruys and Piet Oudolf, have also made us look at border plants in different ways, the former within a strongly architectural framework, the latter through the evocation of a more romantic style, concentrating on the use of plant shape and form.

Preliminary practicalities

What do I want from my border?

It is vital that you clarify the purpose of your border. Is it meant to be a showpiece, or somewhere to grow favourite plants? Should it double as a boundary, running beside a fence or hedge for example, or be placed in a lawn? And will it include tall plants so that it is looked up at, or low ones so that it is looked over?

Next, consider the immediate surroundings. The new border can be used to fill a gap or bare space, for example a right-angled corner between two walls, or to cover a bank or hide an eyesore. John Brookes' designs are particularly helpful when it comes to arranging plants right in front of a building, and often include strongly structural plants to complement their surroundings. Sunny, sheltering, backdrop walls also mean that some borders can incorporate sub-tropical plants, because they like the extra heat and protection (see my and Penelope Hobhouse's designs on pages 134–137 and 110–113). By clarifying the purpose of the border, it becomes clear which type of plants you need.

Positioning borders

The dimensions of your garden determine the maximum size of the border, and there is nothing you can do about that, but you can decide where you put it.

First and foremost, a border needs to be positioned where it can be seen, either from the house or a seating area in the garden. In fact, borders are often designed in conjunction with a seating area or a feature, such as a barbecue. Conventionally, it has been assumed that we need to stand back from a border in order to see it, but recent designs have challenged this approach. They have also blurred the boundaries, in gravel gardens, between the paths and border planting (see Rupert Golby's blue and yellow border and the Pope's dry gravel bed on pages 86–89 and 180–183).

Another development has seen the use of narrow paths through dense planting to offer a more intimate view of the scheme. Such paths are an important feature of contemporary German plantings (see my design on pages 130–133) and, to an extent, of Piet Oudolf's work. In fact, one recent development lets people look down over the planting from raised decking, while planting on banks means you can also look up at the plants (see my design on pages 122–125).

Border backdrops

Borders have traditionally had a backdrop, such as a wall or fence, but this can be very limiting, allowing plants to be looked at only head-on, 'like soldiers on parade', to quote the head of the leading German horticultural research institute. But deciding whether you need a backdrop depends on what you want to grow.

A traditional dark green yew hedge nicely shows off pastel flower colours, but you can get the same effect in an island bed with a distant view of a wall of conifers. Fresh green, blue and yellow flowers look effective against brick walls. Open borders or large island beds, with only a distant backdrop, suit the larger ornamental grasses best, and tall, robust perennials. And where there is no clear division with your neighbour's garden, a new border (even without a backdrop) helps provide privacy and define the end of your garden. Use climbers growing up sturdy trellis panels to enhance the effect.

A bank of poor soil is planted up with stress-tolerant plants in the author's own garden, including mauve *Lavandula stoechas* subsp. *pedunculata* and yellow *Euphorbia seguieriana* subsp. *niciciana*

The early morning
light illuminates the
blues, whites and
greens in a border in
the Rothschild garden
in the South of France
which was designed by
Penelope Hobhouse

The right conditions

While full sun supports the widest range of garden flora,
a wide variety of plants flourish in light, damp or heavy
shade (see John Brookes', Penelope Hobhouse's and my
designs on pages 58–61, 102–105 and 126–129). However,
unless you are drawn to the more subtle beauties of
woodland plants, aim for a site that gets as much sun
as possible.

Lighting

Sites that receive sun all year long offer more scope
for trouble-free gardening and design possibilities.
But thinking about how light hits the plants is crucial,
particularly in the winter when the sun is often at a low
angle. Piet Oudolf has done more than most modern
designers to draw our attention to how light affects the
way we see plants, particularly ornamental grasses
that often needing back-lighting to look their best.

Selecting the right plants for the right site

Soil conditions

The condition of the soil can cause a lot of heartache, especially to new gardeners. Much of this is due to a feeling that only one sort of soil is good for gardening, and that is the fine, crumbly tilth seen on TV garden programmes. But few of us have this, and if you do not it certainly is not a problem.

If you do have extremely good soil it means that you can grow the widest range of plants. Less perfect soils mean you must choose plants that enjoy the prevailing conditions. However, there are some situations that are difficult at the best of times, and they include heavy clay subsoil, extensive tree roots and soil that is full of rubble and rubbish. Where this is impossible to avoid, it will be necessary to improve the soil with large quantities of well-rotted organic matter, for example manure, agricultural waste (such as spent hops), and plant-derived compost, that should be dug in before planting and applied annually as a soil conditioner thereafter. Where soil conditions are very bad, try buying top quality topsoil and grow a border in a raised bed, so that the plants have about 30cm (1ft) of good soil to grow in.

There are two important criteria. The first is, will existing plants nearby have any impact? For example, if there are several large rhododendrons in the background, your choice of border flowers may create a colour clash. Make sure that the border plants look good in relation to each other, and to those nearby (see John Brookes' and my designs on pages 54–57 and 126–129).

The second point is that you must choose plants that will thrive in your border's soil and climate. Areas which often pose a problem to new gardeners include . . .

Hot dry sites, or soils that are light and free-draining

There is a wide selection of drought-resistant plants, most of which flower in spring and/or early summer. They often have attractive evergreen foliage, with popular Mediterranean flora recognizable by its low shrubby growth and grey leaves.

Try a border based on lavender, sage, thyme and rock roses, with the use of gravel. Gravel is a good mulch, reducing evaporation from the soil in dry spells, and is ideal in dry gardens (see John Brookes' contemporary border, Rupert Golby's scented border and the Popes' gravel garden, on pages 62–65, 78–81 and 180–183).

Wet soil

Moist soil can be a boon, allowing many lush-growing plants to flourish, but if water sits in pools when it rains or there is regular flooding, only those species that originate from wetlands will survive. The rest will rot and die.

Wet environments encourage the growth of luxuriant vegetation with lots of tall, rapidly-growing stems, usually with flowers in the latter part of the year like, for example, the big yellow ligularias. A border on such wet soil will probably feature several shrubs tolerant of occasional flooding (willows) and large perennials, many of which have striking foliage and are very colourful in late summer, for example species of sanguisborba and eupatoriums. The Popes are particularly skilful in combining dramatic colours and shapes – even in damp conditions (see their damp border on pages 176–179).

Shade

Few plants from open, sunny habitats will grow satisfactorily in shade, and if they do make good growth they might not flower. There are, however, a large number of plants from woodland habitats that will flourish in shade, especially if it is not very deep or the soil is not dry for long periods. Most are spring flowering, but many have attractive leaves that look good all summer and, since many are evergreen, there is no reason why a shady area should not look good all year. Most flowering woodland plants are low-growing bulbs and perennials, but there are some taller foliage plants, such as bamboos and a few shade-tolerant flowering shrubs, for example species of ribes, sarcococca or, for deep shade, *Danae racemosa*.

A shady border will probably be on the low side but with an interesting variation of foliage colour, shape and texture. (Penelope Hobhouse's design for a north-facing border, on pages 102–103, is a good starting point. Mine, pages 126–129, shows how planting can reflect the gradient from deep to light shade.)

The garden at the Old Rectory, Sudborough, designed by Rupert Golby, features a large natural pond where damp-loving plants thrive

Exposed sites

Wind will damage many plants, making it impossible to grow some common border varieties either because of physical damage (with tall plants being blown over) or because of the desiccation of delicate leaves. Since cold winds are particularly damaging, restrict your plants to those that are reliably hardy. Though this rules out tall perennials, many smaller ones can be used, as can many shrubs, plants with tiny leaves (heathers) and ornamental grasses (*Molinia caerulea*) that simply and beautifully bend in the wind.

Coastal sites

Plants will need to be salt- and wind-tolerant to grow on the coast. Those with silver or grey foliage are often a good choice because the coating of tiny hairs, which provide the distinct colour, is a protective device against desiccation and the salt particles blown in from the sea. When selecting a colour scheme, grey foliage is an obvious starting point, in conjunction with purple or bronze leaves or pastel-coloured flowers.

Coastal gardens do have one big advantage though, because the sea moderates cold winter temperatures. This provides a good environment for frost tender, wind-tolerant evergreens, such as hebes and olearias. They could be the basis of a planting scheme, their attractive evergreen foliage making a wonderful combination with other plants, such as many ornamental grasses. (Penelope Hobhouse's mixed shrub border in full sun, pages 106–109, is a possibility for such a scheme. My steppe planting, pages 122–125, is also suitable for coastal or exposed locations.)

The aesthetics

Which style?

The environment of the site might suggest a starting point for your design, while other elements may provide an inspiration. An old country house, for example, may suggest a cottage garden border, a finely proportioned house might demand something more formal, while a modern house or surroundings suggest a border with many ornamental grasses and other simple, elegant forms. The fine sense of balance created by Penelope Hobhouse's 'repeating plants' (see pages 98–101) and the occasional symmetrical planting in Rupert Golby's designs (pages 74–81) work well in the vicinity of older houses. With contemporary architecture, try the more modernist asymmetry of John Brookes' designs (pages 50–65) which are particularly successful at softening areas dominated by brick and concrete.

You can also opt for a wide range of other choices, such as a Mediterranean-style border, a border based on a particular group of plants (roses), or plants with a similar look (architectural plants), or plants that are richly scented. The final consideration is, do you want the border at its best at particular times (spring, midsummer and early autumn) or staying attractive right through the year? (Rupert Golby is particularly skilled at building plant combinations that always look attractive; see his year-round border on pages 74–77.)

Colour

Most people want to explore the possibilities of a particular colour or combination of colours. This theme can be continued through as much of the year as possible, or just for one season. (Penelope Hobhouse's designs on pages 98–113 have a strong sense of colour harmony, and are well worth studying.)

One-colour borders

They are relatively easy and fun to make, and can look very sophisticated. The Popes have dedicated much of their gardening to exploring the possibilities of monocolour planting, believing that the result creates a strong sense of harmony. Having a single colour also makes people seek out the subtle differences between each plant, in terms of tone and shape.

White has good possibilities for long-term interest, and is delightfully cool. Yellow is a good spring to early autumn possibility, but can have limitations if too many hard golden yellows are used. Blue/mauve is interesting to use because the tones vary significantly, though the number of true blues is limited. And red can be tricky choice, at least until late summer, because there is not a vast amount of choice before then. It is also quite a dark colour en masse, creating a surprisingly sombre effect.

Two-colour borders

Two colour borders involve a bit more skill but also create an image of sophistication. The key to understanding how two-colour borders work is the colour wheel. Colours that are next to each other, such as pink and blue, and yellow and green, are harmonious combinations. Those opposite each other are more startling combinations, such as yellow and blue, orange and purple, and scarlet and green. They can be very striking but are not to everyone's taste.

The blue and yellow combination is quite easy to work with, partly because there are many plants to choose from in these colours, and partly because the colours 'spark off each other' without being strident. You can now also find a wide variety of plants with yellow foliage, for example the grassy *Carex elata* 'Aurea' and the popular tree *Robinia pseudoacacia* 'Frisia', both of which make an excellent background to blue or blue-violet flowers. (Also see Penelope Hobhouse's yellow and blue border backed by a yew hedge, on pages 110–113, which offers several flushes of these two colours through the growing season.)

Blue/violet and pink combinations are also easily created because there is a huge variety of suitable plants from which to choose. It is very much an early to midsummer combination, the classic 'olde English garden' look being shrub roses under-planted with blue/violet and pink geraniums, with nearby catmint and lavender. It may be a cliché, but it certainly is very restful. (The Popes have come up with novel plum and orange colour schemes on pages 170–183. You can easily adopt this idea choosing your own two-colour scheme.)

A red border at Hadspen House in mid-summer: the red of *Crocosmia* 'Lucifer' and *Achillea* 'Feuerland' is complemented by the dark foliage of *Prunus* × *cistena*

Pastel schemes

Pastel schemes using one or more colours can be extended to include bolder shades, such as the magenta *Geranium psilostemon* or purple-red *Knautia macedonica*, or even some of the remarkably deep-coloured dahlias now available. You can either let the strong colours dominate and add the lighter ones for relief, or alternatively use pastels with a few stronger highlights – it is entirely a matter of taste.

Hot schemes

Hot schemes are increasingly popular with their use of bright, jazzy colours. Red, orange and yellow are a popular combination, wonderful for summer and autumn. While there are plenty of yellows available, the number of oranges and good reds is more limited. Tropical climates tend to produce more oranges and reds, but these tender plants tend to flower late in the season though they certainly create quite a spectacle. Adding plants with purple or bronze foliage is also popular because they help to separate the strong colours without diminishing the overall effect.

And do not forget, whichever colour scheme you do choose, it can easily be changed at various times. For example, yellow and blue in spring (using daffodils and scillas) can be followed by pink and blue in early summer (from geraniums and lavenders) that, in turn, is replaced by yellow and blue in late summer (with rudbeckias and asters). The art of creating a good border is making sure there is a constant flow of colour. The best way to achieve this is to visit a garden centre every six weeks or so buying what is in flower. And learn how to avoid putting startling colours next to a feature plant which might detract attention from it. Also learn to use some plants as background fillers to help show off your favourites.

At Hadspen House, the
nodding flowers of
Polygonatum x
hybridum are a subtle
counterpoint to the
exuberant red of this
tulip. The cluster of red
flowers belong to
Euphorbia griffithii
'Fireglow'

The all-season border

Many gardeners want something that always looks good
in high profile positions, around the front door for
example. But a good seasonal spread may mean that
its virtues are spread thinly, so that it never looks
spectacular. Evergreens will inevitably play a large part,
and that can mean that the lack of seasonal change
leads to boredom. The key is to have a wide variety of
evergreens, perhaps using some coloured foliage, or to
pay great attention to plant form and leaf shape and
texture, such as mixing bamboos, ivies and hollies.

Along with the evergreens, include some perennials or
deciduous shrubs that have good form, or interesting leaf
shapes, which will provide spring to autumn interest.
Finally aim to have some really worthwhile flowers that
succeed each other. There probably won't be space for
many combinations that flower altogether so think of one
flowering plant for each month of the growing season and
then consider some leaf/flower combinations that look
good like a pink rose with a silver leaved artemesia.

The one-season border

In situations where it is not vital that everything always
looks good all the time, it can be very rewarding to create
borders that are spectacular for a couple of months with
reduced interest for the rest of the year. An example might
be a shaded area which can be made into a wonderfully
colourful spring border but which is a more restrained
collection of leaf shapes for the rest of the year. Another
example would be a modern variant of the classical
herbaceous border, a late summer to mid-autumn
crescendo of colour and form, but with only a scattering of
bulbs in spring and a few small perennials in early summer.

Those who love colour, will find this approach very
satisfying, an opportunity to create exciting combinations
of saturated colour. Those with space may be able to
combine a backdrop of evergreens and a foreground of
seasonal plantings or islands of short-interest colour
amongst longer season plantings. Penelope Hobhouse is
particularly good at doing this, as her first love,
surprisingly as the author of *Colour in your Garden*
(HarperCollins, 1985), is evergreen shrubs. The areas
that the Popes plant at Hadspen are highly saturated
with colours and tend to need high levels of maintenance
to look good over a long season. Their gravel garden
(pages 180–183) will last over a relatively long season,
whereas their other plans will have a late season

Many shrubs, which by nature have an amorphous shape, can be made to look 'architectural' with some imaginative pruning. In Penelope Hobhouse's garden such shrubs give structure to the otherwise relaxed, informal planting

Height and shape

Plants need combining both for their colours and shapes so that they make a harmonious whole. A border entirely composed of low, hummocky shapes may be necessary on an exposed site, but will be rather dull. A few, dramatically vertical plants can make all the difference, for example the upright yew *Taxus baccata* 'Fastigiata'. (See John Brookes' plan for a small town garden, pages 54–57.) The opposite case, with too many upright growers, will conversely make it difficult to see what is happening behind the plants.

The traditional border has always put the tall plants at the back and the short ones at the front, with island beds having the tall ones in the centre. These principles do not need to be stuck to but it is important to ensure that you can see everything you are growing. For example, interlocking erect and ground-covering perennials provide interesting shapes and visual harmony.

Structure

Borders can be beautifully coloured and arranged but still look a mess. The reason is that there is not enough (or too much) structure. Borders without a few plants providing bold foliage, or composed entirely of plants with amorphous shapes, will be boring. Conversely a border with too many different shapes can be as fussy as one with too many colours.

Plants such as irises and grasses, with their linear leaves, are particularly useful for varying the pace of a border because they contrast with the leaf shapes of most border perennials and shrubs. More dramatic leaf shapes are provided by the likes of yuccas and phormiums (see John Brookes' contemporary border on pages 62–65). Bamboos, large grasses (miscanthus), upright conifers (cypresses), clipped box and yew are also good choices when it comes to injecting architectural shapes into a border.

Foliage

Strongly structural elements play a major role in nearly all the designs in this book. The exceptions are my naturalistic designs (see pages 122–137). Not that they are totally devoid of structure – the structure of ornamental grasses and perennials is just more subtle and seasonal than many of the large-leaved perennials (hostas) and evergreens (bamboos, hollies and phormiums). The strong element of repetition and mingling of varieties, is also an alternative to conventional structure in some naturalistic designs.

A strong development in recent years has been the greater focus given to form and foliage, with hardy exotic or tropical-looking plants becoming very fashionable. Well-sited they can be very dramatic, but they are also in danger of becoming a cliché (or oddity) if they are used where the visually attention-seeking foliage is out of place, for example in rural areas. But in the right place, certainly a sheltered one, it is possible to have a lot of fun with exotica. (In my exotic garden, on pages 134–137, I deliberately go over the top in using these plants.)

Foliage lasts a lot longer than flowers and has more potential than gardeners often realize. Coloured foliage plants have always been popular and a scattering of silver variegation or yellow- or purple-tinged leaves can transform a border over a long season. Such colours can also be used to complement flower colours with, for example, cream variegation looking beautifully cool with white flowers, while gold or yellow complements blue or violet, and purple leaves look stunning with orange or yellow. Light coloured foliage is also a boon in the dark winter months.

Beware, though, of using too many different foliage tints and patterns in one border. To many eyes, gold and silver do not mix, while putting variegated patterns together can look terribly fussy. The keynote is restraint.

The plant categories

Shrubs

Shrubs are bulky and take up space, dividing the border into smaller portions, controlling what can be seen while obscuring other plants. They are essential for height and shape in the winter to early spring period, when most perennials are still underground. The main criticisms are that most shrubs flower early, and far too many look dull for the rest of the year. Also, many have amorphous, uninteresting shapes which make those that do have a distinct form, such as the layered branches of *Viburnum plicatum* 'Mariesii', such valuable garden plants.

In fact, viburnums are some of the most useful spring-flowering shrubs, with roses being the most popular for summer. Rhododendrons and azaleas are really only for those who have acid soil but note that, like all dark evergreens, the former can be oppressive when not in flower.

Climbers

Vital for clothing backdrop walls and fences, climbers can also be allowed to scramble over shrubs. For example, let a small summer-flowering clematis clamber over a spring-flowering shrub, creating interest through two seasons. Climbers can also be grown on supports such as obelisks and wigwams.

Most climbers flower in early summer, but it is increasingly possible to find varieties that flower earlier or later, as the range sold by nurseries becomes more adventurous. Clematis are the largest group of climbers, with something for every taste and almost every season. Honeysuckles are also popular, as are roses, but the latter are often difficult to send in the required direction and do not offer the same coverage as do most climbers. And do not forget the foliage climbers, such as Virginia creeper (*Parthenocissus quinquefolia*) and vines that are attractive over a long season, often with spectacular autumn colours.

Perennials

Perennials are the mainstay of the border, with progressively more coming into flower through the year with the climax in late summer, and a tailing off until mid- or late autumn. The early flowering perennials, such as pulmonarias, geraniums and bergenias, tend to be low and hummocky, while the later ones often have a highly distinctive, upright form, such as asters, goldenrods and sunflowers.

One of the great advantages of perennials is that they quickly get established. It takes years for a shrub to show its full potential, but only a couple for a perennial. They also tend to be easy to propagate by division, providing extra plants for repeat planting which makes them very useful in naturalistic borders like mine, where much of the impact comes from the repetition of a relatively limited number of varieties.

Ornamental grasses

Garden grasses can be divided into two categories: those that are grown for their coloured foliage, such as carex and hakonechloa, and the larger ones that are used for their structural aspects, such as miscanthus and the popular *Stipa gigantea*. Many of the former are evergreen, making them very useful when creating long-season colour combinations and for cheering up exposed situations. The larger ones are marvellous for adding structure to borders, and for a sense of continuity, linking summer to winter, their flowers turning into seed heads that often look highly decorative until late winter. Piet Oudolf's designs use grasses to great effect.

Climbers, shrubs and perennials are used to create this stunning, shocking pink and green border at Hadspen house

[Left] In the yellow border at Hadspen House, the perennial fennel [*Foeniculum vulgare*] is grown through the pampas grass *Cortaderia selloana* 'Aureolineata'

[Right] Sweet peas run up arches over a path through the potager designed by Rupert Golby at the Old Rectory, Sudborough

Bulbs

Bulbs are vital for spring colour, and are generally remarkably easy to grow. Snowdrops, crocuses and daffodils are particularly reliable, forming clumps that increasingly get bigger each year. Bulbs are also easy to dot around other border plants, surrounding late emerging perennials and flowering in front of shrubs, particularly tulips, which in a cool climate have to be treated as an annual. Summer-flowering bulbs, such as lilies, and the autumn-flowering ones, such as colchicums and cyclamen, are equally useful, although it may be more difficult to find space for them amongst fuller later-season planting.

Annuals

Annuals and tender plants used for temporary summer effects, such as pelargoniums and marguerites, are often very colourful over a long summer season, making them essential components of the 'instant border'. A mixed border may well involve leaving spaces between shrubs and perennials so that there is room for different coloured annuals each summer. They can also be used to fill spaces between plants that take several years to reach their full size. Traditional hardy annuals, such as love-in-the-mist (*Nigella damascena*) and pot marigold (*Calendula officinalis*), can be sown directly into the ground.

Vegetables

Though slightly unconventional in the ornamental border, many herbs and vegetables make attractive plants and can be used in a similar way to annuals, filling spaces between perennials. The big disadvantage is that harvesting spoils the pattern. Even so, it is well worth using red lettuce and chicory, ruby-coloured perennial beet or chard, dark-leaved beetroot and purple-leaved basil. Those with attractive flowers, such as scarlet runner beans, can also play a part. (The Popes potager on pages 168–171 is an example of how effective coloured vegetables can be.)

Getting down to it: making and maintaining borders

Planning

Making a plan, even a crude one that is not to scale, will organize your thoughts. It is vital when calculating how many plants you need to buy if you are laying out the border all at once. Most good reference books and some garden centre labels indicate the eventual size of the plant, helping you work out the spacings. Note that it takes perennials two to three years to reach their full size, and shrubs even longer.

Perennials should be planted so that they just touch or slightly overlap after the first or second year, while shrubs should be spaced well apart leaving gaps between for perennials or annuals. Do not place the latter too close to the shrubs' woody growth; leave a gap of 40–50cm (16–20in).

Planning also enables you to work out how best to repeat plants, which is essential if the planting is to have any unity and coherence. A particularly good way of creating a successful border is to choose a theme plant for every one or two-month period through the spring and summer to which every other colour is related. Theme plants could include a large, dominating shrub or climber or, in the case of smaller perennials, a variety that is repeated by scattering several such plants across the border.

Soil preparation and weeding

Much fuss has been made about soil preparation before planting. This is because it was thought that any soil that fell short of a certain standard was deficient and had to be improved. But it is important to note that even quite difficult soils can be used as the starting point for attractive plantings, if the chosen plants actually like those soils. Clay is a good case. Because it is so hard to work, being lumpy and heavy, people tend to regard it as a real problem, but many shrubs actually flourish in it, roses especially, as do many perennials. Clay is a problem for those who need to cultivate the soil on a regular basis when growing vegetables and annuals, but for those making a permanent planting it is a once-only nuisance.

While our ideas on soil are changing, they are not when it comes to weeds. I cannot over-stress the importance of weeding, especially if you know that you have problem weeds, such as ground elder, creeping thistle or bindweed. They are very competitive plants which, if not eliminated, will create problems in the future. Chemical weed control is the best option. Despite claims to the contrary, there is very little evidence that modern herbicides, such as those containing the biodegradable ingredient glyphosate, present any appreciable danger to the environment and, in any case, such herbicides need only be used once.

Care and cultivation

For those who are organic, cover the ground with old carpet weighed down by stones or soil for one growing season and the weeds beneath will die, though some may come up through holes and around the edges. Dig them out, with every last bit of root.

Once the weeds have been eliminated, it is usually possible to start planting, but the soil does need to be moist. Often planting is made easier if the ground is cultivated first, perhaps with a rotovator to break up the soil. Unless this is very poor, there is little point in digging in manure or compost, or adding nutrients such as fertilizers. Most ornamental plants cannot utilize the levels of fertilizers often recommended for them, and the chemicals will only encourage the growth of weeds which use them more effectively.

Since woody plants are slow to establish it is worth making sure that you give them the right conditions. The soil well below the level of the rootball, and to its side, should be broken up to help aerate it, enabling water to drain away quickly and encourage the roots to spread. Care should be taken that the soil level mark on the trunk or stem remains the same as when in the pot.

It also helps, especially when the plants are pot-bound (ie the container is packed with roots that start poking out of the drainage holes), if you gently tease out the roots so that they grow in all directions and not round and round in a downward spiral, providing greater stability. It is now considered potentially harmful to add organic matter to a planting hole because it can encourage waterlogging. Soil returned to the planting hole should be well firmed in and watered to eliminate any air pockets.

Perennials, being much faster to establish, do not need such careful planting. Ideally, on heavy soil, the ground around the planting hole should be broken up if it has not already been done, the roots teased out of the rootball, with the soil then firmed down around them. In fact perennials can be planted with the minimum of care, even in less than ideal ground, provided they are firmly wedged into moist soil.

Getting established

Perhaps more crucial than the planting technique is the timing. In maritime-influenced climates with mild wet winters, the best time to plant is in the autumn or early winter because the plants will get established before there is any risk of summer drought. In regions with severe or prolonged winter cold, woody plants are best planted in the autumn, but perennials are liable to be frost-heaved out of the ground if put in then. Keep them in a cold frame until the spring. Areas with a continental climate tend to have only a very limited window of opportunity for perennial planting, and that is the period immediately after the worst of the winter.

The 'establishment phase' is the first year after planting for perennials, and a somewhat longer period for woody plants. If plants survive this, they will be better able to cope with subsequent difficult conditions or neglect.

All plants must be kept watered during their first year in periods of drought, even plants that are drought-resistant. Watering that is occasional but thorough will do far more good than frequent light watering, which often only wets the top of the soil, encouraging roots to stay there instead of delving downwards. Indeed, there is a point in delaying watering for as long as possible after planting to encourage them to do precisely this.

Weeding is also essential in the first year, otherwise your new plants will be up against stiff competition. Seedlings need to be hoed off, and larger plants hand-pulled or dug out. Weed and grass competition is the worst enemy of young trees and shrubs (as are adjacent, strongly growing ornamental perennials), and it is vitally important that you keep them away from the base of the plants for at least three years after planting.

Both weed competition and drying out can be greatly reduced by using a 3–5cm (1½–2in) deep wood chip mulch around the new plants. It suppresses the weeds and locks moisture in the ground. Take care not to allow the soil and mulch to get mixed up.

Wide columns of yew are used to give structure to the Oudolf's garden in Hummelo, eastern Netherlands. Grasses are combined with perennials to contribute structure and texture.

Maintaining borders

The great herbaceous borders of Edwardian Britain established this kind of planting as an art form, but they did little for its reputation as something that everyone could achieve. Relying on plants that needed a lot of attention, such as Michelmas daisies (*Aster novi-belgii* hybrids), there was an endless, annual round of manuring, staking, weeding and dividing. The Karl Foerster tradition, on the other hand, relied far more on plants that were robust and did not need so much more attention.

Mixed borders (with shrubs) evolved in the way that they did partly because of the need to avoid too much maintenance. Contemporary border styles that almost entirely use perennials, stress the importance of relying on varieties that are robust and low-maintenance. They are able to survive for years without needing to be dug up and divided, do not require an annual fix of a high-nutrient feed and are sufficiently robust to stand up without any staking.

How much work a border requires depends on the choice of plants. More traditional English-style borders with a lot of roses, and perennials with a high-nutrient requirement, such as delphiniums, or seasonal plants, such as dahlias and annuals, require regular feeding if they are to thrive. The traditional practice of heaping on plenty of well-rotted manure in the autumn is a well-established way of doing this. Alternatively, a mulch of garden compost can be used with a slow-release general fertilizer if the soil is not particularly fertile. A more modern variant is to use a shredder to break down dead perennial stems, and pruning clippings, as an autumn mulch.

Part of the philosophy of a contemporary perennial border is that it should be planned with the soil type in mind. If it is poor, use varieties that do not need feeding, such as low-growing and colourful *Salvia nemorosa* and *Geranium sanguineum*. Whatever happens, do not feed taller plants because they might become top-heavy and flop over.

Cutting back

Two tasks dominate the annual maintenance regime of perennial-dominated borders: cutting back dead growth and weeding. In the past, perennials were cut back in the autumn leaving an unattractive expanse of bare earth, but current thinking favours leaving them standing, at least those with interesting structure, until late winter. Regions which have regular hoar frosts will see some spectacular displays as the frost leaves a magic layer of crystals on every surface, while garden birds will be grateful for the seeds and insects left behind in the dead stems. Shrubs may also need pruning, and this is generally done after flowering, but if more drastic pruning is needed, this is best done in the autumn or winter.

Further weeding

In addition to the weeding before planting, it is vital to keep an eye out for weeds throughout the year. Modern thinking aims to have a dense carpet of plants by late spring, so that there is no bare earth left for weed seedlings to colonize; if anything does appear after this, it will need to be pulled out by hand.

In regions with a mild winter there is usually a period between mid-winter and mid-spring when weed seedlings do appear, and grasses in particular start to cover the ground, especially if a mulch has not been used. It is important that they are hoed off before they get established. Perennial weeds regenerating from buried roots are more problematic; the best way to deal with them is with careful use of a glyphosate-based weedkiller that will kill their root systems but leave other plants unharmed. The chemical is inactivated as soon as it touches the soil, and is then broken down by bacteria.

Pests and diseases

We now have a more relaxed attitude to pests and diseases than in the past. Pests and diseases are always very specific, and since modern plantings involve a wide mix of plants, this means that even if one species falls victim then there are plenty of others that will continue to look good. A good mixture of species also restricts the ability of pests and diseases to spread.

However, slugs and snails can do enormous damage to certain plants very early in the season, just as the new leaves are emerging. Even in the wild they can cause local extinctions. There are various products on the market designed to tackle the problem. The most effective means of control is the traditional slug pellet. Claims that the pellets are harmful to wildlife appear to be largely groundless, with a virtual absence of research studies supporting the belief that they are hazardous. However on a precautionary note it still makes sense to minimize their use. Research shows that they only need be used very sparingly: 10 pellets per 1 sq m (1 sq yd) every three weeks, before the plants have filled out for the season, is all that is required.

The yellow border in the
old kitchen garden at
Hadspen House, with a
variety of yellow flowers
and folige, is the most
thoroughly planned one-
colour border at Hadspen,
and reflects Nori and
Sandra Pope's belief that
through its relationship to
green, yellow is a
harmonious colour

The experts' dos and don'ts on making borders

Do not concentrate on colour

Piet Oudolf is particularly worried that new gardeners concentrate on colour at the expense of other factors. But structure is equally important. Take a black and white photograph of your border and see what it looks like without the distractions of colour. The structure (or lack of) really stands out. In fact, many borders will seem an undifferentiated mass, while those with good structure will look almost as good in black and white as they do in colour. John Brookes' plans in particular show how effective a concentration on plant form can be.

Avoid too many shrubs

Many of the shrubs sold in garden centres can become very large with time, overwhelming smaller borders or even whole gardens. Piet Oudolf's designs are particularly refreshing because they largely do without shrubs. This is partly for reasons of space, but also because of what Piet sees as their amorphous shapes that contribute little to the structure of the planting, and their absence of colour after flowering. Penelope Hobhouse, a great believer in shrubs, especially evergreens, adds that many gardeners are wrong to imagine that shrubs are automatically low-maintenance. They most certainly are not if they are too big for the site and constantly need cutting back.

If you do have an established shrub that is too big for its site, note that it can be ruthlessly cut back, to ground level if need be. Despite what many think, shrubs are rarely killed by doing this, and the results are often a rejuvenated plant with better looking foliage and a neater habit.

Designed by Rupert Golby, the rose garden at the Old Rectory, Sudborough, features purple sage, *Salvia officinalis* 'Purpurea', the seed heads of *Allium christophii* and the sparse mauve flowers of *Verbena bonariensis*

Small spaces need big plants

Tall or big plants are particularly effective in small spaces. Build a border around one or two majestic plants and they will have real impact, whereas filling it with miniatures will constantly remind you how small it is. John Brookes' designs are particularly effective at making use of strong plants in small areas. Penelope Hobhouse stresses how height is important in small or city gardens, with verticals adding a new element to a flat space, while trees and pergolas create light and shade.

Avoid bare ground

Aim to have total soil coverage by late spring, and there will be much less space for invading weeds. Ground-covering or clumping perennials, for example the hardy geraniums and the popular *Stachys byzantina* with its wooly, silvery leaves, are particularly good choices for ground cover. A mulch of wood chips can be used to cover the soil, blocking out weeds, especially in the early stages. The gravel used by the Popes and John Brookes is another way to minimize maintenance because weed seeds rarely germinate in the stones. Gravel is also more stylish than chips, more durable over the long term and makes a good backdrop to a wide variety of flower colours.

Do not use too many different varieties

A large number of different plant varieties, especially if there is only one of each, creates an untidy and fussy border, something that was mentioned by all the designers. Such borders are little more than plant collections, the result of what John Brookes calls people 'thinking horticulturally rather than in design terms', while Nori Pope talks about 'people trying to compose a symphony when what is really needed is a chamber piece'. 'Less is more' is a motto that many gardeners should take to heart. Choose a few plants that you like, that look good with each other and succeed in your garden, and work with them.

In their different ways, I think all the contributors have adhered to this idea. John Brookes is a particularly strong exponent of this practice, which works well in conjunction with paving and brickwork. However, while he tends to clump together a few plants, I prefer to intermingle them, imitating the way plants grow in nature. John also suggests buying large perennials and splitting them up to produce several plants that can be either clumped to produce more impact, or repeated to create a satisfying rhythm through the border.

The Herb Garden at the Old Rectory, Sudborough , is framed by a wall of Lavender and full of aromatic herbs and flowers

Do not make borders too small

Far too many gardeners create borders that are just narrow strips. Several of the plans in this book are aimed at encouraging the reader to be bold and to plough up boring stretches of lawn, replacing them with wide borders that stretch right across the garden. The bigger the border the more you can try different effects and plant combinations.

Do not be discouraged by quirky, irregular areas or slopes

Small gardens are often odd shapes, but they are potentially more exciting than a rectangle. The best approach is to decide on one basic border feature that sets the tone for the whole garden, which could be a topiarized shrub or a collection of plants with strong scent or bold foliage.

Slopes can be off-putting, yet looking up at plants or down onto them offers a perspective that is all too rarely seen or appreciated. They do involve hard work, and need to be well planned to reduce maintenance as much as possible by using attractive plants that need little attention (see my plan for a low-maintenance planting on pages 126–129).

Avoid close planting

It is all too easy for new gardeners to pack plants together, but while this initially looks good, it creates long-term problems. Piet Oudolf also points out how easy it is to overcrowd plants in the spring when there is plenty of bare ground, creating the illusion that there is more space than really exists.

If you do want to create a full look very quickly, by all means overplant, but you must be prepared to be ruthless in future years, removing some plants to make room for others to grow and develop. Therefore make a clear distinction when planning between the priority plants that you want to keep, and less important fillers that could be removed later; alternatively, plant three of one particular variety, aiming to keep only one. The removed plants can be used elsewhere in the garden.

John Brookes

More than anyone else, John Brookes has helped turn garden design into a discipline, with his promotion of a professional body (the Society of Garden Designers) and numerous important books on the subject encouraging gardeners to understand the basic principles of planning and designing their plots. And, for many of us, his Chelsea Flower Show gardens of the 1980s and 1990s introduced us to contemporary garden design.

'I design garden *spaces*,' he says. 'Plants *per se* don't thrill me. My early experience working on the journal *Architectural Design* taught me that there had to be some sort of rules.' But while his early books and show gardens stressed the architect's eye, he now feels they over-emphasized structure leading many of us (myself included) to associate his work with bricks and patios. 'All I ever wanted to say,' he adds, 'was that a garden needs a structure despite the fact that it might then be lost in the planting.'

John began his career in commercial horticulture, then worked for three years with Nottingham Parks Department where he ended up in the design office. On leaving Nottingham, he sent some of his drawings to Brenda Colvin who, in the 1950s, was one of Britain's most notable landscape architects. She took him on and, after a university course, he moved on to work in the office of another big name in garden design, Sylvia Crowe. It was after this that he worked as a writer for *Architectural Design*. John then went freelance, since when he has

[Left] Yellow evening primroses [*Oenothera* spp.] with lavender form part of the blue and yellow-dominated planting at Denmans in early to mid-summer. The oenothera, along with the tall *Verbascum bombyciferum* are short-lived but self-sow readily

[Right] Two very large box 'boulders' add a strong sense of shape to relaxed perennial-dominated borders. Purple sage, *Salvia officinalis* 'Purpurea' spills on to the path, helping to blur the distinction between path and border

always balanced writing and lecturing with designing gardens for clients scattered over many countries, including France, Germany, Italy, the USA, Japan, Chile and Argentina.

Perhaps this international range of work has helped bring about the most recent change in John's approach, with great attention now being paid to what he calls the cultural element in horticulture – the importance of relating gardens to the local landscape, and using native plant associations if possible. He is worried that gardens around the world will look increasingly similar if we all grow the same plants.

Not surprisingly, given his architectural bent, John likes formality and structure in gardens, 'not necessarily classical straight lines but fractured formality, Japanese gardens, some French gardens, the gardens of the contemporary Belgian designer Jacques Wirtz (whose formal schemes are a modern working of a traditional idiom), and Islamic gardens, for example those in southern Spain'. 'But,' he adds, 'I don't go to many gardens now and when I do, I see nothing but mistakes. What moves me is landscape and countryside such as around the Sussex Downs where I live. I'd be hard pushed to think of a garden that bowls me over.

'I'm also increasingly interested in leaves – their colour, shape and texture – and in leaving space between the plants so that they can be clearly seen.' Previously he was attracted to the more dramatic leaves of yuccas, phormiums and sumachs – 'that was when I was in my architectural phase – but now I love native, lime-loving wildflowers, and seeing box and yew in the woods. You can learn so much from looking at how wildflowers grow, even if you do not actually use them'.

But it is important to look at the architectural element in John's work, and one way of tackling it is to relate it to the modern movement in art and architecture. John has often been seen as 'a modernist', a label he now rejects, but there is little doubt that one of the reasons for his importance as a garden designer is his relationship to the movement that started with the Bauhaus in the 1930s that favoured clarity of purpose and simplicity in design. In fact, the modern movement passed Britain by and had relatively little effect on garden design, unlike other art forms. But it did influence some garden designers, for example the Brazilian Roberto Burle Marx who, with his bold sweeps of planting and dramatic contrasts of colour and form, was the most prolific and best known proponent in a variety of rural and urban settings.

Talking of modernism, John says: 'I went through a lot of it… it set me up for life, but I am not a minimalist.' He adds, though, that he was influenced by the 'very simple clear cut lines' of Thomas Church's gardens, created during the 1940s and 1950s in California, which so successfully linked house, garden and landscape.

An interest in Islamic gardens has also been an important part of John's life. He describes researching them as 'a hobby of mine', which he indulged in during the 1960s and 1970s, starting off in southern Spain, moving on to Iran and then the Indian sub-continent. His resulting book, *Gardens of Paradise* (Weidenfeld & Nicolson, 1987), remains one of the few modern works that discusses the gardens and landscape of the Muslim world. Reading it now, it comes across as something that was written at a time when dialogue between cultures was easier, and there was more possibility of interesting international work being carried out in the Middle East. The book contains much valuable writing on the basic principles of the Islamic garden and on the general problems of gardening in a semi-desert climate, and one hopes that it will continue to inspire gardeners and designers in the future.

John's own garden at Denmans, near Arundel in West Sussex, has 3.5 acres (1.4 ha) of lawn, trees and carefully orchestrated foliage. Wandering around the garden one bright June day, I felt that I was exploring a very different kind of garden. I stress the word 'wandering' because it does not have any obvious axes or features to propel you in certain directions, something that is emphasised by the flatness of the surrounding countryside, just visible from a few views in the garden.

What first impressed me were the striking plant forms, but not the fashionable, spiky phormiums and yuccas seen everywhere. I loved the perennials with strong shapes such as the verbascums, with their distinctive rosettes and tall spires of yellow flowers, and various species of thistle-like eryngium. John told me how he prefers to 'work down from structure…colour is the last thing, a bonus'.

Yet the strong shapes never overwhelmed because they act as a counterpoint to the many mounds created by the hummocks of sage (*Salvia officinalis*), the low evergreen *Viburnum davidii* and the roughly-textured leaves of *Phlomis russeliana*. There are also many evergreens, many with Mediterranean-type grey leaves, as well as more traditional box. Some of the plants are clipped into dramatically large boulders that add structure and rhythm to an area of looser herbaceous and shrub planting.

What is interesting at Denmans is how few of those quintessentially contemporary plants, the ornamental grasses, he uses. He confesses that 'I have problems with them. I can't make them work in design terms'. As a result he has created a modern, grass-free garden where the prevalence of rounded shapes makes it feel much more Mediterranean in spirit. And the distinctive use of gravel reinforces the Mediterranean atmosphere, with a great river of it wending its way across the grass at one end of the garden, crossed by a stylized wooden bridge.

Since the gravel is part-footway and part-planting area, the edges between the two are blurred, often by plants seeding themselves into the gravel. Here and elsewhere, much of the planting is notably looser than is conventional. This allows well-shaped plants to be appreciated more fully than had they been squeezed into a border. Leaving space for plants to 'spread themselves spontaneously by self-sowing' is also important. Areas of gravel encourage this process, and they also have 'a looser, more informal feeling than grass'.

To me, Denmans evokes a series of open, woodland glades. While walking around I went from sun to shade and back again, with small groups of trees providing shady patches, but they were never so dense as to obstruct the view. Most of the trees are smaller species or have light foliage, and include birches, *Gleditsia triacanthos* and *Robinia pseudoacacia*, all big enough to define spaces while allowing views through at eye level to another open patch of garden beyond.

John has lived at Denmans for about 25 years, but only owned it for the last 10. He came here 'because I liked it, and I was a friend of Joyce Robinson, the then owner, who made the original garden. She was a plantswoman,' says John, 'while I tried to iron out the garden, giving it a simpler design.' Interestingly, John has treated Denmans as if it was a private rather than a client's garden, by which he means 'I never made big positive decisions right at the start, though I did put the pond in; everything else has been added piecemeal'. The little changes here and there, over the years, have gently re-moulded one person's garden into another's.

This is how most gardeners develop their own gardens, and is perhaps a warning that designing your own garden in one go is not such a good idea. The message is clearly that designing a garden is a continual process that has to respond to many factors, including the way in which the plants grow and often die, so creating new possibilities.

Being such a clear and schematic thinker, it is instructive to listen to John describe the different processes of garden design. 'First of all,' he says, 'I decide on mood and character, and try to see things through my client's eye

often with a vague idea of colour. Then I go through the plant categories and make a selection.' He stresses how plantings have to relate to the proportion of the design, and how they will be seen against a backdrop of trees. Then he begins work on the 'skeleton material, moulding the design, building up massed shapes using cotoneasters and viburnums, etc., before moving on to a decorative range of plants, not doing one border at a time, but a bit here and there'. Finally come 'the pretties with perennials, smaller bulbs, sub-shrubs, such as lavender, and finally the infillers like bulbs'. He sums up his work by saying that a strong and simple framework is vital. 'Keep it simple,' he says, 'repeat plants, take out half of what you first thought of, and double up what is left . . . less is more.'

One of his final points is that a garden design must have a relationship to its surroundings. And it is this relationship – dubbed 'visual ecology' – that has most concerned him over the last few years. It is a two-way relationship involving the effect that the garden has on the surroundings, and the reflection of the local environment in the garden. This relationship should not be destroyed by creating, for example, a cottage garden in a modern city centre. In his recent book (*The New Garden*, Dorling Kindersley, 1998), he stresses the importance of local inspiration for the design and the need to repeat elements of the landscape in the garden, softening boundaries, and bringing views into the garden.

The mullein, *Verbascum bombyciferum*, self-sows into the gravel path that runs through this border, making an effective contrast with more amorphous plant shapes and generating a powerful sense of rhythm

A lifelong commitment to clear, simple design has been the
hallmark of John's work, and the core message of the
modern gardening movement. He is distinctive amongst
British designers of his generation in not being a
traditionalist, with little interest in the historical revivalism
or eclecticism that has marked the work of many. And,
unlike many 20th-century British designers, he has not
tied his career to that of the big country house, and to the
essentially backward-looking values of the traditional
land-owning aristocracy who still dominate much British
aspiration, in gardening above all else. Freed from the ties
of tradition, he has been more international in outlook,
and perhaps more clear thinking. Above all he has helped,
and continues to help, move garden design into the 21st
century.

A tropical-
inspired border

plant list

1. *Helenium* 'Moerheim Beauty'   (5)
2. *Campsis* × *tagliabuana* 'Madame Galen' (1)
3. *Ligularia dentata* 'Desdemona'   (3)
4. *Hosta fortunei* 'Gold Standard'   (7)
5. *Hemerocallis* 'Pink Sundae'   (6)
6. *Lysimachia nummularia* 'Aurea'   (12)
7. *Sedum telephium* subsp. *maximum*
   'Atropurpureum' (6)
8. *Iris foetidissima* 'Variegata'   (4)
9. *Salvia officinalis* 'Icterina'   (3)
10. *Lychnis* × *arkwrightii*   (6)
11. *Angelica gigas*   (3)
12. *Hibiscus syriacus* 'Dorothy Crane'   (2)
13. *Canna* 'Di Bartolo'   (8)
14. *Hedera helix* 'Goldheart'   (1)
15. *Eremurus* hybrids   (23)
16. *Tulipa* 'Queen of Sheba'   (25)

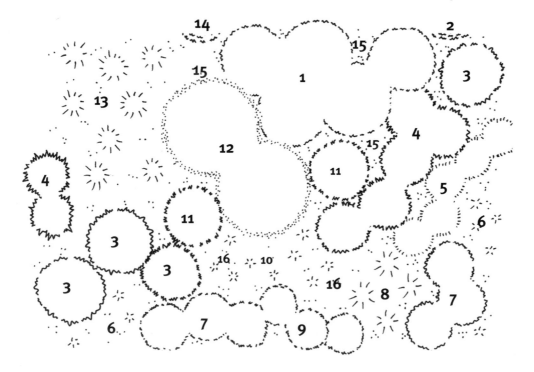

50

What is tropical is in the eye of the beholder. John believes that 'it involves leaf shape and colour, and strong flower colours' but maintains that 'to create the effect in a temperate climate will be something of a pastiche'. Given that many plants with especially distinctive foliage shapes or strong flowers are not particularly hardy, he warns that the plants need to be selected carefully. 'The important thing is to get that tropical clash of colour,' he says, adding 'I love that jungly look.'

He uses two *Hibiscus syriacus* 'Dorothy Crane', exotic-looking white flowers with a red centre, to provide the shrubby bulk at the core of this planting. In early summer a clump of eremurus hybrids thrust their spires skywards, each one packed with thousands of little orange and yellow flowers, while at the front there is a group of the lily-flowered tulip 'Queen of Sheba' with its yellow-edged orange flowers.

At its best during midsummer, the dominant colour theme of this planting is salmon-purple, backed up by a striking combination of foliage colours. The big, gold-leaved *Hosta fortunei* 'Gold Standard' and an underplanting of creeping yellow-leaved *Lysimachia nummularia* 'Aurea' contrast with the purple leaves and orange flowers of *Lychnis* × *arkwrightii*, and the purple foliage of *Angelica gigas* and *Sedum telephium* subsp. *maximum* 'Atropurpureum'.

Midsummer sees the deep red-orange of *Campsis* × *tagliabuana* 'Madame Galen' create a striking backdrop on the wall or fence behind. *Canna* 'Di Bartolo' has a strong colour, combining bronze leaves with deep pink flowers, and is a striking foliage plant that instantly evokes a feeling of the tropics wherever it is planted. With *Ligularia dentata* 'Desdemona', which also combines dramatic foliage and flowers, it is the dominant element in this planting through the summer. 'Desdemona' has jagged

REQUIREMENTS

edged, dark mahogany-green leaves and tall, branching heads of orange daisies. The dark purple umbels of *Angelica gigas* make a striking contrast. The rusty brown daisy-like flowers of *Helenium* 'Moerheim Beauty' bring the summer to a close.

During the winter the yellow-leaved ivy, *Hedera helix* 'Goldheart', maintains something of this planting's strong colour, as do the cream-streaked evergreen *Iris foetidissima* 'Variegata' and the golden-leaved sage, *Salvia officianalis* 'Icterina'.

1. With such strong colours it should be obvious that this is a planting that needs full sun to look its best. The campsis also needs a warm site, preferably against a sunny wall, for its growth to ripen well enough to flower regularly. The only plant that is not hardy is the canna; in mild districts its roots can be covered with a thick mulch to keep out the cold, otherwise it needs to be dug up and the tops cut off, with the rhizomes being stored inside, in a dry, cool frost-free place; replant next spring as the weather warms up.

2. Any reasonably fertile soil, preferably moister rather than drier, will suit the plants. The eremurus needs drier conditions, being a semi-desert plant; also avoid over-crowding.

3. *Angelica gigas* is a biennial, which means seed needs to be sown every year to produce flowers the following year. If you are lucky though, it might self-seed and do the job for you. *Lychnis* × *arkwrightii* is also short-lived, but freely self-seeds. The tulips rarely flower reliably from one year to another, and may need annual replacement.

4. The hosta and ligularia are prone to slug and snail attacks, the spring damage leaving the plants with unsightly holes for the rest of the season. Surrounding the plants with material the molluscs cannot cross, such as egg shells and bark chippings, can help avoid this.

5. Long-term, this planting should cause few problems in its management.

A foliage border for a small town garden

plant list

1. *Cynara cardunculus*	(2)
2. *Buddleia davidii*	(1)
3. *Jasminum nudiflorum*	(1)
4. *Hydrangea villosa*	(1)
5. *Taxus baccata* 'Fastigiata Aurea'	(1)
6. *Santolina pinnata* subsp. *neopoltana*	(6)
7. *Agapanthus* 'Headbourne Hybrids'	(5)
8. *Heuchera micrantha* var. *diversifolia* 'Palace Purple'	(3)
9. *Viburnum davidii*	(2)
10. *Lilium regale*	(8)
11. *Hedera helix* 'Goldheart'	(1)
12. *Pittosporum tobira* 'Variegata'	(1)
13. *Solanum crispum* 'Glasnevin'	(1)
14. *Camellia* 'White Swan'	(2)
15. *Rosa* 'Albéric Barbier'	(1)

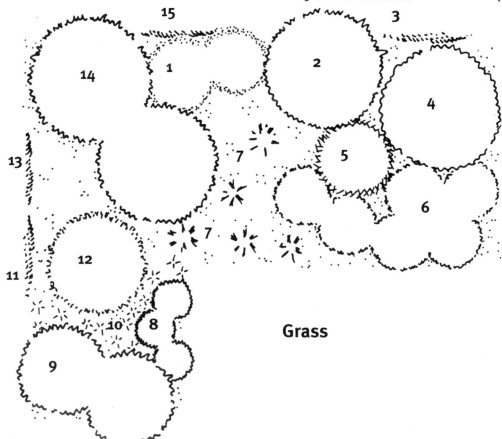

Grass

'This planting,' says John, 'is about furnishing the garden with greenery which I think is more important than flower colour.' One could argue that this is true for any garden, but it is absolutely essential for small town gardens where the freshness of foliage is always at a premium. And small gardens everywhere need to provide interest for as long as possible. Flowers are relatively short-lived and cannot be relied on to provide interest for long.

That is why evergreens form the bulk of this border. An upright Irish yew (*Taxus baccata* 'Fastigiata Aurea') provides a major focus of interest, and is balanced by two of the spring-flowering *Camellia* 'White Swan'. In front of the yew is the low growing, grey-leaved evergreen *Santolina pinnata* subsp *neapolitana* that provides a contrast in foliage colour. The *Pittosporum tobira* 'Variegata', by the side of the camellias, gives year-round interest, and in summer produces masses of sweetly-scented flowers.

The *Hydrangea villosa* behind the yew has strikingly large leaves and pink flower heads in midsummer, while *Buddleia davidii* on the other side is a large shrub that has butterfly-attracting violet flowers. There are a great many cultivars of the buddleia to choose from. The *Agapanthus* 'Headbourne Hybrids' are among the hardiest of these blue-flowering perennials; the strap-like leaves make an effective ground cover, filling gaps between the shrubs.

The dark leaves of *Heuchera micrantha* var. *diversifolia* 'Palace Purple' act as an edging on the other side of the planting, creating a good foil for the creamy-white *Lilium regale*. And *Viburnum davidii*, at the end of this part of the border, is a low-growing shrub with elegant, evergreen leaves and dark berries.

The most dramatic plant here is the perennial *Cynara cardunculus*. There are two in the centre creating a major attraction from spring onwards as their very large, grey, and deeply-toothed leaves begin to emerge, culminating in a dramatic, thistle-like blue flower during summer.

Being surrounded by walls on two sides, there is some scope for climbers. They include the yellow-leaved *Hedera helix* 'Goldheart', *Solanum crispum* 'Glasnevin' with its purple 'potato flowers' in mid- to late summer, the fragrant creamy-coloured rose 'Alberic Barbier' and the winter flowering *Jasminum nudiflorum*.

REQUIREMENTS

1. The plants need full sun, at least for most of the day, and any reasonable soil, although the camellia will not be happy in very hot sites or on thin or alkaline soils.

2. The pittosporum and the solanum are the least hardy. The santolina is best maintained by pruning after flowering, to encourage compact growth.

3. Several of the woody plants can become very large with time, which could ruin the balance and overall feel of the planting. The yew may need trimming to keep it from becoming too bushy, while the buddleias are notorious for getting far too big far too quickly, unless they are cut to ground level every winter; do not worry, they will still make 2–3m (6–9ft) growth in the summer and flower well.

A shady foliage planting

plant list

1. *Primula vulgaris*	(153)
2. *Cyclamen hederifolium*	(20)
3. *Iris foetidissima*	(4)
4. *Helleborus foetidus*	(5)
5. *Geranium sylvaticum* 'Mayflower'	(29)
6. *Symphytum × uplandicum*	(3)
7. *Euphorbia amygdaloides* var. *robbiae*	(12)
8. *Digitalis purpurea* 'Alba'	(9)
9. *Pulmonaria officinalis* 'Cambridge Blue'	(6)
10. *Alchemilla mollis*	(4)
11. *Lilium pardalinum*	(18)
12. *Narcissus* 'W. P. Milner'	(100)

'Since my foliage planting is beneath a tree that casts only light shade, it is damp and not dry shade. Even so, there are several species here that will also do well in dry shade. The natural-looking planting is inevitably orientated to spring and autumn instead of summer.'

Of these *Euphorbia amygdaloides* var. *robbiae* can be invaluable in difficult shade. It has dark evergreen leaves and yellow-green flowers in early spring, and a spreading habit that can be a boon in large shady areas, but it can create problems in smaller ones. *Helleborus foetidus* and *Iris foetidissima* are also evergreens that are reasonably tolerant of drier shade. The hellebore is one of those rare plants that looks best in winter, forming a great mound of rather elegantly divided leaves topped by pale green flowers. The iris has dark, strap-shaped leaves and clusters of orange berries that usually last well through the winter.

Early spring sees the blue flowers of *Pulmonaria officinalis* 'Cambridge Blue' and the pale yellow of several patches of the primrose, *Primula vulgaris*, with the soft yellow flowers of an early daffodil, *Narcissus* 'W. P. Milner'. By late spring the clear blue comfrey, *Symphytum* × *uplandicum*, is in flower, and by early summer there is the violet-blue *Geranium sylvaticum* 'Mayflower', that is followed by the yellow-green *Alchemilla mollis*.

A little later the foxglove, *Digitalis purpurea* 'Alba', produces its tall spikes of white flowers, bringing light into the shade. *Lilium pardalinum*, an unusual orange lily that thrives in damp shade, also flowers in the early to midsummer period. In late summer, *Cyclamen hederifolium* starts to flower, its pink flowers like a miniature version of the Christmas pot plant. While the period after midsummer is relatively flowerless, there is a good selection of different foliage textures and shapes.

[Left] *Euphorbia
amygdaloides* var. *robbiae*

[Right] *Digitalis purpurea*
'Alba'

REQUIREMENTS

1. Any reasonable soil that does not badly dry out in summer will suit all these plants. However, several are quite tolerant of dryish shade, as noted.

2. The digitalis is very short lived but nearly always self-seeds; some of the seedlings will be pink, and this colour will reassert itself over several generations. Pink-flowering seedlings can usually be distinguished from the white ones because they have more of a red flush on the leaves. *Helleborus foetidus* is a relatively short-lived plant too, but also self-seeds well. The geranium also spreads through seedings.

3. The euphorbia and symphytum can be invasive, particularly on fertile soils, which can cause problems; ensure that they are given plenty of space.

4. Since several of these plants self-sow, and therefore change their positions from year to year (some are very vigorous spreaders), this planting may well change from year to year quite considerably. Take care that the less vigorous ingredients, such as the pulmonaria, are not swamped, and that the most vigorous (impossible to predict) do not take over entirely. A firm controlling, weeding hand is vital.

61

A contemporary mixed planting

plant list

1. *Artemisia* 'Powis Castle' (4)
2. *Allium giganteum* (14)
3. *Lavatera thuringiaca* 'Barnsley' (2)
4. *Helictotrichon sempervirens* (2)
5. *Allium aflatunense* (15)
6. *Iris* 'Blue Denim' (4)
7. *Rosa* 'Mutabilis' (3)
8. *Salvia officinalis* 'Purpurascens' (4)
9. *Perovskia atriplicifolia* 'Blue Spire' (3)
10. *Tulipa*, lily-flowered, white (25)
11. *Potentilla fruticosa* 'Katherine Dykes' (5)
12. *Sisyrinchium striatum* (6)
13. *Phormium tenax* (2)
14. *Iris germanica* 'Golden Alps' (3)
15. *Kniphofia caulescens* (4)
16. *Ceanothus thyrsiflorus* var. *repens* (1)

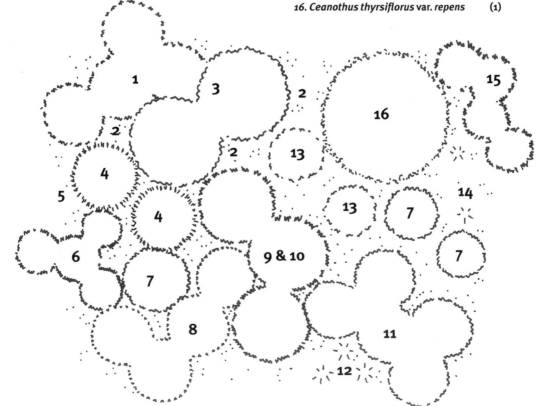

'I haven't defined the medium of the hard landscaping that surrounds this planting because I would like the look to be fluffy at the edges, so that there is no strict line between the border and path,' says John, but it will need to be gravel, shingle or another hard, loose material. One of the unusual and attractive features about John's own garden, in West Sussex, is the way that his gravel paths and plantings in gravel do merge into each other. Redefining accepted conventions is part of his contemporary style.

So too is his move away from perennials and grasses, unlike many modern designers, towards shrubs. He says that, being 'increasingly in Britain, I'm getting a bit bored with perennials and grasses because the joy of the English climate, I believe, is our capacity to grow shrubby plants well'.

This design includes shrubby plants and a central role for strong foliage shapes, a key ingredient of modern designs. Note the rosettes of *Kniphofia caulescens*, a dramatic clump of *Phormium tenax*, bearded iris cultivars, and the iris-like leaves of the *Sisyrinchium striatum,* all of which contrast with the mound-like forms of *Ceanothus thyrsiflorus* var. *repens*, *Salvia officinalis* 'Purpurascens', *Rosa* 'Mutabilis' and *Lavatera thuringiaca* 'Barnsley'.

The scattering of the ornamental onions, *Allium giganteum* and *A. aflatunense*, with their tall drumstick-like flower heads, and the grass *Helictotrichon sempervirens*, with its superb seed heads, add further seasonal elements to the picture. Many of these plants are evergreen or semi-evergreen, with a variety of foliage colours ranging from the dark green of the ceanothus to the purple of the salvia and the silver of *Artemisia* 'Powis Castle'.

The year starts in late spring with white lily-flowered tulips and the purple alliums, followed by blue and yellow irises in early summer, when the scene is dominated by the masses of blue ceanothus flowers. The rose has flowers that quickly change colour from yellow to orange and red, while the sisyrinchium and potentilla are both primrose yellow. The kniphofia's flowers, like the rose's, turn colour as they age, in this case from red to yellow, and generally appear later in the summer while the perovskia's are misty blue-mauve in midsummer. The lavatera flowers profusely all summer with dark pink-eyed, white flowers. Having gravel around these plants will act as a marvellous foil for the different colours, and makes an effective mulch, locking moisture in the ground in dry periods.

REQUIREMENTS

1. Any reasonable well-drained soil will suit these plants, as will any open site that is sheltered from cold winter or spring winds. Cold winters may cut the lavatera to ground level, but it soon recovers. It may occasionally produce branches with pink flowers, and the former must be cut off before more appear and take over.

2. The lavatera is never a long-lived plant, with five years being a reasonable life-span, and the ceanothus may die after 10 years. Also note that both grow very big, as does the phormium, and they should be given plenty of space at the outset. However, this can create temporary problems, because there will initially be gaps to the sides before the plants fill out. Solve the problem using alliums and the sisyrinchiums as temporary fillers, to be removed when the gaps start closing. Once the lavatera and ceanothus die you will have to decide whether to replace them with the same species or try something different.

3. The alliums and the sisyrinchiums can self-sow on some soils, adding a note of spontaneity; indeed the sisyrinchium can sometimes almost become a weed.

[Left] *Perovskia atriplicifolia* **'Blue Spire'**

[Centre] *Artemisia* **'Powis Castle'**

[Right] *Ceanothus thyrsiflorus* var. *repens*

Rupert Golby

'The biggest complement anyone can pay me,' says Rupert Golby, 'is to say that it doesn't look like you've had a designer in here.' One of the younger generation of garden designers, his approach to design is subtle and plant orientated. He says that he likes to think of himself 'as really just gardening for the future', and that he would 'rather approach a garden through plants than through design'. For Rupert, design is very much an extension of horticulture rather than a separate activity.

In many ways, Rupert is working at the very heart of the English gardening tradition, both geographically because he is based in the Cotswolds, home of Hidcote and Kiftsgate, two of the best-loved and most influential English gardens, and metaphorically because he adopts a traditional approach. Nearly all his clients are private, many with historic houses and gardens, although he has also carried out a major restoration project for English Heritage, at Osborne House on the Isle of Wight, working on the walled kitchen garden.

He took up gardening at the age of four when he started growing hollyhocks, and went on to study at the Royal Horticutural Society's Garden at Wisley, and then the Royal Botanic Garden at Kew, both in the UK. One of his first jobs was at Ninfa, in Italy, a romantic garden built around the ruins of a town: 'An extraordinary garden,' he says, 'and a great influence.' Rosemary Verey, for whom he also worked, was another crucial influence. 'She used plants as a painter would, almost without regard for the fact that

they are plants. They were there to be exploited, not tended, which was quite an eye-opener to me.' Rupert also mentions Christopher Lloyd as a source of inspiration. 'I like his unorthodox use of plants … what looks like neglect is in fact intended. By which I mean, for example, his love of dying fern fronds and old lawns seeded with wild flowers.'

Rupert's credo is that: 'A garden has to take its reference from the house.' Once away from the house the garden 'should not creep into the countryside'. He also 'likes to furnish a house with climbers, using multiple plantings growing together, making a billowy rather than a rigorously pruned look'.

Balance and harmony are obviously very important to Rupert, and it is interesting to notice how much symmetry there is in his plans. He adds that he dislikes strong colours because: 'I find them artificial and prefer a tapestry effect.' He is fond of using big blocks of plants in certain places, for example *Acanthus mollis* across the front of a house, but also of creating 'a speckled effect over a large area' by mixing three or so individuals of one particular species.

Evergreens play an important role in Rupert's work, indeed his own house is easily recognized by the big clipped hollies that stand sentinel outside the front door. 'Clients,' he says, 'are increasingly demanding year-round interest, and are more and more intolerant of plants with just one season of interest — which is why I am using greater numbers of evergreens, such as phillyrea and sarcococca.' *Phillyrea angustifolia* is hardly new (it has been in cultivation since the 18th century), but it is now increasingly available because the Italian nursery trade is exporting it in growing numbers to Britain, a good example of how the commercial availability of plants affects garden design.

When designing a planting scheme, Rupert is emphatic that he starts with what the clients want, and that the design is negotiated with them at all stages. 'Then we have to decide what stays in the garden, and then set about linking the old and new plantings. It is also important to decide if an area is to have a short, intense period of interest or a diluted interest over a longer period.'

He finds that most of his clients want a traditional look, and any temptation he has to try something more contemporary inevitably succumbs to the client's desire to play safe. Either that or the architecture of the 'new pseudo-Georgian houses' does not lend itself to anything experimental. He adds: 'I work for a lot of wealthy clients, including a lot of rock stars, who you think would want to be contemporary, but in fact they all want a traditional stone house, and that sets the tone of the garden. All rebel rock stars slot back into wanting the traditional signs of wealth. People,' he continues, 'want restful, peaceful gardens, nothing shocking or jarring, though I try to include some modern ideas.' One relatively recent development is that Rupert finds most of his clients want entertainment venues, like areas for furniture, barbecues etc., incorporated in their gardens; a sign perhaps that the 'garden for living in' concept, pioneered by Thomas Church in 1950s California, really has arrived in Britain.

[Left] The colours of the flowers and foliage in this border have been limited to white, silver and blue with hot pink cosmos for contrast

[Right] Herbs and perennials spill over the path through the pottager at the Old Rectory

Rupert is adamant that he is contemporary because: 'I use many of the huge range of plants that are now available. I like to see unusual or new plants used on a large scale, not just as single specimens. For example, I worked on a garden in Dorset where we put in a whole avenue of cut-leaved beech, *Fagus sylvatica* 'Aspleniifolia'.' His use of tender perennials is also very contemporary. He likes to integrate them with herbaceous plants in borders, salvias, argyranthemums and dahlias, but sometimes uses them on their own. 'They might be weak in early summer,' he says, 'but they are so startling at the end of summer.'

The increasingly popular grasses though, are not necessarily his favourite plants. 'The best way of using them is in terrific quantities, and they can look good with perennials but they look misplaced with shrubs. The main problem is that they are so often dotted around as a gesture.' The use of newly available plants is one way in which an old garden can be 'made to look forward', which Rupert thinks is much better than 'just slavishly putting in plants of the period, and anyway gardens die if you simply preserve them'.

Rupert's view of gardens is that they do not improve as they age (as everyone thinks), but that they gradually die, and need rescuing before it is too late. Most of Rupert's work is in old gardens where there is no question of their being a blank slate; a sensitive approach is needed to restoration, thinning existing planting and making everything more manageable. Much of this work is actually 'very destructive, because gardens are often overplanted or have never been thinned, which is particularly the case with trees. And after thinning they often look so much better'. His sensitivity to plants and landscape is important as gardens are gradually remoulded. 'I do not want to use plants like building blocks, I'd rather make a happy garden rather than a building site. I believe in creating a balance, and that's when the garden becomes a magical place.'

Whether he is working on old or new gardens, he says he is finding that increasing numbers of clients want to take an organic approach to gardening, but without understanding the issues involved. Like most designers he finds it can be a problem. 'One of my biggest gardens is

[Left] Allium seedheads have
been left in the rose garden at the
Old Rectory to provide contrast of
shape with the low mounds of
purple sage and of colour with the
deep red roses

[Right] A shady, green and white
border that relies on foliage
shape and colour will look good
all year round

completely organic, and is a complete nightmare. We have
so many gardens that were designed to be completely
chemical dependent and that are now being run
organically, but this approach is so labour-intensive and
time-consuming. The key issue is the use of herbicides
because unchecked weeds are the great enemy of
ornamental plants in Britain.' Rupert reckons a good
compromise 'is to clean up a garden with herbicides and
then use organic methods after that'. Interestingly, several
committed organic growers have said as much to me,
strictly off the record of course.

Like many plant-influenced designers, Rupert stresses
that 'how a garden is maintained is almost more important
than the original design'. And the vast majority of clients
do want Rupert to be involved after the project has been
completed, often to create projects, but also to monitor
the development of the garden and advise them and their
staff. Advising gardeners can be tricky, but Rupert finds
that 'almost without exception staff appreciate your input,
but you do have to prove yourself by working alongside them'.

Besides paying attention to the plants, Rupert (like all
designers) has to be involved intimately with the hard
landscaping (including paving, stonework and timber,
etc.). But the plants get all the attention. 'How often do
you hear someone go into a garden and say "wonderful
steps", after so much money and effort went into them?'
'But the truth is,' he says, 'that they are vital for each other.'

A discussion of hard landscaping inevitably leads towards
talk about the latest developments in gardening, and the
popular new shows at Chaumont-sur-Loire in France, and
at Westonbirt Arboretum, in Gloucestershire, UK, where
installation art meets garden design in a flurry of
scaffolding poles, mirrors, coloured plastic sheeting,
glass, gravel and new materials. Not surprisingly Rupert is
lukewarm. 'It is good to be provocative, and it makes
people think about what a garden really is, but it is
important that the installations don't get in the way of real
gardening. A lot of it does not contribute to gardening and
some is an intrusion, and there is a danger that the plants
could be sidelined.'

Rupert concludes that 'gardening has changed out of all recognition in the last few years', especially with the growth of make-over TV programmes and media interest in the garden. 'People now feel chanelled into design, whereas in the past they were happy just gardening and growing things, and it was the process of growing that people enjoyed. Many of our greatest gardens were planted by enthusiastic amateurs.'

Perhaps in many ways Rupert represents the true heart of English gardening, someone who, while being aware of the latest trends, prefers to work in a more incremental way, building on what history has bequeathed us rather than going out of his way to plough new furrows. His deep understanding of plants is also something that is fundamental to English garden design.

The vast range of plants that will flourish in the climate of the British Isles means that designers have an almost overwhelming range of species to use, though very few of today's garden designers actually have the knowledge (or inclination) to use them effectively. This, with the fact that the climate of the British Isles is so weed-friendly, means that designers working here will arguably always need to be more horticulturally biased and skillful than in other countries. Whatever new trends affect garden design in Britain, it will always be practitioners like Rupert who will remain the bedrock of the profession.

A border of year-round interest

plant list

1. *Arbutus unedo* (1)
2. *Phillyrea angustifolia* (1)
3. *Rosa* 'Gardenia' (1)
4. *Magnolia grandiflora* 'Exmouth' (1)
5. *Osmanthus* × *burkwoodii* (1)
6. *Photinia* × *fraseri* 'Rubens' (1)
7. *Blechnum tabulare* (1)
8. *Hebe* 'Mrs Winder' (2)
9. *Cornus alba* 'Elegantissima' (2)
10. *Viburnum davidii* (female) (1)
11. *Iris foetidissima* (25)
12. *Ruscus aculeatus* (female) (1)
13. *Daphne tangutica* 'Retusa' (1)
14. *Sarcococca confusa* (1)
15. *Helleborus foetidus* (4)
16. *Bergenia cordifolia* 'Purpurea' (6)
17. *Helleborus argutifolius* (4)

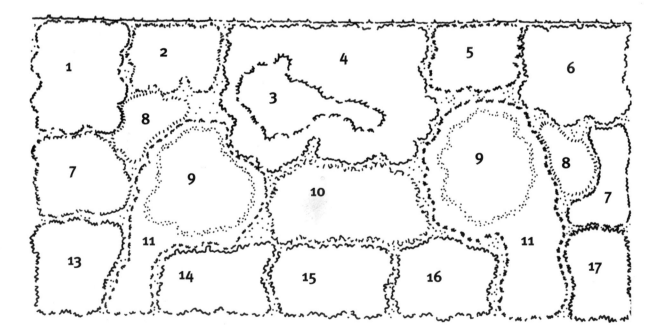

Magnolia grandiflora

Rupert says that having the plantings look good all year is a major priority of many for his clients. 'Borders adjacent to a house, where they are constantly seen, particularly need to be well furnished throughout the year, even in the depths of winter, without necessarily being flower strewn and colourful. It is more important that they should be healthy, well shaped and full.' Evergreens are therefore important, partly because they make 'such a satisfying block against which deciduous plants of winter interest are shown off to advantage, one of the best examples being the red-stemmed *Cornus alba* 'Elegantissima'.'

This particular border features a number of plants with lustrous green leaves at the back, although the foliage of the centrally-placed *Magnolia grandiflora* 'Exmouth' are an interestingly lighter shade, with brown undersides. Once established this species will produce occasional huge and scented white flowers in mid-summer. The osmanthus has deliciously scented white blossom in spring, the arbutus has white lily of the valley-like flowers in early summer followed by red, strangely strawberry-like fruit later, while the photinia has deep mahogany-red young growth in spring.

These evergreens provide a fine backdrop for the red stems of *Cornus alba* 'Elegantissima' in winter and for its cream variegated leaves in summer, and for the fine creamy-white flowers of the rambling rose 'Gardenia'. They need to be held against the wall on wires until the magnolia is large enough to offer support, when the rose can be encouraged to poke through its branches.

Around the cornus are clumps of *Iris foetidissima*, an iris with relatively inconspicuous flowers but striking orange berries in autumn that usually last well into winter, along with its dark green leaves. *Hebe* 'Mrs Winder' has contrasting bronze-purple foliage. Framing the central part of the planting are two plants – *Ruscus aculeatus* and *Blechnum tabulare* – that add considerably to the long season of structural interest. The ruscus has very stiff, dark green leafy stems and an ability to thrive in the most unpromising dry shade, while the blechnum is a fern with strikingly cut, leathery-looking leaves. The latter needs a site that never dries out, and will only really flourish in relatively mild climates. Other ferns, such as dryopteris and polystichum, would be suitable in colder situations.

The centrally-placed *Viburnum davidii* has a neat, low habit, with elegant evergreen leaves and dark blue berries, while *Sarcococca confusa* is another evergreen, low-growing, clump-forming shrub whose main feature is the scented winter flowers. The two species of helleborus are both primarily foliage plants, forming striking clumps of evergreen leaves topped by lime-green flowers in winter, while the bergenia has magenta flowers in early spring and large, red leaves that turn deep bronze-red in winter.

REQUIREMENTS

1. This border is suitable for any aspect other than north-facing, and needs shelter from cold winter winds. Any reasonable soil is fine.

2. All the plants used are notably long-lived; if not crowded and planted at suitable planting distances, many will still be there in 100 years time. The planting distances are crucial because many of the plants will take many years to reach their mature size. Avoid the temptation to plant them closer together than the distances given for their eventual spreads or the more vigorous species will block out the others.

Many of the shrubs along the rear of the border are large growers, but there is a danger that they might initially be planted too close together. If this happens they can be clipped or pruned, but the result may be rather artificial. Selective removal may be the best option.

A border with scented plants and herbs

plant list

1. *Buddleia alternifolia* 'Argentea' (3)
2. *Lonicera periclymenum* 'Cornish Cream' (3)
3. *Foeniculum vulgare* 'Purpureum' (3)
4. *Rosa rubiginosa* (1)
5. *Nepeta sibirica* 'Souvenir d'André Chaudron' (2)
6. *Perovskia atriplicifolia* (2)
7. *Artemisia ludoviciana* subsp. *ludoviciana* var. *latiloba* (2)
8. *Calamintha nepeta* (3)
9. *Rosmarinus officinalis* 'Benenden Blue' (6)
10. *Lilium candidum* (2)
11. *Dictamnus albus* (1)
12. *Hyssopus officinalis* (1)
13. *Thymus vulgaris* (4)
14. *Origanum laevigatum* (1)
15. *Cistus × cyprius* (1)
16. *Allium sphaerocephalon* (10)
17. *Phuopsis stylosa* (1)
18. *Nerine bowdenii* (10)
19. *Salvia officinalis* (2)
20. *Myrrhis odorata* (1)
21. *Euphorbia characias* 'Blue Hills' (1)
22. *Lilium regale* (2)
23. *Verbascum olympicum* (5)
24. *Aquilegia vulgaris* 'Belhaven Blue' (4)
25. *Eryngium alpinum* 'Amethyst' (1)
26. *Atriplex halimus* (1)

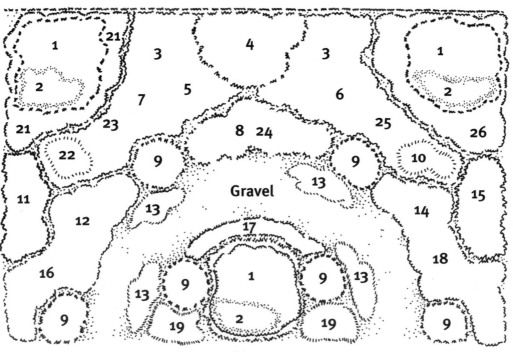

Lilium regale 'Album'

Getting access to fragrant plants is a vital part of this and, indeed, any planting. Consequently this border has a path that curves round allowing exploration right into the bed.

Rupert uses three semi-standard specimens of *Buddleia alternifolia* 'Argentea' that need regular pruning to retain their open, airy habit, and which provide the only element of regularity in this otherwise informal miscellany. His intention is that 'multiple plantings of herbaceous plants should run together and merge with neighbouring combinations to give a massed effect of form, colour and scent'.

Each buddleia is accompanied by a honeysuckle (*Lonicera periclymenum* 'Cornish Cream') which, until the buddleia is large enought to support it, will requite a tripod of canes, and an underplanting. The evergreen *Euphorbia characias* 'Blue Hills' used beneath one of the buddleias flowers very early in the year, with lime-green flowers, and its greyish leaves are echoed by those of the semi-evergreen, silvery leaves of the *Atriplex halimus* below one of the other buddleias. *Myrrhis odorata*, used beneath the third, is a sophisticated cow-parsley with deep green filigree foliage and white flower heads in early summer. The rose is the sweet briar, with small pink flowers and long-lasting scarlet hips, its main feature being the apple-scented foliage.

Most of the other plants here are low-growing species, many of Mediterranean origin, their aromatic foliage being characteristic of the drought-resistant flora of this area. Some, such as rosemary, sage (*Salvia officinalis*), fennel (*Foeniculum vulgare* 'Purpureum') thyme, oreganum and hyssop, double as culinary herbs. Most are low-growing and sprawling, much of their charm arising from the fact that they will intermingle with each other and form irregular mats of foliage across the gravel path. *Phuopsis stylosa* is perhaps a brave choice because it has a strong smell in summer, reminiscent of garlic. Its deep pink flowers in early to midsummer are certainly striking.

Plants with a marked upright habit are very useful as a contrast to low-growing species. The list includes aquilegias, to flower in late spring and early summer, sumptuously scented white lilies (*Lilium candidum* and *L. regale*), the clustered white spikes of *Dictamnus albus*,

[Left] *Phuopsis stylosa*

[Right] *Buddleia alternifolia*
'Argentea'

REQUIREMENTS

the thistle-like *Eryngium alpinum* 'Amethyst' and, most dramatic of all, the tall spires of the mullein (*Verbascum olympicum*). *Perovskia atriplicifolia* also has an upright habit, but is less clearly defined. A number of bulbs also provide a contrast, and they include the dark red-pink of the midsummer flowering *Allium sphaerocephalon* and the bright pink *Nerine bowdenii* in autumn.

The predominant colours are white, blues and mauves, with the occasional pink. The use of gravel provides a good backdrop for these colours and low-maintenance ground cover.

1. Full sun and any reasonable well-drained soil will suit this scheme. Many will also do well on dry or sandy soils. Nerines, in particular, appreciate a hot spot.

2. Gravel's practical advantages are many: it reduces moisture loss and helps prevent weeds from gaining a foothold. However, it encourages some plants to self-sow; amongst the species used here, the verbascum, aquilegia, foeniculum, allium and *Lilium regale* will readily do so, creating attractive drifts. The loose surface also enables surplus seedlings and weeds to be easily pulled out.

3. This should be a successful long-term planting. Some species (the rosemary, cistus and salvia) might eventually become very woody and unattractive and need replacing. Others may die out (the verbascum and foeniculum) but invariably replace themselves with seedlings. Where plants eventually make large clumps they may detract from the design, but they can easily be divided and thinned out.

A border of bold foliage plants

plant list

1. *Miscanthus sinensis* 'Gracillimus' (1)
2. *Eryngium pandanifolium* (1)
3. *Aralia elata* (1)
4. *Macleaya cordata* (1)
5. *Epimedium* × *versicolor* 'Sulphureum' (3)
6. *Acanthus mollis* (5)
7. *Sasa veitchii* (1)
8. *Angelica archangelica* (1)
9. *Phyllostachys nigra* (2)
10. *Levisticum officinale* (1)

Wall

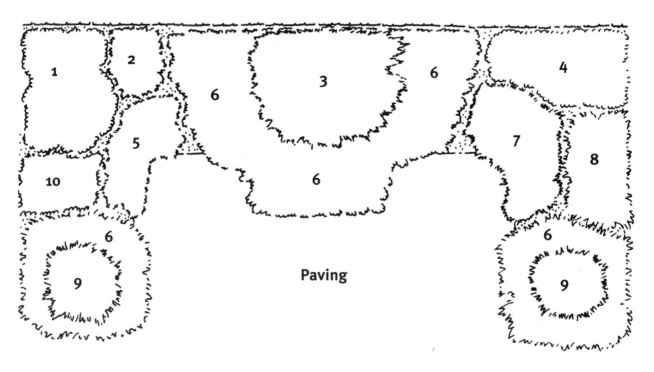

Paving

Rupert describes this border as 'a celebration of foliage, combining a broad spectrum of beautiful leaved plants'. It is ideal for a courtyard or enclosed space where year-round greenery is desired. Different shapes of foliage are contrasted with each other, the result being a very bold planting.

Aralia elata is at the centre and will dominate the planting when mature. It has very large, pinnate leaves and what Rupert calls 'lethally spiked' stems. He describes the *Acanthus mollis* around it as 'forming statuesque iconography'. It is semi-evergreen and is one of the most tolerant and resilient of those perennials that have very striking foliage, and is enhanced in summer by bold white and mauve flower spikes.

Eryngium pandanifolium is another bold perennial with lots of thistle-like flower heads and dramatically toothed leaves. It will be echoed by the similarly tall and bold angelica (*Angelica archangelica*) and lovage (*Levisticum officinale*) to the sides, all three being members of the cow-parsley family. *Macleaya cordata* in the right-hand corner is also large, but it is a gentler looking plant with grey-toned leaves, vaguely resembling fig leaves, the colour being a good contrast with the strong greens of the other plants.

The *Miscanthus sinensis* 'Gracillimus' is an ornamental grass with elegant, plume-like flower and seed spikes from late summer until late winter. The two bamboos that frame the area are the black-stemmed *Phyllostachys nigra*, while the much shorter but broader leaved *Sasa veitchii* fills a corner of the paving. The opposite corner is planted with the perennial *Epimedium* × *versicolor* 'Sulphureum' that forms a dense clump of glossy, bronze-tinted leaves.

REQUIREMENTS

1. The majority of these plants are probably happiest in light shade, in soil that is well drained but does not regularly dry out.

2. Soil moisture is particularly important for the bamboos. Also note that since the *Sasa veitchii* bamboo can spread invasively when mature, you should surround its rooting area with slates, tiles or heavy duty plastic to keep it within bounds.

3. All the other plants are perennials apart from the angelica, which is usually biennial, so young plants need to be planted every year to ensure continuity; allow self-sown seedlings to fill their parents' places.

4. This planting should be long-lived, with competition between spreading clumps of plants the only long-term management problem; the acanthus, in particular, is a rather over-enthusiastic grower, especially in warmer sites.

[Left] *Acanthus spinosus*

[Right] *Miscanthus sinesis*
'Gracillimus'

A border of yellow and blue

plant list

1. *Bupleurum fruticosum* (4)
2. *Anthemis tinctoria* 'E.C. Buxton' (2)
3. *Euphorbia characias* subsp. *characias* 'Humpty Dumpty' (2)
4. *Nepeta govaniana* (1)
5. *Nigella damascena* (10)
6. *Campanula persicifolia* (3)
7. *Camassia leichtlinii* (10)
8. *Eryngium × oliverianum* (2)
9. *Linum perenne* (3)
10. *Achillea taygetea* (2)
11. *Clematis × durandii* (2)
12. *Ceanothus thyrsiflorus* var. *repens* (2)
13. *Clematis integrifolia* 'Pastel Blue' (1)
14. *Kniphofia* 'Little Maid' (4)
15. *Eryngium bourgatii* 'Picos Blue' (3)
16. *Iris pallida* 'Variegata' (5)
17. *Eryngium giganteum* (2)
18. Pot planted with *Solanum rantonnetii* and *Bidens ferulifolia* (1)
19. *Milium effusum* 'Aureum' (6)
20. *Parahebe perfoliata* (2)
21. *Hypericum olympicum* 'Sulphureum' (3)
22. *Veronica longifolia* 'Blauer Sommer' (3)
23. *Melissa officinalis* 'Aurea' (2)
24. *Sisyrinchium striatum* 'Aunt May' (1)
25. *Helictotrichon sempervirens* (2)
26. *Linum narbonense* (2)
27. *Polemonium caeruleum* (3)

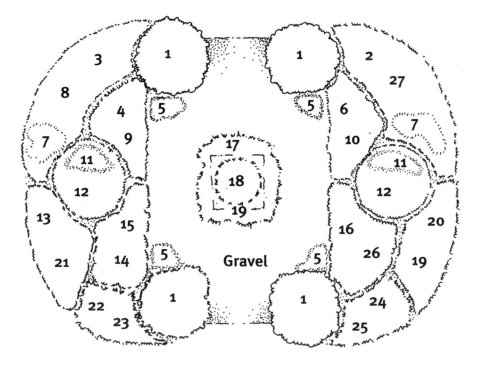

This plan for an island bed provides colour throughout the summer. The dominant theme is yellow (including many less common pale yellows) and blue, with a variety of interesting foliage shapes and textures. Rupert describes it as being 'held down by the use of evergreen shrubs with a low dome-like habit'. His two key plants in this respect are the *Ceanothus thrysiflorus* var. *repens* and *Bupleurum fruticosum*. The former has striking blue flowers in early summer, the latter has greeny-yellow flowers at roughly the same time. The fine texture of the former makes a good contrast with the larger, glossier leaves of the latter.

Early summer is particularly colourful with the blue camassias, *Campanula persicifolia*, the two linum species and *Polemonium caeruleum* in flower, while the pale yellow *Anthemis tinctoria* 'E. C. Buxton', *Nepeta govaniana* and *Hypericum olympicum* 'Sulphureum' will also be in flower. Slightly later, two species of blue eryngium start flowering, while *Kniphofia* 'Little Maid' has primrose yellow spikes of tightly packed tubular flowers, making it

one of the finest of the red hot pokers. Slightly paler is *Sisyrinchium striatum* 'Aunt May' with flowers in whorled spikes. It also has rather iris-like variegated foliage, echoing that of *Iris pallida* 'Variegata'.

The two clematis varieties provide plenty of blue interest throughout the summer: *Clematis × durandii* has dark purple blue flowers and a herbaceous scrambling habit, and can attractively drape itself over the ceanothus, neatly making the same space flower twice. *Clematis integrifolia* 'Pastel Blue' has small nodding flowers and, while not a climber, does need some support, for example using pea sticks.

A number of the plants have coloured or distinctive foliage. Both *Melissa officinalis* 'Aurea' and *Milium effusum* 'Aureum' are yellow tinted, which combines well with the blue flowers, while the grass *Helictotrichon sempervirens* has blue-grey leaves. *Parahebe perfoliata* also has greyish leaves, blue flowers and, like many Australian plants, a very singular appearance, with its leaves arranged on spreading, nodding stems.

REQUIREMENTS

The centre of the planting is gravelled where a raised pot of tender perennials gives added emphasis to the centre of the planting. He suggests using the dark blue-purple *Solanum rantonnetii* with the deep yellow *Bidens ferulifolia* to intensify the colour scheme. 'Miss Willmott's Ghost' (*Eryngium giganteum*) and the yellow grass *Milium effusum* 'Aureum' surround the pot, while the blue-flowered annual *Nigella damascena* is sown in the corners. The idea is that in future years the nigella, the grass and the biennial eryngium will self-seed into the gravel. They will also probably self-seed into the surrounding garden, providing an ever-changing note of spontaneity.

1. Any reasonable soil in full sun will suit this planting, with quite a few of the plants being happy in dry or poor soils, such as the ceanothus, anthemis and linums. The ceanothus and bupleurum may suffer in very frosty areas or if flayed by cold winter winds, although they easily cope with mild, maritime gales.

2. The ceanothus will need replacing often, approximately 8–10 years, while the anthemis might survive for only 2–3 years, though it can be propagated by division or cuttings.

3. The central pot contains one species, the *Bidens ferulifolia*, that is only half-hardy and short-lived, and one tender plant, the solanum, that needs to be brought under cover for the winter. It is possible to train this sometimes untidy and rapid-growing shrub as a standard, allowing a new shoot to replace the old central stem every other year.

[Left] *Camassia leichtlinii*

[Right] *Bupleurum fruticosum*

Penelope Hobhouse

Penelope Hobhouse is well known for her study of colour in the garden and for her involvement in many garden restorations. Alongside a successful career as a writer, she has run a garden design business, overseeing historically oriented restoration projects and creating gardens for private clients in Europe and the USA.

'Most people think I'm a traditionalist, which is not really true,' Penelope declares. 'I'm not so much interested in getting exactly the right colours next to each other as in choosing plants that are going to be happy together.' Indeed, her enthusiasms are wide ranging. She is interested in contemporary nature-inspired planting design, for example, and feels 'passionate' about unusual plants. She is 'very interested in modern architecture', which has influenced her garden designs, 'although it is difficult to say why. I love the new buildings in Chicago – seeing them from many different angles was one of the most exciting days of my life – and the Guggenheim museum in Bilbao.' Knowledge and appreciation of garden history is 'background grammar' to her designs and many of her books show her love of historical research and attention to detail.

Penelope's highest profile project is the garden designed for the late Queen Elizabeth, the Queen Mother, at Walmer Castle, Kent, UK, which like much of her design work is considered 'traditional', yet is more accurately summed up as '20th-century English'. This is the school of Gertrude Jekyll and Vita Sackville-West, where formal structures are

[Left] The 'lollipop' heads of *Robinia pseudacacia* 'Umbraculifera' provide the main structural element in Penelope Hobhouse's current garden

[Right] Masses of butterfly-attracting *Verbena bonariensis* in a border at Walmer Castle, Kent, in mid-summer. Usually dotted around in borders, the long-flowering and drought-tolerant perennial is rarely seen massed in this way

balanced with an almost insouciant cottage-garden style informality, and where the creation of intimate themed spaces is a key element. Pergolas, shrubs and roses provide vertical elements and bulk, perennials fill out spaces, while hedges divide and add definition. 'Gardens,' Penelope has written, 'are about using space, they are "rooms", volumes of cubic space, which relate to their surroundings.' She considers plants to be the most important architectural elements and uses 'small trees with broad, globular or pyramidal heads' to act as '"ceilings" to enhance the room-like effects'. This is

apparent in her own walled garden in Dorset where round-headed specimens of *Robinia pseudoacacia* 'Umbraculifera' are the tallest elements.

Penelope first became interested in gardening when she was in her twenties, after visiting Tintinhull in Somerset, where she was inspired by the strong lines of the layout and was 'bowled over by the colour schemes'. Interestingly, she returned to Tintinhull in later life, living in the house as a tenant of the National Trust. In the meantime, for 12 years she lived at Hadspen House in

Somerset, where her love of gardening and garden history really took off. She worked on the neglected 3.5 hectare (9 acre) garden with Eric Smith, whose expertise in growing and selecting new perennial cultivars helped inspire her own developing plant knowledge. 'I became very interested in plants', and, she adds, 'especially shrubs' because they played an important role in the reclamation and management of the Hadspen garden, where the aim was to establish 'an overall effect of a controlled wilderness'. (The kitchen garden area has since been developed by Nori and Sandra Pope, see pages 162–167.)

Gradually though, Penelope realized that there was a danger in being too concerned simply with the aesthetics of plantings. 'If people don't consider the habitat of a plant, and look only at the picture,' she says, the planting tends to look inappropriate. She is still surprised at how many gardeners do not consider ecology when designing plantings, 'especially since Beth Chatto has set a new standard for doing this. Part of the problem,' Penelope adds, 'is that we lose sight of the importance of the soil when nearly everything is grown in containers; it is not so easy to relate plants to their conditions when they are

bought in a pot.' Indeed, instead of being depressed by the 'waterlogged clay' in her Dorset garden, she says how 'good it has been for me', in 'making me think about choosing plants that will really grow well here'. Penelope clearly loves working, both at her desk, and 'in physically gardening'; only someone who is totally committed to their craft could be so happy about a clay soil.

Designing in the USA brought Penelope face to face with many gardens that used native plants or worked with a more naturalistic aesthetic and incorporated semi-wild areas in the garden. In some projects she found herself creating plantings that had to fit into settings of natural beauty where the 20th-century English look would have been inappropriate. She also met designers who were quite militant in their desire to reject the whole English garden tradition. The vast drifts of grasses and perennials created by seminal American garden designers Wolfgang Oehme and James Van Sweden could not be more different to the hedge-defined 'rooms' of much of Penelope's work. 'I do love the Oehme Van Sweden style,' she says, 'although grasses in Britain and Europe can be more

problematic,' and has even worked with James on one project. However, Penelope is emphatic that a garden is not a natural space, for if it were truly 'natural' it would not be a garden, and no garden will look after itself. 'Wild gardening is some of the most skillful of all', she says. Her experiences led to *Natural Planting* (Pavilion, 1999), her book on the new nature-inspired plantings, interpreted as a contemporary re-working of the ideas of the late-Victorian Irish-born gardening writer William Robinson.

'Structure is so important,' Penelope says, even in wild gardens. For those who think of structure only in terms of formality, it is instructive to hear Penelope outline the various ways in which structure can be used in gardens. 'You do not need a formal garden for structure,' she says, 'some clipped yews or a single enclosing clipped hedge is all that is needed to give a garden a sense of framework. Structure,' she adds, 'can also be created by repeating groups of plants, but not necessarily symmetrically. It's very important that something repeats, even if the planting is too small to have the same thing repeated, there should be something else that hints at a particularly

prominent colour or form.' She stresses too that structure also depends upon having plenty of interesting foliage shapes, with evergreens particularly useful for supplying these. Repetition is something that is key to the naturalistic planting movement too, an element that is particularly striking at the garden of the Weihenstephan Institute, near Munich. This is one of several gardens that Penelope has visited in Germany which explore a very different, essentially naturalistic, aesthetic, and one that has made an especially strong impression on her. Long rectangular beds are planted with a wide variety of perennials, along with some shrubs and annuals, many of them part of systematically organised collections. However a strong visual effect is made through key plants being repeated, so that a remarkably strong rhythm is built up.

Italy, Penelope's greatest foreign love and the primary source of the formal tradition in Western garden history, has taught her valuable lessons: in the Italian Renaissance garden 'all is geometric, in balance and perfectly proportioned', she explains. 'There are allegorical meanings,' she says, 'which few gardens have today.' Like

the Muslim concept of the garden as a spiritual oasis, 'earlier gardens had connections to philosophy and spirituality'. (She has visited Iran three times and is writing a book on Persian gardens.) She is excited by the increasing involvement of new ideas in gardening: 'Cutting edge ideas are excellent and gardens that create links with art and ideas are tremendously important, although the key thing is what impression they make when a visitor first steps inside.' To illustrate this she talks about her visit to Charles Jencks' Garden of Cosmic Possibilities in Scotland, which has become one of the best known allegorical gardens. 'I went by myself and absolutely loved it,' she says, 'although then I didn't have the faintest idea of what it was all about.'

Art and landscape have both inspired Penelope garden design work, with Monet, Turner and Claude all having, she believes, important lessons for gardeners. Landscape is important for her too, 'perhaps even more so than art in museums'. 'Ploughed fields or corn stubble have their own beauty, and I love looking out over the rolling hills of my own Dorset landscape.'

[Left] The use of box hedging to create formal patterns is a very traditional style of gardening. Here it is used to give order to a relaxed perennial planting in Penelope Hobhouse's own garden

[Previous Page] Penelope's informal style uses strongly architectural plants, shaped shrubs and gravel paths to create structure in her garden

Penelope no longer designs gardens, preferring now to concentrate on writing and on consultancy work. The latter she finds 'so much easier' than design, mainly because of the difficulties associated with keeping in touch with how gardens develop. One of the central problems of the garden designers' art is that their work is never truly finished and they are nearly always dependent upon the efforts of others for the fulfillment of their vision. Designers who walk away from their work, never returning, exert no control over how it develops; yet to continue to be involved, as Penelope prefers, assumes that the owners' vision of the garden's development is reasonably consistent with that of the designer and that they are prepared to pay for follow-up and supervisory visits. 'Owners so often mess the gardens around and it can be a problem if, for example, they get too keen, and start cramming in too many plants,' she says. 'Then there are problems of who you deal with, owners, managers, gardeners, and how long they stay in the job.'

Discussing recent developments in popular gardening culture, Penelope describes how she is a 'terrific fan of Alan Titchmarsh', the British TV garden presenter, who introduced the concept of 'make-over' gardens. She confesses that while her 'first feeling was that it was a product not a process', she gradually realized: 'Alan was introducing gardening to a whole new range of people who had never gardened before and his approach has quite revolutionized the nursery trade.' But completely re-making a garden in a short space of time in front of the cameras is harder to take. 'Why all the rush? I don't see why it all has to be done so quickly.'

Penelope's current garden in Dorset includes an inner walled enclosure of some 40 by 40 metres, with a network of formal gravel paths that often merge with areas of gravel-covered bed. The feeling in winter is very Mediterranean, both because of the clipped box and other formal elements, but also because of the emphasis on evergreen foliage. 'I love evergreen shrubs more than anything,' she says. 'In a few years there will be nothing here but greys and greens. I'm quite happy with that, but it is not so easy to sell to other people.' In summer though, the dominance of evergreens is disguised by a variety of deciduous shrubs, perennials and grasses, some growing out over the paths to soften the garden's underlying framework, others busily seeding into the gravel. The high walls act as a shelter from the elements and from the outside world, and help to protect slightly tender species such as *Acacia pravissima* and *Euphorbia mellifera*. It is a garden that combines discipline and modesty with natural exuberance, a fitting balance for reflecting the range of interests of Penelope's garden career.

A rectangular island bed around smoke bushes

plant list

1. *Kniphofia uvaria nobilis* (10)
2. *Helianthus* 'Lemon Queen' (9)
3. *Lysimachia ciliata* 'Firecracker' (9)
4. *Hemerocallis* 'Stafford' (14)
5. *Artemisia* 'Powis Castle' (6)
6. *Cotinus* 'Grace' (2)
7. *Cephalaria gigantea* (7)
8. *Lilium* 'Enchantment' (12)
9. *Alchemilla mollis* (7)
10. *Crocosmia* 'Lucifer' (9)
11. *Eupatorium purpureum* 'Atropurpureum' (9)
12. *Coreopsis verticillata* 'Moonbeam' (9)
13. *Crocosmia* 'Lady Hamilton' (9)
14. *Monarda* 'Purple Ann' (9)
15. *Euphorbia characias* subsp. *wulfenii* (4)
16. *Hemerocallis citrina* (7)
17. *Lysimachia ephemerum* (9)
18. *Potentilla* 'William Rollison' (6)
19. *Foeniculum vulgare* 'Purpureum' (5)
20. *Helianthus* 'Beldermeir' (9)
21. *Euphorbia griffithii* 'Fireglow' (7)
22. *Artemisia ludoviciana* (5)
23. *Crocosmia* 'Star of the East' (9)

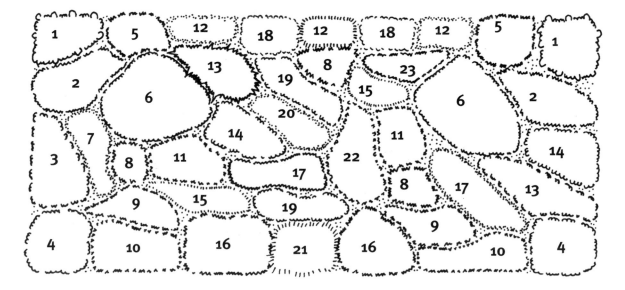

'Because I like enclosed spaces I don't design many island beds,' says Penelope, 'which means that most of the borders I design have a back.' But she concedes that island beds do have some advantages. 'You can look across them and see them from more angles than you can when a border backs on to a wall or hedge. The picture is never static.'

'I designed this particular bed with a lot of purple-bronze foliage, a colour that is not as strong as that of many of the purple-leaved plants that are often used, and that associate well with yellow flowers which are paler yellow on the north side and stronger on the sunnier side.'

A good example of the lighter purple is *Cotinus* 'Grace', a pair of which act as a pivot for the whole bed. It is a shade lighter than the more commonly seen variety 'Royal Purple'. The two cotinus plants are the only true woody shrubs in this bed, and virtually act as its skeleton; even in winter their bare twigs provide some structure.

Late winter sees a couple of *Euphorbia characias* subsp. *wulfenii* slowly begin to unfurl their yellow-green flower heads from out of their grey-leaved clumps. Penelope waxes lyrical about euphorbias, saying how she would like to collect more of them, and how valuable many are in springtime. As spring advances the purple-leaved herbaceous plants in the border begin to make their presence felt, such as *Lysimachia ciliata* 'Firecracker' and *Foeniculum vulgare* 'Purpureum'. And the silver-felted leaves of *Artemisia ludoviciana* make a dramatic contrast to the nearby purples.

In early to midsummer this planting really get into its stride with yellow-green *Alchemilla mollis* and lemon-yellow *Hemerocallis citrina*, for example. Midsummer sees two tall clumps of *Cephalaria gigantea* in flower, an unusual plant because its pale primrose-yellow flowers are a rare colour at the best of times, especially now. At a similar height of 2m (7ft), but flowering slightly later, is *Eupatorium purpureum* 'Atropurpureum', its dull pink, fluffy flower heads making up for their somewhat dirty colour by attracting hordes of butterflies. The purple monardas are another feature at this time, and also attract plenty of insects.

Helianthus 'Lemon Queen' is the star at the end of the growing season, its pale yellow flowers borne over a long period into autumn, a colour that can be a welcome relief from the strong yellows that tend to dominate at this time. In Penelope's design these perennial sunflowers are the only really tall plants at the edges of the bed. Island beds are usually structured so that the taller plants are in the centre and the shorter ones towards the outside. Placing these floriferous plants at the edge helps 'frame the picture'. Their yellow is picked up by the hot colours of the crocosmias that, with the fiery tones of the autumn colours of the cotinus, end the season on a high.

REQUIREMENTS

1. The plants in this border tolerate a wide range of soil conditions but need a sunny open position. Some of the later-flowering perennials, such as the monardas and the eupatorium, may not appreciate a prolonged period of drought. A thick mulch of wood chips or shredded plant material will help conserve moisture in the ground, and ensure that the later-flowering perennials perform well.

2. This is a very good planting for the long-term, with virtually all the species being very long-lived. The only possible exception is the monarda, that has a tendency to die out in the centre, with its new growth creating a new outer edge. In other words, the plant gradually moves, leading to possible competition with neighbouring perennials. When this happens, the monardas need to be dug up in spring and replanted.

3. The main long-term problem is caused by most of the perennials forming large clumps that may compete with each other. Some, such as *Euphorbia griffithii* 'Fireglow' and *Lysimachia ciliata* 'Firecracker', will do this faster than others, and may need to be reduced in size by division after three or four years. On light soils, the artemesia may be invasive. The cotinus may eventually become quite large and need pruning back; this can be done ruthlessly, even to ground level, without any fear of killing it.

A scented winter border in shade, with some spring and summer flowers

[Left] *Philadelphus coronarius* 'Aureus'

[Right] *Daphne odora* 'Aureo-marginata'

plant list

1. Choisya ternata	(1)	*16. Cornus stolonifera* 'Flavirnamea'	(3)
2. Corylopsis pauciflora	(1)	*17. Daphne odora* 'Aureo-marginata'	(1)
3. Sarcococca hookeriana var. *humilis*	(10)	*18. Lonicera tragophylla*	(2)
4. Brunnera macrophylla	(24)	*19. Hedera helix* 'Buttercup'	(5)
5. Arum italicum 'Marmoratum'	(5)	*20. Ilex × altaclerensis* 'Golden King'	(9)
6. Euphorbia schillingii	(5)	*21. Lonicera × purpusii* 'Winter Beauty'	(2)
7. Cotoneaster lacteus	(1)	*22. Hamamelis × intermedia* 'Jelena'	(1)
8. Hamamelis mollis	(1)	*23. Ligustrum ovalifolium* 'Aureum'	(1)
9. Philadelphus 'Belle Etoile'	(3)	*24. Hydrangea petiolaris*	(1)
10. Anemone nemorosa	(25)	*25. Sarcococca hookeriana* var. *digyna*	(5)
11. Symphytum × uplandicum 'Variegatum'	(3)	*26. Philadelphus coronarius* 'Aureus'	(1)
12. Helleborus × hybridus	(18)		
13. Garrya elliptica 'James Roof'	(18)		
14. Viburnum × burkwoodii	(1)		
15. Rhamnus alaternus 'Argenteovariegata'	(1)		

Wall

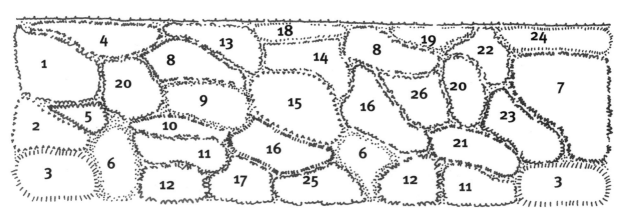

Borders that receive little sunlight, such as those which are north-facing, need shade-tolerant woodland plants if they are to succeed. These include many evergreen winter-flowering shrubs that naturally live in woodland, and that enjoy the bright conditions in winter when most of the trees have dropped their leaves.

The winter-performing shrubs in this border include two hollies (*Ilex × altaclerensis* 'Golden King') that form a golden variegated backbone to the border. Despite the name, they are female and will bear a good crop of berries in the autumn if there are male hollies in the vicinity. The border is further framed by bulky evergreens with the spring-flowering *Choisya ternata* at one end and a red-berried *Cotoneaster lacteus* at the other. The sense of framing is enhanced by the three sarcococca groups at the front; they are evergreen with sweetly scented flowers in late winter.

The two hazels (*Hamamelis*) flower in winter, and the related corylopsis a little later in spring, having curious little blossoms with an extraordinarily sweet and far-carrying scent. The winter-flowering honeysuckle (*Lonicera × purpusii* 'Winter Beauty'), the *Garrya elliptica* 'James Roof' and *Helleborus × hybridus* also flower at this time. Winter interest is further enhanced by the variegated foliage of the centrally-placed *Rhamnus alaternus* 'Argenteovariegata', the golden-variegated *Ligustrum ovalifolium* 'Aureum' and the yellow stems of the dogwood (*Cornus stolonifera* 'Flaviramea').

As winter turns into spring, many of the perennials used in this border start into growth, and being edge-of-woodland plants in bright positions they make strong growth relatively early in the season. They include *Brunnera macrophylla* that flowers in mid-spring, *Arum italicum* 'Marmoratum' with its variegated leaves and *Symphytum × uplandicum* 'Variegatum' with broad, cream-margined leaves. Notice how the bulky, green-leaved brunnera is situated at the rear, filling space at the base of the wall and the shrubs, and how the perennials

with more showy, variegated foliage are sited in a more prominent position at the front.

The spring also sees a steadily spreading carpet of the delicate white flowers of *Anemone nemorosa*, a species that can be slow initially. And, in late spring, *Viburnum × burkwoodii* and *Daphne odora* 'Aureo-marginata' produce their richly scented flowers.

Towards the front of the border are two plants of *Euphorbia schillingii*, Penelope's 'favourite out of all the euphorbias'. Their elegant leaves have a central, creamy vein while the red-flushed stems act as a foil to the greeny-yellow flowers borne in early summer. Also flowering in early summer is the sweetly scented *Philadelphus coronarius* 'Aureus', a relatively compact form that has yellow-tinged leaves which scorch easily in strong sunlight, making it an ideal variety for this shady spot. And on the wall at the rear are two climbers, the yellow-flowering honeysuckle (*Lonicera tragophylla*), and the white, self-clinging *Hydrangea petiolaris*.

[Left] *Hamamelis* ×
intermedia 'Jelena'

[Right] *Hamamelis mollis*

REQUIREMENTS

1. Being mostly woodland plants, these species benefit from a humus rich, free-draining soil that stays moist through the summer. Of all the plants used, the daphne, hamamelis and corylopsis most need these conditions; the latter two have a reputation for doing better on acid or neutral soil.

2. All the shrubs and perennials used are notably long-lived, which means this planting could last for decades. Problems of serious competition will only result if the plants are arranged too closely. Shrubs that become too large, relative to their neighbours, will need pruning to reduce their size at some stage, and some of the perennials, the symphytum especially, will need thinning out. Eventually, depending upon planting distances, the shrubs will tend to intermesh, forming a solid mass. This may be so dense that it denies space or light to the perennials. In the long-term, the diversity of this planting will therefore decrease without any intervention, but it will become lower maintenance.

A mixed shrub border in full sun

plant list

1. *Clematis* 'Bill Mackenzie'	(1)
2. *Polygonatum odoratum* 'Variegatum'	(7)
3. *Nepeta* 'Six Hills Giant'	(10)
4. *Leptospermum* × *grandiflorum*	(1)
5. *Phlomis longifolia*	(5)
6. *Agapanthus campanulatus*	(14)
7. *Cephalaria gigantea*	(14)
8. *Salvia guaranitica* 'Blue Enigma'	(7)
9. *Campanula lactiflora* 'Pritchard's Variety'	(18)
10. *Verbascum chaixii*	(14)
11. *Abutilon vitifolium*	(1)
12. *Bupleurum fruticosum*	(1)
13. *Euphorbia longifolia*	(5)
14. *Alchemilla mollis*	(18)
15. *Verbascum pyramidatum*	(7)
16. *Baptisia australis*	(3)
17. *Lavandula angustifolia* 'Hidcote'	(2)
18. *Stauntonia hexaphylla*	(1)
19. *Salvia uliginosa*	(18)
20. *Rosa* 'Frühlingsgold'	(1)
21. *Clematis* 'Perle d'Azure'	(1)
22. *Ceanothus* 'Italian Skies'	(1)
23. *Clematis tangutica*	(1)
24. *Cytisus battandieri*	(1)
25. *Lilium* 'Golden Splendour'	(24)
26. *Euphorbia schillingii*	(5)
27. *Phlomis fruticosa*	(2)

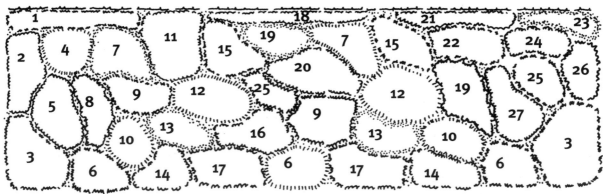

Garden Wall   Garden Wall

This border perhaps represents Penelope Hobouse's interests most clearly. 'It is for a fairly mild climate,' she says, and 'reflects my passion for broad-leaved evergreen shrubs, greys and greens, euphorbias and phlomis,' whose shapes, colours and textures provide structure and a particularly strong sense of continuity. The predominant colour scheme is violet-blue and yellow right through the summer, with enough evergreens to provide winter interest.

The front is framed by lavender and, at the corners, there is a foaming mass of catmint (*Nepeta* 'Six Hills Giant'). The wall at the back is planted with a variety of clematis, including two of the so-called lemon-peel ones ('Bill Mackenzie' and *C. tangutica*) that flower later than most, from mid- to late summer. In the centre is the climber *Stauntonia hexaphylla* with wonderful, scented, creamy flowers in spring and rather exotic-looking, divided leaves. There is a good mixture of plant forms here, many of the shrubs having a mound-like growth habit to contrast with the more upright habit of many of the perennials, especially the starkly upright spikes of two verbascums. 'I love the upright verbascums,' says Penelope, 'and I love them to self-seed, although this cannot be expected if a mulch is used.'

REQUIREMENTS

This border really gets going in early summer, with the pale yellow rose 'Frühlingsgold', several euphorbias, the nepetas and ever-useful *Alchemilla mollis*. Early summer also sees the flowering of the ceanothus, abutilon, pineapple-scented Moroccan broom (*Cytisus battandieri*), and the the herbaceous *Baptisia australis* with its lead-blue, pea-like flowers that are followed by attractive, near-black seed heads.

A little later in summer, the lilies flower and the shrub *Bupleurum fruticosum* has a mass of green-yellow bloom. This is another of Penelope's favourites, and is typical of the Mediterranean, evergreen shrubbery to which she is so drawn but which may be too subtle for some tastes. It forms a subtle centrepiece for this border, and provides a good foil for the stronger colours.

There are some good blues for midsummer, including agapanthus and *Campanula lactiflora*. The *Leptospermum* × *grandiflorum* also flowers about now, making a shrub (or sometimes small tree) that is somewhat tender (like the rest of its genus), although it is obviously a favourite of Penelope's. 'I think it is the hardiest leptospermum and the one most adaptable to alkaline soil. It is also the most reliable and has very good sized white flowers.' While it loves sun and needs good drainage, it must be in a position where it will never dry out.

Late summer and autumn are lit up by the exceptionally clear blue flowers of *Salvia uliginosa* and the deep blue *Salvia guaranitica* 'Blue Enigma', two of many exceptionally rich colours provided by the salvia group.

1. This border is built around plants that appreciate a mild climate. The wall provides protection, reflecting the sun's heat back on to the border, and keeps off strong winds. Interestingly, several of the evergreens, notably the bupleurum and leptospermum, tolerate strong, mild sea winds but hate cold winds. Any reasonable soil will suit the majority of the plants, but it should not be drought prone or some species will suffer. The phlomis, lavandula and ceanothus are the most drought tolerant, the *Salvia uliginosa* the least.

2. This scheme should continue to give pleasure for many years because only a few of the species used are short-lived: the verbascums are little more than biennials but nearly always self-sow, while the abutilon and ceanothus will last for 7–10 years, and the low Mediterranean shrubs – lavander and phlomis – will eventually become scraggily senescent and need replacing. Annual light pruning will help keep them tidy though, giving them a lifespan of 12–15 years. The verbascums will self-sow on most soils, scattering themselves around, that helps create a natural, spontaneous atmosphere. Only occasionally will self-seeding become a problem, but surplus seedlings are easily hoed off.

3. The clematis will benefit from annual pruning, the heaviness of which depends upon how much they need to be restricted in size. In areas that might experience a severe frost, the plant can be protected by a thick winter mulch of straw, well weighted down.

Penelope Hobhouse A mixed shrub border in full sun

A border in sun, backed by a yew hedge

plant list

1. *Thalictrum glaucum*	(10)
2. *Phlox maculata* 'Alpha'	(10)
3. *Geranium* 'Johnson's Blue'	(12)
4. *Anaphalis margaritacea* var. *cinnamomea*	(18)
5. *Kniphofia* 'Wrexham Buttercup'	(10)
6. *Crambe cordifolia*	(10)
7. *Clematis recta*	(2)
8. *Phormium cookianum*	(10)
9. *Anemone* 'Honorine Jobert'	(10)
10. *Lilium regale* var. *album*	(10)
11. *Euphorbia characias* subsp. *wulfenii* 'Lambrook Gold'	(3)
11. *Euphorbia characias* subsp. *wulfenii* 'John Tomlinson'	(3)
12. *Perovskia atriplicifolia*	(24)
13. *Aster* × *frikartii* 'Mönch'	(18)
14. *Galega orientalis*	(10)
14. *Galega officinalis*	(10)
15. *Aconitum carmichaelii* 'Arendsii'	(7)
16. *Gaura lindheimerii*	(16)
17. *Iris pallida*	(18)
18. *Phlomis fruticosa*	(1)
19. *Clematis macropetala*	(2)
20. *Clerodendrum trichotomum*	(1)
21. *Olearia* 'Waikariensis'	(1)

Yew Hedge

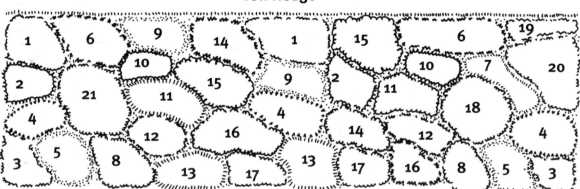

Designed to provide a long summer of blues, yellows and some whites, this border is backed by a yew hedge whose dark foliage makes a splendid backdrop to most colours. It is largely herbaceous, with only three shrubby species. There is *Clerodendrum trichotomum* with white flowers in late summer, followed by its rather extraordinary turquoise berries, and the yellow flowers of *Phlomis fruticosa* and *Olearia* 'Waikariensis'. The olearia is one of the New Zealand daisy bushes and is a particular favourite of Penelope's, being covered in clusters of white daisy-like flowers in midsummer. With the phlomis it creates the evergreen, shrubby pivot of this border. Since they do not drop their dead flowers, both will need dead-heading.

Two cultivars of *Euphorbia characias* subsp. *wulfenii* start the year off in late winter, with *Iris pallida* making early growth. Late spring or early summer sees the small, mauve-blue *Clematis macropetala* at the rear in flower with the lilac-blue iris blooming a little later, followed by *Geranium* 'Johnson's Blue' that has mauve-blue flowers and a tidy, low, clump-forming habit, perfect for the front of the border. Later on there is the white and silver *Anaphalis margaritacea* var. *cinnamomea* and the contrasting architectural spikes of the yellow-flowering *Kniphofia* 'Wrexham Buttercup'. All kniphofias are excellent border plants, especially for their vertical shapes. Their foliage also has a linear quality that contrasts with other leaf shapes in the border.

There are two clumps of the dark-eyed, pink-flowering *Phlox maculata* 'Alpha' in this scheme, that help fill what Penelope describes as 'the awkward gap' in summer, before the big flush of late summer- and autumn-flowering perennials. The two big clumps of *Perovksia atriplicifolia*, with a haze of blue flowers in midsummer, fulfil the same role. *Gaura lindheimeri* is a plant that Penelope is very enthusiastic about because it has good sized white flowers on wiry, branching stems, and looks good until well into autumn. Since the stems are not that visible from a distance, the flowers appear to hover above surrounding plants like butterflies. The flowering season ends with white *Anemone* 'Honorine Jobert' and the blue *Aster × frikartii* 'Mönch'.

Most of the plants die down over winter, leaving the two evergreen shrubs and the spiky, evergreen form of *Phormium cookianum* at the front as the main source of interest. Many plants may be cut back in the autumn, but do leave the perovskias until spring because their attractive, branching stems turn an attractive bleached colour over winter.

REQUIREMENTS

1. Any reasonable soil and an open, somewhat sheltered position will suit the plants well, all of which, with the exception of the gaura, are long-lived.

2. In time, some will outgrow their alloted spaces, particularly the anemones that form very large clumps, while in a mild climate the phormium may become very large. It is difficult to reduce a phormium in size, but all the herbaceous plants are easy to divide and the shrubs can be pruned. The clerodendrum will eventually develop a tree-like habit, creating a certain amount of shade. The geranium, anemone and euphorbias (when young) are the only species that will really thrive in this situation without regular maintenance. The phlox should be divided into sections every few years, creating more new plants.

113

Nöel Kingsbury

In 1994 I decided to travel abroad looking at gardens. I had done some garden design in England but was very disillusioned with most of the contemporary design work. Very little seemed to be forward-looking or experimental, and the emphasis was on evoking the glories of the past, 'tradition' and 'period' being the buzzwords. Frustrated with this lack of creativity I wanted to see what was happening overseas. After visiting Brazil, the USA and Holland (where I first met Piet Oudolf), I went to Germany where I had heard of rumours of a new ecologically based and nature-inspired planting style.

So, one fine June day I found myself in Munich's Westpark, looking down on a shallow amphitheatre of planting. It included many familiar plants – with bearded irises, red valerian, mallows, ornamental grasses and alliums – but all arranged in a way that was totally new to me. Instead of being lined up in the familiar border, they were spread out with an almost field-like generosity. There were broad paths full of people on that public holiday, but also a network of narrow paths that wended their way through the plantings, giving access to all areas, although at first sight these paths were invisible. The overall effect was that a herbaceous border had been crossed with a wildflower meadow. It was overwhelming.

I have termed this style of planting the 'open-border style' because it eliminates the rigid format of the traditional English border, where plants are looked *at* against a backdrop of a fence, wall or hedge. Instead, it makes it

possible to look *over* or even *through* them. Another eye-opener to me was that very few plants were arranged in the blocks that most English-style designers used. I was used to a style that never questioned the prevailing dogma in which, at least in medium-sized or larger borders, plants were set out in multiples, creating blocks. But in this German open border the plants were blended and intermingled, giving an effect that was much more naturalistic and, I think, more subtle, complex and sophisticated.

Those with a small garden may well ask: 'What has all this got to do with me?' More than they may think, I would argue. I have always been struck by how many Dutch front gardens, never very big, are laid out with planting all the way across instead of having narrow borders edging an area of lawn. In other words, if you do not need a lawn and like growing plants, dig it up and create a meadow-like effect. American gardeners with their vast acreages of lawn have even more possibilities.

Creating these open borders requires thinking differently about how plants are used. To create a sense of a unified whole in a large area means you need to repeat plants, and this is most effectively done with those that have a dramatic appearance (for example, kniphofias and verbascums) or which have a long season of interest (many ornamental grasses). Such repetition injects a sense of rhythm and visual unity.

Such aesthetic questions are important, but the key to this approach is plant ecology. The plantings I so admired in Munich, and later in other German cities, were developed specifically for public spaces, and were meant to be low-maintenance and low input. Building on the work of Karl Foerster, the 20th-century German nurseryman and prolific writer who inspired a whole generation of designers and gardeners, the following plans create communities of plants all chosen because their ecological requirements (for water, light and nutrients, etc.) can be readily supplied by the site.

For example, the Westpark planting was an example of steppe planting, named after the grassy environment found in eastern Europe on free-draining soils. Steppe plants have to be able to survive severe winter cold and possible drought. They are not pampered and watered as are traditional English borders. And while their main flowering period is short but spectacular, many are evergreen with attractive grey foliage, giving a long season of interest.

An emphasis on plant communities is central to the German parks approach. This is not surprising because the study of natural plant communities (known as plant sociology) has played a major part in German botany. In the wild, particular plants are found together time and time again, in roughly similar conditions. Such a predictable set of plants can then be classified as a community.

Some of the most popular combinations used in the parks utilize plants found at woodland edges, a rich habitat where plants of both open and shady places can be found together. They are often native to central Europe. Other combinations, as in the steppe plantings, use species growing in similar habitats from a wide range of countries.

Ironically, the fertile, consistently moist soils favoured by traditional gardeners, are the least suitable for the open-border style. This is because weeds thrive in such resource-rich soil while perennials and ornamental grasses have a tendency to compete aggressively against each other, detracting from the look.

[Left] The steppe area in Munich's Westpark in Germany in June, with red valerian, *Centranthus ruber*, and bearded irises the dominant feature.

[Right] Yellow spires of *Verbascum nigrum* dominate a park in Ingolstadt, Bavaria in July, the product of many years self-sowing.

[Left] A border designed by the author includes multi-coloured achillea hybrids and purple *Salvia nemorosa*

[Right] In the author's own garden, late May is dominated by purple *Geranium sylvaticum* 'Birch Lilac', which has been allowed to self-sow, and *Aquilegia vulgaris*

Interestingly, in recent years I have found many of my German colleagues paying a lot of attention to the American prairie as a model of a highly attractive plant community that flourishes on very fertile soils. Experimental work has therefore started on adapting the prairie plant community to public gardens. Prairie species are already familiar to European gardeners because many have been in cultivation as border plants for more than a century. They include monardas, rudbeckias, helianthus (perennial sunflowers) asters and solidagos.

Back home, I have been experimenting with the German approach. The mild and humid climate of the west of England creates both opportunities and problems for a low-maintenance style. The combination of unpredictable, but generally high, rainfall with a long growing season means you can be more flexible about combining plants from different habitats than in mainland Europe. For example, you can combine woodland-edge species (*Geranium endressii*) with dry meadow plants (*Salvia nemorosa*), whereas these plants would be less likely to succeed together in a region where summer and winter are more distinct.

The problems are caused by the long growing season. Most ornamental perennials are winter dormant, but some of the most aggressive weeds are able to grow right through the winter, particularly the tough pasture grasses. Failure to keep such weeds in check means that the desired perennials get swamped. Consequently, in west-coast climates there has to be a greater emphasis on weed control. Plantings that are going to be low maintenance need to be based on robust weed-suppressing perennials, wood chip mulches must be used to inhibit the growth of weed seedlings, and the removal of winter weeds with a glyphosate-based weedkiller may be a necessity.

In addition to plantings for public spaces, I have been able to monitor a long-term experiment with a large, open border, using moisture-loving perennials, at Cowley Manor Hotel, Gloucestershire, UK. Despite several years of neglect while the ownership changed, it has been very successful, with relatively little weed incursion and, despite some species spreading at the expense of others, has remained very attractive. The most aggressive spreaders have included the pink *Geranium × oxonianum*

types, although some asters have been equally vigorous, including *Aster* 'Climax'. However, in a garden they can easily be controlled while in wild gardens their vigour may be welcome.

Elsewhere in Britain, there have been other experiments with naturalistic planting. Nigel Dunnett and James Hitchmough, at the landscape department at the University of Sheffield, in the UK, have been working with a number of approaches using annuals, and perennials in rough grass and coppice (ie. using a combination of perennials and shrubs, the latter being regularly cut to the ground). At Lady Farm, Somerset, UK, owner Judy Pearce and designer Mary Payne have developed a particularly spectacular steppe-style planting where knlphofias make a dramatic appearance studding a slope with their fiery flower spikes, with a wide variety of other perennials and grasses.

The most interesting adventure, though, has been at The Garden House, Devon, UK, where head gardener Keith Wiley has been working for several years with a wide variety of nature-inspired plantings, often informed by his foreign travels. The South African Karoo desert has been the idea behind a very colourful combination of annuals, alpine meadows inspired a merging of a border of perennials with wild grasses, and Crete a stone wall covered with drought-tolerant plants.

Self-sowing is a key part of the appearance of the garden at The Garden House, with plants such as *Verbena bonariensis*, a tall, wiry stemmed, long-flowering species, scattering itself around. This is one of many species which are short-lived but survive through prolific seeding. In the garden this injects a feeling of spontaneity that can never be achieved through design alone, and which is a crucial part of many of the most successful naturalistic plantings. Another key factor is the widespread use of grasses. Since they are strongly linked to wild and semi-natural places, adding a few to a scheme immediately evokes a natural feel.

Naturalistic planting schemes undoubtedly look best on a large scale, which makes them especially suited to public spaces, where sustainable and relatively low-maintenance plantings make a viable alternative to traditional rose beds

and bedding schemes. However, I believe that there is also scope for smaller-scale plantings based on the open border style. If plant height and spread is restricted to less than 30cm (1ft), there are many species that can be used to create very attractive mixtures. Creeping evergreen species with good foliage can be particularly effective if they are allowed to merge with each other, providing a background for taller plants. Varieties of sedum, acaena, cotula and thyme are ideal for this purpose, with small grassy plants, such as forms of festuca and carex, growing out of them. There is a lot of potential here, as yet largely unexplored.

I find the whole area of naturalistic planting design incredibly exciting. There is so much to learn, so many new plants to try, and so many ways of combining them. I believe that gardeners should work with people from other disciplines to realize fully what they are doing. In particular ecologists have so much to teach us about how plants function in their habitats, with major implications for horticultural practice and design. Looking across traditional boundaries is a big part of the excitement.

Miscanthus sinesis 'Silberfeder' is a large, dramatic ornamental grass for the latter part of the growing season, here growing alongside yellow *Coreopsis tripteris*. Both thrive on moist, fertile soils and can be used in low maintenance plantings as they will survive a certain amount of weed competition. The large leaves on the left is the tree *Paulownia tomentosa*, kept as a coppiced shrub

Steppe

plant list

1. Stipa tenuissima	(17)
2. Molinia caerulea 'Edith Dudzus'	(1)
3. Carex comans	(4)
4. Tulipa sprengeri	(50)
5. Allium schoenoprasum	(2)
6. Allium hollandicum	(15)
7. Campanula rotundifolia	(3)
8. Knautia macedonica	(2)
9. Centranthus ruber	(3)
10. Iris germanica	(10)
11. Salvia nemorosa 'Ostfriesland'	(2)
12. Salvia 'Mainacht'	(2)
13. Salvia 'Viola Klose'	(2)
14. Thymus coccineus	(3)
15. Aster amellus 'King George'	(2)
16. Kniphofia 'Little Maid'	(3)
17. Nepeta × *faassenii*	(1)
18. Origanum laevigatum 'Rosenkuppel'	(4)
19. Perovskia atriplicifolia	(2)

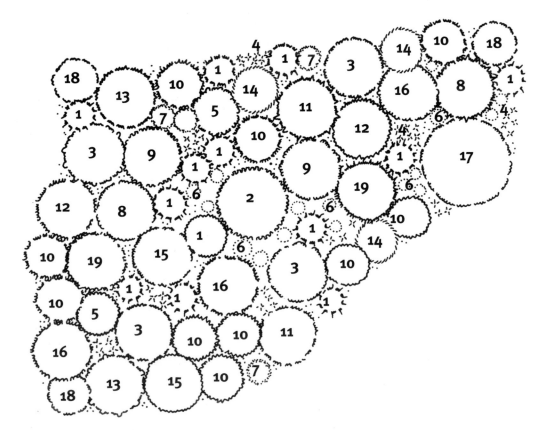

The starting point and inspiration for this hot, dry bank is the steppe, the great, dry grassland of eastern Europe. Not all the plants are actually steppe species but they are all reasonably drought resistant. They are also hardy, which makes this kind of planting more useful than Mediterranean -type schemes where the drought-resistant plants can succumb in bad winters.

Grasses, including the wispy *Stipa tenuissima* and the sedge (*Carex comans*), are the key to the naturalistic look. The former has a good nine months of interest, and the latter is evergreen, giving some winter interest. As with other dry habitats, the best season is spring and early summer, with some species continuing to provide colour until autumn. Since dry land vegetation tends to be sparse, the planting does not need to keep all the ground covered.

The bulbs could be a major feature from late winter until early summer. I have only shown two bulb species, the spring-flowering *Tulipa sprengeri* and the dramatic, early summer-flowering *Allium hollandicum*, with its ball of flowers on top of an upright, bare stem, but many more could be used.

The irises highlight the main early summer-flowering season. When choosing your favourites from the bewildering range of hybrids, make sure that they are medium-sized. They can be accompanied by salvia hybrids and the well-known *Centranthus ruber*. Later on, *Knautia macedonica* starts producing its extraordinary dark red flowers, that often carry on until late summer. *Kniphofia* 'Little Maid' flowers at the same time. While not amongst the most drought-resistant species, it has that rather exotic look that people often expect from dry plantings. Its strikingly upright form is also markedly different from that of the other plants used here. 'Little Maid' is comparatively small but in larger plantings, bigger cultivars with stronger colours could be used.

Late summer and autumn tend to be relatively sombre in dry climates. However, this combination includes an origanum, aster and perovskia that provide good colour at this time. The salvias and the nepeta will also repeat flower now if they are cut back after their main flowering in early summer. Summer rain or watering also helps promote repeat flowering.

In areas with milder winter temperatures, where the minimum rarely dives below −10°C (12°F), these plants could be combined with Mediterranean dwarf shrubs, for example species of cistus, lavender and phlomis etc. This adds a further dimension in form and more winter interest from the grey and silver foliage.

REQUIREMENTS

1. Ideal for a dry site or a thin alkaline soil, this planting is also possible on any well-drained soil, including a slope or bank.

2. Given that there are gaps between many of the plants, weed infiltration may be a problem. On flat or gently sloping sites this can be overcome by using a gravel mulch that will also help conserve moisture in the ground and provide an excellent seed bed for self-sowing species, such as the centranthus and carex. Some weeding of especially vigorous species may be necessary.

3. This is definitely a long-term planting, and any species that do die out after five years or so (possibly the centranthus and salvias) will often self-seed and create replacement plants

4. Irises tend to form large, spreading clumps after a few years, with a decline in vigour, and possible collisions with neighbouring plants. When this happens, they can be dug up when dormant and divided, with some of the sections being replanted.

5. The bearded irises (*Iris germanica*) need to have their roots exposed to the sun in temperate climates. Also, leave gaps for bulbs, particularly those that, like species tulips, need to get a good summer baking if they are to flower again next year.

[Left] *Tulipa sprengeri*

[Right] *Nepeta* × *faassenii*,

A low maintenance, naturalistic planting

plant list

1. *Alchemilla mollis* (6)
2. *Anemone* × *hybrida* 'Honorine Jobert' (3)
3. *Aster divaricatus* (10)
4. *Aster laevis* 'Climax' (1)
5. *Aster lateriflorus* 'Lady in Black' (2)
6. *Brunnera macrophylla* (2)
7. *Calamagrostis* × *acutifolia* 'Karl Foerster' (2)
8. *Carex comans* (6)
9. *Eupatorium rugosum* 'Braunlaub' (7)
10. *Euphorbia palustris* (1)
11. *Geranium* × *oxonianum* 'Claridge Druce' (3)
12. *Geranium endressii* (3)
13. *Geranium* 'Johnson's Blue' (4)
14. *Geranium* 'Spinners' (3)
15. *Geranium versicolor* (7)
16. *Geranium* × *oxonianum* 'Wargrave Pink' (2)
17. *Luzula sylvatica* 'Marginata' (9)
18. *Persicaria amplexicaulis* (4)
19. *Persicaria bistorta* 'Superba' (4)
20. *Rudbeckia fulgida* (9)
21. *Vinca major* (8)
22. *Galanthus nivalis* (50)
23. *Narcissus* 'Liberty Bells' (50)

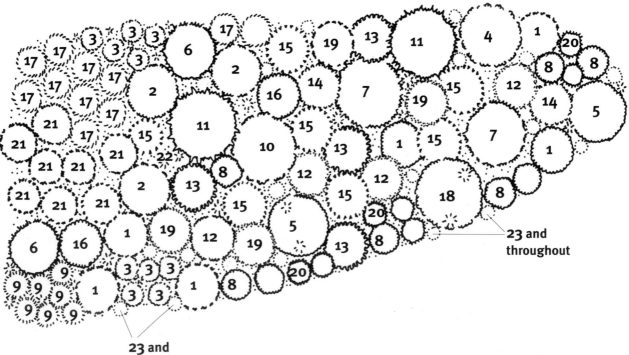

23 and throughout

23 and throughout

This design is intended for a site (for example, a slope) that is difficult to maintain. Instead of using grass that would have to be mown, or shrubs that can look dull for much of the year, use robust perennials that are good at looking after themselves and which effectively smother weeds.

Another feature is the way in which different plant combinations are used as the distance from the tree increases. The area around the base of the tree is shady and dry, where only the most robust species will grow. They include the glossy evergreen *Luzula sylvatica* 'Marginata', that eventually forms tight mats, and the evergreen periwinkle (*Vinca major*), that has blue flowers in spring.

Where light and soil moisture levels begin to increase away from the tree, there are two white, late summer-flowering perennials, *Eupatorium rugosum* 'Braunlaub'

and *Aster divaricatus*. These plants are all grouped together to ensure that they form solid clumps with time, otherwise they might compete with each other, which can lead to one variety smothering the others.

In the lighter shade under the outer canopy of the tree are four key plants with a variety of geraniums. The four are *Brunnera macrophylla*, with blue flowers in spring and large, weed-smothering leaves, *Anemone* × *hybrida* 'Honorine Jobert', with pure white flowers in late summer and autumn, *Persicaria bistorta* 'Superba', with pink flower spikes in late spring, and the low-growing, lime-green *Alchemilla mollis*, with lime green flowers.

The pink geraniums provide the backbone of this planting. They include *Geranium* × *oxonianum* 'Claridge Druce', *G. endressii*, *G.* × *oxonianum* 'Wargrave pink' and *G. versicolor*. They are very useful as weed-smothering ground-cover, especially for west coast gardens where a long growing season sees plenty of evergreen weeds, such as grasses and creeping buttercup. The geraniums' semi-evergreen nature allows them to compete against such weeds, and their repeat-flowering habit makes them very decorative. Two of the slightly less vigorous blue geraniums ('Johnson's Blue' and 'Spinners') are included for contrast.

The other elements in the planting fall into two categories, the taller upright plants and the front of border plants. The former provide variation in height, structural interest and give colour at times when the geraniums are not at their best. The latter provide a tidy edge to the planting on the lower side, which is the most visible one in this garden.

The main structural plant among the tall uprights is *Calamagrostis* × *acutiflora* 'Karl Foerster', its bolt upright flower and seed heads making a striking feature from early summer to late winter. *Euphorbia palustris* provides a mound of yellow-green flowers in spring and some good autumn colour, while *Persicaria amplexicaulis* develops into a similar shape with masses of deep pinky-red spikes in the latter part of the season. Finally there are two asters, the very vigorous, clump-forming, purple-blue *A. laevis* 'Climax' and *A. lateriflorus* 'Lady in Black' that, by late summer, forms an almost shrub-like shape, covered in attractive dark foliage, before smothering itself with tiny, pale pink flowers in autumn.

The front of border plants include a bronze evergreen sedge (*Carex comans*), and the dark-eyed yellow *Rudbeckia fulgida* that flowers during the autumn. Both are short plants that can always be relied upon to look tidy.

The bare ground of perennial-based plantings can be unattractive in spring, but bulbs make all the difference. Here snowdrops (*Galanthus nivalis*) are scattered in clumps, with a spring-flowering daffodil (*Narcissus* 'Liberty Bells'). Smaller daffodils are better than larger ones because the somewhat untidy leaves left after flowering are less noticeable.

REQUIREMENTS

1. Any reasonable soil in good sunlight is suitable for this design, but not where there is too much tree shade. Most of the species used are tolerant of a wide range of conditions, with only prolonged drought, waterlogging or very poor soil being unsuitable. Being robust growers, no soil preparation is generally required, apart from weeding.

2. This is a low-maintenance scheme requiring only one session of work a year after the first year. With the exception of the vinca and luzula, all the plants produce a substantial quantity of dead growth at the end of the season, which should be cut off and composted. The resulting compost can be applied as a mulch the year after.

3. Although the plant selection should suppress weeds quite effectively, there may sometimes be a problem (largely from grasses) in the late winter to mid-spring period. Given the slope, the best way to deal with the weeds is to use a glyphosate-based weed killer immediately after cutting back, carefully 'spot-spraying' the weeds.

4. In the long-term, there will be quite a bit of jockeying for position by these mostly vigorous plants. The only plants likely to suffer adversely are the smaller species at the front, the carex and rudbeckia. Plants impinging on them can be dug up and divided to limit their size and spread.

A prairie-style planting

plant list

1. *Aster cordifolius* 'Little Carlow' (4)
2. *Aster laevis* 'Arcturus' (2)
3. *Aster turbinellus* (3)
4. *Aster umbellatus* (2)
5. *Eupatorium fistulosum* (4)
6. *Geranium phaeum* 'Lily Lovell' (6)
7. *Geranium psilostemon* (3)
8. *Geranium sylvaticum* 'Birch Lilac' (10)
9. *Helianthus* 'Lemon Queen' (10)
10. *Helianthus* 'Sheila's Sunshine' (5)
11. *Lysimachia ciliata* 'Firecracker' (3)
12. *Miscanthus sinensis* 'Rotsilber' (1)
13. *Miscanthus sinensis* 'Silberfeder' (1)
14. *Molinia caerulea* 'Transparent' (3)
15. *Monarda fistulosa* (9)
16. *Rudbeckia* 'Juligold' (3)
17. *Solidago rugosa* 'Feuerwerke' (3)
18. *Vernonia crinita* (3)
19. *Veronica longifolia* (3)
20. *Veronicastrum virginicum* (3)
21. *Ajuga reptans* 'Caitlin's Giant' (2)
22. *Narcissus* 'February Gold' (50)

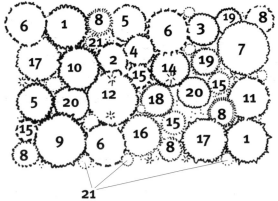

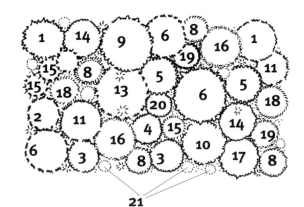

22 planted throughout

The North American prairie once covered a vast area with an incredibly rich plant community, a relatively limited number of grasses and a large number of tall, flowering herbaceous plants. Now almost entirely destroyed to make way for agriculture and urban development, remnants of the prairie have become an inspiration for contemporary naturalistic plantings.

This planting combines North American late-flowering prairie perennials with some lower-growing and earlier-flowering Eurasian species for a longer season of interest,

as well as some Eurasian grasses. The plan is designed for a site that fronts a lawn and backs onto decking, with a boardwalk connecting the two. The boardwalk is an invitation into the scheme, and provides an intimate sight of the planting. 'Into' really is the right word because the late-flowering varieties used are from 1.8–3.5m (5ft–11ft) high.

Narcissus 'February Gold' has been used to provide spring interest with the dark-leaved *Ajuga reptans* 'Caitlin's Giant'. Small narcissi and other dwarf bulbs are a good way of making later-flowering perennial plantings

interesting in spring and will be dormant by the time the perennials start to shade the ground. The evergreen ajuga provides winter interest and blue flowers in spring; it is one of the few creeping perennials that seems able to survive in the dense shade cast by the taller plants. It will eventually form sparse ground cover.

Late spring sees the deep mauve *Geranium sylvaticum* 'Birch Lilac' in flower, with emerging clumps of dark leaved *Lysimachia ciliata* 'Firecracker' and dark blue *Geranium phaeum* 'Lily Lovell'. By early summer the magenta *Geranium psilostemon* and pale blue *Veronica longifolia* and *Veronicastrum virginicum* will be making a striking combination, before the flowering of *Monarda fistulosa* kicks off the real prairie season.

The monarda has pale violet flowers but any of its hybrids, in shades of red, pink and mauve, could be used instead. From late summer until the first hard frosts, the dominant theme is yellow and blue-violet. Golden yellows will be provided by *Rudbeckia* 'Juligold' and *Solidago rugosa* 'Feuerwerke', the pale, almost primrose-yellows by

Helianthus 'Lemon Queen' and *H*. 'Sheila's Sunshine', and blue/violets by *Aster cordifolius* 'Little Carlow', *A. laevis* 'Arcturus' and *A. turbinellus*. At the very end of the season, *Vernonia crinita* contributes its distinctive red-tinged violet flowers. Also flowering now is the creamy *Aster umbellatus* and the flesh-pink *Eupatorium fistulosum* . All these late perennials are excellent butterfly-attracting plants.

A genuine prairie planting is dominated by grasses (prairie is nearly always made using a seed mix of grasses and perennials, but it can also be evoked using large grasses and perennials from a variety of different areas which must be tall and late flowering). However, here grasses are used as an additional decorative element, their winter appearance being especially valuable. Though not strictly speaking prairie grasses, they are reliable and easily available. The miscanthus cultivars are the main winter feature, but some of the other perennials have strong enough stems to withstand the winter, and can appear quite attractive. Their seed heads are potentially a good food source for birds.

[Left] Golden-yellow
Solidago rugosa
dominates this autumnal
planting of perennials.
Pale yellow *Helianthus*
'Lemon Queen' is
to the left

REQUIREMENTS

1. A site in full sun is important for this planting, with a soil that is reasonably fertile and moisture-retaining but not waterlogged.

2. The only maintenance, apart from early season weeding, is the annual cutting back of dead stems – which needs to be completed in late winter before the bulbs start to emerge. There will be plenty of dead growth for composting, but if it is going to overwhelm a modest compost heap, shred it. Then scatter the remains over the soil as a mulch to recycle nutrients.

3. Many prairie plants do not start to grow until late spring, which might mean that in regions with mild winters and a long growing season, the bare soil surface becomes a seedbed for weeds. The danger is they might get established before the bulk of the plants start to grow. This can be largely prevented by using a 3–5cm (1½–2in) deep woodchip mulch between the plants.

A glyphosate-based weedkiller can be used to kill any surviving weeds by spot-spraying them, preferably just after cutting back the perennials. Or they can be dug out by hand, but take care not to mix the mulch and the soil, ruining the effect of the former.

4. All plants here, with the exception of the monarda, form long-lived, solid clumps. However the monarda will tend to send out 'runners', resulting in the plant re-locating itself. If the border eventually becomes somewhat crowded, dig up the plant clumps and reduce them by division, using the excess sections elsewhere in the garden.

An exotic border

plant list

1. Acanthus mollis	(1)
2. Aralia racemosa	(1)
3. Bergenia cordifolia	(9)
4. Crocosmia 'Lucifer'	(2)
5. Helleborus argutifolius	(2)
6. Hosta sieboldiana 'Elegans'	(4)
7. Ligularia stenocephala 'The Rocket'	(1)
8. Ligularia dentata	(1)
9. Petasites japonicus 'Giganteus'	(1)
10. Asplenium scolopendrium	(5)
11. Polystichum setiferum	(2)
12. Indocalamus tesselatus	(1)
13. Luzula sylvatica 'Marginata'	(5)
14. Miscanthus floridulus	(1)
15. Euphorbia mellifera	(1)
16. Fatsia japonica	(1)
17. Musa basjoo	(1)
18. Paulownia tomentosa	(1)
19. Salix magnifica	(1)
20. Trachycarpus fortunei	(1)
21. Viburnum davidii	(2)
22. Aristolochia macrophylla	(1)
23. Clematis armandii	(1)

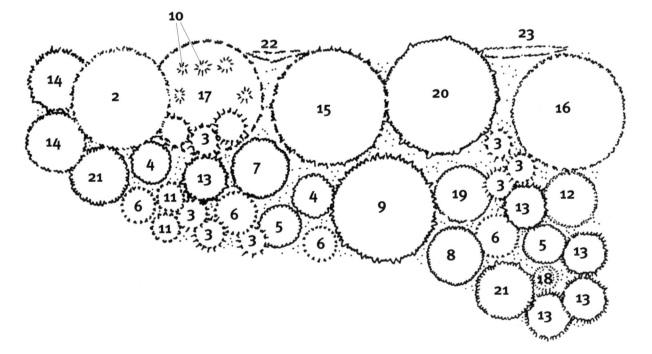

This border, designed for a south- or west-facing corner between two sheltering walls, brings together a variety of hardy plants with foliage that is luxuriant enough to convince most that they might be in the tropics. One tender species, the banana (*Musa basjoo*), is included, and is worth all efforts to protect it over winter for its spectacularly exotic appearance.

Since many of the best hardy exotica are big plants, space is needed. However, in some cases it is possible to restrict their size by pruning and other techniques. To compensate, I have tried to include plenty of smaller and more common, usually herbaceous, plants with lush foliage. When used in combination they can look quite exotic. They are also able to fill smaller spaces and act as ground cover.

The scene is set by the bamboo with its particularly broad, tropical-looking leaves and the hardy palm (*Trachycarpus*). During winter, when the bamboo has been wrapped up against the cold, the evergreen fatsia and the rounded shrub *Euphorbia mellifera* will still be here to create the right impression. A number of the smaller plants are also evergreen. They include the bergenia, hellebore and luzula. *Luzula sylvatica* is a quite exceptional plant, and with its broad leaves looks very exotic and makes effective ground cover in difficult, dry shade. The evergreen hart's tongue fern (*Asplenium scolopendrium*) is very tolerant of deep shade and can be spectacular *en masse*.

Midsummer to autumn is the best period for this border, with the ligularias flowering and the almost sugar cane-like giant grass, *Miscanthus floridulus*, reaching its maximum height of 3m (10ft). The deciduous shrubs (the paulownia and salix) will also be at their best. I say shrubs, but these two are naturally small trees. Here, however, they are kept shorter by pollarding and coppicing. These traditional techniques involve cutting back very hard to a point either well above ground level (pollarding) or close to ground level (coppicing). Not only do they keep large plants within bounds, but annual pruning results in dramatically larger-than-normal leaves. In fact visitors to my garden ask more about these plants than any other.

REQUIREMENTS

1. A site sheltered from strong winds is essential because the large leaves easily get damaged. Protection from severe frosts is not so vital, except for the euphorbia and bamboo. A fertile soil that stays reasonably moist in summer is important, especially for the ligularia and hosta.

2. The pruning of the salix and the paulownia has been mentioned. After coppicing there will be 2m (6ft) and more of growth. Pollard the paulownia at about 2m (6ft) above ground level and it will make its annual growth on top of this, creating a more tree-like effect than with the coppiced plants, while creating space to grow herbaceous plants below.

3. The giant-leaved petasites is spectacular, but especially on moist soils is dangerously invasive. However, it can be kept within bounds if planted within a barrier of heavy-duty plastic sheeting, buried vertically to a depth of 30cm (1ft). The same technique can also be used to keep the bamboo from spreading.

[Left] *Crocosmia*
'Lucifer'

[Centre] *Asplenium scolopendrium*

[Right] *Trachycarpus fortunei*

4. *Musa basjoo* will need protection in most gardens, particularly in the early years. The roots will survive at least −10°C [12F], but the best results are gained if the less hardy stems are protected. Wrap them in sheets of bubble-plastic, secured by wire or string, over winter. Eventually the plant will flower, bear little inedible bananas and then die, but not before producing several daughter stems, building up a substantial clump.

5. Given these management techniques this border should look good for many years. Eventually some of the perennials and ground-cover plants will become too large and compete for space, but they can easily be thinned out.

Piet Oudolf

The Dutch designer, Piet Oudolf, has become one of the most enthusiastically received and talked about designers today. I believe this is largely because he has achieved the harmonious balancing of geometric structure and seemingly unrestrained natural growth that many find so inherently satisfying. Much of his work really is doing something new: he uses new plants and new forms, with a distinctly contemporary take on old themes.

The debate between the formal and informal in gardening is one of the most enduring in garden design history. At times, though, it has been not just a source of discord but of important, creative energy. The relationship between the two has tended to be dialectical, and the evolution of the 20th-century English style, the product of Vita Sackville-West, Gertrude Jekyll and others, has achieved its popularity and status because it accomplished some sort of reconciliation in this formal versus informal debate.

Strong formal structure in the form of hedges, *allées* and geometry filled with informal burgeoning vegetation such as herbaceous borders, shrubs, roses and exuberant climbers give us the carefree sense of the idealized, rose-bedecked cottage garden and the clarity and definition of classical order. Piet Oudolf is doing the same, but in a strikingly contemporary way.

After a career designing gardens in the Netherlands, Piet has now gone international. With his colleague, Arne Maynard, he won the Best Show Garden Award at

the Chelsea Flower Show, 2000, and with landscape architect Kathryn Gustafson he has designed a planting scheme for the lakeside Millennium Park complex, in Chicago, USA. He now combines working on larger public projects with private gardens.

Piet started training as a landscape gardener at age of 25. His first influence was inevitably Mien Ruys, the Bauhaus-trained designer whose architectural and modernist garden style dominated Dutch design for much of the 20th century, but who was actually very passionate about plants. 'She was everywhere, the only garden designer in Holland who was talking about plants and plantings while the others just talked about design,' Piet says. 'But by copying her, everyone clichéd what she did and her inventions lost their meaning.'

Piet's own passion for plants received a boost when he first came to England in 1977 and visited Alan Bloom's Dell Garden, in Norfolk, and Hidcote, in Gloucestershire, among other places. 'I loved the atmosphere of these gardens, the kind of dreamland, and the plants I had never seen,' he says.

At the start of his career Piet had been working in the densely populated western part of Holland. But, in 1982, he and his family moved to the more sparsely populated eastern province of Gelderland, and spent several years converting an old farmhouse in Hummelo. They also laid the groundwork for a nursery (run by his wife, Anja).

Piet was increasingly frustrated at not being able to obtain the plants he wanted for his designs, and decided to provide his own.

A key part of the next few years was spent finding these plants. In England, the Beth Chatto Nursery, in Essex, had plenty to offer, 'besides inspiring me,' he says, 'by the way that she ran the nursery... in fact she gave us the idea of setting up the nursery in the first place.' From here and elsewhere the Oudolfs bought geraniums, hellebores and lavateras, etc. German nurseries were also a valuable source of plants, in particular that of Ernst Pagels, in Ost Friesland, just across the border. Pagels had been a student of the highly influential nurseryman and writer Karl Foerster, whom Piet describes as 'my hero for his unconventional way of looking at plants'.

Piet and Anja also travelled in the Balkans collecting plants, a region especially rich in plant life, finding some particularly fine hellebores in Bosnia-Hercegovina just before the war broke out. There were as yet few customers at their nursery, Piet had temporarily stopped doing design work, and the only income was from Anja selling grasses and cut flowers to local florists. But the nursery soon took off and, in Britain, Piet was frequently known as the 'nurseryman who designs gardens' instead of the designer who had set up his own nursery.

Besides finding plants of wild origin, Piet has done a lot of work on plant selection, concentrating particularly on

asters, astrantias, monardas and sanguisorbas. Plant selection is a classic example of Dutch co-operation because Piet pays a local farmer to trial plants for him, so that he can later make a selection of the best, leaving the remainder to be ploughed in at the end of the season. Thorough and ruthless plant selection is essential. 'I need only the best,' he says.

Whereas Piet's earlier, pre-Hummelo work was strongly architectural, his later work has focused on a dramatic use of perennials, in conjunction with and counter-pointed by distinctly modern structural features.

He also emphasises that perennials have a distinct, unique structure of their own. Although colour combinations are often striking, it is, he says 'the perennials' structure that is the most important aspect in designing with them'. Plants are arranged according to the shape of their flower heads, or the overall shape of the plant. Much use is made of grasses and other plants that gardeners have previously tended to ignore, such as astrantias, sanguisorbas and umbellifers (members of the *Apiaceae* or cow-parsley family). Whatever their distinct colours, their primary appeal to Piet lies in their form and shape.

The key to understanding his exuberant combinations of perennials lies in appreciating his balance of plant structures. Piet tends to divide his perennials into categories: spires (narrow upright stems, such as digitalis), umbels (flattish, plate-like flower heads, such as achillea), buttons (scabious), and balls (alliums). These shapes are then combined to create contrasts with each other, starting with the largest and most strongly structural plants, which are often the grasses, or large perennials, such as *Eupatorium purpureum*.

He also believes that there is an important role for species with a much softer visual texture (for example, many of the grasses), or plants he describes as having 'transparency'. They include *Verbena bonariensis* and the grass *Stipa gigantea* which, though large, are nearly all stem, making it possible to see through them to the plants behind. He also likes what he calls 'filler plants'. They include the hardy geraniums that, while lacking structure, contribute flower colour, especially in the early part of the summer, before the more structural perennials have got into their stride.

At Bury Court Piet Oudolf has created a series of borders within the framework of an old farmyard. A stylized meadow of *Deschampsia cespitosa* 'Goldtau', on the right, provides a dramatic centrepiece

[Left] Mounds of *Origanum laevigatum* 'Herrenhausen', Sedum hybrid 'Munstead Red', *Astilbe chinensis* var. *taquetii* 'Purpurlanze' and monarda

[Right] The 'Dream park' at Enköping in Sweden, where large clumps of perennials, such as *Aconogonon* 'Johanneswolke', are used in a series of sinuous borders

In winter he likes the dead remains of the perennials to be left standing for as long as possible because he believes that this is when structure really counts. He is only partly joking when he says that 'a plant is only worth growing if it looks good when it is dead.' A meticulous photographer of his work, he was one of the first to appreciate the almost monochrome beauty of dead perennials in the winter frost and fog. The sharply defined seed heads of echinacea, sanguisorba, monarda and phlomis stand out in some of his designs against the indistinct forms of grass foliage or blackened eupatorium leaves. Everything looks like it ought to be familiar, but shorn of colour and petals, it can be very difficult to identify individual plants.

If all of this suggests that colour is not important, that is not true. Piet especially seems to like the mysterious dark red of *Astrantia* 'Hadspen Blood', *A. major* 'Claret' and *Cirsium rivulare* 'Atropurpureum'. But despite saying 'I am not a colour gardener' there is no doubt that Piet, at least subconsciously, is very good at creating effective colour combinations, often using strong pastels.

Piet's place in the history of garden and landscape design puts him firmly in the movement that seeks to bring back the wild and natural into the human habitat. 'My biggest inspiration is nature, not copying it but capturing the emotion,' he says. 'What I try to do is create an image of nature.' This can be particularly appreciated in late summer or autumn, when borders in his designs can almost overwhelm the onlooker with huge perennials and grasses. 'It is good to feel awe in front of plants,' he adds.

The partnership of James Van Sweden and Wolfgang Oehme in the USA is also part of this natural movement, and has been taken up by many designers in Germany.

But do not forget the other side to the Oudolf garden, which is formality. Not the clichéd formality of the classical European garden, with its right angles and straight lines, but something more contemporary and much more daring. Piet's own garden is the best place to understand this aspect of his work.

The first part of his garden features a strong diagonal path, the second a central axial one. Unlike the central axes of classical formality, with which other axes or features meet at right angles, this one has a staggered row of yew columns to either side, and runs through two asymmetric elliptical beds, filled with low ground-cover plants. It is an example of zig-zag symmetry, encouraging the viewer to look from side to side instead of ahead.

Whereas classical formality, with its dependence on right angles, tends to get to the focal points too quickly, thus being inappropriate for smaller spaces, Piet's approach makes the viewer slow down and appreciate what is on both sides. It is an effect that the art historian and gardener Sir Roy Strong describes as 'wonky baroque'.

Piet's first commission in Britain, the garden at Bury Court in Hampshire, is centred around a large area of lawn, and the diagonal thrust of its main path leads to a view over the surrounding countryside. Extensive borders of perennials and further paths entice the visitor away on either side and on to Piet's first gravel bed planting, with some wonderfully spiky eryngiums. This is a good place to appreciate a particularly characteristic Oudolf feature, the use of formal block planting.

Whereas the 20th-century English style used clipped trees essentially as a skeleton, turning them into hedges or regularly spaced geometric shapes, Piet's technique is to use them, and other formal features, to create static blocks of planting. They become an alternative to the much more dynamic and naturalistic perennial borders. Two examples at Bury Court include abstract shapes of box and a circular steel framework, like the outline of a drum, that is gradually being filled with *Cornus mas*, which is being trained up like a hedge.

Increasingly, Piet is being asked to create public plantings. Drömparken (Dream Park) in Enköping, Sweden, was the first large park he worked on, followed by extensive plantings at the Pensthorpe Waterfowl Trust at Fakenham, Norfolk, UK. In both, informal drifts of perennials are combined in large beds between gently winding paths, with no formal elements. His more recent commission at the Royal Horticultural Society's Garden, Surrey, UK, has seen him go in a completely new direction, dividing a very large double border into a series of rigid diagonal strips, each about 2m (6ft) wide, and composed of a mixture of three or four perennial varieties.

A corner planting for summer

plant list

1. *Achillea* 'Summerwine' (2)
2. *Deschampsia cespitosa* 'Goldtau' (1)
3. *Geranium* × *oxonianum* 'Rose Clair' (3)
4. *Geranium* 'Sirak' (3)
5. *Sedum* 'Bertram Anderson' (4)
6. *Eryngium alpinum* 'Blue Star' (2)
7. *Lythrum salicaria* 'Blush' (4)
8. *Baptisia australis* (2)
9. *Veronica spicata* 'Erika' (5)
10. *Sidalcea* 'Elsie Heugh' (4)
11. *Knautia macedonica* (5)
12. *Sesleria autumnalis* (1)
13. *Stachys monieri* 'Hummelo' (5)
14. *Iris sibirica* 'Light Blue' (4)
15. *Salvia* 'Mainacht' (2)
16. *Geum rivale* 'Leonard' (5)
17. *Liatris spicata* (6)
18. *Monarda* 'Scorpion' (1)
19. *Achillea* 'Hella Glashof' (2)
20. *Kalimeris incisa* (3)
21. *Astrantia major* 'Claret' (5)
22. *Aconitum* 'Newry Blue' (4)
23. *Briza media* 'Limouzi' (3)
24. *Papaver orientale* 'Karine' (2)

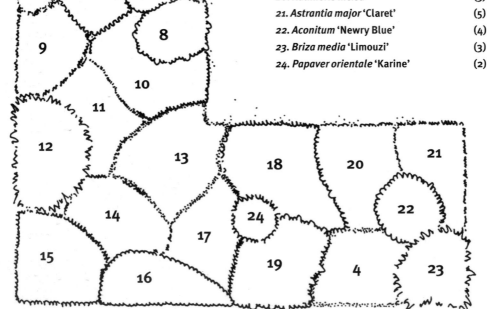

Baptisia australis

This border is designed to fit into a perpendicular space, perhaps around the corner of a house. Being highly visible it is vital that plants provide a long season of interest and continue to look, at the very least, acceptable after flowering. The design combines summer interest with some extra winter value.

The early to midsummer period sees the large pale pink flowers of the Oriental poppy (*Papaver orientale* 'Karine') with pale pink *Geranium* × *oxonianum* 'Rose Clair', the 1m (3ft) high reddish-pink *Veronica spicata* 'Erika', deep blue *Salvia* 'Mainacht' and *Iris sibirica* 'Light Blue'. A little later the achilleas start to flower, and include the deep wine-red 'Summerwine' and pale yellow 'Hella Glashof'.

During midsummer two upright perennials, the pale pink *Lythrum salicaria* 'Blush' and pale pink *Sidalcea* 'Elsie Heugh' take over, complemented by the steely grey-blue of *Baptisia australis* and the vivid violet of *Monarda* 'Scorpion'. The red-flowering *Sedum* 'Bertram Anderson' is the last to begin flowering, in late summer or early autumn, although the dark purple of its leaves has been a feature since spring.

Many of the plants selected have distinctive flower head shapes that continue to look strong well after the flowers have died. *Liatris spicata*, *Aconitum* 'Newry Blue' and *Veronica spicata* 'Erika' have distinctive spires, while *Salvia* 'Mainacht' has a more compact habit, with its masses of small, spike-like heads. Even in winter some species continue to look distinctive.

REQUIREMENTS

1. Full sun and free-draining fertile soil that can be relied upon never to dry out seriously is needed for this scheme to thrive. Fertility can be maintained by an annual (or biennial) spreading of compost, or well-rotted manure, over the soil in winter. Alternatively, shredded plant remains can be used as a winter mulch.

2. While the plants have been selected for their long period of interest, some mid-season tidying up or dead-heading may be necessary. The astrantia's dead flowers are definitely untidy looking, and the *Geranium × oxonianum* 'Rose Clair' has a habit of collapsing after flowering, necessitating a hard cut-back, but it will soon regrow to flower again in late summer. The rest will remain relatively tidy.

Come the autumn, how much and when to cut back is up to you. Many gardeners prefer to cut back dead plants selectively, removing the remains only of those that are definitely untidy, leaving those that have some structure and interest. But all should be cut back by late winter to avoid damaging any emerging bulbs.

This plant selection illustrates how the different growths of perennials have implications for the gardener. Some, eg.the lythrum, stay as a tight clump, the pale yellow *Geum rivale* 'Leonard's Variety' forms a tight, low clump that spreads outwards only slowly, while others, eg. the geraniums, spread more rapidly and might need digging up and dividing every few years to keep them in check.

The monarda is rather a special case because it dies out in the centre but new growth radiates outwards, necessitating occasional replanting of the wandering shoots in spring. Some of the species here may self-sow, notably the astrantia and the salvia, but there is only likely to be a problem with excessive seeding on lighter soils.

3. All the plants are long-lived, with the exception of the achilleas that are both relatively short-lived and very sensitive to winter damp. They can be kept going by lifting and dividing them every other autumn, replanting the younger shoots and discarding the old, woody material.

[Left] *Veronica spicata* 'Erika'

[Centre] *Sidalcea* 'Elsie Heugh'

[Right] *Astrantia major* 'Claret'

A circular planting for summer, with winter interest

plant list

1. *Calamintha nepeta* subsp. *nepeta* (2)
2. *Selinum wallichianum* (2)
3. *Aster ericoides* 'Blue Star' (2)
4. *Sedum* 'Matrona' (4)
5. *Perovskia atriplicifolia* 'Blue Spire' (3)
6. *Molinia caerulea* subsp. *caerulea* 'Moorhexe' (2)
7. *Monarda* 'Scorpion' (2)
8. *Eupatorium purpureum* subsp. *maculatum* 'Atropurpureum' (1)
9. *Foeniculum vulgare* 'Giant Bronze' (4)
10. *Liatris spicata* (6)
11. *Echinacea purpurea* 'Rubinglow' (3)
12. *Veronicastrum virginica* 'Fascination' (3)
13. *Achillea* 'Credo' (3)
14. *Scabiosa japonica* var. *alpina* (4)
15. *Schizachyrium scoparium* 'The Blues' (2)
16. *Stachys monieri* 'Hummelo' (5)
17. *Miscanthus sinensis* 'Malepartus' (1)
18. *Helenium* 'Rubinzwerg' (5)
19. *Origanum* 'Rosenkuppel' (2)
20. *Nepeta racemosa* 'Walker's Low' (2)
21. *Veronicastrum virginica* 'Temptation' (3)
22. *Phlox paniculata* 'Rosa Pastell' (5)
23. *Cimicifuga simplex* 'Pritchard's Giant' (2)
24. *Limonium latifolium* (1)

Looking its best primarily in late summer, this planting should continue to offer interest until early winter. Its overall design reflects that of the traditional island bed, with the tallest plants in the centre and the shortest on the outside. Needing good light, it makes a magnificent planting for a large lawn or other flat area where there is nothing else of comparable height nearby. The flower colours are essentially blue/violet and pink.

Flowering starts in early summer with the lavender-coloured catmint (*Nepeta racemosa* 'Walker's Low'), lilac *Stachys monieri* 'Hummelo', sulphur-yellow *Achillea* 'Credo' and the upright blue spires of *Veronicastrum virginicum*.

Most of the other species will flower in mid- to late summer, with extra autumn flowers from the pale pink *Sedum* 'Matrona' and the *Aster ericoides* 'Blue Star'

Height is a key element. In early summer, there is little over 40cm (16in) high, but later the 1.5m (4ft) spires of the veronica and the dark bronze heads of the fennel (*Foeniculum vulgare* 'Giant Bronze') make a strong impact. By late summer the taller species in the centre will be in excess of 2m (6ft) high. *Eupatorium purpureum* 'Atropurpureum' in particular has impressive bulk as well as height, its dark pink flowers acting as a magnet for butterflies. Next to it, *Miscanthus sinensis* 'Malepartus' should begin to produce its reed-like flower stems at the same time and continue to look majestic through the winter, especially if it receives low winter sunlight. The other tall element is *Cimicifuga simplex* 'Pritchard's Giant', with long narrow spikes of white flowers above the impressively divided leaves.

Flower shapes provide some effective contrasts, for example the big, pink daisies of *Echinacea purpurea* 'Rubinglow' with the upright veronica behind it, and the yellow umbel shapes of *Achillea* 'Credo' to one side. Another good shape and colour combination comes from the lavender-blue wispy panicles of *Perovskia atriplicifolia* behind the solid, almost dumpy pink umbels of *Sedum* 'Matrona'. Many of the species have seed heads that provide extra winter attractions.

It is also worth noting that two of the plants are set very close together so that their shapes mingle. Both *Origanum* 'Rosenkuppel' and *Limonium latifolium* flower in mid- to late summer, the former having bunches of pink flowers and reddish bracts that continue to look good for many weeks after the flowers have died, and the latter a head of many tiny, lavender-coloured flowers. The origanum sends up occasional runners some distance from the parent plant, creating a rather attractive effect as new clusters appear scattered amongst other plants.

Besides the tall miscanthus, there are two shorter grasses. *Molinia caerulea* 'Moorhexe' grows 70cm (2 1/2ft) high with flowers and seed heads on tall stems that are initially vertical before arching outwards, and the slightly shorter *Schizachrium scoparium* 'The Blues' has blue-tinged foliage that turns pink or reddish in the autumn.

REQUIREMENTS

1. Full sun and an open site is needed for this scheme to flourish. Provide free-draining, fertile soil, but note that many species need ground that rarely dries out. The cimicifuga may be a problem in some areas because it needs cool conditions, the leaves reacting to heat or drought by turning brown. At high altitudes or latitudes it may be grown in sun, elsewhere it always flowers reliably, and in Piet's opinion the scorched leaves can easily be ignored. The achillea may be a problem because winter wet on some soils, eg. heavy clay ones, or where drainage is less than perfect, can cause the plant to rot.

2. The plants are mostly long-lived and cannot be expected to cause particular long-term management problems. The monarda may need replanting if its young shoots wander too far. the fennel may not survive the winter but will almost certainly self-sow around, and the phlox will need dividing and replanting after a number of years.

[Left] *Liatris spicata*

[Centre] *Veronicastrum virginicum* 'Fascination'

[Right] *Stachys monieri* 'Hummelo' with *Echinacea*

Gravel garden

plant list

1. *Dianthus amuriensis*   (20)
2. *Stipa pulcherrima*   (2)
3. *Acaena* 'Copper Carpet'   (10)
4. *Thymus serpyllum*   (4)
5. *Sedum* 'Fuldaglut'   (12)
6. *Santolina pinnata* subsp. *neapolitana*
   'Edward Bowles'   (9)
7. *Stachys byzantina* 'Big Ears'   (15)
8. *Eryngium bourgatii*   (2)
9. *Sedum ruprechtii*   (8)

10. *Geranium cinereum* 'Ballerina'   (5)
11. *Stipa gigantea*   (1)
12. *Ferula communis*   (6)
13. *Euphorbia seguieriana* subsp. *niciciana* (6)
14. *Dictamnus albus*   (6)
15. *Imperata cylindrica*   (12)
16. *Tulipa hageri* 'Splendens'   (30)
17. *Crocus sieberi*   (100)
18. *Eryngium decaisneum*   (2)

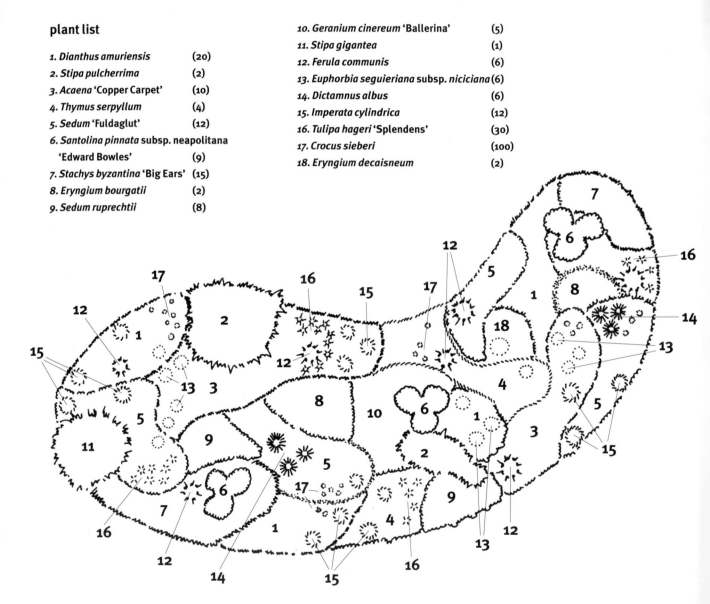

Ideal for a hot dry site, this planting aims at a scattered planting on gravel, with an emphasis on interesting evergreen foliage colours, a variety of textures and some dramatic shapes. Note how a limited palette of plants is used, and the way in which they are repeated, creating a natural rhythm.

Each drift will need a large batch of plants; you decide how many. If a fairly dense carpeting effect is wanted, plants can be set out at the distances suggested, but if a more sparse effect is sought with more gravel showing, use fewer plants. Note that some, notably the acaena, stachys and thyme, are strong spreaders.

The bushy, silver evergreen *Santolina pinnata* subsp. 'Edward Bowles' with creamy-white summer flowers and the low carpeting, silver-grey-leaved *Stachys* 'Big Ears' give winter interest, and contrast with the bronze-copper coloured *Acaena* 'Copper Carpet' (also called 'Kupferteppich'). Spring sees the pink-lilac *Crocus sieberi* and later scarlet *Tulipa hageri* 'Splendens' in flower.

In late spring and early summer, the flowering will be at its height. The carpets of *Thymus serpyllum* have pink flowers, *Geranium cinereum* 'Ballerina' has pink flowers intricately veined with a dark red-pink, and *Dianthus amuriensis* is mauve. In contrast, *Euphorbia seguieriana* subsp. *niciciana* forms mats of grey foliage covered with heads of greeny-yellow flowers for weeks on end.

The low, spiny-looking *Eryngium bourgatii* blooms a little later, its flowers being unusual, dark steel-blue over low grey foliage. *Stipa pulcherrima* also performs from early to midsummer, and is the most spectacular of all grasses with long awns, up to 60cm (2ft) long on each spikelet, that seem to float in the air, forever in motion. This magical effect only lasts a few weeks, after which the seeds blow away. *Stipa gigantea* looks good from early summer to late autumn, with its far-flung, oat-like panicles dangling from 1.5m (4ft) high stems. Though large, the plant is effectively transparent because it is easy to see through the stems. Another feature is *Dictamnus albus*, dotted around the planting with spikes of cream flowers. It produces so much volatile oil that on calm summer evenings you can put a match to it, causing a brief flair-up (with luck) which leaves the plant unscathed.

There is then little in flower until late summer or autumn, when the yellow *Sedum ruprechtii*, the carpeting, purple-leaved and red-flowering *Sedum* 'Fuldaglut' and the spectacular *Eryngium decaisneum* flower. The last thrusts out a 2–3m (6–10ft) flower spike topped by thimble-shaped, purple-brown heads. The other giant in the gravel bed is *Ferula communis*, that may take several years to build up a mound of dark feathery foliage, before producing a yellow flower head atop a 3m (10ft) high stem.

This scheme also includes some plants of the blood grass (*Imperata cylindrica*), whose deep red colour is spectacular when back-lit, making a striking contrast to the other plants here at the end of the year.

REQUIREMENTS

1. This gravel bed is designed for an average, fertile but potentially dry site with free-draining (possibly stony or sandy) soil. Gravel should be chosen to complement the colour of the plants' foliage, and be applied after planting to a depth of around 3–5cm (1½–2in).

2. All the plants are reasonably long-lived although in nature the ferula is monocarpic (i.e. it dies after flowering). In cultivation this does not seem to happen, possibly because growing conditions are generally better in the garden. Long-term, beware the spreading tendencies of the thyme, stachys and acaena; if their growth is too exuberant and they start to smother other plants, their unwanted, offending growth can be easily pulled up.

3. The imperata is not reliably hardy in severe winters, but could be protected with a layer of straw or bracken weighed down with stones or bricks.

[Left] *Imperata cylindrica*

[Right] *Ferula communis*

An early flowering border with good foliage

plant list

1. *Geranium phaeum* 'Album' (6)
2. *Hosta* 'Halcyon' (2)
3. *Astrantia major* 'Claret' (12)
4. *Luzula sylvatica* 'Wälder' (3)
5. *Geranium psilostemon* (5)
6. *Digitalis grandiflora* (10)
7. *Epimedium grandiflorum* (5)
8. *Geranium* × *oxonianum* 'Claridge Druce' (5)
9. *Cimicifuga simplex* 'Brunette' (4)
10. *Rodgersia* 'Die Anmutige' (2)
11. *Uvularia grandiflora* (2)
12. *Podophyllum hexandrum* 'Majus' (2)
13. *Carex muskingumensis* (1)
14. *Anemone rivularis* (3)
15. *Polystichum setiferum* 'Dahlem' (1)
16. *Hakonechloa macra* (1)
17. *Heuchera* 'Palace Purple' (3)
18. *Smilacina racemosa* (3)
19. *Geranium* 'Sirak' (5)

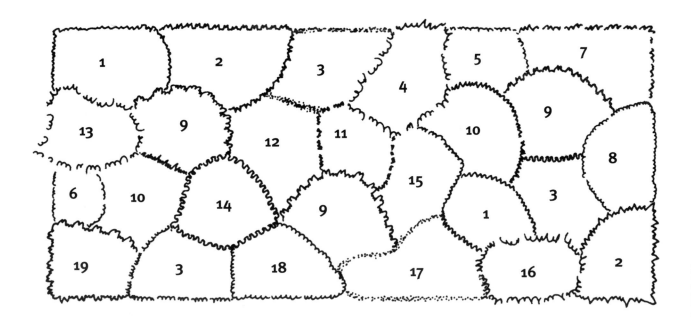

The plants in this scheme come from woodland-edge habitats, where they tend to flower early in the year but compensate by generally having good quality foliage. The best sites are under the outer canopy of a tree, on the shady side of a house, or on a slope facing away from the sun.

Late spring sees the pure white of *Geranium phaeum* 'Album', the lilac-pink of *Geranium* 'Sirak', white *Anemone rivularis*, and the dark red of *Astrantia major* 'Claret' among the fresh young growth of the fern *Polystichium setiferum* 'Dahlem', *Hosta* 'Halcyon', *Cimicifuga simplex* 'Brunette', *Podophyllym hexandrum* 'Majus' and *Rodgersia* 'Die Anmutige'.

Uvularia grandiflora is a woodland plant that also flowers around now, with elegant, yellow, bell-shaped flowers hanging from the upper part of upright 75cm (2½ft) high stems. The related *Smilacina racemosa* has upright stems, briefly complemented by a head of white flowers, and also has elegant foliage. *Digitalis grandiflora* sends up its spikes of large, pale yellow foxgloves somewhat later, while *Geranium × oxonianum* 'Claridge Druce' covers itself in deep pink flowers and the rodgersias produce their rather dramatic panicles, packed with thousands of tiny, creamy flowers.

The astrantia should flower several times through the season, and the *Geranium × oxonianum* 'Claridge Druce' will always flower again in late summer, and into the autumn if the ground has enough moisture. The start of the later part of the season features three plants of *Cimicifuga simplex* 'Brunette' with 2m (6ft) high stems carrying long, bending spikes of white flowers.

The joy of this planting lies in the variety of foliage shapes, with the main element being a contrast between large, bold leaves and finely divided ones. An additional element is the contrast between the various shades of green and the dark bronze-brown of the three cimicifugas, and the dark purple of *Heuchera* 'Palace Purple', the rodgersias and *Epimedium grandiflorum*.

The large-leaved plants include the hosta, rodgersia and the podophyllum. They contrast with the finely-divided polystichium fronds, the coarsely-divided leaves of the cimicifuga and the grassy linearity of the sedge (*Carex muskingumensis*) and the grass *Hakonechloa macra*. The former is a deep fresh green, and makes up for often being somewhat untidy by its healthy, vigorous look, and an unusual tufted growth pattern. The latter, however, always looks attractively neatly combed. *Luzula sylvatica* 'Wälder' is also linear in character, forming dense carpets of low tufted growth.

Only a couple of species here are evergreen, the luzula and polystichum, with the carex keeping its leaves until relatively late in mild climates.

Smilacina racemosa

REQUIREMENTS

1. The ideal site for this scheme receives a few hours of sun a day, or gets dappled sun beneath the outer canopy of deciduous trees. The soil should be free-draining without experiencing drought. Most of the plants will also flourish on soils that are definitely on the moist side, the hosta and rodgersia appreciating this particularly and being the first to suffer in dry conditions. Sites with tree roots that dry out the soil, or that are so close to buildings that rainfall is restricted, are not suitable unless irrigation is installed.

   The plants used that are most tolerant of dry shade include *Geranium phaeum*, the luzula and polystichum. The relative tolerance of the latter makes this a particularly useful fern.

2. An annual cutting down and removal of dead growth is the only regular maintenance needed. Several of the plants, the smilacina, podophyllum and uvularia particularly, also benefit from a humus-rich soil with plenty of organic matter. Composted plants could be applied as a winter mulch or, alternatively, they could be shredded and used as a mulch without composting.

3. The digitalis is the only short-lived or biennial species here, but on all soils, apart from very heavy ones, it will regenerate through self-sowing. *Geranium × oxonianum* 'Claridge Druce' is the only really potentially invasive species; it is a very strong grower and can seed itself around extensively. Cutting it back after flowering results in a tidier plant, and dividing it every few years will help keep it within bounds. The other species are long-lived and do not present any particular problems.

Nori and Sandra Pope

Since Nori and Sandra Pope took over the garden at Hadspen House, Somerset, UK, in 1987, it has become one of the most talked about gardens in Europe. The Popes' experimental colour plantings show a boldness and emotional depth that exceeds anything seen before.

The Canadian couple had seen the semi-derelict kitchen garden while on holiday and, hearing that it was up for rent, made the bold step of taking it on as a business, setting up a nursery and, within a few years, opening the garden to the public. 'Being Canadian,' emphasizes Nori, 'means that we don't come encumbered with so much history and are not hindered by so many boundaries.'

The area in which the Popes work at Hadspen was not designed for ornamental gardening, but they saw the neglected site as a 'romantic frame waiting for a painting'. The south-facing aspect suits an adventurous approach, and contains warm, sunny walls built in a D-shape, that originally would have sheltered peaches and early vegetables, and a terrace (the site of a long-demolished greenhouse) dramatically positioned above a large tank, that is now a lily pond bordered by lush, waterside plants.

The setting of hills and woodland seems to embrace the garden, which looks out over the mellow Somerset countryside. Shrubs planted by Penelope Hobhouse, who had lived there until 10 years before, provide the structure in parts of the garden, while a collection of hostas and other foliage perennials are a legacy of the late Eric Smith,

a plant breeder of legendary repute who Penelope took under her wing.

In his teenage years, Nori was as an apprentice gardener to an old Austrian nurseryman, in British Columbia, Canada, and learnt his gardening skills in a traditional setting before studying graphic arts. He returned to gardening professionally after his studies, and only thought about applying the lessons he had learnt at college when he met Sandra, who wanted to create a red garden. 'Sandra introduced me to colour, and when courting her I bought every red plant known to man.'

Creating the garden together is central to the Popes' achievement. The stereotypical gardening couple splits the work between the man who designs the framework and does the hard landscaping, and the woman who does the planting, but the Popes' gardening relationship is much more complex and subtle. Fundamental to their shared passion for colour is the knowledge that, on the whole, women can distinguish colours to a much finer degree than most men, and can remember them more accurately. Sandra's eye reigns supreme.

When talking to the Popes it is also clear that they are equally comfortable in different disciplines. 'We make no separation,' Nori says, 'between art, music and gardening.' And when discussing their approach to colour he and Sandra move from one subject to another with consummate ease, often using musical terms because 'gardening does not have its own language'. Sandra adds: 'If you take colour as the theme, then combinations of colour are the melody and we build on that thematically, arranging numbers of plants in ascending or descending order. It's the same way that someone composing a piece of music would build on, say, a chord to create a whole symphony.' She emphasizes that they don't 'just think about colour' but see it is a starting point. 'Colour is so diverse – you can make a monochrome border, or create one with harmonies and contrasts.'

It is the Popes' use of monochrome plantings that has created the biggest stir in the gardening community. They created a series of related monochrome themes in the long border against the semi-circular brick wall and a dramatic double yellow border with not only a wide variety of yellow

[left] A section of a red border at Hadspen House contains the annual *Zinnia peruviana* and *Crocosmia* 'Lucifer'

[Right] The famous yellow border

flowers, but also yellow-tinged and variegated foliage. Here, plants are grouped so that there are 'two tunes, related but distinct, twisted together visually'. They run through the yellow border, with clumps of ascending numbers of plants up the border on one side, with descending numbers in each clump on the other.

'A single-colour planting is essentially about harmony,' explains Nori, 'while mixed colours cancel each other out.' Freed from the task of having to see many different colours, the eye can then concentrate on appreciating other aspects of a planting, including the different flower shapes, and the subtle differences between the shades. However, recognizing that too much of one colour will saturate the eye, some relief is provided by a few blue flowers among the yellows.

They contrast their work with that of Christopher Lloyd whose garden at Great Dixter, East Sussex, UK, is very much about exploring contrasts, sometimes to the extent of deliberately provoking his visitors. For example he has juxtaposed orange and pink, a combination that most gardeners would shy away from. As a result Great Dixter is

a high energy garden, with little respite from visual stimulation, which Nori compares with modern dissonant composers such as Bartok. Colour changes at Hadspen are made more gradually and, with closely controlled tonal shifts and underlying melodies, are more akin to 19th-century symphonies.

'We use layers of music in the garden,' says Sandra, and when I ask about specific inspirations, Nori cites Mahler and Goretsky. On another occasion Nori says that he 'wanted to plant Mahler's 2nd Symphony'. He adds: 'You could give plants individual notes and then compose a border based on a piece of music; and then maybe plant another border and compose a musical piece based on your scheme.'

In painting, he lists Monet's use of rhythm, Rothko's use of colour, Bonnard's use of shadow and light, and 'any of the pointillists'. But whereas 'Monet and Renoir made gardens and interpreted them as paintings,' Sandra explains, 'we base gardens on paintings.' Nori adds that Monet's later work is a like a fabric, a mixture of colours. '
I find that inspirational,' he says.

Having explored single-colour plantings so thoroughly, the Popes are now moving on to different colour combinations. In order to maintain harmony, Nori suggests that combinations are made in 'half-tone jumps', for example using peach and yellow, or purple and blue. 'But if there is more than one combination,' he warns, 'it can become a jumble.'

Sandra adds that simply putting colours together does not get you very far. 'You have to look at what you can do with the plants,' she says. 'Do they, for example, provide the colour I want when I want? But plants selected for particular colour combinations should also be looked at within the context of the whole season. Do they have good winter stems, or berries, for example?' To some extent the limitations of a particular colour scheme may be overcome by intensive management, and Hadspen is no low-maintenance garden, as Sandra explains. 'We manipulate plants a lot, and cut them back when they have finished, and then plant out seasonal plants like argyranthemums and tulips.'

Tulips are indispensable for colour early in the season, as are dahlias later in the year. 'We have always loved tulips,' Nori explains, 'as do the mice,' adds Sandra. 'And we like single roses because so many old ones go so soggy in a wet English summer.' Few genera offer such a variety of colours as do the dahlias, many with a sumptuous, velvety depth. They are used in many different parts of the garden to concentrate the colour in a section of the themed border, and to extend its glory until the first frosts.

Annuals also enable the Popes to experiment with new schemes every year. They like to create rapid effects because they enjoy the fact that: 'Once it works that's also the end of it; gardening is an ephemeral process and next year you have to start again.' Vegetables are annuals too, and a vegetable area has long been a feature of the central part of the largest open space within the walled garden at Hadspen.

Concentrating on using varieties with coloured foliage, the Popes' vegetable garden is like no other, with purple kales, the glowing stems of ruby chard, dark-stemmed 'Sugar Dot' sweet corn and red-leaved lettuces. The Popes have even done some of their own plant selection with vegetables, producing the chard 'Hadspen Golden', whose broad golden-yellow stems glow in the low winter sun, and a cross between ruby chard and beetroot 'Bulls Blood', whose large leaves and stems are dark purple-red.

Nori has always been a bit of a plant collector, and this has been turned to good use in the couple's constant desire to, as he puts it, 'push the edge of what is possible' with colour. Working with the subtleties of colour requires a great deal of sifting through what is available and, as more plants come on the market, the range of possibilities increases. Of all the colours, the Popes are particularly fond of plum, the blend of red, blue and black.

Historically there has been a limited number of plum-coloured flowers, but recent plant selection has resulted in more, enabling the Popes to develop their most daring colour combinations. Plum with red foliage can be almost mournful, while green foliage highlights it and feels refreshing. Very dark plum shades combined with silver and grey foliage create a sense of drama and vibrancy. With orange, as in their plantings for this book, there is excitement with near-tropical lushness.

At their own home, near Hadspen, they are experimenting in a long thin border with 'plum, apricot, red, purple and blue, in a very wild style'. Their friend Piet Oudolf has dubbed it 'a meadow in a strip', using plants with lots of small leaves rather than dark or bold ones, so 'that the planting is sympathetic to the landscape'. The relationship with landscape is something that is beginning to occupy the Popes at Hadspen, too, as they look to its future development, aiming to simplify it and extend the garden into the landscape.

They are also on the lookout for new, large plants. 'Compact is not a word we want to hear,' says Nori. When I spoke to them they were very pleased with a recent acquisition, the seed of an enormous wild marigold they found in Kerala, India. 'There is a huge amount of exploration still to be done with colour,' Sandra adds, stressing again that 'new plants mean new combinations'.

Confident that they are just at the beginning, Nori and Sandra will no doubt carry on creating inspiring new plant combinations at Hadspen, agreeing very occasionally to design plantings for public places, for example a border at the Botanic Gardens, Oxford, UK, which is intended to be at its best in spring and autumn. They also act as consultants to a select number of garden designers and landscape architects, advising them on plant selection and combinations. The four plantings they have designed for this book, all based on a theme of orange and plum-purple, demonstrate their exciting use of colour.

Decorative vegetable garden in orange and plum

[Left] The vegetable garden at Hadspen with beds of fennel, lettuces and, in the background, angelica

[Right] Lettuce 'Bijou'

plant list

1. Lettuce 'Parella Red'	(20)	11. *Tagetes patula*	(30)
2. Chard 'Hadspen Golden'	(20)	12. Amaranthus 'Hopi Red'	(30)
3. Cabbage 'Red Jewel'	(8)	13. Sunflower 'Orange Sun'	(20)
4. Tomato 'Golden Sunrise'	(8)	14. Zinnia 'Orange Cajun'	(30)
5. Beetroot 'Bull's Blood'	(30)	15. Lettuce 'Bijou'	(20)
6. Aubergine 'Bambino'	(8)	16. *Tropaeolum majus* hybrid	(30)
7. Courgette 'Gold Rush'	(4)	17. *Tropaeolum majus* Alaska Series	(2)
8. Kale 'Redbor'	(20)	18. Winter squash 'Kuri'	(2)
9. *Calendula officinalis*	(30)	19. Purple podded runner beans	(2)
10. Basil 'Dark Opal'	(30)	20. Sweet pea 'Beaujolais'	(2)

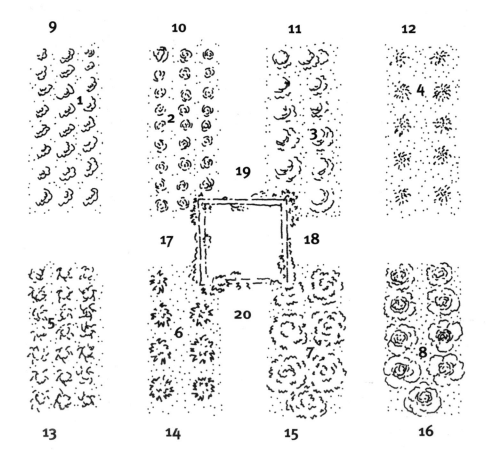

Gone are the days when vegetables were consigned to a part of the garden never to be viewed, except when digging or harvesting. Vegetables are now accepted as being beautiful in their own right, and varieties are being bred with coloured leaves or stems, or with fruit that is differently coloured to conventional varieties. This vibrant potager translates the Pope's theories about colour from the border to the vegetable garden, with vegetables and some flowers being laid out in beds, with a central pergola planted with flowers and vegetables.

The orange and plum colour scheme is effective with vegetables because so many have dark foliage – amaranthus, basil, beetroot, cabbage, kale and lettuce – while the runner bean has purple pods. The others here have orange flowers or fruit and, in the case of the courgette, yellow flowers and fruit. Chard 'Hadspen

Golden', one of several developed by the Popes, has orange stems and, like all chards, provides a nutritious spinach-like vegetable for almost 12 months of the year, both stems and leaves being edible. Amaranthus is a leaf vegetable that is eaten all over the tropics, and is a particular favourite in the Caribbean where it is known as 'callalloo'. Squash 'Kuri' is tangerine-orange while the sweet pea 'Beaujolais' has burgundy-red flowers.

The flowers are not just decorative. The English marigold (*Calendula officinalis*) can be eaten in salads, while the nasturtium (*Tropaeolum majus* hybrid) has hot tasting leaves that can be judiciously added to salads. Its seed pods can also be used in salads, and even pickled.

With a potager like this, the key to cultivation lies in the distinction between those vegetables and herbs that are

hardy and those that are half-hardy. Hardy kinds can be sown in the ground where they are to grow in spring, whereas half-hardy kinds need to be sown inside, in a greenhouse or on a light windowsill, well before they are planted out after the last frost. English marigold is a hardy annual, as is the beetroot, kale, chard and the two varieties of lettuce and nasturtium. The amaranthus and sunflower can be sown in late spring, but will make better growth if they are started off inside. All the others need a warm start inside, with the aubergine needing to be sown in early spring if it is to have any chance of producing fruit.

With all vegetables, particularly the half-hardy kinds, it is vital that the instructions on the packet are followed, and that they are sown at the times and temperatures recommended. The sweet pea has hard seed that germinates better if the seed coat is nicked with a knife, but ideally sow it in the autumn, and stand the pots out in a cold frame where they will survive the winter cold.

The vegetables can be harvested throughout the summer, with the lettuce being sown in succession to avoid any gaps, or leaves can be taken as and when required, without digging up the whole plant. It will be possible to harvest the chard throughout the winter if it is not too cold, while the kale will stand any amount of cold, making it one of the most useful winter vegetables.

REQUIREMENTS

1. Like all vegetables, these varieties benefit from plenty of sun, water and nutients. An open site that gets sun for most of the day is very important, as is fertile soil that never dries out. The soil should ideally be well-fed and supplied with plenty of organic matter: use well-rotted manure or garden compost in the autumn, and a general -purpose organic fertilizer before planting in the spring.

2. This is obviously a planting for one year only. If you like it so much that you want to repeat it next year or try a similar scheme, change the positions of the plants. Crop rotation is fundamental to good vegetable garden practice, and is discussed in detail in all books on vegetable gardening. Esentially it means you must not grow the same crop on the same patch of ground more than once in three years. It ensures that pests and diseases do not build up in the soil.

[Left] Courgette 'Gold Rush'

[Right] Kale 'Redbor'

[Left] *Miscanthus sinensis*
'Malepartus'

[Right] *Carex flagellifera*

[Below] *Dahlia*
'David Howard'

An autumn border in orange and plum

plant list

1. *Heuchera* 'Bressingham Bronze'	(12)
2. *Dahlia* 'David Howard'	(5)
3. *Chrysanthemum* 'Mary Stoker'	(3)
4. *Amaranthus* 'Hopi Red'	(20)
5. *Cosmos sulphureus* 'Sunset'	(12)
6. *Miscanthus sinensis* 'Malepartus'	(5)
7. *Cosmos astrosanguineus*	(6)
8. *Helianthus* 'Velvet Queen'	(7)
9. *Rosa moyesii* 'Geranium'	(1)
10. *Dahlia* 'Ellen Houston'	(5)
11. *Helenium* 'Chipperfield Orange'	(3)
12. *Acer platanoides* 'Crimson King'	(1)
13. *Foeniculum vulgare* 'Purpureum'	(7)
14. *Buddleia* × *weyeriana*	(1)
15. *Helenium* 'Moerheim Beauty'	(3)
16. *Chrysanthemum* 'Shelly'	(3)
17. *Carex flagellifera*	(5)
18. *Atriplex hortensis* var. *rubra*	(30)
19. *Helianthus* 'Floristan'	(7)

18 planted throughout

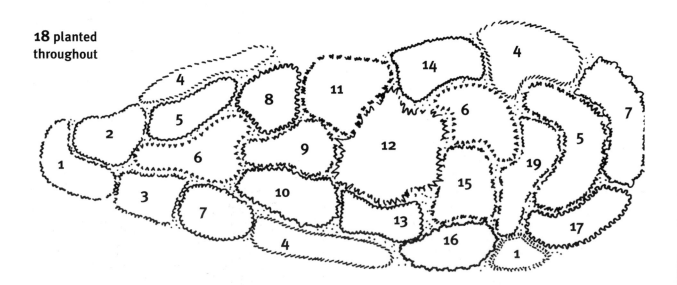

'Hot colours are prevalent at this time of year,' says Sandra. Certainly it does seem that there are more colours like red and orange in late summer and autumn, and this planting is designed to make the most of the various oranges using shrubs, perennials, grasses and annuals.

The centrepiece of the border is a maple (*Acer platanoides* 'Crimson King') that has deep crimson leaves, turning orange in autumn, and which is kept pollarded (ie. it has its branches cut back to the trunk every two years to keep it small). Next to it is *Buddleia × weyeriana* with panicles of pale orange flowers through summer, into the autumn. There is also a *Rosa moyesii* 'Geranium' that produces scarlet hips.

Apart from these woody plants, everything else in this border is a perennial or an annual, reflecting the fact that late-season colour primarily comes from non-woody plants. Members of the daisy family contribute some of the best colours in the orange part of the spectrum, especially at this time of year. They include *Chrysanthemum* 'Shelly' (deep copper) and *C.* 'Mary Stoker' (single, palest apricot), *Helenium* 'Moerheim Beauty' (rich browny-red) and *H.* 'Chipperfield Orange' – all are hardy perennials, and can be regarded as permanent parts of the planting.

The dahlias include 'David Howard' (amber-orange) and 'Ellen Houston' (orange), both of which are half-hardy, needing lifting and protecting under cover over winter. There are two sunflowers, *Helianthus* 'Floristan' (red-orange) and *H.* 'Velvet Queen' (dark burgundy-brown),

REQUIREMENTS

and *Cosmos sulphureus* 'Sunset' (amber-orange), all of which are annuals. The predominately orange tones of the flowers are balanced by the purple and plum-tinged foliage of the maple, by *Amaranthus* 'Hopi Red', the bronze fennel (*Foeniculum vulgare* 'Purpureum'), *Atriplex hortensis* var. *rubra* and *Heuchera* 'Bressingham Bronze'.

The effect of the striking colours is enhanced by interesting textural elements. Look at the tight red flower and seed heads of the amaranthus, the rosettes of the fine brown grass, the foliage of *Carex flagellifera* and the very dark, light-absorbing matt foliage of the fennel. The stately grass *Miscanthus sinensis* 'Malepartus' has red-tinged flower panicles, while its more subtle shades and grassy texture add a calming note to these strong colours.

Scent plays its part too, with *Cosmos atrosanguineus* providing mysterious dark red flowers and the most delicious scent of chocolate, an endless source of interest and amusement.

[Left] *Cosmos atrosanguineus*

[Right] A border designed by the Popes in the Oxford Botanic Garden in early autumn with blazing *Dahlia* 'David Howard' and *Helenium* 'Chipperfield Orange'

1. Any site which receives full sun on a reasonably fertile, moisture-retentive soil will support these plants.

2. This combination includes permanent woody and herbaceous plants, and seasonal plants. The dahlias need protecting over winter, as will the *Cosmos atrosanguineus* in cold winter gardens, while the amaranthus and atriplex are hardy annuals, and the *Cosmos sulphureus* is a half-hardy annual (sow its seed under cover in spring). The atriplex and amaranthus can usually be guaranteed to self-seed, and will reappear every year scattered throughout the border. Both can be used as a spinach-like leaf vegetable.

3. The perennial elements will ensure a good long-term result, although the buddleia will grow large and may need ruthless pruning, even annual cutting back to the ground, if required, to stop it becoming too big.

A damp border in orange and plum

plant list

1. *Tropaeolum speciosum*	(3)
2. *Corylus maxima* 'Purpurea'	(1)
3. *Rhododendron* 'Brazil'	(1)
4. *Veratrum nigrum*	(5)
5. *Canna* 'Lesotho Lill'	(5)
6. *Ligularia dentata* 'Desdemona'	(5)
7. *Euphorbia griffithii* 'Fireglow'	(5)
8. *Lilium henryi*	(12)
9. *Phormium tenax*	(5)
10. *Angelica gigas*	(9)
11. *Trollius chinensis* 'Golden Queen'	(5)
12. *Primula bulleyana*	(15)
13. *Meconopsis cambrica*	(30)
14. *Plantago major* 'Rubrifolia'	(10)
15. *Mimulus cardinalis*	(10)
16. *Epimedium* × *warleyense*	(10)
17. *Geum* 'Georgenberg'	(10)
18. *Hemerocallis fulva*	(4)

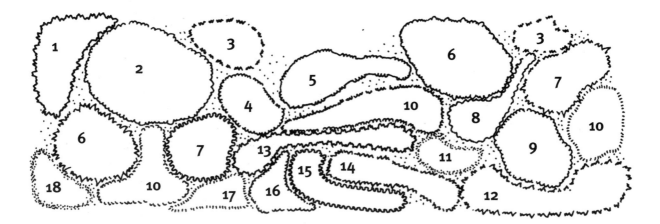

'People usually think of green as being the predominant colour in damp places, says Sandra, 'and this combination of orange and plum is not often seen. It's an opportunity to make a hot and lush border.

The planting brings together striking plant forms, often characteristic of species that thrive in moist habitats, and a dramatic colour combination of hot colours and purples. The border's evergreen lynchpin is *Phormium tenax*, with its copper-coloured, sword-like leaves. During the growing season a number of herbaceous species with bold foliage complement it. They include *Veratrum nigrum,* with its unusual, pleated leaves, the orange *Canna* 'Lesotho Lill', with broad, tropical-looking foliage and *Angelica gigas*, a biennial cow-parsley relative with dark purple flowers, plum-tinged foliage and an architectural form.

The purple-leaved hazel (*Corylus maxima* 'Purpurea') exerts a powerful influence on the border throughout the summer, although the fiery appearance of the azalea (*Rhododendron* 'Brazil') will act as a dramatic contrast during early summer when it is flowering. The dark foliage theme is carried further by *Ligularia dentata* 'Desdemona',

with its large mahogany leaves and orange flowers, and the plantain (*Plantago major* 'Rubrifolia').

The orange theme starts in spring with the delicate flowers of *Epimedium* × *warleyense*, whose fresh green leaves add a light touch among so much dark foliage. It extends into late spring with *Trollius chinensis* 'Golden Queen', the short-lived and often self-seeding *Meconopsis cambrica* and the delightful, soft orange *Geum* 'Georgenburg'.

Euphorbia griffithii 'Fireglow' is a darker, almost red colour, while *Hemerocallis fulva* is a yellow, with a much more elegant appearance than most of the day lilies. Early to midsummer sees the dull orange turk's cap flowers of that tallest of lilies, *Lilium henryi*, the orange-red of *Mimulus cardinalis* creeping along at the front, and the warm tones of *Primula bulleyana*, one of the candelabra species, so-called because the flowers appear in whorls up the stems. The clump of cannas provides a strong central stand of orange for mid- to late summer, and the season ends with the spectacular scarlet of *Tropaeolum speciosum* climbing over the purple hazel.

[Left] *Crocosmia* 'Star of the East' with *Carex flagellifera*

[Right] *Angelica gigas*

REQUIREMENTS

1. Most of the plants need soil that is moist but definitely not waterlogged, although the ligularia copes well in very wet soil. The azalea and the tropaeoleum need acid soil. Light shade probably offers the most suitable conditions for the majority of plants, but if the soil never dries out they should flourish in full sun.

2. *Angelica gigas* is biennial, and seed should be sown annually for flowering the following year. The canna is not hardy; in mild climates it may be protected over winter by an insulating layer of straw, but in colder areas it is better to lift the tubers and store them in a frost-free place inside.

3. Most of the plants are long-lived and, eventually, some will form extensive patches. The epimedium and geum make useful ground-cover, but the *Euphorbia griffithii* might eventually take up too much space and need thinning out. Others are less long-lived, but have the capacity to self-sow and regenerate themselves.

The meconopsis and mimulus survive for only a few years but they self-sow well (occasionally to nuisance proportions), while the primula builds into clumps and self-sows. The end result may well be an exuberant mass of new plants. Rarely, however, will all spread equally well, and in time one will predominate, possibly at the expense of others. So be ready with the hoe to thin out any excess seedlings of the more dominant species.

[Below] *Crocosmia* 'Star of the East'

REQUIREMENTS

1. This scheme is for a sunny site because the strong colours look best in good light, and because many of the species used are from relatively warm climates. The planting is a mix of reliably hardy, long-lived species, one-season annuals and tender perennials that need protecting over winter. This means that the colour scheme has a solid, permanent framework, including varieties with purple foliage, such as the cotinus and the fennel, for the background, and elements that can be changed every year. An annual exercise in creativity is the result, when you must decide what works well with the framework plants.

2. The dahlia is half-hardy, and needs to be lifted after the first frost and stored in a frost-free place, and the arctotis needs lifting and looking after in a conservatory, or you can take cuttings in late summer and overwinter them inside. The mina and the tithonia are also half-hardy but are normally treated as annuals, being raised from seed indoors in spring, and planted out after the last frost. The eschscholzia is a hardy annual and will often self-sow itself, and in mild winters even survives for a second year. Although the achillea is totally hardy, it will not survive mild wet winters, damp being the major problem.

3. Gravel is a key part of this composition, but it needs to be in a colour that will complement the plants' flower and leaf colours; for example, soft yellow gravel will work much better than grey. It is normally applied after planting, filling the gaps between the plants to a depth of 3–5cm (1½–2in). If any planting is carried out after the gravel has been applied, care must be taken to avoid mixing the soil and gravel. Once appreciable quantities of soil get mixed in, there is a greater likelihood of unwanted weeds getting established.

[Above Left] *Cotinus* 'Grace'

[Above Right] *Kniphofia caulescens*

Acknowledgements

Cassell Illustrated would like to thank the following photographers for permission to reproduce their pictures:

Mark Bolton (4, 9, 16, 18, 19, 25, 26–27, 28, 29, 36–37, 39, 40–41, 43, 45, 46–47, 49 (middle and bottom), 51 (bottom), 55, 59, 60, 61, 67, 68, 69, 70, 71, 76, 77, 84, 92, 94–95, 96, 103 (left), 104, 105, 107, 109 (top left), 110, 113, 115, 120–121, 127, 132, 136, 137, 140–141, 145 (top), 148 (right), 151, 152 (right), 155 (right), 157, 163, 164, 166, 169 (left), 173, 174, 175, 178, 179, 182, 183, 184–185); John Brookes (49 (top)); Garden Picture Library: (51 (top left, John Glover), 52 (Howard Rice), 65 (right, Juliette Wade), 75 (Howard Rice), 79 (Jacqui Hurst), 85 (Jerry Pavia) 87 (left Neil Holmes, right David Russell), 88 (Brian Carter), 99 (left J. S. Sira, right Howard Rice), 101 (John Glover), 109 (top right Jerry Pavia, bottom J. S. Sira), 123 (Georgia Glynn-Smith), 124 (John Glover), 125 (Neil Holmes), 129 (left Jo Whitworth, right Howard Rice), 131 (top Brian Carter, bottom right John Glover), 135 (Howard Rice), 147 (Howard Rice), 148 (left Chris Burrows), 152 (left Roger Hyam), 155 (left Sunniva Harte), 156 (Howard Rice), 169 (right Emma Peios), 170 (Mayer/Le Scanff), 171 (Clive Nicholls), 181 (Sunniva Harte)); Harpur Garden Library (14, 51 (top left), 56, 63, 64, 65 (left), 72, 80, 81, 83, 89, 91, 93, 103 (right), 149, 153, 159, 160, 177); Noël Kingsbury (11, 116, 117, 118); Andrew Lawson (32, 44, 139, 145 (bottom)); Marianne Majerus (13, 20, 23, 35, 119, 131 (bottom left), 165); Clive Nicholls (6, 8, 142, 143)